SELF-DETERMINATION IN HEALTH CARE

This book is well-researched and referenced; the analysis is clear and coherent, and the chapters read well together. The hypothesis is lucidly defined and rigorously established; it is an original contribution to scholarship in the field. I thoroughly enjoyed reading it.

Remigius N. Nwabueze
Associate Professor of Law, University of Southampton, UK

I am pleased to endorse this book, which explores the subject of consent to medical treatment in an interesting and novel way. The author offers an alternative 'property' model as a basis for generating a fresh understanding of the subject in the new climate of greater deference to patient choice. The book will be a valuable contribution to knowledge in this field.

Vivienne Harpwood
Professor of Healthcare Law, Cardiff University, UK

To my son
Zealinjo Joshua Edozien

Self-determination in Health Care

A Property Approach to the Protection of Patients' Rights

LEROY C. EDOZIEN
University of Manchester, UK

Routledge
Taylor & Francis Group
LONDON AND NEW YORK

First published 2015 by Ashgate Publishing

2 Park Square, Milton Park, Abingdon, Oxfordshire OX14 4RN
52 Vanderbilt Avenue, New York, NY 10017

Routledge is an imprint of the Taylor & Francis Group, an informa business

First issued in paperback 2020

British Library Cataloguing in Publication Data
A catalogue record for this book is available from the British Library.

Library of Congress Cataloging-in-Publication Data
Edozien, Leroy C. author.
Self-determination in health care : a property approach to the protection of patients' rights / By Leroy C. Edozien.
pages cm
Includes bibliographical references and index.
ISBN 978-1-4724-6198-8 (hardback : alk. paper) 1. Informed consent (Medical law)–Great Britain. 2. Informed consent (Medical law)–United States. 3. Patients–Legal status, laws, etc.–Great Britain. 4. Patients–Legal status, laws, etc.–United States. I. Title.
K3611.I5E36 2015
344.4104'12--dc23

2014046613

ISBN 978-1-4724-6198-8 (hbk)
ISBN 978-0-367-59884-6 (pbk)

Contents

List of Figures and Tables

Figures

Tables

About the Author

Leroy C. Edozien holds qualifications in the basic sciences, Medicine and Law from universities in Ibadan, London and Glasgow and is a member of postgraduate medical colleges in West Africa, Ireland and London. He is a consultant obstetrician and gynaecologist at St Mary's Hospital, Manchester and Manchester Academic Health Science Centre.

Acknowledgements

I am hugely indebted to Professor Sheila McLean, Emeritus Professor of Law and Ethics in Medicine, University of Glasgow, for her support, direction and encouragement throughout the long gestation of this work.

The work is primarily in the field of law, but it has foundations in ethics, philosophy and the social sciences. I am grateful to Professor Robin Downie, Emeritus Professor of Moral Philosophy, University of Glasgow, who helped me find a road map for navigating this terrain.

The work is informed by, and builds on, the work and contributions of numerous scholars, authors, judges and the lay public, and I am indebted to all.

I am thankful to my family and friends for their support.

Above all, I am grateful to the Omniscient for this and many other blessings.

Preface

I have endeavoured to provide a theoretical framework for the concepts underpinning this book but have been mindful of the fact that this is not a treatise in philosophy or bioethics. A prior assumption is made that protecting patient self-determination is a good and desirable thing, and only a token effort is made to justify this assumption. Doing otherwise would have made the book cumbersome.

The terrain covered in this work is vast. In compiling footnotes, I have imbibed the wisdom of Baroness O'Neill who asserts that '[i]n bioethics massive footnoting often indicates insecurity rather than authority, and frequently directs the reader to sources that reiterate rather than establish central points'.[1]

Representing two constituencies – law and medicine – I have tried to be faithful to both, in terms of end product. A purely academic tome may serve its immediate purpose, but it is always more fulfilling if the product has the potential to find practical application. I aimed from the outset to develop an idea that has a firm theoretical basis but is relevant and applicable in legal and clinical practice. It is my hope that, by situating my property analysis in a context of both jurisprudence and medical professionalism, a measure of success has been achieved in this regard.

Cases from various jurisdictions (England, Scotland, Australia, Canada and the USA) have been cited and, for cases outside the United Kingdom, it has been made clear which jurisdiction is concerned; however, it was not the intention in this book to describe or examine the law of consent in each of these jurisdictions, and the citations are meant simply to illustrate fundamental concepts.

It is common in the legal literature to refer to the patient's right to determine what happens to their body, and what treatment they wish to have or to decline, as autonomy. The word 'autonomy' is capable of myriad interpretations, and could be controversial. For this reason, 'autonomy' has been avoided as much as possible in this work and the term 'patient self-determination' has been adopted as an alternative. Wherever 'autonomy' appears in the book, it should be taken as synonymous (and interchangeable) with 'self-determination'. It is explained in

1 O'Neill O, *Autonomy and Trust in Bioethics*. Cambridge: Cambridge University Press 2002, p. xi.

Chapter 2 that patient self-determination is taken in this work to mean the right of the competent patient to make decisions about his/her medical treatment.

This work is no more than an attempt at proof-of-concept, introducing the concept of proprietary rights in the patient's expectations from a consultation and showing that the concept has the potential to be applied in legal and clinical practice. Much further work, well beyond the scope of this book, needs to be done to take the concept forward.

Leroy C. Edozien

Chapter 1
Introduction

> There is a growing demand among patients for more responsive consultations with doctors that will enable them to participate in clinical decision-making.[1]

Traditionally health care was delivered on the basis that the doctor knew what was best for the patient. This tradition could be traced back to the Hippocratic Oath in which the doctor pledges to use those 'regimens which will benefit my patients according to my greatest ability and judgement'.[2] Decisions about what treatment should be given and when and how the treatment would be delivered were in the hands of the doctor.[3] This tradition – medical paternalism – is ebbing, and gradually being superseded by a modern approach which places the patient at the centre of care.[4] In contemporary medical and legal practice it is acknowledged that patients have a right to be proactively involved in decisions about their treatment and that a breach of this right is a breach of the patient's bodily integrity.[5] For this right to be respected in clinical practice, consultations with doctors have to be responsive, as stated in the epigraph above.

Historically, consent has been the medium by which the doctor ensures that the treatment he/she provides does not violate the patient's bodily integrity. It must be stated at the outset that consent is not regarded in this book as a right or, as Brownsword puts it, a free-standing ethic;[6] rather it is the medium by which the law protects the patient's right to bodily integrity.

Consent has served its purpose and continues to play a major role in medical consultations but, with the movement from medical paternalism to proactive patient involvement in decision-making, and with increasing use

---

1 Rosen R and Dewer S, *On Being a Doctor: Redefining Medical Professionalism For Better Patient Care*. London: King's Fund 2004, p. 2.

2 Hippocratic oath; available at. http://www.nlm.nih.gov/hmd/greek/greek_oath.html. Accessed 1 November 2014.

3 In this book 'treatment' includes physical examination, ancillary investigations and the gamut of physical, psychological and pharmacological interventions employed to cure disease and/or promote well-being.

4 Kravitz RL and Melnikow J, Engaging patients in medical decision making (2001) 323 BMJ 584.

5 General Medical Council, Consent: Patients and *Doctors Making Decisions Together*. London: GMC 2008.

6 Brownsword R, The cult of consent: fixation and fallacy (2004) 15 King's College Law Journal 223–253, at p. 225.

of rights discourse, questions are now being asked as to whether the consent model remains fit for purpose and whether there are alternative models which offer advantages where consent has limitations.[7] The law, as reflected in judicial pronouncements, seeks to protect the self-determination ('autonomy') of the individual through consent but critics have doubted that the law actually achieves what it sets out to do in this regard.[8] For a start, there is no uniform conception of autonomy in law, ethics and philosophy. Even if an agreed conception of autonomy were to be articulated for medical law and bioethics, Manson and O'Neil assert that the prevailing approach to consent does not protect self-determination,[9] and McLean states that 'the law has developed in such a manner as to be systematically incapable, or perhaps unwilling, to find a formula that can support the preferred account'.[10] Given that, arguably, consent as currently operationalised does not protect the patient's right to self-determination, other critics have sought to develop more nuanced models of consent.[11]

What is quite clear, and more or less universally agreed, is that consent as currently applied by the courts and by clinicians is inadequate in serving the intended purpose, and an alternative approach needs to be considered. It may well be, however, that the answer lies not in a refashioning of consent but in consideration of a different model. I would argue that, for various reasons, producing more sophisticated accounts of consent may not be the answer. In a nutshell, the argument is as follows.

Firstly, while the consent model has its strengths, it has fundamental flaws that warrant consideration of alternative model(s). Secondly, as a general principle when a tool, system or strategy is not delivering the required end-product, consequent to fundamental flaws, it is often more productive to think laterally and consider alternative approaches, rather than persist with efforts to rescue the failing one. Sticking to the failing model when the situation calls for an alternative model could become a fixation, and it is well recognised in psychology and business that fixation increases the probability of poor judgment, poor decision-making, error and adverse outcomes.[12] Fixation with

7 See Manson NC and O'Neill O, *Rethinking Informed Consent in Bioethics*. Cambridge: Cambridge University Press 2007; Maclean A, *Autonomy, Informed Consent and Medical Law: A Relational Challenge*. Cambridge: Cambridge University Press 2009; McLean SAM, *Autonomy, Consent and the Law*. Abingdon: Routledge 2010; Maclean A, From *Sidaway* to *Pearce* and beyond: is the legal regulation of consent any better following a quarter of a century of judicial scrutiny? (2012) 20 Med L Rev 108–129.

8 Maclean, From *Sidaway* to *Pearce* and beyond; McLean, *Autonomy, Consent and the Law*.

9 Manson and O'Neill, *Rethinking Informed Consent*.

10 McLean, *Autonomy, Consent and the Law*, p. 95.

11 Manson and O'Neill, *Rethinking Informed Consent*; Maclean, *Autonomy, Informed Consent and Medical Law*.

12 Murphy JD, *Flawless Execution: Use the Techniques and Systems of America's Fighter Pilots to Perform at Your Peak and Win the Battles of the Business World*. New York: Regan Books 2005,

consent in the face of contemporary developments in medical law could have similar consequences, and it will be argued in this book that the judicial thinking and outcome in the celebrated case of *Chester* v. *Afshar*[13] reflected fixation with the consent model.

Thirdly, while the more nuanced conceptions of consent may have ethical and philosophical sophistication, they do not provide a readily applicable *legal* framework. The ethical foundations of consent are important, but the primary focus of this book is on the legal protection of the patient's right to self-determination.

Finally, the limits of the consent model have to do not only with the theoretical construct but also with the gap between the paradigm of consent espoused in theory and the paradigm that is operationalised in clinical practice. No matter how much theorising is done about consent, the desired goal of protecting the patient's right to self-determination will not be achieved if the legal framework for achieving this has no bearing on the attitudes and behaviour of clinicians.[14] Conversely, a legal framework that is in harmony with the context of clinical practice is more likely to serve the patient's interests effectively. In other words, any framework that aims to secure and enhance the protection of patient self-determination should be embedded in the core of medical professionalism if it is to be maximally effective. It is argued in this book that the limitations of the consent model (and especially the diluted paradigm of consent operationalised in clinical practice) are potentially avoidable in a new model, and that the new model should be embedded not only in the common law but also in medical professionalism. It will also be argued that, given recent guidance from professional bodies and regulators, the model advocated in this book is more likely to be embedded in clinical practice than the consent model has been – because the recent professional guidance has at its core the underlying principles of the proposed model.

In the light of the criticisms and limitations of the consent model, this book explores the potential benefits of a property-based approach to protecting

---

pp. 118–122. Also Job M, 'Hey – what's happening here?' In *Air Disaster* vol 1. Fyshwick ACT: Aerospace Publications 1994, pp. 98–111.

13 *Chester* v. *Afshar* [2004] UKHL 41; [2005] 1 AC 134; [2004] 3 WLR 927.

14 It has been said that 'one of the goals of tort law is to influence how doctors and other healthcare professionals act and to encourage higher standards of care'. Heywood R, Macaskill A and Williams K, Informed consent in hospital practice: health professionals' perspectives and legal reflections (2010) 18 Med L Rev 152–184, citing Fanning JB, Uneasy lies the neck that wears a stethoscope: some observations on defensive medicine (2008) 24 Professional Negligence 93; Symonds A, Reactions to perceived risk: defensiveness in clinical practice (2003) 9 Clinical Risk 182; McFarlane G, Clinical negligence – risk management and reporting (2001) 2 J Personal Injury Law 164.

the patient's right to self-determination. The property model comprises the following elements:

- the patient's right to self-determination is protected as a distinct legal right
- the patient's right to bodily integrity is a proprietary right
- the patient also has a proprietary right in his/her legitimate expectation of involvement in decision-making about their own treatment
- correlative to the patient's proprietary rights, the doctor has a fiduciary duty to enable the patient to make an informed decision, by providing relevant information
- pursuant to this fiduciary duty, the doctor–patient consultation is transactional (rather than the unidirectional passive transfer of data – described as the conduit paradigm[15] of information disclosure – that is practised in consent discussions)
- there is a bilateral distribution of responsibilities between doctor and patient: the doctor has a responsibility to take reasonable steps to ensure that the patient understands the information provided, and the patient takes responsibility for the information communicated to the doctor and also for his/her own decision.

It could be said of the property model, as was said of the doctrine of informed consent by an academic commentator, that it 'weaves social policy, communication theory, patient-doctor interactions and medical ethics into a complex legal tapestry'.[16]

Taking as my starting point the position that treating patients without reference to, or in disregard of, their views and preferences is anathema in contemporary clinical practice, I compare the subsisting consent model and the proposed property model. I begin with a discussion of the patient's right to self-determination, drawing on concepts of medical paternalism, anti-paternalism and consumerism (Chapter 2). An attempt has been made to substantially elucidate the concept of paternalism because this is the antithesis of what the consent and property models both seek to entrench. Breach of the duty of care in tort cannot arise in the absence of a relationship, so the nature of the doctor–patient relationship is also explored in this chapter. An essential element of the proposed property model is a doctor–patient relationship in which the doctor, acting in a fiduciary capacity, provides the patient with information on the nature of the condition and possible interventions, and assists the patient in determining which medical interventions fit with the patient's articulated values, with the patient retaining ultimate decisional control.

15 A scholarly exposition of the conduit paradigm is given by Manson and O'Neill, *Rethinking Informed Consent.*

16 Carnerie F, Crisis and informed consent: analysis of a law-medicine malocclusion (1986) 12 Am J Law & Med 55–97, at p. 56.

This is followed by a discussion of the legal and ethical aspects of the consent model (Chapters 3 and 4) and analysis of the limitations of this model (Chapter 5). Property has many meanings, and it is important to establish the meaning and context of the term as it applies in this analysis. This is done in Chapter 6.

In applying property analysis to the subject of self-determination in health-care decision-making, there are two possible approaches. The more trodden path is to consider one's body as one's own property. The alternative approach, an untravelled road which will be explored in this book, is to regard the patient's legitimate expectations from a medical consultation and the associated right to proactive involvement in decision-making as constituting a proprietary right. The association of property discourse with commodification of the human body will be a stumbling block in any attempt to promote a property model in doctor–patient consultations. Chapter 7 attempts to remove this stumbling block by elucidating the issue of property rights in the human body and in body parts and particles. A key point in this discussion is that property (as understood in this book) defines a relationship, not a thing. To move further away from the reification of property, a novel theory of proprietary rights in the doctor–patient consultation is developed in Chapter 8. This theory ascribes proprietary rights to the expectations that arise from the doctor–patient consultation. Since both the law and ordinary usage commonly associate the term 'property' with tangibles, it is suggested that the term 'proprietary right' should be adopted in preference to 'property' or 'property right' when applying property analysis to the doctor–patient transaction and, in particular, the patient's right to be the ultimate decision-maker in their treatment.

The property model will confer no advantage unless it overcomes the limitations of the consent model, and this is discussed in Chapters 9 and 10. The property model has the advantage over the consent model in that it does not require the occurrence of harm for a claim to arise; thus, there is no requirement to prove causation – a major stumbling block in consent cases.

It is argued that patient involvement in medical decision-making is about more than just halting medical paternalism, and that the patient's right to self-determination is worthy of protection as a legal right in itself (that is, as a distinct legal right), regardless of whether the patient has suffered any harm as a result of a breach of that right. The property model is a mechanism for achieving this. Possible implications of the adoption of the property model – such as widening the legal scope of the fiduciary duty of the doctor and expansion of the tort of battery – are discussed.

The theories discussed and developed in the preceding chapters provide an interpretative framework for analysing case law. In Chapter 9, legal issues in key consent cases are re-visited using this framework, and the judicial decision in each of these cases is analysed in the context of the property model.

Property analysis is not the only alternative to consent. Arguably, human rights law and contract law are feasible mechanisms for enshrining legal protection of the right to self-determination. It is submitted that human rights law is unable to protect this right with the rigour that the property model offers, while application of contract law could potentially subvert the doctor–patient relationship and, in any case, the doctrine of consideration could be an obstacle.

Consent analysis may be helpful in protecting the patient against medical paternalism but, due to intrinsic and extrinsic limitations, cannot go far enough in equipping the patient for a more proactive role in decision-making. Furthermore, the patient faces formidable obstacles in obtaining an appropriate remedy when the right to self-determination is interfered with. In other words, while the consent model is more of a shield for the doctor than a sword for the patient,[17] the property model may well provide both a shield and a sword for the protection of patient self-determination in medical decision-making.

The book concludes, in Chapter 10, with the assertion that the property model has potential to promote patient involvement in health-care decision-making, subject to its further development.

Choosing the Right Paradigm

In order to appraise consent and self-determination in a realistic and pragmatic rather than abstract way, we must examine the concepts not in isolation but within the context of public policy. Public policy discussions may be framed in metaphors, and it has been said that 'an extensive repertoire of metaphors appears to be helpful in the pursuit of productive discourse about health'.[18]

This book adopts an ecology paradigm modelled on the ecological metaphor described by George Annas,[19] who identifies two other metaphors in health care. He describes the military metaphor as having the most pervasive influence in the practice of medicine and gives the following examples:

> Medicine is a battle against death. Diseases attack the body, uniformed physicians intervene. We are almost constantly engaged in wars on various diseases, such as cancer and AIDS. Physicians, who are mostly specialists backed by allied health professionals, and trained to be aggressive, fight invading diseases with weapons designed to knock them out. Physicians give orders in the trenches and on the

17 An analogy originally used in relation to the doctrine of estoppel ('a shield not a sword') as it cannot be used on its own as the basis of an action.

18 Marinker M, Health policy and the constructive conversationalist. In Marinker M, *Constructive Conversations about Health.* Oxford: Radcliffe 2006, pp. 1–16, at p. 8.

19 Annas GJ, *Some Choice – Law, Medicine and the Market.* New York: Oxford University Press 1998.

> front lines and use their armamentaria in search of breakthroughs. Treatments are conventional or heroic, and the brave patients soldier on as gallant fighters who hope to conquer their diseases. We engage in triage in the emergency department, invasive procedures in the operating theater, and even in defensive medicine when a legal enemy is suspected.[20]

He goes on to argue that the military metaphor encourages us to over-mobilise and ignore costs, and just as military superpowers engage in the arms race, so health-care providers engage in a race to catch up with the latest technology. The patient's body is seen as a battlefield and clinicians concentrate on the physical.[21] Applying this to the subject matter of this book, consent procedures in clinical practice are often like well-rehearsed military drills, and a patient faced with a consent form to sign is often like the military personnel mindful of the culture to obey now, complain later.

The other metaphor is the market metaphor which has consumer choice as its mantra. Clinicians in the contemporary National Health Service (NHS) are familiar with the provider side of this metaphor in which managers, cost-cutting and value-for-money reign supreme. Emphasis is on efficiency, customer satisfaction and competition between health-care providers. Annas criticises this metaphor for being just as dysfunctional as the military metaphor.[22] He is critical of the ideology of medicine being displaced by the ideology of the marketplace. One must stress, however, that displacing the ideology of medicine with the ideology of the marketplace is a separate matter to, and should be distinguished from, the concept of transferring learning from the marketplace to the health-care arena. Health professionals can learn and borrow ideas (including the freedom of the consumer to make his/her own decisions based on his/her values) from the marketplace; this does not necessarily mean that one ideology is replaced by the other.

Annas' preferred metaphor is the ecology metaphor, a metaphor that places greater emphasis on the community than on individuals:

> Ecologists use words like integrity, balance, natural, limited (resources), quality (of life), diversity, renewable, sustainable, responsibility (for future generations), stewardship, community, and conservation. The concepts embedded in these words and others common to the ecology movement could, if applied to health

20 Ibid., p. 45.

21 The use of military metaphor has also been criticised elsewhere: Wiggins NM, Stop using military metaphors for disease (2012) BMJ 345: e4706.

22 Annas, *Some Choice*.

> care, have a profound impact on the way the debate about it is conducted and on plans for change that are seen as reasonable.[23]

Control and conformity in health care are in tune with the military and market metaphors, whereas retreat from individualism and promotion of the communal spirit are encouraged by the ecological metaphor.

The ecology paradigm has been chosen for this book because ecology values the relationship of individuals with each other and with the wider environment, and property is conceptualised in this book as defining relationships rather than things. Also, just as ecology regards biodiversity as enriching rather than diminishing nature, the increasing heterogeneity of social and cultural values in modern society are regarded in this book as enhancing the importance of self-determination. The key implication of adopting an ecology paradigm in this book is that I subscribe to McLean's view regarding the individualist account of self-determination, that 'it too may be described as socially contextualised'.[24] As will be seen in Chapter 2, the conception of self-determination adopted in this book more or less decries the atomism associated with absolute autonomy, and takes account of social responsibility and communal good. It would thus appear to be consistent with, or at least lean towards, the ecology paradigm. The notion of property adopted in Chapters 5 and 6 also fits with this paradigm.

On the surface, it might appear that the ecology paradigm is out of tune with the drive for individual choice in health care. In this regard, the ecology paradigm is confronted head-on by rights discourse. In *The Silent World of Doctor and Patient*, Katz states that:

> The history of the physician-patient relationship from ancient times to the present … bears testimony to physicians' inattention to the patient's right and need to make their own decisions.[25]

This historical position has evolved; contemporary health care emphasises patients' rights and places patients at the centre of the health-care system.[26] "Patients' choice" has become a mantra – but Annas feels that choice has been trivialised because the rhetoric of choice has not been tied to the language of rights: 'Human rights language is much richer and more inclusive than choice language.'[27] Rights language and choice language both have problems, the former carrying the connotation of a right to demand a particular treatment

23 Ibid., p. 48.

24 McLean, *Autonomy, Consent and the Law*, p. 30.

25 Katz J, *The Silent World of Doctor and Patient.* New York: Free Press 1984, p. 28.

26 Department of Health, *The NHS Plan: A Plan for Investment, A Plan for Reform.* Cm 4818-I. London: The Stationery Office 2000.

27 Annas, *Some Choice*, p. 249.

and the latter connoting selection from an à la carte menu provided by the doctor.[28]

In the discussion of self-determination that follows (Chapter 2), it is made clear that self-determination is not absolute and, on the other hand, is more than the mere expression of choice.[29] Choice, however, is perhaps the most visible dimension of self-determination; decision-making invariably ends with a choice (or preference), and in health care the freedom to make an informed choice from a range of treatment options (or to refuse all) is the hallmark of patient self-determination.

If rights discourse is a rich medium for advancing self-determination, then property analysis has a lot to offer – after all property rights have traditionally been highly valued by society, and accorded strong legal protection.

As with absolute autonomy, rights discourse becomes burdensome when isolated from the overall interests of society. This tension between individual rights and communal interest is apparent in Chapter 2 where the concept of self-determination is discussed.

Issues beyond the Scope of this Book

The consent and property models are not mutually exclusive. They both acknowledge the primacy of the patient's right to self-determination, and oblige the doctor to obtain the patient's informed agreement before proceeding with treatment. I do not argue in this book that consent must necessarily be jettisoned; what this book does is to offer an alternative model which retains the strengths of the consent model but potentially offers stronger *legal* protection to patient self-determination.

Also, the scope of the book is limited to establishing the principle that the patient's legitimate expectation of involvement in decision-making about his/her care can be a proprietary right[30] (the conceptual argument), and should be regarded as such (the consequential argument, i.e. that no untoward legal or ethical consequences flow from application of the property model). Detailed description of how the law can operationalise this principle is beyond the scope of this work.

In this book, clinical decision-making refers to the selection of a course of action regarding the treatment of a patient. In some cases this would entail making a choice between treatment alternatives. In other cases, it may simply

28 Described by Baroness O'Neill as 'mere choice'. O'Neill, *Autonomy and Trust in Bioethics*. Cambridge; Cambridge University Press 2002, p. 28.

29 See also the definition of consumerism in Chapter 2, pp. 32–33.

30 Or an object of property.

entail choosing whether or not to proceed with one particular treatment (i.e. a choice of treatment or no treatment). Processes involving cognition, intuition and emotion are involved in decision-making, but an exploration of these processes is also outside the scope of this work. Their importance is, however, recognised in the central position which the property model accords to the transactional form of doctor–patient communication.

Chapter 2
Patient Involvement in Decision-making: The Right to Self-determination

> In modern law medical paternalism no longer rules.[1]

> The dye is now cast: the rhetoric, if not the reality, of the relationship between physician and patient has been irrevocably changed by contemporary recognition of the importance of patient self-determination.[2]

To set the context for an analysis of the consent and property models, the concept of patient self-determination is discussed in this chapter. Firstly, the conception of self-determination adopted in this book is clarified; then the basis for protecting self-determination (that patients want it, that it is associated with better clinical and health outcomes, and that it is a fundamental right) is outlined. As conceived in this book, patient self-determination comprises (a) the right to bodily integrity and (b) the right to make decisions regarding treatment.

The ways in which patient self-determination may be suppressed or expressed are described. Patient self-determination may be suppressed by medical paternalism or by instrumentalisation (the use of persons as instruments to achieve the doctor's goals, as happened in the Tuskegee and Willowbrook scandals[3]). The latter could be regarded as a crime, and so it has been excluded from further discussion, and attention is focused on paternalism.

Self-determination is expressed when the patient, rather than the doctor, is the ultimate arbiter of what treatment may or may not be given, and when. It is shown in this chapter that this decisional authority is moving from the hands of the doctor to those of the patient, but a lot more needs to be done. The progression from paternalism to 'patient-centred care' is described and current

---

1 Lord Steyn in *Chester (Respondent)* v. *Afshar (Appellant)* [2004] UKHL 41, at para 16.

2 McLean SAM, *Autonomy, Consent and the Law*. Abingdon: Routledge 2010, p. 31.

3 Brandt, AM, Racism and research: the case of the Tuskegee Syphilis Study (1978) 8 Hastings Cent Rep 21–29; Rothman DJ, Were Tuskegee & Willowbrook 'studies in nature'? (1982) 12 Hastings Cent Rep 5–7.

initiatives to promote patient self-determination in the UK National Health Service are outlined.

The protection of patient self-determination entails the following elements: (a) recognition of, and respect for, the patient's right to decide what treatment to have or not to have; (b) provision of an enabling climate for the patient to make self-determined choices (ensuring effective communication and building trust); and (c) having regard for the context (social, cultural, emotional, etc.) in which the patient has to make his or her decision. In keeping with the ecology paradigm adopted in Chapter 1, self-determination is viewed not in isolation but in the context of the doctor–patient relationship. This relationship is critical to the fulfilment of the three elements listed above. The literature on various models of the relationship is briefly reviewed and it is concluded that the 'collaborative' approach to doctor–patient consultation offers the best protection for patient self-determination as defined in this book.

Patient Sovereignty

The underlying principle of this book is that every person has a right to self-determination in respect of the medical treatment that they receive. This right was famously affirmed by Cardozo J in the landmark US case of *Schloendoff* v. *Society of New York Hospital*:

> … every human being of adult years and sound mind has a right to determine what shall be done with his own body; and a surgeon who performs an operation without his patient's consent, commits an assault.[4]

It was reaffirmed by Lord Donaldson MR in the UK case *Re T*:

> An adult patient who … suffers from no mental incapacity has an absolute right to choose whether to consent to medical treatment, to refuse it or to choose one rather than another of the treatments being offered … This right of choice is not limited to decisions which others might regard as sensible. It exists notwithstanding that the reasons for making the choice are rational, irrational, unknown or even non-existent.[5]

In the same vein, Butler-Sloss said in *Re MB* that:

4 *Schloendoff* v. *Society of New York Hospital* 105 NE 92 (1914), at 105.
5 *Re T (Adult: Refusal of Treatment)* (1992) 4 All ER 649, at 652.

> A mentally competent patient has an absolute right to refuse to consent to medical treatment for any reason, rational or irrational, or for no reason at all, even where that decision may lead to his or her own death.[6]

This right is commonly referred to in legal and other texts as 'autonomy' but the term is somewhat amorphous, each school of thought moulding it to suit their purpose. For example, philosophers view autonomy as an attribute of personhood, while psychologists regard it as a behaviour.[7] Even among philosophers, concepts of autonomy vary. Autonomy could refer to freedom from control by others. It could also mean freedom from any factor which prevents one from making a choice consistent with one's values. In health care, the word autonomy is used with various interpretations.[8] As Switankowsky put it, autonomy is 'a philosophical concept that is riddled with psychological complexities and individual peculiarities'.[9]

When a judge uses the term he/she probably takes it as no more than a shorthand for the right of the patient to decide what may or may not be done to his/her body. It is unlikely that the judge has considered any philosophical analyses of the term or anticipates that his/her use of the term will be subjected to such analysis. Coggon, for example, has noted that '[i]t is rare for a judge to provide an explicit, philosophical investigation of autonomy'.[10]

In order to avoid (to the extent that this is possible) some of the confusion associated with the diverse interpretations of the word 'autonomy', the term self-determination is used as an alternative to autonomy in this book. The essence of self-determination is the notion of a person who is able to decide, choose or act on the basis of his/her own volition rather than the dictates of another person or group of persons. Self-determination in health care is the antithesis of paternalism. As Lord Scarman put it, patient self-determination is 'no more and no less than the right of a patient to determine for himself whether he will or will not accept the doctor's advice'.[11]

At this juncture, it is worth clarifying the relationship between self-determination and the principle of bodily integrity, the latter being a common starting point for defining consent to treatment. The principle of bodily integrity

6 *Re MB* 38 BMLR 175.

7 Bergsma J and Thomasma DC, *Autonomy and Clinical Medicine: Renewing the Health Professional Relation with the Patient.* Dordrecht: Kluwer Academic 2000, p. 109.

8 Slowther A, The concept of autonomy and its interpretation in health care (2007) 2 Clinical Ethics 173–175.

9 Switankowsky IS, *A New Paradigm for Informed Consent.* Lanham, Md.: University Press of America 1998, p. xvii.

10 Coggon J, Varied and principled understandings of autonomy in English law: justifiable inconsistency of blinkered moralism? (2007) 15 Health Care Anal 235–255, at p. 236.

11 *Sidaway* v. *Board of Governors of Bethlem Royal Hospital* [1985] 1 All ER 643 HL, at 649.

holds the human body to be inviolate; a person's body cannot be interfered with by another without that person's willing agreement. It is protected by Article 3 of the Universal Declaration of Human Rights which states that '[e]veryone has the right to life, liberty and security of person', and by constitutional provisions in some countries.[12] This principle is one of the two components of self-determination (as defined in this book), the other component being decisional control. As Petersen puts it:

> Self-determination is broader than bodily integrity in the sense that it concerns not only an individual's body but also his or her actions and choices – including whether to engage in sexual relations, to marry or to bear children.[13]

The distinction between bodily integrity and self-determination was made in passing by Robert Walker LJ in an English case:

> Every human being's right to life carries with it, as an intrinsic part of it, rights of bodily integrity and autonomy – the right to have one's own body whole and intact and (upon reaching an age of understanding) to take decisions about one's body.[14]

This distinction is important in the context of this book because self-determination could be expressed (or suppressed) in clinical situations that do not necessarily entail touching the body. In such situations, there may be no physical violation of the patient's bodily integrity, but decisional control is taken away from the patient, thus breaching his/her right to self-determination.

All accounts of self-determination have one thing in common: the individual should have a right to make his/her own decision/choice and should be allowed to exercise that right. Where they differ is in relation to two other elements: firstly whether a decision has to be rational for it to be a true expression of self-determination; secondly, whether, in expressing self-determination, the individual is obliged to consider third party interests.

Accounts that make rational decision-making a prerequisite for self-determination are excluded from further consideration in this book because the law, as it currently stands (see quotes above), does not require a patient's decision to be rational in order for it to be accepted as legitimate, and any

---

12 For example, article 40 of the constitution of the Republic of Ireland.

13 Petersen CJ, Reproduction and family planning: individual right or public policy? In Wacks R (ed), *Hong Kong, China and 1997: Essays in Legal Theory*. Hong Kong: Hong Kong University Press, pp. 261–306, at p. 268.

14 Robert Walker LJ, in *Re A (Minors) (Conjoined Twins: Separation)* [2000] Lloyd's Rep Med 425, at 494.

argument for this aspect of common law to be changed is outside the scope of this work.

Taking account of third party interests is presented in the literature as a key difference between the individualistic model of autonomy and the relational model.[15] One could, however, argue that, in practice, the difference between the two accounts is not as substantial as is sometimes portrayed. In Chapter 6 the point is made that the notion of property in a coconut anywhere on an island is, at least in practical terms, meaningless to the man who is the sole inhabitant of that island – property is a function of the *relationship* we have with persons around us. In a similar way, self-determination is a function of our social interactions and experiences. The very idea of having individuals make their own decisions stems from the fact that each individual has different life experiences, interests, priorities, values and so on, all the result of interactions with other members of the community. There would be no basis for recognising individualism if we were all just individual anatomical and physiological entities (in other words, biological clones), devoid of any social identity. The idea of self-determination being a function of the patient's social interactions and experiences fits with the ecology paradigm adopted in Chapter 1. It goes without saying, therefore, that any absolutely and purely individualistic notion of self-determination is rejected by this author.

The pragmatic question is to what extent should individuals be allowed to make their own decisions, unfettered by what the rest of the community thinks or wants? In other words, where should the balance between individual rights and communal interests lie? Lord Mustill referred to this balance in *R* v. *Brown*, albeit without specifying where the line is drawn:

> ... the state should interfere with the right of an individual to live his or her life as he or she may choose no more than is necessary to ensure a proper balance between the specific interests of the individual and the general interests of the individuals who together comprise the populace at large.[16]

Few in the western world would contest the right of the individual to self-governance.[17] What is controversial, however, is where the line is drawn between this right and the interests of the community. In other words, to use a term that I return to in my adopted model of property (Chapter 6), what should be the *stringency of protection* of this right?

---

15 Nedelsky J, *Law's Relations: A Relational Theory of Self, Autonomy, and Law*. New York and Oxford: Oxford University Press 2012.

16 R v. *Brown* [1993] 2 All ER 75, at 116.

17 This book focuses on health care decision-making in the western world. It is conceded that some Asian, African and Islamic traditions and scholarship may abhor individual rights.

The extremist views on this question are moral individualism at one end and communitarianism at the other. Moral individualism[18] holds that persons are egoistic and each person should determine what counts as moral good on his/her own, without reference to objective standards.[19] To some minds (but not to this author) moral individualism could be taken as homologous with self-determination. As stated above, this notion of self-determination is rejected.

At the other end is communitarianism (as a philosophical concept rather than a political ideology) which emphasises the need to balance individual rights and interests with those of the community as a whole, and argues that individual people (or citizens) are shaped by the cultures and values of their communities. Unlike classical liberalism, which construes communities as aggregates of atomistic and egoistic individuals, it emphasises the role of the community in defining and shaping individuals.[20]

McLean regards the gap between these extremes as narrower than portrayed in the literature.[21] Further she points out (and this is consonant with the ecology paradigm adopted in this book) that:

> The lessons that the individualistic account can learn from the relational one are that the moral worth of decisions is predicted not only by the mere *exercise* of choice but potentially also by the *impact* of that choice on others.[22]

Studies have shown that patients make treatment decisions based on their social experiences, emotions, relationships and values.[23] The question is not whether decision-making should be influenced by other-regarding considerations; we expect the individual's decision to be influenced by experiences and relationships. Rather the question is whether the individual having made their decision, the decision should be followed to the letter or be modified by the doctor in the light of communitarian considerations. The issue becomes less contentious if contextualised against the predominant political tradition. In the western world

18 Hellsten S, *In Defense of Moral Individualism*. Helsinki: Philosophical Society of Finland 1997.

19 As discussed later, the courts are often challenged as to whether to apply subjective or objective standards in determining whether a patient's right to self-determination has been breached.

20 Here I am referring to communitarianism as it would apply in a multicultural western state. I have excluded consideration of some Asian and African communities where the individual has virtually no rights and the communal interests always trump those of any individual.

21 McLean, *Autonomy, Consent and the Law*.

22 Ibid., p. 28 (emphases in original).

23 van Kleffens T, van Baarsen B and van Leeuwen E, The medical practice of patient autonomy and cancer treatment refusals: a patients' and physicians' perspective (2004) 58 Soc Sci Med 2325–2336; Sinding C and Wiernikowski J, Treatment decision-making and its discontents (2009) 48 Social Work in Health Care 614–634.

this tradition is democracy, which gives each individual the same right to elect the political leadership and encourages equal participation of all citizens in governance. In democracies, the individual is the unit of society, but individuals are also subject to the laws and customs of society.

The conception of self-determination adopted in this book can therefore be encapsulated as follows. The patient has a right to determine what shall be done with his/her own body. Recognition of this right should manifest as proactive involvement of the patient in decision-making regarding his/her treatment. Acknowledging and acting in accordance with the extent to which a patient wishes to participate (or not participate) in making decisions is part of regard for that patient's self-determination. In making their decisions, patients will be guided to varying degrees (from zero to maximum, as self-determined) by the opinion of their doctor and their personal experiences, values and relationships, but ultimately the decision should be theirs except where they have specifically and voluntarily opted to have the decision made for them by the doctor (excluding cases of incapacity, which are outside the scope of this book).

Involving Patients in Decision-making: What Does it Mean?

While it is widely acknowledged that patients should be involved in decisions about their treatment, there is no uniform articulation of what this means in practice.[24] A patient may be 'involved' in the process but not be the one making the final decision. I submit that in such cases, the right to self-determination has not been upheld, except where the patient has specifically and voluntarily delegated to the doctor the responsibility for making the final decision.

What is important is the exercise of self-determination, as distinct from the question of who has made the final decision. Respecting the extent to which a patient wishes to participate (or not participate) in making decisions is part of respect for that patient's self-determination. So long as the patient has been fully involved in the process of reaching a decision and is in control of *how* the choice of treatment is finally made, self-determination has been upheld. So long as this process has been applied and the chosen treatment is acceptable to the patient, the issue of *who* actually made the choice (patient or doctor) is a secondary matter. In other words, the patient's right to self-determination is also expressed when he/she voluntarily delegates decision-making responsibilities to the doctor.

24 Edwards A and Elwyn G, Inside the black box of shared decision making – distinguishing between the process of involvement and who makes the decision (2006) 9 Health Expectations 307–320.

Patient involvement in treatment decision-making is commonly construed in terms of doctor–patient communication and the patient's use of information to select a preferred treatment option. This construal has been criticised for being too narrow,[25] but any exploration of patient involvement beyond this construal is outwith the scope of this work. The concepts underlying the property model proposed in this book are, however, congruent with the 'stages and competences of involving patients in healthcare decisions' enunciated by Elwyn *et al.*, reproduced in Figure 2.1.

1. Implicit or explicit involvement of patients in decision-making process.
2. Explore ideas, fears and expectations of the problem and possible treatments.
3. Portrayal of equipoise and options.
4. Identify preferred format and provide tailor-made information.
5. Checking process: understanding of information and reactions (e.g. ideas, fears and expectations of possible options).
6. Checking process: acceptance of process and decision-making role preference, involving the patient to the extent they desire to be involved.
7. Make, discuss or defer decisions.
8. Arrange follow-up.

Figure 2.1 Stages and competences of involving patients in health-care decisions

Source: Elwyn *et al.*[26]

25 Entwistle VA and Watt IS, Patient involvement in treatment decision-making: the case for a broader conceptual framework (2006) 63 Patient Educ Couns 268–278.

26 Elwyn G, Edwards A, Kinnersley P and Grol R, Shared decision making and the concept of equipoise: the competences of involving patients in healthcare choices (2000) 50 Br J Gen Pract 892–897.

The Basis for Protecting Self-determination

If judicial or legislative intervention to enhance patient involvement in decision-making is to be advocated, there must be further justification for this, other than saying that paternalism is bad. Patients should be involved in making decisions about their treatment because they have a right to bodily integrity, because it is usually their wish to be involved[27] and this increases their satisfaction with care provided,[28] and because it is in their health interests to be involved.[29] Also, if trust in health professionals and in the health system has been eroded, as observed by O'Neill,[30] enhanced patient involvement in decision-making is one way of regaining confidence and trust. Above all, it is argued in Chapter 9 that the right to self-determination is so fundamental that it deserves protection as a distinct right.

Patients Want to Be Involved

Studies show that the majority of patients want to be involved in decision-making regarding their treatment.[31] National patient surveys involving a total of more than one million patients in England showed that 'involvement in

27 Say R, Murtagh M and Thomson R, Patients' preference for involvement in medical decision making: a narrative review (2006) 60 Patient Educ Couns 102–114.

28 Little P, Everitt H, Williamson I, Warner G, Moore M, Gould C, Ferrier K and Payne S, Observational study of effect of patient centredness and positive approach on outcomes in general practice consultations (2001) 323 BMJ 908–911.

29 Britten N, Stevenson F, Barry C, Barber N and Bradley C, Misunderstandings in general practice prescribing decisions: qualitative study (2000) 320 BMJ 1246–1250; Fallowfield LJ, Hall A, Maguire P, Baum M and A'Hern RP, Psychological effects of being offered choice of surgery for breast cancer (1994) 309 BMJ 448; Greenfield S, Kaplan SH, Ware JE Jr, Yano EM and Frank HJ, Patients' participation in medical care: effects on blood sugar control and quality of life in diabetes (1988) 3 J Gen Intern Med 448–457; Heisler M, Bouknight RR, Hayward RA, Smith DM and Kerr EA, The relative importance of physician communication, participatory decision making, and patient understanding in diabetes self-management (2002) 17 J Gen Intern Med 243–252; Jahng KH, Martin LR, Golin CE and Di Matteo MR, Preferences for medical collaboration: patient-physician congruence and patient outcomes (2005) 57 Patient Educ Couns 308–314; Kaplan S, Greenfield S and Ware JE Jr, Assessing the effects of physician-patient interactions on the outcomes of chronic disease (1989) 27 Medical Care S110–S127; Mandelblatt J, Kreling B, Figeuriedo M and Feng S, What is the impact of shared decision making on treatment and outcomes for older women with breast cancer? (2006) 24 J Clin Oncol 4908–4913; Mead N, Bower P and Hann M, The impact of general practitioners' patient-centredness on patients' post-consultation satisfaction and enablement (2002) 55 Soc Sci Med 283–299; Schulman BA, Active patient orientation and outcomes in hypertensive treatment (1979) 17 Medical Care 267–280.

30 O'Neill O, *Autonomy and Trust in Bioethics*. Cambridge; Cambridge University Press 2002.

31 McKinstry B, Do patients wish to be involved in decision making in the consultation? A cross sectional survey with video vignettes (2000) 321 BMJ 867–71; Coulter A, *Trends in Patients' Experience of the NHS*. Oxford: Picker Institute Europe 2005; Richards N and Coulter A,

decisions and respect for preferences' is one of the aspects of health care that patients consider to be most important.[32]

The surveys showed, however, that many patients were not involved as much as they would like to be in decisions about their care and treatment, that '[a]lthough most patients are treated with dignity and respect by NHS staff, there are signs that care is still too often delivered in a paternalistic manner, with many patients given little opportunity to express their preferences or influence decisions about their care'.[33] For example, one-third of outpatients said they had not received a clear explanation of treatment risks and just over half of stroke patients said they had not been involved as much as they wanted in decisions about their care and treatment in hospital, including 19 per cent who said they were not involved at all.[34]

The authors of one study concluded that 'people vary substantially in their preferences for participation in decision making'[35] but their study actually showed that '[n]early all respondents (96%) preferred to be offered choices and to be asked their opinions'.[36] Clearly, the vast majority of patients (close to 100 per cent) want to participate in decision-making, so what can be concluded from this study is not that there is substantial variability in preferences for participation but that there is near unanimity in expression of a wish to be involved in decision-making. There are studies that report that many patients do not wish to be make decisions about their care.[37] A closer look, however, indicates that what the patients are actually rejecting is mere, sheer choice. The same patients also say they would like to be informed about their treatment. The correct interpretation of these findings is that the patients do not want the doctor to just present options and leave them to choose one. Rather, they want the doctor to provide information and to explain why one option is recommended over the other, given the patient's own circumstances. In this transaction, the patient develops trust in the doctor and may express his/her self determination by opting to go with the choice recommended by the doctor.

Is the NHS Becoming More Patient-centred? Trends from the National Surveys of NHS Patients in England 2002–07. Oxford: Picker Institute Europe 2007.

32 Coulter, *Trends in Patients' Experience of the NHS*, p. 2.

33 Ibid., p. 11.

34 Ibid.

35 Levinson W, Kao A, Kuby A and Thisted RA, Not all patients want to participate in decision making: a national study of public preferences (2005) 20 J Gen Intern Med 531–535, at p. 531.

36 Ibid.

37 Vick S and Scott A, Agency in health care: examining patients' preferences for attributes of the doctor-patient relationship (1998) 17 J Health Econ 587–605.

Medical Paternalism: The Antithesis to Patient Self-determination

Although neither the Hippocratic Oath nor its modern incarnation, the Declaration of Geneva,[38] makes reference to the patient's preferences or views, it would be unfair and incorrect to say that doctors never took any cognisance of a patient's views. They did. The point is that the patient's views were not formally recognised as paramount, were not always specifically elicited, and were always trumped by what the doctor considered to be best for the patient. Even when the patient was engaged in decision-making, it was not because the doctor perceived an ethical or legal obligation to uphold the patient's right to self-determination; rather it was because such patient involvement produced better health outcomes.[39]

No doubt, there is an inequality between patient and doctor regarding knowledge of, and insight into, the patient's medical condition. This difference places the doctor in a position of power over the patient; thus, it is sometimes said that there is a fiduciary relationship.[40] Most doctors would argue that this power has historically been exercised in a benign and benevolent manner, and that the doctor sought to do what was best for the patient. It could be argued that patients too accepted this; after all, doctors have always topped the polls of professionals most trusted by the public.[41] Patients trusted the doctor to do what was best for them, and did not need to be coerced by the doctor into accepting the clinical recommendation. From time to time there was legal

38 Declaration of Geneva; available at http://www.wma.net/en/30publications/10policies/g1/index.html.pdf. Accessed 2 November 2014. The Declaration was adopted by the 2nd General Assembly of the World Medical Association, Geneva, Switzerland, September 1948 and amended by the 22nd World Medical Assembly, Sydney, Australia, August 1968, the 35th World Medical Assembly, Venice, Italy, October 1983 and the 46th WMA General Assembly, Stockholm, Sweden, September 1994, and editorially revised at the 170th Council Session, Divonne-les-Bains, France, May 2005 and the 173rd Council Session, Divonne-les-Bains, France, May 2006. Despite numerous amendments, specific reference to the patient's right to choose, accept or refuse treatment has not been included. However, the World Medical Association International Code of Medical Ethics (http://www.wma.net/e/policy/c8.htm) states that '[a] physician shall respect a competent patient's right to accept or refuse treatment'.

39 Kaplan, Greenfield and Ware, Assessing the effects of physician-patient interactions.

40 The question whether or not a fiduciary relationship exists is discussed in Chapter 7.

41 The periodic Ipsos MORI survey shows that doctors are top of the table when the public is asked whom they generally trust to tell the truth. The former British Prime Minister Tony Blair spoke of how he had been angry to see doctors have such high ratings in the public opinion polls. It must be noted, however, that these polls are about trust of doctors as a group, not the trust that a patient has in his/her individual doctor (which is what 'trust' in the rest of this book refers to). See http://www.ipsos-mori.com/researchpublications/researcharchive/2818/Doctors-are-most-trusted-profession-politicians-least-trusted.aspx. Accessed 2 November 2014.

or ethical challenge[42] to this state of affairs but by and large this 'beneficent authoritarianism' (as Pellegrino and Thomasma[43] termed it) held sway.

With time, however, commentators and ultimately the public began to oppose what was described as medical paternalism.[44] Paternalism is the philosophy of acting in the perceived best interests of the patient irrespective of whether this line of action contradicts the patient's own wishes. It assumes that the patient is not able to decide for him/herself how best to pursue his/her own good, and could take the form of interference with the patient's freedom of action, withholding of information or deliberate misinformation. It is argued that paternalism erodes the patient's self-determination, violates the humanity of the patient and compromises healing.[45] Vocal critics of paternalism asserted as follows:

> … every act of paternalism will involve violating the principle of autonomy with regard to an individual without his/her consent and for the individual's benefit … it is not automatically right to produce benefit for another without consent.[46]

A focus on cure rather than care was decried. Medical paternalism, it is argued, assumes that the medical good is the highest good, overriding all other values; it 'subsumes all the patient's good under only one good – the medical good'.[47] Patients have values beyond the medical good, and these values could be just as important as, or indeed more important than, the medical good, and respect for the full range of values is an essential element of healing or caring. Furthermore, even the medical good is not constant, and doctors may have variable opinions and preferences among treatment options.

The patient should be free to decide what is best for him/herself based on adequate knowledge of the available treatment options. The doctor's responsibility is to provide this information as clearly and as truthfully as possible, and to respect the choice of the patient whether or not this appears

42 In the eighteenth century, for example, a surgeon was sued for disuniting a patient's healing fracture without his consent – *Slater* v. *Baker and Stapleton* (1787) 95 English Reports 860, [1767] 2 Wils K B 359. The court found that it was 'improper to disunite the callus without consent'.

43 Pellegrino ED and Thomasma DC, *For the Patient's Good: The Restoration of Beneficence in Healthcare*. Oxford: Oxford University Press 1988, p. 5.

44 Buchanan A, Medical paternalism (1978) 7 Philos Public Aff 370–90.

45 Lord Steyn in *Chester*.

46 Veatch RM and Spicer CM, Against paternalism in the patient-physician relationship. In Gillon R (ed), *Principles of Healthcare Ethics*. Chichester: John Wiley 1994, pp. 409–19, at pp. 410 and 416.

47 Pellegrino and Thomasma, *For the Patient's Good*, pp. 23–24.

rational. Indeed, it has been argued that to violate a person's self-determination 'is not to heal, but to wound, his or her humanity'.[48]

Defence of Paternalism

While some reject the suggestion that there are any potential benefits of paternalism,[49] others assert that:

> The sick still generally come to their physicians for expertise and reassurance, not knowledge and power. They want to be fixed and reassured, not educated and forced to make decisions about matters with which they are quite unfamiliar.[50]

Defenders of paternalism also say that:

> Failure to be paternalistic, in the proper sense of the word, deprives the patient and the family of real care in the time of their greatest need. Doctors have no need apologetically to defend paternalism.[51]

The qualifier ('in the proper sense of the word') is worth noting. To Shinebourne and Bush, the proper sense of the word is derived from the literal meaning: medical paternalism is simply the doctor acting like a father would to his children; but they also say that 'medical condescension ... is not implicit in the word paternalism'[52] and that '[p]aternalism does not have to imply disrespect for autonomy'.[53] Their definition of paternalism is different from the one adopted in this book (see above), which requires the doctor to act in the patient's perceived best interests *irrespective of whether this action contradicts the patient's own wishes*. Definitional problems account for incorrect statements such as saying that 'the reaction of sick doctors can ironically be to prefer paternalism to personal autonomy'[54] (meaning that when doctors are themselves ill, they want the doctors treating them to act paternalistically). Reading the original research work on which this statement is based,[55] it becomes clear that what the sick

48 Ibid., pp. 23–25.

49 Hayry H, *The Limits of Medical Paternalism*. London: Routledge 1991.

50 Wear S, *Informed Consent – Patient Autonomy and Clinical Beneficence within Health Care*, 2nd edn. Washington DC: Georgetown University Press 1998, p. 2.

51 Shinebourne EA and Bush A, For paternalism in the doctor-patient relationship. In Gillon R (ed), *Principles of Healthcare Ethics*. Chichester: John Wiley 1994, pp. 399–408, at p. 407.

52 Ibid., p. 400.

53 Ibid., p. 401.

54 Stirrat GM and Gill R, Autonomy in medical ethics after O'Neill (2005) 31 J Med Ethics 127–130.

55 Spiro HM and Mandell HN, When doctors get sick (1998) 128 Ann Intern Med 152–154.

doctors prefer to autonomy is beneficence, not paternalism; they want the treating doctors to make any decisions considered to be in their best interests but this is different from saying that they want this action *irrespective of whether it contradicts their own wishes.*

The position of the paternalist has been stated as follows:

> Patients come to physicians to be healed (or at least, restored to function and relieved of suffering as much as possible). Given this over-riding agenda, the primacy of which both parties agree upon, anything that enhances healing is appropriate, anything that diminishes or undermines it is to be avoided. What enhances it seems quite clear: the *trust* that brings that patient in and generates acceptance, compliance, and cooperation with the physician's recommendations. As to decision making, effective and appropriate management of illness dictates that this is the physician's function, often there is a clear and primary treatment of choice and the patient comes to the physician to have this identified and provided.
>
> There were other ways to enhance this process as well. Patients also came seeking reassurance, and the physician was loath not to provide it, even if he diverged from or stopped short of the truth. It was, and still is, a common belief among health care professionals that the more hopeful or optimistic patient does better therapeutically – responds better *physiologically* – than the more pessimistic, less hopeful patient. If strong reassurance enhances therapeutic response or, more specifically, if accentuating the positive and downplaying the negative is therapeutically efficacious, then it would be an abuse of the patient's trust and best interests not to do it.
>
> On this view, truth telling can be counter-therapeutic and the whole new ethos quite misguided. Even now, physicians who are consciously committed to patient autonomy routinely err on the side of emphasizing the benefits of treatment and the likelihood of success.[56]

One reason commonly cited for paternalistically withholding information from patients or misleading them is the fear that this information could induce anxiety in the patient. Higgs dismisses this attempt to justify paternalism:

> … the argument that lies are justified to prevent anxiety carries its own rebuttal. The antidote to fear is not silence but open discussion … Were trust to decline so that patients did not believe what was being said to them, not only reassurance but also genuine support during an illness would become impossible … The

56 Wear, *Informed Consent*, pp. 33–34.

> presumption remains that competent people must be allowed to choose for themselves. If they do not have the information on which to base a choice, or even a realization that a choice is necessary at all, it seems hard not to see this in itself as a major harm.[57]

In a robust analysis, Allen Buchanan identifies and debunks three arguments advanced in support of doctors paternalistically withholding information from patients.[58] The first of these arguments is the 'Prevention of Harm Argument'. This argument posits that if giving the patient information X will do great harm to him/her, the doctor is obliged by the duty of care not to give the patient this information. Buchanan states that for this argument to be valid, the doctor must show that, on balance, giving information X will do greater harm to the patient than withholding the information will.[59] Also the argument assumes that the patient will be successfully deceived and does not take account of the possible consequences (distress, distrust) of the patient suspecting or finding out that information has been withheld. A second argument is the 'Contract Version of the Prevention of Harm Argument'. The argument here is that the terms of the contractual physician–patient relationship are such that the patient authorises the physician to minimise harm to the patient by whatever means the physician deems necessary. Leaving aside the contentious issue of whether the doctor–patient relationship can rightly be described as contractual, one counterpoint to this argument is that every contract has its boundaries or limits and if the patient does not have full information, how can he/she know that the limits of the contract are being respected by the doctor? The third argument is the 'Argument from the Inability to Understand' which is based on the premise that the physician is justified in withholding information when the patient is unable to understand the information. The question arises: what harm would the patient suffer if given information that he/she cannot understand? This question takes us back to the first argument dismissed above.

Strong and Weak Paternalism

In medical paternalism the doctor acts in line with what he/she considers to be the best interests of the patient, irrespective of whether this line of action contradicts the patient's own wishes. Sometimes this paternalistic act arises when the patient is too young or has limited intelligence or education, or for other reasons is not in a position to appreciate the consequences of their

57 Higgs R, Truth-telling. In Kuhse H and Singer P (eds), *A Companion to Bioethics*, 2nd edn. Chichester: Wiley-Blackwell 2009, pp. 520–529, at p. 523.

58 Buchanan, Medical paternalism.

59 Ibid.

choice. When these conditions prevail and the clinician intervenes to act in the best interests of the patient, this is referred to as limited or weak paternalism.[60] Treatment delivered in an emergency situation is sometimes classified as weak paternalism, but I would argue that such treatment is not paternalism but beneficence.[61] In such situations the doctor is not acting without regard for the patient's preference.

In other situations the patient may suffer harm in the absence of the proposed medical intervention, and a clinician acting to protect the patient against their wish is manifesting 'strong paternalism'.[62] This form of paternalism has also been termed 'best-interest paternalism'.[63] In weak paternalism, the physician is disregarding a patient's preference or action that is substantially non-autonomous. The subject of this book is the patient who is in a position to make decisions about his or her own treatment, so the focus is on strong rather than weak paternalism.

Beauchamp and Childress list the following conditions that justify strong paternalism:

1. A patient is at risk of a significant, preventable harm.

2. The paternalistic action will probably prevent the harm.

3. The projected benefits to the patient of the paternalistic action outweigh its risks to the patient.

The least autonomy-restrictive alternative that will secure the benefits and reduce the risks is adopted.[64] These conditions point to the balance which the doctor has to make between his/her obligation to help and the requirement to respect the patient's self-determination, but the authors appear to be suggesting that it is okay to assert or to respect the patient's self-determination so long as the doctor does not foresee that this would result in significant harm to the patient – in other words, protect self-determination, but be paternalistic when you see that respecting the patient's preference could harm the patient. This view is not different from the 'Prevention of Harm Argument' rebutted above. In addition to the counter-arguments made in respect of this argument, there is the issue of what actually constitutes harm to the patient. In *Re C* the

60 Beauchamp TL and Childress JF, *Principles of Biomedical Ethics*, 5th edn. Oxford: Oxford University Press 2001, p. 181. Also Feinberg J, Legal paternalism (1971) 1 Can J Philos 105–124.

61 Beauchamp and Childress, *Principles of Biomedical Ethics*, p. 8.

62 Ibid.

63 Engelhardt HT Jr, *The Foundations of Bioethics*. Oxford: Oxford University Press 1986, p. 283.

64 Beauchamp and Childress, *Principles of Biomedical Ethics*, p. 186.

doctors' view was that the patient would be harmed if he did not agree to have his foot amputated.[65] The patient's own view was that he would be harmed (psychologically as well as physically) by having to live with one foot; he would rather die with two. Another (and less contentious) example is that of a patient who declines chemotherapy, preferring to die rather than suffer the side effects of the treatment.

Paternalism Distinguished from Beneficence

Paternalism is often described in terms that suggest it soothes the ego of power-hungry doctors and is intrinsically bad for the patient.[66] On the other hand, doctors and their advocates sometimes justify paternalism on the basis of non-maleficence and beneficence,[67] two of the four ethical principles enunciated by Beauchamp and Childress (the other two being autonomy and justice).[68] The principle of beneficence requires that we take positive steps to help others. In some situations it becomes an obligation rather than a moral ideal. In medicine, it has always been taken that the obligation to help others is the core tenet of the profession – after all, the reason why people go to a doctor is to obtain help.

Here, it must be emphasised that beneficence is not synonymous with paternalism. Beneficence is the ethical requirement to act in the best interests of the patient whereas paternalism, as defined in this book, is acting in the perceived best interests of the patient *irrespective of whether this line of action contradicts the patient's own wishes*. In other words, what distinguishes beneficence from paternalism is that the latter could entail acting in the absence of, or without reference to, the patient's consent, or even against the patient's wishes. Paternalism, by definition, entails infraction of self-determination; beneficence, on the contrary, includes respect for self-determination.

It must be stressed also that paternalism transcends the mere actions or practices of the health professional: Buchanan recognises this when he states that 'what is at issue is a paradigm, a way of conceiving the physician-patient relationship'.[69] This means that paternalism is a manifestation of the *values* and *attitudes* of the doctor, and therefore lies at the core of the doctor's concept of professionalism.[70]

---

65 *Re C (Refusal of Medical Treatment)* [1994] 1 WLR 290–296.

66 Hayry, *Limits of Medical Paternalism*.

67 Shinebourne and Bush, For paternalism in the doctor-patient relationship.

68 Beauchamp and Childress *Principles of Biomedical Ethics*.

69 Buchanan, Medical paternalism, p. 387. The doctor–patient relationship is discussed below.

70 This is one reason why I argue that any alternative to the consent model should be rooted in medical professionalism.

The same could be said of beneficence. Downie and Macnaughton assert that when doctors are 'beneficent' (seeking the best interests of their patients) it does not necessarily follow that they are upholding a moral good; rather, it is the values and attitudes (i.e. professionalism) that they bring into play that count:

> Our argument can be put simply. What is the basic professional duty of the doctor? It is to treat patients according to their best medical interests. This is not the moral duty of beneficence; it is simply a job description. Or if you want to insist that it is the moral duty of beneficence then it is one to be found in most jobs. The 'lollipop' or road crossings lady helps the children to cross the road to school. That is her job description. Call it the moral duty of beneficence if you like. The garage mechanic mends your puncture. Call it beneficence if you like, but it is just part of what he does for a living. Aristotle maintains that all actions aim at some good, but he doesn't mean a moral good. The 'good' at which all actions aim is just the point of the action. In the case of medicine that point is the best medical interests of the patient. To pursue that aim does not put you in the ranks of the saints and martyrs, or even of the moderately morally good; it is just what you do for a living. Moral assessment applies to how doctors do their jobs, not to the bare fact that that is the job they do.
>
> The significance of this argument, if it is accepted, is considerable. It has been a rarely questioned assumption that doctors, in pursuing the best interests of their patients or in acting towards them in a beneficent manner are showing morally good or indeed altruistic or supererogatory moral qualities. Yet every working person from the waitress to the bus driver might with as much justification claim that they aim at the best interests of whatever or whoever is the object of their activity. Why then should doctors make such a fuss about it, and claim a halo? The answer to this is complex … at least part of the answer is the belief that medicine is a profession and professions have ethical characteristics which are lacking in trades, industries and business.[71]

Professionalism, the framework of values and behaviour that defines the relationship between doctors and patients, will be a key factor in the implementation of any new model which aims to enhance patients' involvement in health-care decision-making. Referring to the model of clinical practice in which treatment is given only with the consent of patients and they are not treated paternalistically, O'Neill said:

71 Downie RS and Macnaughton RJ, *Bioethics and the Humanities: Attitudes and Perceptions.* Abingdon: Routledge-Cavendish 2007, p. 40.

> This revised model of doctor–patient interaction demands more than a simple change of attitude on the part of doctors, or of patients. It also requires huge changes in the terms and conditions of medical practice and ways of ensuring that treatment is given only where patients have consented.[72]

The issue of professionalism is revisited in Chapter 8, as it is an important element in the proposed property model for protection of patient self-determination.

Socio-political Currents that have Induced or Accelerated the Kick against Medical Paternalism

In the last two decades there has been a progressive retreat from medical paternalism. The socio-political currents that induced or augmented this retreat include the ascendency of rights thinking, higher levels of public awareness and education, advances in science and technology, and public knowledge of the fallibility of doctors.

The Ascendancy of Rights Thinking; Consumerism

Perhaps the most powerful factor in the progressive subjugation of paternalism is the ascendancy of rights thinking in today's world. The doctrine of human rights has its origins in the philosophy that individuals hold certain rights simply because they are individual human beings.[73] Self-determination is closely linked with natural rights; indeed, self-determination can be regarded as a foundational natural right. As Madhok recounts:

> ... it is often held that the object of human rights is to enhance the autonomy of the individual through safeguarding the security, liberty and political rights of persons.[74]

The concept of natural rights, entitlements possessed by individuals that others are constrained to acknowledge and respect, has been in existence for centuries but gained formal recognition when the Universal Declaration of Human

72 O'Neill, *Autonomy and Trust in Bioethics*, p. 19.

73 Clapham A, *Human Rights: A Very Short Introduction*. Oxford: Oxford University Press 2007, p. 5.

74 Madhok S, Autonomy and human rights. In Smith RKM and van den Anker C, *The Essentials of Human Rights*. London: Hodder Arnold 2005, pp. 20–24, at p. 20.

Rights was adopted by the United Nations in 1948.[75] Human rights, descendants of natural rights, have increasingly become key elements of legal and political systems. Issues such as access to health care, distribution of health resources and protection of reproductive health rights are commonly framed in human rights terms. In the United Kingdom, this development reached its apotheosis with the enactment of the Human Rights Act in 1998.[76]

The *raison d'être* of human rights is the prevention of abuse of power.[77] It is, therefore, not surprising that claims relating to self-determination and related issues are commonly couched in the language of rights. As observed by Jones:

> Claiming or asserting rights has become the common mode by which people seek to promote an interest or advance a cause. That is to be explained, in part, by the special force possessed by the language of rights. If we are concerned that people should be able to speak freely, or to choose their own careers, or to vote, or to marry the person of their choice, or to have an abortion, or to hunt animals, or to determine their own lifestyle, or to work, or to strike, or not to suffer discrimination, or to receive medical treatment, or not to receive medical treatment, or to live, or to die, it is much more forceful to say that people have rights to do all of those things than to say merely that it is desirable or good that they should be able to do them. In coming to think of these things as rights, we shift them out of the realm of the merely desirable and into the domain of the morally essential.[78]

Arguably, property analysis also shifts its subject matter from the realms of the desirable to the domain of the *legally* essential – society tends to ascribe property to that which is highly prized and which is central to one's life as an independent person.

Rights thinking in the health-care sector is manifested in the American Hospital Association's 1972 publication *A Patient's Bill of Rights*,[79] which (among other rights) affirmed the patient's right to be given information and to give meaningful consent before treatment, and the UK government publication *The Patient's Charter*,[80] which set standards of care for National Health Service (NHS) hospitals.

---

75 United Nations, *The Universal Declaration of Human Rights*; available at http://www.un.org/en/documents/udhr/index.shtml. Accessed 2 November 2014.

76 Human Rights Act [1998] (c.42).

77 Woodiwiss A, *Human Rights*. Abingdon: Routledge 2005, p. 4.

78 Jones P, *Rights*. London: Macmillan 1994, pp. 3–4.

79 American Hospital Association. The Patient Care Partnership. Understanding Expectations, Rights and Responsibilities. AHA; 2003. Available at http://www.aha.org/advocacyissues/communicatingpts/pt-care-partnership.shtml. Accessed 17 April 2015.

80 Department of Health, *The Patient's Charter*. London: DH 1991.

The ascendancy of rights thinking has had an impact on judicial thinking. In the past it was assumed that under the English common law, a man could not be guilty of raping his wife, but in *R* v. *R* the House of Lords held that a woman had the right to give or withhold consent to sexual intercourse with her husband.[81] In *R* v. *D*, the House of Lords ruled that the position of paramountcy in the family accorded the father, which previously afforded him a lawful excuse for forcibly taking away his unmarried child, had been overtaken by social currents which exalted the child's consent.[82] Similarly, a mother's traditional role in determining what treatment her child would have was over-ridden in *Gillick* v. *West Norfolk and Wisbech Area Health Authority* where the House of Lords upheld the child's right to decide for herself (with certain limitations).[83] These examples show that the law evolves to stay in line with social norms, and give cause for optimism that the courts could in due course apply an alternative model to cases involving patient participation in decision-making.[84]

O'Neill states that to cite human rights as the reason for respecting individual autonomy we must first justify human rights, and that while adoption and ratification of human rights declarations may provide political legitimacy, they do not provide ethical justification.[85] Ethical justification, she points out, can be achieved via two routes: grounding human rights in the good of man or grounding human rights in human obligations. The former is less inviting, because it is open to disagreements on what constitutes the good and how the various components of human good should be prioritised. Her preferred route is the latter, and she describes rights and obligations as being analogous to the white and black squares on a chessboard. O'Neill also cautions that if rights rhetoric is to be taken seriously then the corresponding obligations should also be taken seriously.[86] Her concern about 'a disconnected rhetoric of rights'[87] is understandable, but it is a criticism that applies in the spheres of politics, political science and sociology, and not necessarily in the legal arena. It is trite in law that rights carry corresponding obligations, and in determining whether the rights of an individual have been breached, the courts would usually look at the corresponding obligations. The property model that I propose in this book is like the chessboard in O'Neill's analogy; it emphasises both rights and obligations, these being complementary white and black squares.

81 R v. R [1991] 2 All ER 257 (CA); [1991] 4 All ER 481 (HL).

82 R v. *D* [1984] 2 All ER 449.

83 *Gillick* v. *West Norfolk and Wisbech Area Health Authority* [1985] 3 All ER 402.

84 In Chapter 9 I describe how judicial thinking on the patient's right to self-determination vis-à-vis physician disclosure standards has evolved with social norms.

85 O'Neill, *Autonomy and Trust in Bioethics*, p. 75.

86 Ibid., pp. 78–82.

87 Ibid., p. 80. Meaning that rights are disconnected from obligations.

A focus on obligations emphasises what action needs to be taken; it draws attention to relationships rather than to individuals. This is particularly important in health-care decision-making; here, it can be argued that maintaining an collaborative relationship between doctor and patient is a corollary to, and facilitates, protection of the rights of the individual patient. The ecology paradigm adopted in Chapter 1 situates the individual's rights in the context of the doctor–patient relationship, rather than in isolation. As will be shown in Chapter 5, one of the criticisms of the consent model is that it pays insufficient attention to obligations. The question of whether this criticism is overcome by the property model is addressed in Chapter 9.

Society's preoccupation with rights has given rise to consumerism in society at large. This has spread from the corporate sector to health services, and it is feared that it could have adverse implications for the doctor–patient relationship.[88] As with the concepts of self-determination and property described here, the concept of consumerism is capable of taking a variety of meanings when applied to health care. Haug and Lavin state that:

> In simple terms, consumerism in medicine means challenging the physician's ability to make unilateral decisions – demanding a share in reaching closure on diagnosis and working out treatment plans.[89]

Put in these terms, consumerism is seemingly innocuous and can be regarded as simply a shorthand term for protection of patient self-determination. In upholding the patient's right to make self-determining decisions regarding his or her treatment, the UK Supreme Court recently acknowledged that patients are 'widely treated as consumers exercising choices'.[90] Other commentators use a different interpretation of consumerism.[91] Morgan, for example, described a consumerist relationship as that 'in which power relationships are reversed: with the patient taking the active role and the doctor adopting a fairly passive role, acceding to the patient's requests for a second opinion, referral to hospital, a sick note, and so on'.[92] This is much further removed from paternalism than the definition given by Haug and Lavin – challenging the doctor's unilateral

88 Downie RS, The doctor-patient relationship. In Gillon R (ed), *Principles of Health Care Ethics*. Chichester: John Wiley 1994, pp. 343–352.

89 Haug M and Lavin B, *Consumerism in Medicine: Challenging Physician Authority*. London: Sage 1983, pp. 16–17.

90 *Montgomery (Appellant) v Lanarkshire Health Board (Respondent)* (Scotland) [2015] UKSC 11, at para 75.

91 Morgan M, The doctor-patient relationship. In Scrambler G (ed), *Sociology as Applied to Medicine*, 5th edn. Edinburgh: Saunders 2003, pp. 49–65; Randall F and Downie R, *The Philosophy of Palliative Care: Critique and Reconstruction*. Oxford: Oxford University Press 2006.

92 Morgan, Doctor-patient relationship, p. 54.

authority in making decisions is one thing, advocating a passive (or indeed submissive) role for the doctor is another. The latter implies abandonment of medical professionalism, the doctor acting merely as a shop attendant supplying whatever the client wants from the shelf.

Some studies show that while most patients want adequate information about their disease and treatment, not many wish to assume *sole* responsibility for decision-making (emphasis mine).[93] This has led to the comment that 'proponents of a strong consumerist approach to patient participation in health care decisions may be surprised by the way in which the behaviour of sick people deviates from the expected or desired response'.[94]

Randall and Downie take a broader view of consumerism, based on its application in a free market economy. In their conception, consumerism entails consumer access to a choice of goods or services competitively provided by suppliers who are obliged to provide adequate information on, and ensure the safety of, their products; the customer pays for the goods or services, takes responsibility for what he/she has purchased and obtains redress if the goods were misrepresented by the supplier. They say that since it is the doctor, not the patient, who takes responsibility (legal and moral) for the treatment received by the patient, 'there is not now, and not likely to be in the near future, a true consumerism in healthcare'.[95] Elsewhere, Downie and Macnaughton make the same point in these words:

> … neither governments nor medicine seem willing or even aware of the final step towards true consumerist ethics – responsibility. If I receive adequate information in the marketplace, and put my money down, then, as a consumer, I am responsible for my choice. Neither governments nor the public seem willing to take the final step, and accept that patients are responsible for their choices in medicine as much as in the marketplace. Doctors remain responsible even if it is the patient who has made the choice.[96]

In Chapter 9, it is argued that in contemporary medical practice, the right to self-determination should carry with it obligations on the part of doctor and patient, and that the patient's obligations include taking some responsibility for the treatment received. Bilateral distribution of responsibility between doctor and patient is an element of the property model presented in this book.

93 Fallowfield LJ, Hall A, Maguire P, Baum M and A'Hern RP, A question of choice: results of a prospective 3-year follow-up study of women with breast cancer (1994) 3 The Breast 202–208.

94 Ibid., p. 206.

95 Randall and Downie, *Philosophy of Palliative Care*, p. 63.

96 Downie and Macnaughton, *Bioethics and the Humanities*, p. 117.

Involving patients in the decision-making process is often abbreviated to 'offering choice'.[97] Indeed, the expectation of choice underlies a postmodernist theory of consent:

> Social and economic forces ensure that everyone in wealthy societies is a consumer. We expect to be offered choices – of groceries, shoes, radio channels, or holidays – and do not suddenly change when we become ill or injured. Doctors are among the leading purveyors of choices from before the cradle to the grave: prenatal screening; analgesia during childbirth; growth treatments; prostate surgery or watchful waiting; organ transplant or acceptance of death. Much treatment is not for serious disease but for convenience, such as to hasten recovery from minor illness. Even consent to major surgery, like hysterectomy or spinal fusion, may be influenced more by personal preferences than by clinical judgment.[98]

As is the case with 'autonomy' and 'property', however, 'choice' can be used or interpreted in different ways. It has been observed that '[t]he attempt to clarify what we mean when we speak about choice in healthcare is a task as complex as dealing with the history of ideas in the philosophical realm'.[99]

The narrow construction of patient self-determination as a mere question of choice smacks of a flagrantly consumerist approach. Patient self-determination is not upheld simply by presenting the patient with an à la carte menu of treatment options or, in some cases, 'a menu of one item'.[100] Apart from not promoting the conception of self-determination enunciated below, there are ethical objections to promotion of 'mere, sheer choice':[101]

> Why should all choices – even those not based on an adequate grasp of others' proposals – be protected at all costs? Is it of no importance that choices may be good or bad, right or wrong, kind or callous, prudent or risky, informed or ignorant? Or that choices may be based on misleading views of others' proposals, or of the realities, risks and benefits of consenting to – or refusing – those proposals? Does it not matter that individuals may accept proposals for

97 Richards MA, Ramirez AJ, Degner LF, Fallowfield LJ, Maher EJ and Neuberger J, Offering choice of treatment to patients with cancers: a review based on a symposium held at the 10th annual conference of the British Psychosocial Oncology Group, December 1993 (1995) 31 European Journal of Cancer 112–116.

98 Alderson P and Goodey C, Theories of consent (1998) 317 BMJ 1313–1315, at p. 1315.

99 Moro G, Choice. In Marinker M, *Constructive Conversations about Health*. Oxford: Radcliffe 2006, pp. 51–61, at p. 51.

100 O'Neill, *Autonomy and Trust in Bioethics*, p. 38.

101 Manson NC and O'Neill O, *Rethinking Informed Consent in Bioethics*. Cambridge: Cambridge University Press 2007, p. 70.

> action that are likely to injure them, may 'go along' with manipulative proposals, or may succumb to 'offers they can't refuse'? Respect for mere choice has been widely, and in our view plausibly, viewed as a shaky and questionable justification for invasive treatment.[102]

The conception of self-determination adopted in this book transcends mere choice. On the other hand, it appears that judgment of what is or is not mere choice is value-laden and any choice that is risky, callous, wrong or capable of causing harm to the patient is at risk of being labelled mere choice. It will be argued in Chapters 9 and 10 that the property model has the potential to avoid the ethical problems associated with mere choice while also not preventing the self-determining patient from making an informed choice that may in the eyes of others appear risky or irrational.

Public Awareness; Advances in Technology

Arguably, the emergence of consumerist perspectives in public services[103] and increasing emphasis on choice in health-care delivery[104] are in large measure due to the populace being more informed. The emergence of a more educated, enlightened citizenry is one of the social factors cited by proponents[105] who advance the deprofessionalisation hypothesis[106] as the explanation for the changing status of professionals in modern society. Haug stated that:

> By limiting access to training, leaders of the medical elite have generally sought to contain the spread of their fund of esoteric knowledge, keeping it from the unqualified and uninitiated. This endeavour has only been partially successful Despite the continued discovery of new technologies and medical breakthroughs, the media have popularized a great deal of the increasing fund of medical knowledge, and made it accessible to a public whose rising educational level permits many people to grasp it, at least in its main outlines.[107]

102 Ibid.

103 Clarke J, Newman J, Westmarland L, Smith N and Vidler E, *Creating Citizen-Consumers: Changing Publics and Changing Public Services*. London: Sage 2007.

104 Greener I, Towards a history of choice in UK health policy (2009) 31 Sociology of Health and Illness 309 324.

105 Haug MR, A re-examination of the hypothesis of physician deprofessionalization (1988) 66 Milbank Quarterly 48–56.

106 Freidson E, The changing nature of professional control (1984) 10 Ann Rev Sociology 1–20.

107 Haug, Re-examination of the hypothesis of physician deprofessionalization, p. 50.

The public are much more (and better) informed today than at any other time in history. This is due partly to higher average levels of education, but more importantly to the ready availability and accessibility of information through the mass media and the World Wide Web. This has reduced (but not eliminated) the information gradient between doctor and patient.[108] The internet has been associated with the following potential advantages:

> … helping patients make informed health care choices (with potential to decrease health care disparities), shared decision-making with a collaborative, teamwork approach, more efficient use of clinical time, augmenting of physician-provided information, online support groups, and/or access to patients' own health information.[109]

Studies show that younger and better-educated patients desire a more active role in decision-making whereas less well-educated patients are in greater awe of doctors.[110] The informed patient is in a better position to be actively involved in decision-making related to his or her health. On the other hand, a steep information gradient between doctor and patient encourages paternalism.

Whereas in the past most medical interventions owed their effectiveness to the placebo effect, twentieth-century medicine offered a range of effective therapeutic options, thanks to advances in technology. This means that opportunities have arisen for the doctor to present patients with options and to discuss the relative merits and adverse effects of each option, especially in those cases where there is no clearly superior option. These opportunities, however, are meaningful to the patient only if he/she understands the options being presented and is in a position to make an informed choice consistent with his/her values, circumstances and world view. The term 'preference sensitive'[111] has been used to describe the rising number of conditions where there is not one but a range of acceptable treatment options and the best choice depends on the patient's goals and circumstances.

Another factor associated with technological advancement and reduction in the information gradient between doctor and patient is the relative decline

---

108 McMullan M, Patients using the internet to obtain health information: how this affects the patient-health professional relationship (2006) 63 Patient Educ Couns 24–28; Trotter MI and Morgan DW, Patients' use of the Internet for health related matters: a study of Internet usage in 2000 and 2006 (2008) 14 Health Informatics J 175–181.

109 Wald HS, Dube CE and Anthony DC, Untangling the Web – the impact of internet use on health care and the physician-patient relationship (2007) 68 Patient Educ Couns 218–224.

110 Say, Murtagh and Thomson, Patients' preference for involvement in medical decision making; Vick and Scott, Agency in health care.

111 Wennberg JE, *Tracking Medicine: A Researcher's Quest to Understand Health Care.* Oxford: Oxford University Press 2010.

of acute illness and rise of chronic conditions. Increasing numbers of patients are living with conditions such as diabetes, stroke, age-related degenerative disease and heart disease, and many of these patients have become experts in the management of their condition.[112]

Finally, public awareness of the fallibility of doctors has increased, due to well-publicised medical mistakes and scandals. This has induced many patients to question the doctor's recommendations and to play a more proactive role in decisions about their care. Fewer patients would now, as Lord Justice Dunn said in *Sidaway*, 'prefer to put themselves unreservedly in the hand of their doctors'.[113] The world has moved a long way since the days when Sir John Donaldson, also in *Sidaway*, felt that the prudent patient was probably 'a fairly rare bird'.[114] The man and woman on the Clapham omnibus (identified by Sir John as the 'natural habitat' of the prudent patient) are today aware of their rights and ready to assert them.

The following account from Australia could be said to apply in most of the western world:

> When the participants were asked whether they thought the social status of medical practitioners in Australian society had changed over time, nearly everyone agreed that it had. A common observation put forward by the participants was that while doctors may still be generally respected in Australia, they are now subject to more criticism. In doing so, regardless of their age, the participants routinely drew comparisons between the medical practitioners they remembered from their childhood, and those they had dealings with today. An almost mythological account was given of a kindly (almost invariably middle-aged, white male) doctor, the traditional archetype of the 'family doctor' ... These days, it was often contended, this ideal figure of the 'family doctor' had been challenged by increasing publicity around medical negligence or mistakes, sexual harassment or assault of patients by doctors, medical fraud and so on.[115]

It is not only the public's attitude that has been influenced by the scandals; the attitude of the judiciary to the medical profession has also been affected.[116] Lord Woolf identified the scandals and the resultant dent in the 'presumption

112 Tyreman S, The expert patient: outline of UK government paper (2005) 8 Med Health Care Philos 149–151.

113 *Sidaway* v. *Board of Governors of Bethlem Royal Hospital* [1984] 2 WLR at 795.

114 *Sidaway* v. *Board of Governors of Bethlem Royal Hospital* [1984] 2 WLR at 791.

115 Lupton D, Consumerism, reflexivity and the medical encounter (1997) 45 Soc Sci Med 373–381, at p. 376.

116 Lord Woolf, Are the courts excessively deferential to the medical profession? 2001 9 Med L Rev 1–16.

of beneficence'[117] as one of the reasons behind the change to a less deferential attitude to the medical profession by the judiciary.

Curtains for Paternalism

The currents described above have served to accelerate a retreat from paternalism that commenced in the second half of the twentieth century, following atrocities committed by medical doctors during the Second World War. This retreat was accompanied by increasing emphasis on consent procedures.[118] At first glance, it would appear that this emphasis was driven by a determination to restrain paternalism. Stephen Wear argues, however, that the agenda of those advocating this shift in the early days had less to do with the positive goal of enhancing patient self-determination, and more with concerns about research subjects and the outlandish practices of certain physicians.[119] It is noteworthy that although the Nuremberg Court and society's objection to unethical experiments marked the beginning of the march against medical paternalism, the medical community also reacted against such experiments.[120]

Concern about research subjects arose notably in relation to the involvement of Nazi doctors in unethical practices and about the way institutionalised patients were treated.[121] There were also the notorious Tuskegee experiment,[122] where southern blacks with syphilis were left untreated so that the natural course of the disease could be studied, and the Willowbrook experiment,[123] where patients were intentionally infected with hepatitis. What is significant about these cases is that the doctors were not acting in the best interests of their patients. Thus, when campaigners rose to assert the self-determination of patients, they did so not because of paternalism on the part of ordinary medical practitioners, but because of the unethical practices of errant doctors. Interestingly, the same paradigm applies in contemporary medicine where concern about errant doctors such as Shipman[124] has led to reforms or proposed reforms that affect

117 Ibid., p. 3.

118 Shultz MM, From informed consent to patient choice: a new protected interest (1985) 95 Yale LJ 219–299.

119 Wear, *Informed Consent.* At pp. 30-32

120 Ibid.

121 Jonathan Moreno gives a detailed and authoritative account of state-sponsored secret experiments on humans not only during the Second World War but even up to the latter part of the twentieth century, in *Undue Risk: Secret State Experiments on Humans.* New York: Routledge 2001.

122 Ibid., p. 68.

123 Ibid., p. 69.

124 Shipman Inquiry, *Fifth Report. Safeguarding Patients: Lessons from the Past – Proposals for the Future*, Cm 6394. *London: The Stationery Office 2004.* See also Dyer O, Shipman murdered more than

the way medicine is practised by the vast majority of law-abiding and well-meaning doctors.[125]

From these beginnings the movement for protection of patient self-determination by means of consent gained momentum through a series of well-publicised cases concerning prolongation of life in intensive-care units (when one school of thought felt that the patient should be allowed to die with dignity),[126] blood transfusions administered to Jehovah's Witnesses against their will[127] and court-authorised Caesarean sections performed against the will of the women.[128] These cases reach the heart of patient self-determination.

In the UK a major step forward was taken with the publication in 2000 of *The NHS Plan*, which set out the government's proposals for creating a 'patient-centred service' in which patients would be fully involved in decisions relating to their care.[129] Ten years later, the coalition Government published its health white paper, *Equity and Excellence: Liberating the NHS*,[130] which outlined plans to make patient experience a measurable outcome of care, with an ethos of 'no decision about me without me' and 'shared decision-making'[131] becoming the norm.

The NHS Constitution, first published in 2009,[132] spells out the rights and responsibilities of patients and service providers, including the patient's right to

---

200 patients, inquiry finds (2002) 325 BMJ 181.

125 The fifth report of the Shipman inquiry made 109 recommendations (Shipman Inquiry, *Fifth Report. Safeguarding Patients: Lessons from the Past – Proposals for the Future*, Cm 6394-I, II, III. London: The Stationery Office 2004). The inquiry led to changes in regulation of professionals contained in the White Paper, *Trust, Assurance and Safety – the Regulation of Health Professionals in the 21st Century*. London: Department of Health, February 2007. See also Holden J and O'Donnell S, Shipman proposals will alter general practice profoundly (2003) 326 BMJ 280 and the General Medical Council (Licence to Practise and Revalidation) Regulations Order of Council 2012.

126 *Airedale NHS Trust* v. *Bland* (1993) 1 ALL ER 821 (HL); [1993] 2 WLR 316.

127 *John F Kennedy Memorial Hospital* v. *Heston* 279 A 2d 670 (N.J. 1971).

128 Lord Justice Thorpe, Consent for Caesarean section: Part 2 – autonomy, capacity, best interests, reasonable force and procedural guidelines (1999) 5 Clinical Risk 209–212. See also Stauch M, Court-authorised Caesareans and the principle of patient autonomy (1997) 6 Nott LJ 74.

129 Department of Health, *The NHS Plan: A Plan for Investment, a Plan for Reform*. London: The Stationery Office, 2000.

130 Department of Health, *Equity and Excellence: Liberating the NHS*. London: The Stationery Office 2010.

131 Shared medical decision-making is defined as 'a process of communication in which the physician and patient use unbiased and complete information on the risks and benefits associated with all viable treatment alternatives and information from the patient on personal factors that might make one treatment alternative more preferable than the others to come to a treatment decision.' Moulton B and King JS, Aligning ethics with medical decision-making: the quest for informed patient choice (2010) 38 J Law Med Ethics 85–97, at p. 89.

132 Health Act 2009. Chapter 1, section 1; available at http://www.legislation.gov.uk/ukpga/2009/21/section/1. Accessed 2 November 2014.

make choices about his/her care. The Constitution does not create new rights but collates the rights that were previously created by primary and secondary legislation. From a list of 11 rights enshrined in this Constitution, the three considered most important by respondents in a national survey of patients were involvement in decisions about treatment, information about treatment and being treated with dignity and respect.[133] The Health and Social Care Act 2012 places a duty on the NHS Commissioning Board and Clinical Commissioning Groups to involve patients in decision-making,[134] and the Report of the Mid Staffordshire NHS Foundation Trust Public Inquiry reaffirmed both the importance of the NHS Constitution and the need to place patients at the centre of care.[135]

The government is also making efforts to promote public awareness and facilitate provision of information to enhance engagement of patients – for example, through the website NHS Choices.[136] This website, which recorded its 500 millionth visit at the end of 2012,[137] combines patient information with opportunities for patients to give feedback on their care.

Retreat from Medical Paternalism: The Profession's Response

There is evidence that medical professionalism has been responsive to the challenge posed by these socio-political currents.[138] Professional bodies from Europe and America jointly published a Physicians' Charter in 2002 which affirmed that twenty-first-century medical professionalism rested on three fundamental principles: primacy of patient welfare, patient autonomy and social justice.[139] Analogies for the doctor–patient relationship have changed from that

---

133 Patients Association, The *NHS Constitution: Fact or Fiction?* Harrow: Patients Association 2012, p. 21.

134 Health and Social Care Act 2012, section 26 (14U and 14V); available at http://www.legislation.gov.uk/ukpga/2012/7/section/126/enacted. Accessed 2 November 2014.

135 Francis R, *Report of the Mid Staffordshire NHS Foundation Trust Public Inquiry*. London: The Stationery Office 2013.

136 http://www.nhs.uk/Pages/HomePage.aspx. Accessed 2 November 2014. See also http://www.nhs.uk/choiceintheNHS/Treatments/Pages/Treatments.aspx. Accessed 2 November 2014.

137 Gann B, From NHS Choices to the integrated customer service platform (2013) 30 Health Info Libr J 1–3.

138 Taylor K, Paternalism, participation and partnership – the evolution of patient centeredness in the consultation (2009) 74 Patient Educ Couns 150–155.

139 Medical Professionalism Project, Medical professionalism in the new millennium: a physicians' charter (2002) 359 The Lancet 520–522. See also ABIM Foundation (American Board of Internal Medicine), ACP-ASIM Foundation (American College of Physicians-

of the priest in 1968[140] to that of a mountain guide in 2007,[141] and the code of practice published by the General Medical Council recognises the primacy of patient autonomy.[142] Both the General Medical Council[143] and the royal postgraduate medical colleges[144] have published guidelines on consent which assert the patient's primary role in decision-making. Clinical governance,[145] a framework for ensuring the quality of patient-centred care, has been embedded in the National Health Service, and patient involvement in decision-making is at the core of this framework.[146] McLean even goes as far as commenting that:

> It is paradoxical that once embraced by the professions, the importance of respect for autonomy seems to have been taken more seriously by them than by the law.[147]

It is too early, however, to sing the Nunc Dimittis for paternalism for there is an incongruence between the seriousness with which the principle of self-determination is taken by the profession and the extent to which this principle is actually upheld on the shop floor.[148] As observed by one commentator, '[w]hile the medical community has espoused the value of autonomy in principle, much more work must be done to promote patient autonomy in practice'[149] and 'clinical evaluation research studies suggest that patients are routinely asked to make decisions about treatment choices in the face of what can only be described as avoidable ignorance'.[150] There has been progress in involving

American Society of Internal Medicine) and European Federation of Internal Medicine, Medical professionalism in the new millennium: a physician charter (2002) 136 Ann Intern Med 243–246.

140 Byrne PS, The passing of the 'eight' train (1968) 15 J R Coll Gen Pract 409–427.

141 Hilton S, Education and the changing face of medical professionalism: from priest to mountain guide (2008) 58 Br J Gen Pract 353–361.

142 General Medical Council, *Good Medical Practice*. London: GMC 2013.

143 General Medical Council, *Consent: Patients and Doctors Making Decisions Together*. London: GMC 2008.

144 Royal College of Obstetricians and Gynaecologists, *Obtaining Valid Consent*, 2nd edn, Clinical Governance Advice 6. London: RCOG 2008.

145 http://www.flyingstart.scot.nhs.uk/learning-programmes/safe-practice/clinical-governance.aspx. Accessed 2 November 2014. See also http://www.healthcareimprovementscotland.org/previous_resources/standards/clinical_governance_and_risk_m.aspx. Accessed 2 November 2014.

146 NHS Greater Glasgow and Clyde, *Integrating Patient Focus and Public Involvement into Clinical Governance*. Learning Note 2. October 2008.

147 McLean, *Autonomy, Consent and the Law*, p. 96.

148 Legare F, Ratte S, Gravel K and Graham ID, Barriers and facilitators to implementing shared decision-making in clinical practice: update of a systematic review of health professionals' perceptions (2008) 73 Patient Educ Couns 526–535.

149 Moulton and King, Aligning ethics with medical decision-making, p. 87.

150 Ibid., p. 88.

patients in informed decision-making but more work needs to be done.[151] In a survey of NHS patients conducted in 2010, 48 per cent of inpatients said they would have liked more involvement in decisions about their care.[152] This is despite the introduction of the NHS Constitution. The Patients Association found that many patients were unaware of many of the rights and responsibilities described in the NHS Constitution.[153] Over 98 per cent of respondents in a survey reported that they had been treated by the NHS without being notified of the NHS Constitution's existence.[154] The review of the Secretary of State for Health on the effect of the NHS Constitution reported that less than a third (27 per cent) of the public are aware of the Constitution and only 1 per cent of NHS staff report being asked about it.[155]

Moulton and King are critical of this failure to apply in practice what is espoused in principle:

> While physicians, health services researchers, and medical ethicists have advocated the incorporation of shared decision-making into mainstream medical practice for decades, few physicians have successfully integrated the process into their practice. The failure to recognize the provider's ethical imperative to align patient knowledge and patient treatment choices in cases of preference sensitive care is jarring.[156]

A lot more needs to be done to protect the patient's right to self-determination. This will require both a change in the orientation of clinicians and a more robust means of providing remedy when the patient's right has been breached.

Will the Pendulum Swing Back?

It was suggested more than two decades ago that 'solo fee-for-service practice in a competitive situation was more likely to be client-dependent than colleague-

---

151 van den Brink-Muinen A, van Dulmen SM, de Haes HC, Visser AP, Schellevis FG and Bensing JM, Has patients' involvement in the decision-making process changed over time? (2006) 9 Health Expectations 333–342.

152 Care Quality Commission, *Briefing Note: Inpatient Survey Results 2010*. Care Quality Commission 2011; available at www.nhssurveys.org/survey/1016.

153 Patients Association, *Information, What Information? Information Challenges of Shared Decision Making*. Harrow: Patients Association 2011.

154 Patients Association, *The NHS Constitution: Fact or Fiction?* Harrow: Patients Association 2012.

155 Department of Health, *Report on the Effect of the NHS Constitution*. London: The Stationery Office 2012.

156 Moulton and King, Aligning ethics with medical decision-making, p. 95.

dependent'.[157] In other words, where doctors work with other colleagues and require their cooperation and approval, their performance is more likely to conform to that of other doctors than with the expectations of patients; working in an isolated environment, the doctor is less susceptible to such countervailing pressures from colleagues. If this is true, then current shifts in health-care provision have implications for patient self-determination. General practitioners (GPs) are now mostly in group practice and the days of the single-handed GP practice are numbered. Polyclinics are being promoted.[158] In the acute sector, small units are closing down and bigger hospitals are being built. All of this may mean that the twenty-first-century approach to the delivery of health care could be more attuned to professional autonomy than to patient self-determination. If that is the case, then the need to safeguard patient self-determination is even more pressing.

Health-care resources are finite and rationing is inescapable in contemporary health care. This often means that health-care providers are unable to accede to a patient's wishes or offer a full range of therapeutic options.[159] The principles of non-maleficence and equitable utilisation of limited resources could also be employed to justify refusal of a patient's request when treatment is considered ineffective in prolonging life, improving quality of life or providing a physiological benefit.[160] A 45-year-old woman cannot, on the basis of self-determination, demand assisted reproduction on the National Health Service where the results of such treatment are not considered to justify the cost.

Sometimes a physician is concerned that granting a patient's request could result in the patient suffering harm. A good example would be the rising tide of Caesarean section on maternal request. It is well established that while vaginal delivery may weaken the pelvic floor, it is safer in all other respects (post-operative pain, injury to pelvic organs, infection, thrombosis, death) than Caesarean section. On the basis of the medical evidence, Caesarean section should not be performed simply on the basis of maternal request. Granting this request could expose the woman to avoidable harm, but respect for her self-determination (according to one school) demands that her informed

---

157 Freidson E, *Profession of Medicine: A Study of the Sociology of Applied Knowledge*. London: University of Chicago Press 1988, p. 189.

158 Imison C, Naylor C and Maybin J, *Under One Roof: Will Polyclinics Deliver Integrated Care?* London: King's Fund 2008.

159 See, for example, the news item 'Cancer drug "too expensive for NHS"' at http://www.theguardian.com/society/2012/feb/02/cancer-drug-too-expensive-nhs, and the *Guardian* op-ed piece of 4 January 2008, 'Expensive drugs on the NHS are not a right' at http://www.theguardian.com/society/joepublic/2008/jan/04/manythingsvexmeabout. Both sites accessed 2 November 2014.

160 For a discussion of the physician's role in health-care rationing, see 'The physician as gatekeeper', Chapter 14 in Pellegrino and Thomasma, *For the Patient's Good*, pp. 172–189.

choice should be implemented. As with the case of the middle-aged woman who demands fertility treatment on the NHS, society (or government and/or professionals) may determine that Caesarean section on maternal request (i.e. in the absence of medical indications) is a misuse of commonwealth resources. Situations such as this are more common in the United States where 'managed care' operates to limit the choices available to patients. This has led some commentators to say that the paternalism of the individual doctor has been replaced by a 'new paternalism'.[161]

Another consequence of the new approach to health-care delivery is that the patient is treated by not just one doctor but by a team of doctors and other practitioners, sometimes receiving conflicting information from different members of the team and not infrequently finding that no one has had sufficient contact with him or her to be in a position to understand his or her values and thinking. This situation has implications for consent and self-determination, for unless health professionals give consistent and meaningful information relevant to the circumstances and needs of the particular patient, true consent cannot be obtained.

Patient Involvement in Decision-making: Not Black or White, Blue or Red

Discussions of self-determination in health care are commonly framed in dichotomous or extremist terms. For a start, there is a tendency to present the subject as if there were only two absolutes; at one end, medical paternalism, at the other, patient sovereignty – with the expectation or assumption that one extreme must ride triumphant, even roughshod, over the other. In reality, day-to-day clinical practice manifests a delicate interplay between the imperatives of beneficence[162] and patient self determination.

Secondly, the subject is commonly presented in an adversarial framework, as a joust between doctors in the red corner (paternalism) and society in the blue corner (self-determination) of the boxing ring. The responsive nature of medical professionalism, as described above, negates this outdated presentation.

Thirdly, the medical consultation is often framed as either a scenario where the patient's illness diminishes his/her capacity to make a value-based decision[163] or one where the doctor determines what is right and/or presents a limited

161 Chervenak FA and McCullough LB, The threat of the new managed practice of medicine to patients' autonomy (1995) 6 J Clin Ethics 320–323.

162 Beneficence is distinguished from paternalism earlier in this chapter.

163 Komrad MS, A defence of medical paternalism: maximising patients' autonomy (1983) 9 J Med Ethics 38–44.

number of options and 'the patient's role is only to say "yes" – or to do without treatment'.[164] This narrow framing conceals a lot that lies between these two extremes. With advances in science and technology, it is increasingly common to have a wide range of treatment options available to the patient for a particular condition, including surgical and non-surgical treatment. In many cases, there is no one treatment that, on the basis of scientific evidence, is clearly the superior option. A woman presenting to her doctor with troublesome menstrual bleeding is unlikely have her self-determination substantially diminished by her medical condition; she can make an informed choice from a range of options, each of which carries its own effectiveness, advantages and risks. Whether she opts for surgical or non-surgical treatment and, if the former, what type of operation, is likely to be determined by her attitude to surgery and the perceived effects of the various options on her occupation, family life, sexuality and other non-clinical factors. Similarly, for many chronic medical conditions a range of surgical, pharmacological, physical and psychological therapies have been developed, and the patient has to make informed decisions about which treatment to have or not have. In these cases the issue of self-determination is more substantial than in those where the patient is very ill or where there is only one treatment and it is a case of accepting or refusing it.

Reinforcing these dichotomies is an extremism: in bioethics there has been a near-universal tendency towards excessive preoccupation with paternalism. McCullough has decried inaccuracies in historical accounts which, in the relatively short life of bioethics, have depicted paternalism as an uncontested attribute of medical practice dating back to Hippocrates.[165] While his attempt to set the historical record straight is laudable, what is perhaps more instructive is his insightful observation on the effect that inordinate preoccupation with paternalism has had on the march of bioethics. As a result of this preoccupation, bioethics lost the opportunity to critically address in depth the dynamics of the doctor's power as a professional and as an agent of a health-care organisation; rather bioethics has simply been about keeping this power in check. As a result, he concludes, patients have been denied the benefits afforded by a professional fiduciary relationship with their doctor and a contractual relationship has been fostered. Extending this observation further, it can be said that preoccupation with consent has meant that attention is focused on the doctor's duty not to touch the patient without authorisation, without adequate attention to the

164 O'Neill, *Autonomy and Trust in Bioethics*, p. 26.

165 McCullough LB, Was bioethics founded on historical and conceptual mistakes about medical paternalism? (2011) 25 Bioethics 66–74.

patient's right to make decisions and to power relations between doctor and patient.[166]

Self-determination and Models of the Doctor–Patient Relationship

Patients say that the extent to which they are able to make decisions about their treatment is largely dependent on the style of communication adopted by their doctor.[167] The doctor–patient relationship is a critical factor in upholding or truncating self-determination. It is, therefore, appropriate at this juncture to look more closely at models of the doctor–patient relationship.

This relationship has been described as 'the prototype of all professional relationships'[168] and as a 'quasi-mystical relationship'.[169] The nature of this relationship has implications for health outcomes, and the paternalistic form discussed above is only one of a number of forms that this relationship could take.

Various models have been used to characterise the relationship.[170] One approach is based on the doctor's style of consultation: some doctors treat a disease rather than a patient (the scientific model);[171] some see their role as providing the menu from which the patient can choose (the consumerist model);[172] some define the consultation in terms of rights and duties (the contractual model)[173] and others simply take the patient as a person who has

166 In chapter 9 it will be argued that the property model is capable of doing better in this regard.

167 Barry C, Bradley CP, Britten N, Stevenson FA and Barber N, Patients' unvoiced agendas in general practice consultations: qualitative study (2000) 320 BMJ 1246–1250.

168 O'Neill, *Autonomy and Trust in Bioethics*, p. 17.

169 Bergsma and Thomasma, *Autonomy and Clinical Medicine*, p. 111.

170 Szasz TS and Hollender MH, The basic models of the doctor-patient relationship (1956) 97 Arch Intern Med 585–592.

171 The eminent physician, William Osler is credited with saying that 'The good physician treats the disease; the great physician treats the patient who has the disease.'

172 For further discussion of consumerism in health care, see Chadwick R, Genetics, choice and responsibility (1999) 1 Health, Risk and Society 293—300; Shaw I and Aldridge A, Consumerism, health and social order (2003) 2 Social Policy & Society 35–43; Lippman A, Choice as a risk to women's health (1999) 1 Health, Risk and Society 281–291; Lupton D, Consumerism, reflexivity and the medical encounter. (1997) 45 Social Science and Medicine 373–81.

See Emanuel and Emanuel's 'informative model' discussed below and Downie and Calman's paradigms of consent discussed in Chapter 3.

173 A contractual model of doctor–patient relationship is proffered in Veatch, *A Theory of Medical Ethics*. New York: Basic Books 1983. In Chapter 7 we address the question whether property analysis advances a contractual or a fiduciary doctor–patient relationship.

come to enlist assistance in sorting a problem or concern (the humanistic model).[174]

Another approach is based on the power gradient between doctor and patient. Morgan described four types of doctor–patient relationship (paternalistic, consumerist, mutuality and default), classified according to whether the patient and the doctor have high or low control of the consultation.[175] A consumerist relationship is the direct opposite of the paternalistic one, the patient dictating the tune while the doctor acquiesces to the patient's demands. A relationship of mutuality is one where doctor and patient are equals, each bringing something to the table. In a 'default' relationship, the doctor cedes control to the patient but the latter remains passive.

Ezekiel and Linda Emmanuel propose four models of the physician–patient relationship: paternalistic, informative, interpretive, deliberative.[176] In the paternalistic model, the physician acts as the patient's guardian, articulating and implementing what is best for the patient, regardless of the patient's preferences. In this model, self-determination is no more than patient assent to the physician's opinion of what is best.

In the informative model, the physician provides the patient with all relevant information and options and the patient selects the option he or she wants. This model draws a line between facts and values. The patient's values are well defined and known; what the patient lacks is facts. It is the physician's obligation to provide all the available facts, and the patient's values then determine what treatments are to be given. The physician is merely a technical expert, and there is no role for the physician's values, the physician's understanding of the patient's values or his or her judgment of the worth of the patient's values. As consumerism par excellence this model exalts choice, but self-determination (as articulated in the ecology paradigm) is not just all about choice; it is deeper than mere choice, a point illustrated graphically in the following anecdote narrated by Bergsma and Thomasma:

> Convinced of the merits of autonomy-emphasis, a friend once decided to 'go for broke' with autonomy in his family practice. Eventually patients abandoned him, arguing that he was himself 'abandoning' his role as a doctor by putting too much stress on their own decisions. He then took care of young people on a commune farm and was hired by a university. Soon that too fell through and

---

174 For a voyage through the waters of autonomy using the humanistic boat, see Bergsma and Thomasma, *Autonomy and Clinical Medicine*.

175 Morgan, Doctor-patient relationship, p. 54. Morgan cites the original source of this classification as Stewart M and Rotter D (eds), *Communicating with Medical Patients*. London: Sage 1989.

176 Emanuel EJ and Emanuel LL, Four models of the physician-patient relationship (1992) 267 JAMA 2221–2226.

> he went out west to care for Indians on a Reservation. This story demonstrates both the commitments of the physician to support autonomy and care for the underserved, but also that simply placing decision-making in the hands of the patient does not recognize the deeper aspects of autonomy we have argued. This physician, enlightened as he was, still identified autonomy only with choice.[177]

The third model is the interpretive model, in which the physician acts as counsellor or adviser, provides the patient with information on the nature of the condition and possible interventions, and assists the patient in determining which medical interventions fit with the patient's articulated values.

In the deliberative model, the physician acts as a teacher or mentor, engaging the patient in dialogue on what course of action would be best. Not only does the physician indicate what the patient could do but, knowing the patient and wishing what is best, the physician indicates what the patient should do. This model is similar to the 'shared decision-making' paradigm of consent discussed in Chapter 3. The problem with this model is that decision-making still ultimately rests with the doctor rather than the patient.

The authors state that a fifth model, the instrumental model, could be added to these four but hasten to dismiss this model as an aberration. The instrumental model disregards the patient's values completely; the patient's values are irrelevant; the physician aims for some goal independent of the patient, such as the good of society or furtherance of scientific knowledge. The Tuskegee (where southern blacks with syphilis were left untreated so that the natural course of the disease could be studied) and Willowbrook (where patients were intentionally infected with hepatitis) scandals are examples of the instrumental model in action.[178]

Ezekiel and Linda Emanuel note that the legal doctrine of informed consent appears to promote the informative model; whereas, in their view, the deliberative model may be the most appropriate in most clinical encounters.[179]

In the same vein, Charles and colleagues describe four models of decision-making in the doctor–patient relationship: paternalistic, informed, shared and intermediate.[180] The paternalistic model is the 'doctor-knows-best' model. In the informed model, the doctor provides all the relevant information on treatment options and risks, but deliberation and decision-making are the sole prerogative of the patient. In the shared model, the doctor and patient share

177 Bergsma and Thomasma, *Autonomy and Clinical Medicine*, p. 127.

178 Brandt, Racism and research; Krugman S and Giles JP, Viral hepatitis: new light on an old disease (1970) 212 JAMA 1019–1029.

179 Emanuel and Emanuel, Four models of the physician-patient relationship.

180 Charles C, Whelan T and Gafni A, What do we mean by partnership in making decisions about treatment? (1999) 319 BMJ 780–782.

decision-making and reach a consensus on the way forward. The intermediate model is a hybrid of the above models.

Veatch also described four models, similar to the above: priestly, engineering, collegial and contractual.[181] In the engineering model, the patient has full power and the doctor merely provides technical advice. The priestly model is paternalism and the engineering model is consumerism, so both are rejected in this thesis. The collegial model is shared decision-making, where there is supposedly an equal partnership, but this appears to make light of the information gradient between doctor and patient which negates the idea of equal partnership; also the right to self-determination cannot truly be said to be protected unless it is the patient who actually makes the decision. The contractual model explicitly recognises that there is a power gradient between doctor and patient, but in this model the patient retains control over decisions. Rights and duties are central to this model but medical professionalism takes a back seat.

Bergsma and Thomasma describe three vertical models and three horizontal models.[182] The vertical models – models in which one pole or the other dominates the relationship – are paternalism (the physician acts for the good of the patient even in the absence of their consent, or even against their wishes), patient autonomy (the doctor respects the independent decision-making of the patient even when the doctor disagrees with the decision or finds it unconscionable) and entrepreneurial (medicine run as a profit-making enterprise).

In the horizontal models – contract, covenant and negotiation – there is face-to-face dialogue on the patient's problems, and about the roles played by both parties in addressing these problems. A contract model, exemplified by the use of advance directives, reduces the likelihood that the patient's intention will be frustrated, but contracts cannot cover all contingencies. Also, the doctor may limit themselves to the terms of the contract and not feel obliged or inclined to do anything 'extra'. It can be said that the contract model is founded on mistrust.

The covenant model has its roots not in self-determination but in charity and cultural or religious values such as the sacredness of human life. It is arguable that this could be a horizontal model only if doctor and patient both resile from imposing their cultural or religious values on the other party.

Clarke and colleagues have drawn attention to limitations of the models described above.[183] Firstly, these models of medical decision-making have treated the patient *alone* outside of his or her social context as the subject in the

---

181 Veatch RM, *The Patient-Physician Relation: The Patient as Partner, Part 2*. Bloomington: Indiana University Press 1991.

182 Bergsma and Thomasma, *Autonomy and Clinical Medicine*, pp. 121–140.

183 Clarke G, Hall R and Rosencrance G, Physician-patient relations: no more models (2004) 4 Am J Bioeth W16–W19.

physician–patient relationship, whereas many patients prefer family or friends to be involved and want advice from a spouse, son or daughter before they make the final decision. Here we see the ecology metaphor in practice. Clarke *et al.* are concerned that as long as the physician–patient model is that of an individual autonomous patient and a single physician in a decision-making context, the preferences of these patients will be ignored.[184] They found in their own study that patients differ significantly from one another in what they expect from their physicians with regard to communication, and 78.4 per cent of the 51 patients interviewed said they would want a family member or friend present when a physician comes to discuss an operation. The authors concluded that the 'strong preferences we found for involving family and friends in physician-patient communication should lead to a reconsideration of the concept of patient autonomy'[185] and that 'to aim for conformity to a "best" or preferred model of physician-patient decision-making may actually undermine patient autonomy'.[186] The point made by Clarke and colleagues is valid but the solution is not so much a 'reconsideration of the concept of autonomy' but repositioning self-determination in an ecological context – as discussed above.

In analysing the merits of the consent approach or any other approach to protecting patient self-determination, it is important to be clear about the underlying model of patient–doctor relationship. As will be mentioned again in discussion of the relevant case law in Chapter 9, Lord Bridge invoked the 'realities of the doctor/patient relationship'[187] as one reason why a doctrine enforcing the patient's right to self-determination would be 'quite impracticable in application'.[188] His view of the relationship, however, is a vertical and paternalistic one, which is antithetical to the collaborative model espoused in this book. In the same case, another judge, Lord Templeman, described the relationship as contractual.[189]

The existence of a variety of models of the doctor–patient relationship is itself an indication that the needs of patients are not uniform, and consent tailored to meet the exigencies of counter-paternalism may not meet the needs of all – as this is not a case of one size fits all. It is perhaps more helpful if the models of patient–doctor relationship described by various scholars are seen as describing the range of approaches that a doctor may take during a consultation, rather than characterising the relationship per se.

The model of doctor-patient relationship that best fits with the notion of self-determination espoused in this book is one in which both parties form a

184 Ibid.

185 Ibid., p. W18.

186 Ibid.

187 *Sidaway* v. *Board of Governors of Bethlem Royal Hospital* [1985] 2 WLR at 500.

188 Ibid., 503–504.

189 Ibid., 508.

collaborative; the doctor provides the patient with information on the nature of the condition and possible interventions, and assists the patient in determining which medical interventions fit with the patient's articulated values and, although the patient is open to persuasion, the patient retains decisional control.

Conclusion: Self-determination Triumphs, Beneficence Survives

In the light of the above narrative, there appears to be no irrefutable defence for paternalism in contemporary medical practice. I conclude that paternalism (specifically, strong paternalism) is unacceptable in contemporary medical practice in the western world. The drivers of anti-paternalism outlined above are here to stay and a return to paternalism is not foreseeable. Competent patients should be involved in decision-making regarding their care, and their choices and decisions should be respected by the doctor.

Strong paternalism should not be encouraged; on the contrary self-determination should always be protected, albeit within an 'ecological' framework, one that takes cognisance of the relevant communal and contextual factors.

In the past, a doctor could perform a Caesarean section against the wishes of a woman in situations where the doctor recognised that not doing the operation could result in serious harm (e.g. rupture of the womb) or death to the woman or her baby.[190] This was paradigmatic of paternalism. In contemporary practice, the doctor undertaking a Caesarean section without the consent of the woman will be breaking the law.[191] Legally and otherwise, paternalism is abhorred in contemporary health care, and protection of the patient's self-determination has become a legal and moral imperative: 'In modern law medical paternalism no longer rules.'[192]

This is not to say that beneficence, so central to traditional medical practice, no longer has a place. A doctor will continue to be guided by the principle of beneficence, but can no longer act beneficently *in defiance of the patient's wish* on the grounds that respecting the patient's wish could result in harm.

Beneficence is sometimes either conflated with paternalism or presented as the justification for paternalism.[193] It must be noted, however, that respect for self-determination is not incompatible with beneficence; indeed respect for self-determination can be regarded as part of beneficence: by upholding a

190 Stauch, Court-authorised Caesareans.

191 Lord Justice Thorpe, Consent for Caesarean section: Part 2.

192 Lord Steyn in *Chester (Respondent)* v. *Afshar (Appellant)* [2004] UKHL 41, at para 16.

193 Schermer M, *The Different Faces of Autonomy: Patient Autonomy in Ethical Theory and Hospital Practice*. Dordrecht; Kluwer Academic 2002.

patient's self-determination, the doctor is contributing to their welfare. Respect for self-determination also reflects professionalism. Pellegrino and Thomasma developed the concept of 'beneficence-in-trust' to describe the role of the doctor acting in the best interest of the individual while keeping in trust their moral values.[194]

National policies and professional guidance have increasingly recognised the patient's right to self-determination, but the espoused principles of patient engagement have not been fully implemented in clinical practice. The law should give patients adequate protection in this regard, and provide adequate remedy when their right to make decisions is trampled on. Whether the existing provisions in English law can be regarded as affording adequate protection is a matter that will be returned to in later chapters.

It does not follow that a patient can demand any particular treatment or that the doctor is obliged to accede to this demand. While protecting the patient's self-determination is a cardinal goal, the overall interests and values of society (and often the patient) inform the pursuit of this goal.

The consent model has been said to be the standard mechanism for protecting the patient's self-determination, but a property model could be an alternative or complementary model, and in the next chapters I set out to compare both models against the background of an ecology paradigm. In keeping with this paradigm, a collaborative model of doctor–patient relationship is favoured. The informational model is rejected for being too consumerist and out of tune with medical professionalism. The deliberative and shared decision-making or joint investigation models, while consistent with medical tradition and professionalism, fight shy of explicitly underscoring the patient's right of self-determination.

It has been observed that the rhetoric, but perhaps not the reality, of the doctor–patient relationship has been changed by contemporary recognition of the importance of patient self-determination.[195] In subsequent chapters I explore the question of whether the consent or the property approach is more consistent with a model of the doctor–patient relationship in which the doctor, acting in a fiduciary capacity, provides the patient with information on the nature of the condition and possible interventions, and assists the patient in determining which medical interventions fit with the patient's articulated values.

194 Pellegrino and Thomasma, *For the Patient's Good*.

195 McLean, *Autonomy, Consent and the Law*, p. 31.

Chapter 3
Basic Principles of the Law of Consent

> Judges and legal scholars have long asserted the importance of patient autonomy in medical decision making. Yet autonomy has never been recognized as a legally protectable interest.[1]

In Chapter 2 an account was given of how developments in ethics and society at large progressively led to the erosion of paternalism and the ascendance (if not quite triumph) of the principle of self-determination. The mechanism by which this principle is protected in law is the law of consent, and legal developments have, in parallel with ethical and social developments, shaped our understanding of consent. In this chapter the basic principles of consent law are reviewed and an attempt is made to show how case law has responded to rapidly evolving ethical and social perspectives. The chapter sets the backdrop for the analysis that follows in later chapters.

Should the Focus be on Patient or Doctor?

One of the earliest legal references to consent appears to be the 1767 case of *Slater* v. *Baker and Stapleton* where the courts imposed liability on a surgeon who failed to obtain consent.[2] However, it was not until the twentieth century, starting with the US case of *Schloendorff* v. *Society of New York Hospital*, that legal cases on consent began to flourish.[3] As more and more cases reached the courts, the law became more and more complex. Whereas the law at the time of *Slater* did not go beyond a requirement that the surgeon should not treat a patient without the patient's authorisation, the law today requires the physician not just to obtain the patient's assent but to provide sufficient information, seek to ensure that the patient understands, recognise quite specifically what the patient agrees to or does not agree to, respect any refusals and avoid a string of factors

---

1 Shultz MM, From informed consent to patient choice: a new protected interest (1985) 95 Yale LJ 219–299, at p. 219.

2 *Slater* v. *Baker and Stapleton* 95 Eng Rep 860 KB 1767.

3 *Mary E Schloendorff* v. *Society of New York Hospital* 211 NY 125, 105 NE 92 (1914).

such as duress and deception which could vitiate consent.[4] These requirements form the basis of the distinction that Faden and Beauchamp make between the legal and moral foundations of consent:

> The law's approach springs from a pragmatic theory. Although the patient is granted a right to consent or refuse, the focus is on the physician, who holds a duty and who risks liability by failure to fulfil the duty. Moral philosophy's approach springs from a principle of respect for autonomy that focuses on the patient or subject, who has a right to make an autonomous choice.[5]

In other words, the law's approach to consent focuses heavily on the duties of the doctor, while ethics and moral philosophy focus more on the patient's autonomous choice. The point has been made above that it is not pragmatic for the law to concern itself with whether a particular choice is autonomous; nevertheless, I will argue (see Chapter 9) that, if the patient's right to self-determination is to be protected, the law should have this right as its starting point.

The Legal Development of Consent: Battery and Negligence

In English law, a doctor undertaking treatment without consent may be liable for assault or battery or face an action in negligence.[6] Battery and negligence are both torts; assault could be a crime. Battery is an intentional, unauthorised touching of another person, *irrespective of whether any injury results and irrespective of whether or not the defendant acted in good faith*.[7] Assault is an intentional act which induces in the victim an apprehension of imminent harm or offensive contact, but the term 'assault' 'is now, in both ordinary legal usage and in statutes, regularly used to cover both assault and battery'.[8] In Scots law no distinction is made between assault and battery but this brief review of battery and negligence takes an English law perspective, as the key consent cases (*Sidaway* v. *Board of Governors of the Bethlem Royal Hospital and the Maudsley Hospital*[9] and *Chester* v.

4 Hockton A, *The Law of Consent to Medical Treatment*. London: Sweet & Maxwell 2002.

5 Faden RR and Beauchamp TL, in collaboration with King NMP, *A History and Theory of Informed Consent*. Oxford: Oxford University Press 1986, p. 4.

6 Lord Browne-Wilkinson in *Airedale NHS Trust* v. *Bland* [1993] 1 All ER 821, 881.

7 In other words, an intention to cause harm is not a prerequisite; see *Wilson* v. *Pringle* [1986] 2 All ER 440, at 445.

8 Lord Slynn in *R* v. *Brown* [1993] 2 All ER 75 HL.

9 *Sidaway* v. *Board of Governors of the Bethlem Royal Hospital and the Maudsley Hospital* [1985] AC 871.

Afshar[10]) informing the comparative analysis of the consent and property models (Chapter 9) are from the English jurisdiction. Although the English law perspective is taken, cases from other jurisdictions are cited where they help illustrate the various applications of the consent model.

Assault is a common law crime if there was evil intent on the part of the perpetrator or recklessness in causing the victim to apprehend imminent violence.[11] In relation to consent, doctors usually do not have the necessary evil intent, so there may be no criminal action, but they may face a civil action. For a civil law action there is no requirement to prove that the assault caused any damage, and the plaintiff only has to show that there was non-consensual touching.[12]

The doctor commits a trespass against the person (i.e. a battery or assault) if he/she treats that person without prior valid consent, whether or not his/her motive was hostile. This includes the situation where a doctor obtains consent from the patient to perform one type of treatment and subsequently performs a substantially different treatment for which consent was not obtained. This was what happened in the iconic US case of Mary Schloendorff, who was admitted into hospital in January 1908 for an examination under anaesthetic to assess the cause of her abdominal pain.[13] While she was under anaesthetic, the surgeon removed a fibroid that had been found during the examination. There were post-operative complications and the patient sued the hospital. The case was decided in favour of the defendant at first instance and intermediate levels, and an appeal was heard at the state's highest court, the Court of Appeal. This was where the judge made the following statement on consent, part of which is often quoted:

> In the case at hand, the wrong complained of is not *merely* negligence. It is trespass. Every human being of adult years and sound mind has a right to determine what shall be done with his own body; and a surgeon who performs an operation without his patient's consent commits an assault, for which he is liable in damages.[14] (emphasis mine)

In another case, a woman asked to be injected in her right arm but was injected in her left arm, and she won damages in battery.[15] In another case that arose

10 *Chester* v. *Afshar* [2004] UKHL 41; [2005] 1 AC 134; [2004] 3 WLR. 927; [2004] 4 All ER 587.

11 Offences Against the Person Act 1861, ss 18, 20, 47.

12 Deakin S, Johnston A and Markesinis B QC, *Markesinis and Deakin's Tort Law*, 7th edn. Oxford: Oxford University Press 2012, ch. 4.

13 *Mary E Schloendorff* v. *Society of New York Hospital* (1914) 211 NY 125; 105 NE 92.

14 Ibid.

15 *Allan* v. *New Mount Sinai Hospital* (1980) 28 OR 356.

from a clerical error, the doctor was held liable in battery for operating on the patient's back instead of a toe.[16] An action in battery was successful when a woman who went in for a minor gynaecological operation suffered an injury to the womb and was sterilised.[17] Examples from American jurisdictions where battery has been established as a consequence of consent being exceeded include consent given for a hernia operation but the doctor also removed both ovaries,[18] myelogram[19] involving a spinal puncture performed where consent had been for the simpler electromyogram[20]and a mastectomy being performed whereas the patient had only consented to exploratory surgery.[21]

In practice an action in battery is only brought when the doctor has deviated completely from the terms of consent, or where consent was obtained by misrepresentation (see below). Most consent cases take the form of an action in *negligence*, where the claimant seeks to establish that the defendant has breached a legal duty of care and that this breach has resulted in injury. Such a duty of care is presumed to be owed by a doctor to his/her patients, and this duty includes providing information.[22]

Differences between Battery and Negligence

There are important differences between an action in negligence and an allegation of battery. Two differences relate to damage (harm). Negligence requires proof that the breach of duty (in this case, failure to inform) caused injury; in battery there is no need to prove that harm occurred. As Lord Scarman put it, 'damage is the gist of the action in the tort of negligence'.[23] Where harm occurs in battery, the defendant is liable for all damage that results from his or her action, while in negligence, the defendant is liable only for reasonably foreseeable harm.[24]

A further difference between battery and negligence in the context of consent is that a broad explanation of the treatment will usually be adequate defence to an allegation of battery, but more detailed discussion will usually be

16 *Schweitzer* v. *Central Hospital* (1974) 53 DLR (3d) 494.

17 *Devi* v. *West Midlands AHA* (1980) CLY 687.

18 *Zoterell* v. *Repp* (1915) 187 Mich 319 153 N.W. 692

19 An image of the spine and spinal cord.

20 A test that measures the electrical activity in a muscle. See *Berkey* v. *Anderson* (1969) supra, 1 Cal App 3d 790.

21 *Corn* v. *French* (1955) 71 Nev 280 [289 P.2d 173].

22 *Sidaway* v. *Board of Governors of the Bethlem Royal Hospital and the Maudsley Hospital* [1985] AC 871.

23 Ibid., 883. Repeated verbatim (albeit without credit to the original source) by Lord Steyn in *Chester (Respondent)* v. *Afshar (Appellant)* [2004] UKHL 41.

24 Deakin, Johnston and Markesinis, *Markesinis and Deakin's Tort Law*.

required in order to meet the duty of care in negligence.[25] In *Chatterton* v. *Gerson* the claimant suffered numbness after a procedure to treat the chronic pain that she had in a scar.[26] After a repeat procedure, also performed by Dr Gerson, she lost sensation in her right leg. Mrs Chatterton claimed trespass to the person in that there was no valid consent, since the implications of the procedures were not explained to her. She also claimed in negligence that the doctor had breached his duty of care by not providing sufficient information. Bristow J declared that 'once the patient is informed in broad terms of the nature of the procedure which is intended, and gives her consent, that consent is real'[27] and the cause of action for alleged failure to disclose risks is negligence, not trespass.

Another difference is that by definition battery entails touching, so will not be applicable in consent cases (particularly refusal of treatment) where there has been no touching, whereas bodily invasion is not a prerequisite for establishing negligence. *Truman* v. *Thomas* exemplifies this difference.[28] A woman who had repeatedly refused smear tests died of cervical cancer and her children sued the doctor for failing to warn her of the risks of not having this test. Such a case could not establish liability in battery as there was no touching, but could be brought in negligence as the duty of care mandates discussion of the risks and benefits of alternative treatments, including the alternative of no treatment.

Thus, battery is inadequate for protection of patients' choice in the vast and growing proportion of medical decision-making and treatment – for example, whether or not to take cholesterol-lowering medication – that does not entail physical contact.

Lastly, in cases founded on battery, the onus lies on the doctor to prove that the patient consented to the treatment, whereas in negligence it is for the claimant patient to prove that he/she did not give a true consent.[29]

---

25 Per Bristow J, in *Chatterton* v. *Gerson* [1981] 1 All ER 257. Reaffirmed by McCullough J in *Davis* v. *Barking Havering and Brentwood Health Authority* [1993] 4 Med LR 85.

26 *Chatterton* v. *Gerson* [1981] 1 All ER 257. See also [1981] QB 432 (QBD).

27 *Chatterton* v. *Gerson* [1981] QB 432 (QBD), at 432.

28 *Truman* v. *Thomas* 165 Cal. Rptr. 308, 611 P.2d 902 (Cal 1980).

29 Geisen D, *International Medical Malpractice Law: A Comparative Law Study of Civil Liability Arising from Medical Care*. London: Nijhoff 1988, p. 264.

Table 3.1 Negligence distinguished from battery

Battery	Negligence
Body must be touched	Bodily invasion not a prerequisite
No need to prove harm	There must be harm
Defendant liable for all damage	Liable only for reasonably foreseeable harm resulting from action
Burden on doctor to prove consent was obtained	Claimant to prove that he/she did not give consent

Battery in Disclosure Cases: The Position of English Courts

English courts have been reluctant to apply battery law in cases involving alleged non-disclosure of information to patients. In *Sidaway*, Lord Scarman specifically denounced as 'deplorable' the application of battery in claims for non-disclosure.[30] By doing so, he endorsed the view expressed by Bristow J in *Chatterton* v. *Gerson*[31] and Hirst J in *Hills* v. *Porter*.[32] May J also considered such an action deplorable when he dismissed a claim in battery brought by persons who had been treated with human growth hormone (the Creutzfeldt-Jakob disease litigation).[33]

One reason why the courts have taken this position is that battery is an intentional tort. Cases of non-disclosure, even if negligent, are generally not the result of an intention to harm. Courts also consider it unfair to attach a stigma to doctors who have acted in good faith. Where there is evidence that the health-care professional did not act in good faith, however, the courts have not hesitated in finding him or her liable in battery. In *Appleton and Others* v. *Garrett* the claimants brought an action against an NHS dentist who, for fraudulent reasons, had grossly over-treated patients.[34] Extensive treatment was carried out on teeth that were in pristine condition. He was found liable for battery. The court found that had the dentist properly explained the treatments and the need for them to the claimants they would not have consented to these treatments.

30 *Sidaway* v. *Board of Governors of Bethlem Royal Hospital and the Maudsley Hospital* [1985] 1 AC 871, at 883.

31 *Chatterton* v. *Gerson* [1981] 1 All ER 257.

32 *Hills* v. *Potter* [1983] 3 All ER 716; [1984] 1 WLR 641, at 653.

33 *The Creutzfeldt-Jakob Disease Litigation* [1995] 54 BMLR 1 (QBD).

34 *Appleton and Others* v. *Garrett* 34 BMLR 23 (QBD).

All eight claimants were awarded aggravated damages for pain, suffering and loss of amenity.

Battery in Disclosure Cases: The Position in Other Jurisdictions

In some American jurisdictions, when a patient was not given prior warning of a potential complication (the occurrence of which was not an integral part of the treatment procedure but merely a known risk) and this risk materialised, the courts had tended to decide such cases in battery rather than negligence. Examples include failure to warn a patient a spinal operation involved an inherent risk of permanent paralysis[35] and failure to warn of danger of radiation burns.[36] The epochal judgment in *Natanson* v. *Kline* shifted the thrust from battery to negligence.[37] Mrs Natanson suffered burns as a result of radiation therapy after mastectomy, and sued the radiologist, Dr Kline, for failing to warn of the nature and risks of the treatment. It was ruled that action relating to consent cases of this nature should be brought under negligence law rather than battery.

An opportunity arose in *Cobbs* v. *Grant* for the California Supreme Court to clarify its position.[38] Mr Cobbs' spleen was ruptured during an operation for a duodenal ulcer in the hands of Dr Grant, and he needed a second operation to remove the spleen. Subsequently, he developed a gastric ulcer. Dr Grant had not warned him that the initial operation carried a 5 per cent chance of injury to the spleen and that the operation carried a chance of inducing other ulcers. Regarding the form of action to be brought in such cases, the court said:

> The battery theory should be reserved for those circumstances when a doctor performs an operation to which the patient has not consented. When the patient gives permission to perform one type of treatment and the doctor performs another, the requisite element of deliberate intent to deviate from the consent given is present. However, when the patient consents to certain treatment and the doctor performs that treatment but an undisclosed inherent complication with a low probability occurs, no intentional deviation from the consent given appears; rather, the doctor in obtaining consent may have failed to meet his due care duty to disclose pertinent information. In that situation the action should be pleaded in negligence.[39]

---

35 *Gray* v. *Grunnagle* (1966) 423 Pa 144 223 A.2d 663.

36 *Belcher* v. *Carter* (1967) 13 Ohio App.2d 113 [42 Ohio Ops.2d 218, 234 NE2d 311].

37 *Natanson* v. *Kline* (1960) 187 Kan 186 [354 P.2d 670].

38 *Cobbs* v. *Grant* 8 Cal. 3d 229, 502 P.2d 1, 104 Cal. Rptr. 505 (1972). 8 Cal. 3d at 240-241; 502 P.2d at 8; 104 Cal. Rptr. at 512.

39 *Cobbs* v. *Grant* 8 Cal. 3d at 240–241; 502 P.2d at 8; 104 Cal. Rptr. at 512.

Resurgence of Battery?

This exposition of the shift from battery to negligence is relevant because in Chapter 9 I will assess whether property analysis could either facilitate or inhibit a reversal of this shift. Although it is not currently fashionable for the tort of battery to be employed in the context of consent, it has been speculated that developments in human rights law could encourage the use of this avenue.[40]

Such speculation could be fuelled by academic commentators, like Kennedy who argued that:

> patients' interests could well be better protected if the tort of battery were held to have a wider application. In particular, questions of what has come to be known as 'informed consent' could well be differently analysed and decided. A patient may have consented on the 'nature and purpose' test, but the information provided by the doctor may be so inadequate, in that it failed to respect the patient's right to know, so as to be able to choose, that the consent should be regarded as entirely invalid. Such an extension to the tort of battery would restore the law's protection of the symbolic harm represented by the complaint that the patient's right to know was not respected. It would, in other words, reflect a response based upon rights.[41]

The goal of enabling patients to exercise their right of self-determination is handicapped by the narrow interpretation of consent in the tort of battery. Many years after Kennedy's call for expansion of this tort, little has happened in this direction. Perhaps the key to unlocking this door is property analysis – we return to this in Chapter 9 where an argument is made for patient self-determination to be protected as a fundamental right, independent of any injury that may or may not result from infraction of this right. Meanwhile attention is focused on negligence, and in the rest of this chapter I discuss the requirements for valid consent, then the concept of informed consent.

40 Hockton, *Law of Consent to Medical Treatment*, pp. 17 and 29.

41 Kennedy I, The fiduciary relationship and its application to doctors and patients. In Birks P (ed), *Wrongs and Remedies in the Twenty-First Century*. Oxford: Clarendon Press 1996, pp. 111–140, at p. 113.

Valid Consent

For consent to be valid the following must apply:

a) The patient must have the *capacity or competence* to make the decision.
b) There must be no *undue influence.*
c) The patient must have been given [or offered] *sufficient information* about the proposed treatment.[42]

In theory each of these requirements is simple and clear enough. In practice, their application is more complex and, as discussed below, the courts have not always provided clear-cut and consistent guidance.

In addition to these requirements which are cited in all standard descriptions of consent law and practice, one would add that there should be no misrepresentation. In *Sidaway*, Sir John Donaldson MR said that 'if the consent is obtained by fraud or by misrepresentation of the nature of what is to be done … it can be said that an apparent consent is not a true consent'.[43] In *Salgo*, Bray J. warned that 'the physician may not minimise the known dangers of the procedure or operation in order to induce his patient's request'.[44] In *R* v. *Tabassum* it was held that consent to breast examination was vitiated by fraud, as the defendant had misled the women into believing that he was a doctor.[45] In *Appleton and Ors* v. *Garrett* a dentist concealed information for financial gain and Dyson J. held that there was no valid consent (see above).[46]

The Bristol Inquiry recommended that where the procedure is experimental or innovative or the clinician inexperienced, the patient should be informed as part of the consent process.[47] It is arguable that failure to comply with this recommendation could count as concealment of information for the personal gain of the doctor or hospital.

---

42 British Medical Association, *Medical Ethics Today: The BMA's Handbook of Ethics and Law*, 2nd edn. London: BMJ Books 2004.

43 *Sidaway* v. *Board of Governors of the Bethlem Royal and the Maudsley Hospital* [1984] 2 WLR 778, at 790.

44 *Salgo* v. *Leland Stanford Jr. University Board of Trustees* 154 Cal.App.2d 560 (1957) 317 P.2d 170, at 578.

45 R v. *Tabassum* [2000] Lloyd's Rep Med 404.

46 *Appleton and Ors* v. *Garrett* [1997] 8 Med LR 75.

47 The Bristol Royal Infirmary Inquiry, *Learning from Bristol: The Report of the Public Inquiry into Children's Heart Surgery at the Bristol Royal Infirmary 1984–1995*. Recommendation 102, p. 449. Available at http://www.bristol-inquiry.org.uk/final_report/the_report.pdf. Accessed 13 October 2012.

Competence[48]

As has been pointed out, competence 'is not an all or nothing notion, as the legal definition suggests'.[49] In clear-cut cases, where a patient is in a coma or severely mentally handicapped, he/she is clearly incompetent. At the other extreme is the highly knowledgeable and articulate patient with well-defined values and goals, who is able convincingly to communicate his/her wishes to the clinician. Most patients fall between the two extremes and determining competence to consent to a particular procedure is not always easy. The situation is compounded by the fact that a patient may be competent to give consent for one intervention but not for another. Strictly speaking a competent person must have a coherent set of beliefs that shapes his or her values or attitudes in a consistent way.[50] In the absence of this coherent set of values, it is arguable that an authentic decision regarding medical treatment cannot be made. The assessment of competence is an onerous task for the clinician who must determine whether the patient is capable of retaining the information, weighing the options on balance against his or her values, beliefs and attitudes, and arriving at a decision.[51] It has been observed that clinicians often do not proceed beyond a casual evaluation of patient competence due to time constraints, lack of communication and sometimes lack of education. On the other hand it is fair to say that a detailed assessment of competence is not necessary in all cases. An adult is presumed to be competent and a full assessment of competence is required only in those cases where the clinician has reason to rebut this presumption.[52]

Undue Influence

For consent to be valid it must be given without undue influence.[53] The Law Commission said that purported consent could be invalidated by 'compulsion (that is physical force), coercive threats or offers ("duress") and defective beliefs induced by fraud or mistake'.[54] Coercion does not appear to be a major issue in clinical practice, but more subtle forms of undue influence are encountered.

48 Here, 'competence' is used as interchangeable with 'capacity'. Strictly, however, clinicians assess *decisional capacity* but *legal competence* can only be determined by a court.

49 Switankowsky IS, *A New Paradigm for Informed Consent.* Lanham, Md.: University Press of America 1998, p. 18.

50 Drake JF, The many faces of competency (1985) 15 Hastings Cent Rep 17–21.

51 Ibid.

52 *Re B (Adult: Refusal of Medical Treatment)* [2002] 2 All ER 449.

53 *Re T (Adult: Refusal of Treatment)* [1992] 3 WLR 782, at 799.

54 The Law Commission, *Consent in the Criminal Law: A Consultation Paper*, Issue 139 of the Law Commission Consultation Paper Series. London: HM Stationery Office 1995, p. 260.

Tales of women who have been manipulated into having an unnecessary hysterectomy dramatically reflect 'misinformed' consent[55] and it may well be that these extreme cases are the tip of an iceberg, with the less extreme or dramatic cases remaining hidden beneath the surface. The manipulation does not have to be ill-motivated for it to vitiate consent.

A distinction is made between narrow and broad meanings of voluntary action, between truly volitional and constrained volitional actions.[56] In the narrow definition of voluntary action, the subject simply exercises a choice between alternatives; in the broader meaning, the subject's action is involuntary when his/her will is not taken away but his/her choice is unduly influenced. Take the case of a person who is held at gun point and opts to hand over his money rather than be shot. This is a choice he has made himself, but he is acting at the behest of the gun holder and does not have an independent reason for that action. He acted voluntarily in the narrow sense of the word but involuntarily in the broader sense – a constrained volitional action. In relation to patients' decision-making in clinical practice, some decisions may appear to be volitional but are actually constrained volitional decisions.

Health-care providers do not literally hold their patients at gun point, but in some situations (such as when submitting to an interventional procedure) a patient may not have an independent reason for taking a particular action and only does so in deference to the awesome figure of the medical establishment. The patient's apparent agreement to the procedure in such situations has been said to be assent rather than consent but while this description makes a good point, it does not go far enough in capturing the patient's captive situation. This type of agreement, which is common in medical practice, should be described as a constrained volitional agreement to treatment.

Professional guidance[57] on consent cautions against undue influence. In its guidance, the General Medical Council advises doctors:

> You must give information about risk in a balanced way. You should avoid bias, and you should explain the expected benefits as well as the potential burdens and risks of any proposed investigation or treatment.[58]

> You must respect a patient's decision to refuse an investigation or treatment, even if you think their decision is wrong or irrational. You should explain your concerns clearly to the patient and outline the possible consequences of their

55 Cloutier-Steele L, *Misinformed Consent: Women's Stories about Unnecessary Hysterectomy.* Chester, NJ: Next Decade 2003.

56 Wertheimer A, *Coercion.* Princeton: Princeton University Press 1990, pp. 6–7.

57 General Medical Council, *Consent: Patients and Doctors Making Decisions Together.* London: GMC 2008.

58 Ibid., p. 17, para 33.

> decision. You must not, however, put pressure on a patient to accept your advice.[59]

It is not always easy to determine where persuasion ends and undue influence begins. In *Re T (Adult: Refusal of Medical Treatment)* Lord Justice Butler-Sloss said that '[t]he degree of pressure to turn persuasion or appeals to affection into undue influence may be very little',[60] but in the same case Lord Donaldson said that it did not matter how strong the persuasion was, so long as it did not overbear the independence of the patient's decision.[61] The case involved a 34-year-old pregnant woman who, following a road traffic accident, developed a lung abscess and needed surgery but declined blood transfusion. Her mother was a Jehovah's Witness but she herself was not one. Reversing the decision of the lower court, the Court of Appeal held that her refusal of blood transfusion was not binding on medical staff because her mother had unduly influenced her. Since the court agreed it was wholly acceptable that a patient should be persuaded by a third party so long as the final decision was the patient's, health professionals should not be discouraged from using persuasion where necessary.

The informational model of the doctor–patient relationship would not condone persuasion, but in Chapter 2 this model was discountenanced as being too consumerist and out of tune with medical professionalism. Persuasion is consistent with the collaborative model of the doctor–patient relationship and with medical beneficence; it also fits with the ecology paradigm underlying this book. The collaborative model obliges a doctor, for example, to try to persuade a patient to accept blood transfusion but such persuasion must not be allowed to degenerate into coercion. Faden and Beauchamp regard the use of persuasion as 'an acceptable form of influence in informed consent contexts'.[62] The courts, too, acknowledge that the doctor has a role beyond mere provision of options:

> … the patient, being unlearned in medical sciences, has an abject dependence upon and trust in his physician for the information upon which he relies during the decisional process, thus *raising an obligation in the physician that transcends arms-length transactions.*[63] (emphasis mine)

Undue influence could of course come from the patient's family,[64] but that is outside the scope of this analysis.

59 Ibid., p. 19, para 43.

60 *Re T (Adult: Refusal of Medical Treatment)* [1992] 4 All ER 649 (CA), at 667–668.

61 *Re T (Adult: Refusal of Treatment)* [1992] 3 WLR 782, at 799.

62 Faden and Beauchamp, *History and Theory of Informed Consent*, p. 373.

63 Judge in *Arato* v. *Avedon*, 5 Cal. 4th 1172; 23 Cal. Rptr.2d 131; 858 P.2d 598 (1993).

64 *Re T (Adult: Refusal of Medical Treatment)* [1992] 4 All ER 649 (CA); [1992] 3 WLR 782.

'Informed Consent' – the Term

The term 'informed consent' is frequently used in clinical practice and in the literature, and two authoritative books[65] use the term in their title, despite the authors of one of the books recognising the term as a pleonasm.[66] It is important to distinguish between 'informed consent' as a doctrine and 'informed consent' used imprecisely to mean a valid consent, one where the broad nature of the treatment proposed has been explained to the patient. This latter use of the term has been described as unhelpful since the requirement that consent be informed is only one of the ingredients of valid consent.[67] It is arguable that the phrase is tautologous, as consent must always be informed if it is to be legally and ethically acceptable. In everyday life, people give meaningful consent (or assent) to various activities (e.g. agreeing to participate in a social activity) without having full information, but in legal usage, consent has to be informed in order to be valid.

Jackson finds the term problematic because it is ambiguous, does not tell how much information should be provided, may make doctors over-burden patients with too much information and emphasises information provision at the expense of understanding.[68] She expands on the ambiguity of the term as follows:

> … the expression 'informed consent' may be both ambiguous and misleading. It is, for example, commonly used as a convenient shorthand for two separate legal duties: the duty to obtain the patient's consent before treatment, and the duty to ensure that the patient has been adequately informed about the risks and benefits of their therapeutic options. Nor is it clear whether the word 'informed' refers to the doctor's behaviour or the patient's state of mind. Is consent 'informed' if information has simply been provided before consent is given, regardless of whether the patient has in fact read, listened to, or understood anything? Or must the consent itself have been 'informed' by the patient's prior consideration of all relevant material factors?[69]

---

65 Manson NC and O'Neill O, *Rethinking Informed Consent in Bioethics*. Cambridge: Cambridge University Press 2007; Maclean A, *Autonomy, Informed Consent and Medical Law: A Relational Challenge*. Cambridge: Cambridge University Press 2009.

66 Manson and O'Neill, *Rethinking Informed Consent in Bioethics*, p. 89.

67 Kennedy I and Grubb A, *Medical Law: Text with Materials*, 2nd edn. London: Butterworths 1994, p. 151.

68 Jackson E, 'Informed consent' to medical treatment and the impotence of tort. In McLean, SAM (ed) *First Do No Harm: Law, Ethics and Healthcare*. Aldershot: Ashgate 2006, pp. 273–286.

69 Ibid., p. 273.

Commentators from outside the UK have similarly criticised this term,[70] and in this book it is used only when directly quoting other texts. The point (made rhetorically in the passage quoted above) about the importance of taking steps to check that the patient understands the information provided is revisited in Chapter 9.

Informed Consent – the Doctrine

As a legal term, 'informed consent' refers to the doctrine, developed in the United States, which underlies the amount of information that a patient should be given in addition to the 'broad nature' of the treatment. Even when used in this sense, the term could be problematic and some commentators have avoided it, preferring terms such as 'real' or 'meaningful' consent,[71] but other critics suggest that these alternatives are equally unhelpful to the extent that they 'would render proof of causation still more difficult for claimants, and would enable doctors to justify non-disclosure on the basis of vague fears that the claimant was then incapable of making a sensible or rational decision'.[72] This criticism, however, errs in assuming that 'real' or 'meaningful' implies 'sensible' or 'rational' consent.

The phrase 'informed consent' originated in 1957 from *amicus curiae* submitted by the American College of Surgeons to the California Court of Appeals in *Salgo* v. *Leland Stanford Jr. University Board of Trustees*.[73] Martin Salgo sued his doctors for negligently failing to warn him of the risk of paralysis resulting from translumbar aortography.[74] The court sowed the seed[75] of the doctrine of 'informed consent' when it held that the doctor owed a duty to the patient to disclose 'any facts which are necessary to form the basis of an intelligent consent by the patient to the proposed treatment'.[76]

The seed of 'informed consent' germinated as a doctrine in *Canterbury* v. *Spence*, where it was held that it was for the court to determine the extent of,

70 Skegg PDG, English medical law and 'informed consent': an antipodean assessment and alternative (1999) 7 Med LR 135–65, at 138.

71 McLean SAM, *A Patient's Right to Know*. Aldershot: Dartmouth 1989, p. 102.

72 Healy J, *Medical Negligence: Common Law Perspectives*. London: Sweet & Maxwell 1999, p. 125.

73 *Salgo* v. *Leland Stanford Jr. University Board of Trustees* [1957] 317 P.2d 170.

74 Imaging of the aorta, involving injection of a dye into the aorta via a needle inserted near the spine.

75 It was no more than a seed because while the court required full disclosure, it also said this should be consistent with the physician's discretion.

76 *Salgo* v. *Leland Stanford Jr. University Board of Trustees* [1957] 317 P.2d 170. Per Bray J. at 180.

and any breach of, the doctor's duty to inform.[77] The claimant was a 19-year-old man with severe pain between his shoulder blades who was referred to a neurosurgeon. The doctor told him that he would have to undergo an operation (laminectomy) to correct a suspected ruptured disc. The patient did not object to the operation or ask any questions, but in answer to his mother's question the doctor said the operation was not any more serious than any other operation. The day after the operation, the claimant fell from his hospital bed; he was paralysed in the lower half of his body and became permanently disabled. The claimant sued the doctor and hospital on the ground that the doctor was negligent in failing to disclose a risk of serious disability inherent in the procedure. In a landmark decision, Robinson J upheld the claim that the 1 per cent risk of paralysis should have been disclosed. Significantly, the court decided that the standard for determining whether adequate information had been given was not that of professional opinion but of the reasonable patient.

In *Sidaway*, Lord Scarman summarised the doctrine as follows:

> … where there is a 'real' or 'material' risk inherent in the proposed operation (however competently and skilfully performed) the question whether and to what extent a patient should be warned before he gives his consent is to be answered not by reference to medical practice but by accepting as a matter of law that, subject to all proper exceptions (of which the court, not the profession, is the judge), a patient has a right to be informed of the risks inherent in the treatment which is proposed. The profession, it is said, should not be judge in its own cause; or, less emotively but more correctly, the courts should not allow medical opinion as to what is best for the patient to override the patient's right to decide for himself whether he will submit to the treatment offered him.[78]

In a nutshell, the doctrine mandates full disclosure of material risks to the patient, and the standard of disclosure is to be determined not by the medical profession but by the court, taking account of the patient's expectations. The full disclosure is not, however, referenced to the particular patient; it is full only in so far as it includes all that a hypothetical 'reasonable patient' would want to be told. The doctrine is American in origin and application, and Robertson suggests that expanding the liability of doctors was at the root of its development.[79] As the key point of divergence or controversy between jurisdictions that embrace the doctrine and those that do not is the standard for assessing the quality and quantity of disclosure, this issue is addressed in more depth in the paragraphs below.

---

77 *Canterbury* v. *Spence* [1972] 464 F.2d 772.

78 *Sidaway* v. *Bethlem Royal Hospital Governors* (1985)1 All ER 643, at 645.

79 Robertson G, Informed consent to medical treatment (1981) 97 LQR 102.

Standards of Disclosure: What Constitutes Sufficient Information?

For consent to be valid, the patient must be given sufficient information, but what constitutes sufficient information? Over the years two standards have been employed: (a) the professional standard or responsible doctor standard and (b) the reasonable person or prudent patient standard. The professional standard takes us back to the paternalistic model where the physician decides what should or should not be disclosed, with more emphasis on beneficence and much less on autonomy.[80] This standard does not sit well with the principle of self-determination that the consent model purports to protect.

The prudent patient standard obligates the clinician to disclose information that any reasonable person would require to make a rational decision. Some courts have applied it not just in relation to the nature of treatment, but in determining the extent to which the risks of treatment should be disclosed to the patient by the clinician.[81]

In his landmark decision in the US case of *Canterbury* v. *Spence*, Robinson J. broke ground that the courts had been disinclined to explore previously.[82] Firstly, he departed from the 'professional standard', which was hitherto the test for disclosure. Secondly, he provided new guidelines regarding materiality of risk and the contentious issues of therapeutic privilege and causation. Before *Canterbury* v. *Spence*, the test for negligence in relation to information disclosure was the 'professional standard', also known as the 'reasonable' or 'prudent' doctor standard. Under this standard, the validity of an apparent consent depended on whether a responsible body of physicians (even if this was a minority one) regarded disclosure, or non-disclosure, of the particular information as professionally acceptable. One of the implications of this test was that it allowed policy considerations to override self-determination. Also, in adopting this test the courts failed to distinguish between the strictly medical aspects of clinical practice (such as making a diagnosis) and the non-medical (such as communicating with the patient). McLean, among others, has emphasised the importance of making this distinction between the 'technical' and 'moral' aspects of medical behaviour.[83] On this issue, Robinson J said:

> Prevailing medical practice, we have maintained, has evidentiary value in determinations as to what the specific criteria measuring challenged professional conduct are and whether they have been met, but does not itself define the

80 For an erudite analysis of paternalism versus patient autonomy in relation to information disclosure, see McLean, *Patient's Right to Know*.

81 *Rogers* v. *Whitaker* [1992] 109 ALR 625; *Canterbury* v. *Spence* [1972] 464 F.2d 772; *Pearce* v. *United Bristol Healthcare NHS Trust* [1999] PIQR P53.

82 *Canterbury* v. *Spence* [1972] 464 F.2d 772.

83 McLean, *Patient's Right to Know*, pp. 22–25.

> standard. That has been our position in treatment cases, where the physician's performance is ordinarily to be adjudicated by the special medical standard of due care. We see no logic in a different rule for nondisclosure cases, where the governing standard is much more largely divorced from professional considerations. And surely in nondisclosure cases the factfinder is not invariably functioning in an area of such technical complexity that it must be bound to medical custom as an inexorable application of the community standard of reasonable care.[84]

Robinson J explained why the professional standard did not apply:

> There are, in our view, formidable obstacles to acceptance of the notion that the physician's obligation to disclose is either germinated or limited by medical practice. To begin with, the reality of any discernible custom reflecting a professional concensus [*sic*] on communication of option and risk information to patients is open to serious doubt. We sense the danger that what in fact is no custom at all may be taken as an affirmative custom to maintain silence, and that physician-witnesses to the so-called custom may state merely their personal opinions as to what they or others would do under given conditions. We cannot gloss over the inconsistency between reliance on a general practice respecting divulgence and, on the other hand, realization that the myriad of variables among patients makes each case so different that its omission can rationally be justified only by the effect of its individual circumstances. Nor can we ignore the fact that to bind the disclosure obligation to medical usage is to arrogate the decision on revelation to the physician alone. Respect for the patient's right of self-determination on particular therapy demands a standard set by law for physicians rather than one which physicians may or may not impose upon themselves.[85]

This judgment should not spawn triumphalism among proponents of autonomy, however. As has been pointed out,[86] the judgment was based not just on the right to self-determination but also on the absence of logical justification for following the professional standard at all times (e.g. experts may state merely their personal views; and the myriad of variables makes each patient so different). Also, the court in *Canterbury* has been criticised for being equivocal about the protection of patients' choice through formulation of an appropriate standard.[87] While primacy of self-determination calls for a subjective test of causation, the court

84 *Canterbury* v. *Spence,* [1972] 464 F.2d 772, at para 27.
85 Ibid., para 24.
86 Healy, *Medical Negligence*, pp. 92–93.
87 Ibid., p. 90.

opted for an objective prudent patient test. This may be less than ideal, but it is pragmatic. It could be argued that reliance on a subjective test would have placed too much weight on the patient's unverifiable word, thereby encouraging unnecessary litigation and leaving doctors vulnerable. This balance between the ideal and the pragmatic also underlies the court's views on materiality. The test for determining whether a particular peril must be divulged is its materiality to the patient's decision. A risk is material 'when a reasonable person, in what the physician knows or should know to be the patient's position, would be likely to attach significance to the risk or cluster of risks in deciding whether or not to forego the proposed therapy'.[88] The main factors are the incidence of injury and the degree of harm threatened. Even a very small chance of death or serious disablement, therefore, may well be significant.

In less than a decade, ten jurisdictions in the United States had adopted the principles behind *Canterbury*;[89] but a backlash soon followed – a medical malpractice insurance crisis forced many states to beat a retreat from the doctrine of informed consent, via legislation that either affirmed the professional standard or set statutory limits.[90] The primary purpose of these statutes was to limit the financial consequences of litigation.

In Canada, the Supreme Court clarified the law in the case of *Reibl* v. *Hughes*.[91] The claimant suffered from headaches and hypertension and was referred to a neurosurgeon who advised an operation. The surgeon did not tell the patient that the operation involved a 4 per cent risk of death and a further 10 per cent risk of having a stroke. The operation was performed competently, but the patient suffered a massive stroke which left him paralysed. He sued in battery and negligence. The court rejected the professional standard and affirmed the duty of the doctor to disclose any material risks and any special or unusual risks. On the issue of causation, the court opted for the objective test but modified it by investing the prudent patient with the attributes of the claimant (who was at no immediate risk without the operation and was within one and a half years of earning pension benefits). A prudent person in this position would probably have opted not to undergo surgery, given a 10 per cent risk of a stroke.

Robertson pointed out that in 25 of the 46 cases (56 per cent) decided in the ten years following *Reibl*, the claimants failed to show that the breach of duty to inform caused the loss.[92] This is largely attributable to the adoption of the objective test, albeit subjectivised in varying degrees in the post-*Reibl* cases.

88 *Canterbury* v. *Spence* (464 F.2d 772) 1972.

89 Healy, *Medical Negligence*, p. 100.

90 Ibid., pp.100–101.

91 *Reibl* v. *Hughes* [1980] 114 DLR (3d) 1.

92 Robertson G, Informed consent 10 years later: the impact of *Reibl v Hughes* [1991] 70 Can Bar Rev 423, at 428.

Robertson's review also showed that, contrary to expectations, *Reibl* did not open the floodgates to successful negligence claims.

The abandonment of the professional standard was underscored in *White* v. *Turner*, a case concerning breast reduction surgery:

> No longer does the medical profession alone collectively determine, by its own practices, the amount of information a patient should have in order to decide whether to undergo an operation.[93]

The duty of the doctor to disclose all material or unusual risks, and that of the courts to determine this materiality, was reiterated by the New Brunswick Court of Appeal in *Kitchen* v. *Mullen*.[94] The claimant was given a blood product after a tooth extraction. This carries a small risk of transmission of hepatitis about which he had not been warned but which materialised. All three judges held that the risk should have been disclosed, but the action failed on the element of causation. This element has been a seemingly insurmountable hurdle in Canadian cases where the doctrine of informed consent was applied à la *Reibl*. In *Considine* v. *Camp Hill Hospital*,[95] *Ferguson* v. *Hamilton Civic Hospitals*[96] and *Casey* v. *Provan*[97] material risks were not disclosed and the claimants respectively claimed for urinary incontinence, stroke and loss of voice but all failed because causation was not established.[98]

A more patient-friendly application of the doctrine of informed consent is to be found in the celebrated Australian case of *Rogers* v. *Whittaker*.[99] The plaintiff who had been blind in the right eye from birth was advised by the defendant to undergo an operation on this eye to improve her sight. The 1 in 14,000 risk of sympathetic ophthalmia in the healthy left eye was not disclosed. This risk materialised and she lost the sight in that eye. The court not only adopted the prudent patient test from *Canterbury* but went as far as adopting a subjective approach to the test (i.e. 'what did this particular patient need to know?' and not 'what did a reasonable person in her position need to know?'). The surgeon's appeal was dismissed.

---

93 *White* v. *Turner* [1981] 120 DLR (3d) 269, at 269.

94 *Kitchen* v. *Mullen* [1990] 1 Med LR 352.

95 *Considine* v. *Camp Hill Hospital* [1982] 133 DLR (3d) 11.

96 *Ferguson* v. *Hamilton Civic Hospitals* [1983] 114 DLR (3d) 214.

97 *Casey* v. *Provan* [1984] 11 DLR 706.

98 In Chapter 9 it will be shown that one way of skipping or removing the causation hurdle is to adopt the property model.

99 *Rogers* v. *Whittaker* [1992] 109 ALR 625.

Does the Prudent Patient Standard Encumber Clinicians?

Disclosure of information does not depend on medical skill so it would appear sensible for the standard of disclosure to be determined not by medical professionals but by patients. If patients set the standard an additional burden is placed on the physician, who has to make extra effort to find out what a reasonable patient would want to know. However, there is reason to believe that in clinical practice the professional standard is beginning to approximate to the reasonable patient standard. Various professional bodies now provide guidance to doctors on standards of information disclosure, and practically all of these documents address the kind of information that the objective patient would want to be given.[100] It remains to be established whether the apparent rise of the prudent patient standard has led to better communication between clinician and patient.

Subjective or Objective Prudent Patient?

Application of the prudent patient standard does not necessarily resolve the controversy, for there is also tension between the *objective* patient standard and the *subjective* patient standard. If the principle of autonomy-respecting consent is to be followed strictly, then it is the subjective patient standard that should be applied.

McLean emphasises the failure of the objective standard to protect self-determination:

> … the aggrieved patient might nonetheless conclude that the standard that emerges from them is still not ideally suited to the protection of his or her own autonomy. The individual patient will have interests and needs which might bear little relationship to the 'prudent patient', however conceptualized. Autonomy is essentially a personal concept, which is supposed to take account of the individual's own interests and concerns – not those of some homogenised, fictional character.[101]

In the same vein, Giesen asserts that:

---

100 General Medical Council, *Consent*; British Medical Association, *Consent Tool Kit*, 5th edn. Undated; available at http://bma.org.uk/practical-support-at-work/ethics/consent-tool-kit. Accessed 2 November 2014; Royal College of Obstetricians and Gynaecologists, *Obtaining Valid Consent*, 2nd edn, Clinical Governance Advice 6. London: RCOG Press 2008; American College of Obstetricians and Gynaecologists, *Informed Consent*, ACOG Committee Opinion no. 439. Washington DC: ACOG 2009; Royal College of Surgeons, *Good Surgical Practice*. London, 2014.

101 McLean SAM, *Autonomy, Consent and the Law*. Abingdon: Routledge 2010, p. 83.

> to the degree that the decision of the average, 'reasonable' patient would differ from the perhaps idiosyncratic decision of a particular patient, the law's 'objective' standard fails to support that particular patient's right of self-determination.[102]

Applying the subjective test could potentially open the floodgates to litigation, since the benefit of hindsight could be exploited. The case of *Chester* v. *Afshar* suggests, however, that this may not necessarily be so: the claimant could have said (with the benefit of hindsight) that had she been warned of the risk of cauda equina syndrome[103] she would not have undergone the operation, but she did not say so.[104] She truthfully admitted that she would still have had the operation (but on another day, after thinking about it and seeking the views of others).

Also, adoption of the subjective standard does not mean that the patient's claims will automatically be believed: the Australian case *Ellis* v. *Wallsend District Hospital* establishes that the courts will still test the patient's evidence for credibility – but this case predates *Chester* and was not endorsed in that case.[105]

There is also the potential problem that the physician would have to have an extensive conversation with the patient for every intervention proposed, but this problem only materialises where there is a focus on quantity rather than quality of information. Meeting the informational needs of the particular patient does not necessarily require more extensive conversations. On the contrary, such conversations could result in cognitive overload, which may compromise patient self-determination. The requirement is for tailored information, information tailored to the needs of the patient (including any questions asked by the patient), and not for a treatise on the treatment being offered.

The issue is revisited in Chapter 9. For now, attention is turned to how English courts have addressed the doctrine of consent.

English Law and the Doctrine of Consent

The doctrine of informed consent does not technically apply in English or Scots law. In the discussion below, I concentrate on English case law because it is the English cases that form the basis of my comparison of the consent and property models.

102 Geisen, *International Medical Malpractice Law*, p. 298.

103 Condition in which there is loss of function of the nerve roots below the termination of the spinal cord.

104 *Chester* v. *Afshar* [2004] UKHL 41; [2005] 1 AC 134; [2004] 3 WLR 927; [2004] 4 All ER 587 HL.

105 *Ellis* v. *Wallsend District Hospital* [1990] 2 Med LR 103.

English law does not require full disclosure of all possible risks. The position was stated by Bristow J in *Chatterton* v. *Gerson*[106] as follows:

> ...once the patient is informed in broad terms of the nature of the procedure which is intended, and gives her consent, that consent is real....[107]

Also, English courts have historically stuck to the professional standard for disclosure, and thereby allowed medical opinion as to what is best for the patient to override the patient's right to self-determination. The standard for assessing the care given by a doctor was articulated by McNair in his direction to the jury in the case of *Bolam* v. *Friern Hospital Management Committee.*[108] Mr Bolam was advised by the doctor to have electroconvulsive therapy (ECT), but was not warned of the small risk of suffering a fracture as a complication of this treatment. Unfortunately this risk materialised. He sued for negligence but lost. McNair J said that:

> A doctor is not guilty of negligence if he has acted in accordance with a practice accepted as proper by a responsible body of medical men skilled in that particular art.[109]

This was subsequently endorsed by the House of Lords[110] and came to be known as the *Bolam* test. The application of the test to diagnosis and treatment was unquestionable, but it was uncertain whether it also applied to the disclosure of information.

Hatcher v. *Black* was the first English case on non-disclosure of risk prior to surgical treatment.[111] The claimant, having been assured pre-operatively that there was no risk to her voice, suffered vocal cord paralysis following surgery to correct a toxic goitre. The defendant was vindicated on the strength of the professional standard as well as causation. In directing the jury, Lord Denning said:

> ... none of the doctors called as witnesses have suggested that the surgeon was wrong ... If they do not condemn him, why should you?[112]

---

106 *Chatterton* v. *Gerson* [1981] QB 432, [1981] 1 All ER 257 (QBD).

107 *Chatterton* v. *Gerson* [1981] QB 432, at 443.

108 *Bolam* v. *Friern Hospital Management Committee* [1957] WLR 582.

109 Ibid., 587–588.

110 *Whitehouse* v. *Jordan* [1981] 1 WLR 246; *Maynard* v. *West Midlands RHA* [1985] 1 All ER 635.

111 *Hatcher* v. *Black* [1954] CLY 2289.

112 *The Times*, 2 July 1954.

Although such Denningesque *obiter dicta* would not usually be the basis for legal precedent, it gives an indication of the respect with which the medical profession was regarded in the 1950s.

A series of subsequent cases at first instance addressed the issue of information disclosure but laid down no firm principles.[113] Before the issue reached appellate level, there were two opportunities (*Chatterton* v. *Gerson*[114] and *Hills* v. *Potter*[115]) to address it at first instance courts. In both of these cases, the claimants sued in trespass and in negligence for non-disclosure of risks inherent in their respective surgical operations, and in each case it was held that the defendant had followed accepted medical practice. In the first case the patient, Miss Chatterton, suffered numbness after an operation that was meant to relieve her of pain in a post-operative scar. She sued in both battery and negligence, alleging that the doctor did not warn her of the risk of numbness and muscle weakness. Bristow J declined to apply the doctrine of informed consent and the claim failed. Similarly, Hirst J in *Hills* v. *Potter* declined counsel's argument for the doctrine of informed consent to be applied, saying: 'I hold that the proper standard is the medical standard, in accordance with Bolam's case.'[116]

What was until March 2015 the definitive position was elaborated by the House of Lords in *Sidaway* v. *Board of Governors of Bethlem Royal and the Maudsley Hospital*.[117] In 1973, Mrs Amy Doris Sidaway underwent an operation to relieve the pressure on a nerve root that had been identified as the cause of the persistent pain in her right arm and shoulder. The risks of the operation included a 2 per cent risk of nerve root damage and a less than 1 per cent risk of damage to the spinal cord. Unfortunately, the latter risk eventuated and she suffered paralysis. She sued on the ground that she had not been informed of the risk of spinal cord injury and claimed that, had she been informed of this risk, she would not have undergone the operation.

At first instance, the trial judge dismissed the case. The Court of Appeal (Sir John Donaldson, Master of the Rolls, Justice Dunn and Justice Browne-Wilkinson) unanimously dismissed Mrs Sidaway's appeal.[118] Regrettably, their decision not to adopt the doctrine of informed consent was not based on a forensic analysis of the doctrine but on time-honoured deference to the medical profession and on assumptions that would be regarded with incredulity in today's world. For example, Sir John said that '[i]t is a rare patient who wants to know what may go wrong in terms of what part of his body may actually

---

113 For example, *Wells* v. *Surrey Area Health Authority*, *The Times*, 29 July 1978.

114 *Chatterton* v. *Gerson* [1981] 1 All ER 257.

115 *Hills* v. *Potter* [1983] 3 All ER 716.

116 Ibid.

117 *Sidaway* v. *Board of Governors of Bethlem Royal and the Maudsley Hospital* [1985] 1 All ER 643; [1985] 1 AC 900, HL.

118 *Sidaway* v. *Bethlem Royal Hospital Governors*, 1 All ER 1018 (1984).

be damaged',[119] and Justice Dunn said that most patients 'would prefer to put themselves unreservedly in the hands of doctors'.[120] No one can seriously argue that such statements are sustainable in today's world. In an article strongly criticising the Court of Appeal decision, Annas said that it seemed 'unreasonable … to permit the doctor's interest in doing what he or she thinks best to outweigh the patient's interest in making critical decisions about his or her own body'.[121]

The case went to the House of Lords but again the claim failed. The decision of the House of Lords was predictable,[122] given its decisions in two cases (*Whitehouse* v. *Jordan*[123] and *Maynard* v. *West Midlands RHA*[124]) where the court upheld the principle that a doctor is not liable if he had acted in accordance with a practice accepted as proper by a responsible body of fellow professionals. As there was a responsible body of medical opinion which would not have warned the claimant of the risk of spinal cord injury, Mrs Sidaway's appeal was dismissed. The Law Lords, by a majority of four to one, endorsed the rejection in *Chatterton* and *Hills* of the applicability of the doctrine of informed consent in English law. In addressing this issue, Lord Bridge said:

> The important question which this appeal raises is whether the law imposes any, and if so what, different criterion as the measure of the medical man's duty of care to his patient when giving advice with respect to a proposed course of treatment. It is clearly right to recognise that a conscious adult patient of sound mind is entitled to decide for himself whether or not he will submit to a particular course of treatment proposed by the doctor, most significantly surgical treatment under general anaesthesia. This entitlement is the foundation of the doctrine of 'informed consent' which has led in certain American jurisdictions to decisions, and in the Supreme Court of Canada, to dicta, on which the appellant relies, which would oust the Bolam test and substitute an 'objective' test of a doctor's duty to advise the patient of the advantages and disadvantages of undergoing the treatment proposed and more particularly to advise the patient of the risks involved.[125]

119 Ibid.

120 *Sidaway* v. *Bethlem Royal Hospital Governors* [1984] 2 WLR, at 795.

121 Annas GJ, Why the British courts rejected the American doctrine of informed consent (and what British physicians should do about it) (1984) 74 Am J Public Health 1286–1288, at p. 1287.

122 Legal Correspondent, Consent to treatment: the medical standard reaffirmed. (1984) 288 BMJ 802–803.

123 *Whitehouse* v. *Jordan* [1981] 1 All ER 267.

124 *Maynard* v. *West Midlands Regional Health Authority* [1985] 1 All ER 635.

125 *Sidaway* v. *Board of Governors of Bethlem Royal and the Maudsley Hospital* [1985] 1 All ER 643, at 662–663.

He went on to dismiss the doctrine:

> I recognise the logical force of the *Canterbury* doctrine, proceeding from the premise that the patient's right to make his own decision must at all costs be safeguarded against the kind of medical paternalism which assumes that 'doctor knows best'. But, with all respect, I regard the doctrine as quite impractical in application.[126]

Lord Diplock also rejected the doctrine of informed consent:

> The juristic basis of the proposed situation which originates in certain state court jurisdictions in the United States of America and has found some favour in modified form by the Supreme Court of Canada appears to me, with great respect, to be contrary to English law. Its foundation is the doctrine of 'informed consent' which was originally based on the assumption in *Canterbury v Spence*.[127]

Lord Scarman was the only judge who favoured adoption of the doctrine:

> My Lords, I think the *Canterbury* propositions reflect a legal truth which too much judicial reliance on medical judgement tends to obscure. In a medical negligence case where the issue is as to the advice and information given to the patient as to the treatment proposed, the available options, and the risk, the court is concerned primarily with a patient's right. If one considers the scope of the doctor's duty by beginning with the right of the patient to make his own decision whether he will or will not undergo the treatment proposed, the right to be informed of significant risk and the doctor's corresponding duty are easy to understand; for the proper implementation of the right requires that the doctor be under a duty to inform his patient of the material risks inherent in the treatment. And it is plainly right that a doctor may avoid liability for failure to warn of a material risk if he can show that he reasonably believed that communication to the patient of the existence of the risk would be detrimental to the health … of his patient.[128]

In summary, the court decided that in cases of alleged inadequate disclosure of risks, the *Bolam* test applied. Why was there a reluctance to embrace the doctrine of informed consent? An explanation might be found in Lord Bridge's speech. He gives three reasons: the doctrine does not take full cognisance of the variety of factors that influence a doctor's clinical judgment; it is unrealistic

126 Ibid.
127 Ibid., 643.
128 Ibid., 654.

to separate the primary medical problem from the issue of disclosure; and the objective test leaves it to the judge to decide what a reasonable person would do (which encourages uncertainty in litigation). This reasoning has been criticised as being 'deeply flawed and uninformed in many respects'.[129] The first of Lord Bridge's reasons exalts paternalism and underestimates the propensity of the medical profession to close ranks. The second reason fosters the custom of deference to doctors (see below) and the third reason ignores the fact that far from being imprecise, *Canterbury* affords a meticulous analysis of the relevant principles. In defence of Lord Bridge, it must be accepted that adoption of the professional standard does not mean total surrender to the medical profession. As the learned judge asserted, the court might in certain circumstances come to the conclusion that disclosure of a particular risk was so obviously necessary to an informed choice on the part of the patient that no reasonably prudent medical man would fail to make it – and this was confirmed in *Bolitho* v. *City and Hackney Health Authority* (discussed below).[130]

In retrospect, it appears that a major (perhaps the primary) reason for the failure of the English courts to embrace the doctrine of informed consent was their deference to the medical profession. The Right Honorable the Lord Woolf acknowledged this 'over-deference'[131] and said that *Sidaway* will now have to be read in a different light:

> A doctor's decision not to disclose risks will now have to be subjected to logical analysis, and if he has withheld without a good reason information that should have been disclosed then he will be liable even though his decision may have been consonant with ordinary professional practice.[132]

It should be noted that although the doctrine of informed consent does not formally apply in English law judges still use the term loosely, even at the level of the House of Lords (Supreme Court): in *Chester* v. *Afshar*, Lord Steyn used the term in the sense of valid consent.[133]

England, Scotland, Ireland and some US states appear to be the only jurisdictions that were, or still are, reluctant to jettison the professional standard of disclosure. This is not entirely surprising. Historically, American judicial and socio-cultural tradition has placed issues of individual rights on a high pedestal. At the other end of the spectrum, there has been a tendency, in the British tradition, for individual rights to be subjugated to societal imperatives, and

129 *Canterbury* v. *Spence* (464 F.2d 772) 1972, Healy J at 139.

130 *Bolitho* v. *City and Hackney Health Authority* [1997] 4 All ER 771.

131 Lord Woolf, Are the courts excessively deferential to the medical profession? (2001) 9 Med L Rev 1–16.

132 Ibid., p. 11.

133 *Chester (Respondent)* v. *Afshar (Appellant)* [2004] UKHL 41, para 14.

'British courts routinely pay less verbal attention to the language of human rights'.[134] English disclosure case law generally manifests a reluctance to depart from the professional standard, but there is now case law indicating a shift to the reasonable patient standard.[135]

Following *Sidaway*, the professional standard was reiterated even more brazenly in *Blyth* v. *Bloomsbury Health Authority*.[136] The claimant had asked questions about Depo-Provera® (Pharmacia & UpJohn), the contraceptive injection she had been given, but did not receive comprehensive information. The Court of Appeal, deferring to medical opinion, found in favour of the defendant. The same court again applied the professional standard in the case of *Gold* v. *Haringey Health Authority*.[137] Mrs Gold was not warned of the possibility of failed sterilisation, but her claim failed because at that time some gynaecologists did not warn patients of this risk.

A Scottish judge unequivocally upheld the professional standard in *Moyes* v. *Lothian Health Board*:[138]

> As I see it, the law in both Scotland and England has come down firmly against the view that the doctor's duty to the patient involves at all costs obtaining the informed consent of the patient to specific medical treatments … I can read nothing in the majority view in *Sidaway* which suggests that the extent and quality of warning to be given by a doctor to his patient should not in the last resort be governed by medical criteria.[139]

The Shifting Position of UK Courts

Arguably, the law and judicial interpretation should reflect societal values and norms.[140] Indeed, Lord Woolf asserts that the courts move with the times, albeit slowly:

> … there had developed an increasing awareness of patients' rights. The public's expectations of what the profession should achieve have grown. Like it or not, we have moved from a society which was concerned primarily with the duty

134 See McLean, *Patient's Right to Know*, p. 101.

135 *Pearce* v. *United Bristol Healthcare NHS Trust* [1999] PIQR P53. *Montgomery (Appellant) v Lanarkshire Health Board (Respondent) (Scotland)* [2015] UKSC 11

136 *Blyth* v. *Bloomsbury Health Authority* [1993] 4 Med LR 151.

137 *Gold* v. *Haringey Health Authority* [1987] 3 WLR 649.

138 *Moyes* v. *Lothian Health Board* [1990] 1 Med LR 468; (1990) SLT 444.

139 *Moyes* v. *Lothian Health Board* (1990) SLT 444. Per Lord Caplan at 449.

140 Lin TE, Social norms and judicial decision making: examining the role of narratives in same-sex adoption cases (1999) 99 Columbia Law Rev 739–794.

> individuals owed to society to one which is concerned primarily with the rights of the individual. You may find this difficult to accept, but judges do move with the times, even if more slowly than some would like. The move to a right-based society has fundamentally changed the behaviour of the courts.[141]

Over the years, consumer advocacy has been on the ascendancy in the UK, and in the health sector found expression in the Patient's Charter, which was launched in 1991 by the John Major government and replaced by the NHS Constitution in 2013.[142] It is therefore not surprising that there has been a progressive shift from the professional standard. In *Smith* v. *Tunbridge Wells Health Authority*, it was held that disclosure of the risk was the only reasonable course of action, despite medical support for non-disclosure by the defendant.[143] Another first instance decision was that in *McAllister* v. *Lewisham and North Southwark Health Authority*.[144] In this case, the patient suffered a postoperative hemiplegia, the risk of which had not been disclosed. Rougier J assessed each expert's view and concluded that the warnings given by the defendant had been inadequate. In *Newell and Newell* v. *Goldenberg*, Mantell J found a doctor negligent for not disclosing the risk of failed sterilisation, opining that the 'Bolam principle provides a defence for those who lag behind the times. It cannot serve those who know better.'[145] Other cases manifesting a retreat from the professional standard include *Gascoine* v. *Ian Sheridan & Co and Latham*[146] and *Lybert* v. *Warrington Health Authority*.[147]

It may be that fear of opening the floodgates of litigation was a further unspoken reason for English courts being reluctant to adopt the doctrine of informed consent, and Lords Kerr and Reed referred to this fear (only to dismiss it) in *Montgomery v Lanarkshire Health Board (Scotland)*.[148] If so, then as the doctrine has not necessarily opened the floodgates in other jurisdictions, it seemed plausible that English courts would continue to ease away from their traditional position. The House of Lords' decision in *Bolitho* v. *City and Hackney Health Authority*,[149] and the Civil Procedure Rules, laid down as a result of the Woolf reforms,[150] both require expert witness opinion to withstand the scrutiny

141 Lord Woolf, Are the courts excessively deferential to the medical profession?, p. 3.

142 See en.wikipedia.org/wiki/Patient's_charter.

143 *Smith* v. *Tunbridge Wells Health Authority* [1994] 5 Med LR 334.

144 *McAllister* v. *Lewisham and North Southwark Health Authority* [1994] 5 Med LR 343.

145 *Newell and Newell* v. *Goldenberg* [1995] 6 Med LR 371, at 374.

146 *Gascoine* v. *Ian Sheridan & Co and Latham* [1994] 5 Med LR 437.

147 *Lybert* v. *Warrington Health Authority* [1996] 7 Med LR 71. See also Jones MA, Failed sterilization and omission to warn: the causation problem (1998) 4 Clinical Risk 12–16.

148 *Montgomery (Appellant) v Lanarkshire Health Board (Respondent) (Scotland)* [2015] UKSC 11. On appeal from: [2013] CSIH 3; [2010] CSIH 104.

149 *Bolitho* v. *City and Hackney Health Authority* [1997] 4 All ER 771.

150 Lord Woolf, *Access to Justice: Final Report to the Lord Chancellor by Lord Woolf*. London: HMSO, July 1996.

of logic, , and signalled further retreat from the professional standard, although it should be noted that *Bolitho* was not a case about consent.

Bolitho relates to treatment received by 2-year-old Patrick Nigel Bolitho who suffered respiratory failure, cardiac arrest and concomitant brain damage. A doctor who had been informed of his condition failed to attend, and a breach of the duty of care was established. Difficulties arose, however, regarding causation. The doctor said in her evidence, and this was accepted by the court, that if she had attended she would not have intubated Patrick Bolitho. Experts called by the claimant and defendant gave opposing views as to whether intubation would have affected outcome. The High Court, Court of Appeal and House of Lords all found in favour of the defendant as the case progressed through the litigation process and this was largely because the evidence of the expert called by the defence could not be dismissed as illogical. Lord Browne-Wilkinson said in his judgment:

> … in cases of diagnosis and treatment there are cases where, despite a body of professional opinion sanctioning the defendant's conduct, the defendant can properly be held liable for negligence (I am not here considering questions of disclosure of risk). In my judgment that is because, in some cases, it cannot be demonstrated to the judge's satisfaction that the body of opinion relied on is reasonable or responsible. In particular, where there are questions of assessment of the relative risks and benefits of adopting a medical practice, a reasonable view necessarily presupposes that the relative risks and benefits have been weighed by the experts in forming their opinions. But if, in a rare case, it can be demonstrated that the professional opinion is not capable of withstanding logical analysis, the judge is entitled to hold that the body of opinion is not reasonable or responsible.[151]

This signalled a shift from the professional standard, and suggests a significant departure from the stance taken by the same judge in *Sidaway* (at Court of Appeal stage) when he stood stoutly for the professional standard:

> If the disclosure of the risks results in prejudicing the ability of the doctor to cure and the confidence of the patient in the doctor, the existence of a duty to disclose such risks would positively militate against the main purpose of the relationship … trust and confidence may be severely shaken by a formal communication of risks.[152]

151 *Bolitho* v. *City and Hackney Health Authority* [1997] 4 All ER 771, at 773.

152 *Sidaway* v. *Bethlem Royal Hospital Governors* [1984] 1 All ER 1018.

Although *Bolitho* is credited with introducing the requirement for professional opinion to be capable of withstanding logical analysis, the fact is that this requirement existed long before *Bolitho*. In *Hills* v. *Potter*, Mr Justice Hirst said:

> In every case the court must be satisfied that the standard contended for on [the doctors'] behalf accords with that upheld by a substantial body of medical opinion, and that this body of medical opinion *is both respectable and responsible*, and experienced in this particular field of medicine.[153] (emphasis mine)

Subsequently, in *Sidaway*, the Court of Appeal per Sir John Donaldson added the qualification 'rightly' to Justice Hirst's principle:

> The duty is fulfilled … if the doctor acts in accordance with a practice *rightly* accepted as proper by a body of skilled and experienced medical men.[154]

Thus even when the courts have a adopted the professional standard of care they 'will always reserve to themselves the right to scrutinize expert medical evidence with a view to establishing in each case whether the standards *practised* by the profession conform to the standard of reasonable care *demanded* by the law'.[155]

The retreat from the professional standard was to be continued in the cases that followed. In *Pearce* v. *United Bristol Healthcare NHS Trust*, the Court of Appeal explored the extent of a doctor's duty to give adequate information to the patient about the risks of treatment.[156] The claimant had gone 14 days past her estimated date of confinement when she had a consultation with her obstetrician during which she begged to be admitted for induction of labour or Caesarean delivery. The obstetrician explained the risks of induction of labour and Caesarean section, and recommended normal birth without any form of medical intervention. Seven days later, the claimant was admitted for delivery but the baby had died *in utero*. She brought an action against the hospital, claiming that the obstetrician was negligent in not advising her of the small risk associated with waiting for labour to start spontaneously after 42 weeks' gestation. The judge dismissed the case and the claimant appealed.

Although he did not decide the appeal in favour of the claimant (evidence having shown that the increased risk of stillbirth as a result of the additional delay that occurred was no more than 0.1–0.2 per cent), Lord Woolf said that

153 *Hills* v. *Potter* [1984] 1 WLR 641, at 653.

154 *Sidaway* v. *Board of Governors of the Bethlem Royal Hospital and the Maudsley Hospital* [1984] QB 493, at 514.

155 Geisen, *International Medical Malpractice Law*, p. 287.

156 *Pearce* v. *United Bristol Healthcare NHS Trust* [1999] 48 BMLR 118, and [1999] PIQRP 53.

he was applying both *Bolam* and *Bolitho* to the matter of disclosure of risk, and he made it clear that doctors must disclose risks which the reasonable patient would expect to be disclosed:

> … if there is a significant risk which would affect the judgement of a reasonable patient, then … it is the responsibility of a doctor to inform the patient of that risk if the information is needed so that the patient can determine … what course he or she should adopt.[157]

What began as a gradual shift assumed seismic dimensions in *Chester* v. *Afshar*, where the House of Lords felt compelled to modify the traditional rules of causation in order to grant remedy to a claimant who had not been fully informed of the risks inherent in an operation that she was going to have anyway, regardless of the risks.[158] This case is discussed further in Chapter 9 but the facts are stated here to demonstrate how judicial thinking is moving with the times.

It could be argued that previous retreats described above were no more than just a modification of the prudent doctor standard but *Chester* v. *Afshar* established that English courts were now prepared to pay more than mere lip service to the patient's need for information. The claimant underwent neurosurgery in the hands of the defendant. The court found that he did not inform her of the 1–2 per cent risk of cauda equina syndrome. Unfortunately this risk materialised. An action in negligence followed and the judge at first instance found in favour of the claimant. This judgment was upheld by the Court of Appeal. The House of Lords found that application of the 'but for' test would have resulted in the claimant being denied a remedy for the surgeon's failure adequately to inform her of the risks of the operation. That the court was prepared to deviate from the traditional application of this test in order to find in favour of the patient is an indication of how committed it was to upholding the claimant's right to be informed. *Chester* marks a significant departure from the professional standard and establishes beyond doubt the willingness of the English judiciary to accord the highest priority to self-determination in medical decision-making. This willingness led the court to adopt jurisprudential contortions in order to find for the claimant – which in turn throws into sharp relief the inadequacy of the consent model.

If *Sidaway* marked the apotheosis of the professional standard in English law, *Montgomery* marked its nadir. The claimant ('pursuer' in Scots law), who was only 5 feet tall and had diabetes, suffered a difficult delivery of her first

157 Ibid., 59.

158 *Chester* v. *Afshar* [2004] UKHL 41; [2005] 1 AC 134; [2004] 3 WLR 927; [2004] 4 All ER 587.

baby. The baby was big (birth weight: 4.25 kilograms), and there was shoulder dystocia (difficulty in delivering the shoulders after the baby's head had been delivered). An interval of 12 minutes elapsed between emergence of the head and delivery of the rest of the baby, during which time the baby suffered hypoxic brain damage and concomitant cerebral palsy, as well as a brachial plexus injury (Erb palsy). There were contentious issues relating to intrapartum care, but the kernel of the case related to antenatal care, particularly the disclosure of risk. Her obstetrician had not informed her of the risk of shoulder dystocia, because she had not asked specifically about risks, because the obstetrician considered that the risk of serious injury to the baby was very slight, and because the obstetrician was concerned that disclosure of this risk would elicit a request for an elective Caesarean section. The pursuer contended that in the antenatal period no ordinarily competent obstetrician acting with reasonable skill and care would have: (1) failed to advise the pursuer of the risks of vaginal delivery; (2) failed to inform the pursuer of the risks during vaginal delivery of shoulder dystocia; and (3) failed to offer the pursuer the option of delivery by Caesarean section.

Experts instructed by the pursuer and the defendant gave contrasting opinions on whether it was acceptable practice for an obstetrician not to disclose the risk of shoulder dystocia to a woman in Nadine Montgomery's position. The judge at first instance, applying the professional standard, found in favour of the defendant.[159] An appeal to the UK Supreme Court followed. In upholding the appeal, the court opined that 'the analysis of the law by the majority in Sidaway is unsatisfactory'[160] and clarified the current position:

> The correct position, in relation to the risks of injury involved in treatment, can now be seen to be substantially that adopted in Sidaway by Lord Scarman, and by Lord Woolf MR in Pearce, subject to the refinement made by the High Court of Australia in *Rogers v Whitaker* ... An adult person of sound mind is entitled to decide which, if any, of the available forms of treatment to undergo, and her consent must be obtained before treatment interfering with her bodily integrity is undertaken. The doctor is therefore under a duty to take reasonable care to ensure that the patient is aware of any material risks involved in any recommended treatment, and of any reasonable alternative or variant treatments. The test of materiality is whether, in the circumstances of the particular case, a reasonable person in the patient's position would be likely to attach significance

159 *Nadine Montgomery* v. *Lanarkshire Health Board* [2010] CSOH 104 and this was upheld on appeal by the Inner House of the Scottish Court of Session. *NM* v. *Lanarkshire Health Board* [2013] CSIH 3; 2013 SC 245.

160 *Montgomery (Appellant)* v. *Lanarkshire Health Board (Respondent) (Scotland)* [2015] UKSC 11, at para 86.

to the risk, or the doctor is or should reasonably be aware that the particular patient would be likely to attach significance to it. [Para 87]

It appears that the parting of ways between the UK courts and the professional standard (as far as disclosure of information is concerned) is now complete. Some uncertainty remains, however, as to whether an objective or a subjective test applies in the particular situation.

Conclusions

The legal mechanism for protecting the patient's right to self-determination is consent. A doctor undertaking treatment without consent may be liable for battery or face an action in negligence. The courts have been reluctant to take the battery route, mainly for fear of pouring odium on doctors acting with good intentions. There is a school of thought, however, that advocates expansion of the tort of battery to 'reflect a legal response based on rights',[161] and it has been suggested that this tort 'may be due for a fresh lease of life'[162] with the rising profile of rights in English law.[163]

The more common route is an action in negligence. Here, there is usually no dispute about the right of the patient to be informed, but controversy surrounds the standard for determining adequacy of disclosure. Although the UK has traditionally deferred to the medical profession in this regard, there has been a shift towards adoption of the patient's right rather than the doctor's opinion as the starting point for determining adequacy of disclosure. Even then, the courts will often fail to protect patient self-determination – because of the adoption of an objective rather than subjective test of what the patient would want to know. Thus, there are legal shortcomings in the consent model as far as protection of patient self-determination is concerned. Also, as indicated in the quote at the beginning of this chapter, self-determination *per se* has not been recognizsed as a legally protectable interest. There may also be ethical shortcomings and it is to this question that attention is turned in the next chapter.

161 Kennedy, Fiduciary relationship, p. 114.

162 Hockton, *Law of Consent to Medical Treatment*, p. 29.

163 This suggestion is revisited in Chapter 9.

Chapter 4
Ethical Underpinnings and Justification of Consent

> Consent is … the cutting edge of the patient autonomy movement.[1]

> Consent is much more complex than theorists originally believed it to be.[2]

There is an obvious legal justification for consent – unconsented-to touching is an assault, as discussed in Chapter 3 – but the purpose of consent is not just to protect doctors from litigious patients. To set the context for further analysis of the consent model, it is worth exploring the ethical justifications for consent.

The question has been asked why consent is such an important requirement in health care, whereas it is not in other areas of human activity.[3] Wear says, for example, that statistics regarding divorce are not routinely trotted out as part of the marriage ceremony.[4] Similarly, a salesman is not obliged to ask if the purchaser really wants the product, and a formal declaration of consent is not required prior to purchase of the product.

Freedom to Pursue Personal Goals

One argument for the necessity of consent in health care is that illness itself restricts freedom and consent helps to *restore the sense of freedom and self-determination* that is undermined by illness.[5] In other words, consent is necessary not simply as an antidote to medical paternalism, but in a broader sense for enhancement of well-being and protection of the patient's freedom. This argument could itself be tricky, in the sense that potentially it unintentionally provides justification for medical paternalism – if an ill person is weakened and unable to take control, then the clinician should assist him/her by making decisions. Nevertheless,

---

1 Wear S, *Informed Consent – Patient Autonomy and Clinical Beneficence within Health Care*, 2nd edn. Washington DC: Georgetown University Press 1998, p. 2.

2 Swintankowsky IS, *A New Paradigm for Informed Consent*, Lanham, Md.: University Press of America 1998, p. x.

3 Wear, *Informed Consent*, p. 40.

4 Ibid., p. 41.

5 Ibid., p. 42.

the concept of freedom in relation to consent is an important one, for the importance of consent is that it facilitates the freedom to make choices that reflect the individual's own values, beliefs and life experiences. No matter how well-intentioned a clinician may be, he/she is not usually in a position to share the same values, attitudes and beliefs as the patient. In modern societies with advanced technology, depersonalisation and multiculturalism, there is increased heterogeneity of ideas, attitudes and cultures, which means that we are as individuals perhaps less likely to share attitudes, beliefs and cultures with each other. This, by the way, is another argument for preferring the subjective application of the prudent patient test to the objective application.

Attitudes, beliefs and culture are key ingredients in formulating personal goals, such as those relating to one's family, professional or social life. Personal goals are an important, but often underestimated, determinant of decisions or choices made by patients. For example, the goal to attend a family wedding later in the year may be important enough to make a patient opt for conservative rather than surgical treatment. Sometimes trade-offs are critical elements in the decision-making process. A pregnant woman who needs an urgent surgical operation for cervical or ovarian cancer may wish to defer the operation until after she has given birth to the baby, rather than have the operation immediately and lose the pregnancy, with the full understanding that delaying the operation could adversely affect the outcome of treatment. Schwartz and Bergus state that:

> Although decision researchers always emphasize the importance of goals in decision making, goals are rarely considered explicitly because they are unique to each decision maker, and it is often assumed that only the decision maker has good insight into his own goals. The incorporation of goals into medical decisions, although *amenable to systematization*, thus remains in large part an art practiced by physicians who excel in communication with patients in the clinical other encounter.[6] (emphasis mine)[7]

Related to goals are constraints – social, economic or other factors which limit patients' decision-making. An example would be the patient who is constrained from accepting blood transfusion because of his/her religion. In the consent transaction, it is important for doctors to explore their patients' goals and for patients to make their constraints known to the doctor. As will be discussed

6 Schwartz A and Bergus G, *Medical Decision Making: A Physician's Guide*. Cambridge: Cambridge University Press 2008, p. 6.

7 In chapter 9, it will be argued that the property model, through transactional consultation and bilateral distribution of responsibility, facilitates this systematised incorporation of patients' goals into medical decision-making.

in Chapter 9, this mutually rewarding exercise could help to determine what *tailored* and *relevant* information the doctor should provide (as opposed to a blanket full disclosure of information or what Manson and O'Neill refer to as 'explicit and specific consent'[8]).

Protection from 'Strangers'

Apart from the traditional anti-paternalism justification of consent, changes in the nature of health-care systems necessitate mechanisms for protecting the patient's right of self-determination. The delivery of medicine is increasingly following an assembly-line pattern; almost gone are the days of the good old-fashioned doctor who knew the entire family. Almost gone also is the hospital generalist who had a holistic view of the patient's problems. These days, the patient is likely to be treated by a team of sub-specialists and a variety of health professionals. O'Neill, quoting Rothman,[9] refers to them as 'strangers by the bedside.[10] O'Neill suggests that these developments in delivery of medical care break the traditional bonds of trust between doctors and patients.[11] Trust aside, there is a potential threat to consent in this situation. If the authority gradient between patient and doctor was steep in the traditional setting, the gradient is even steeper when the patient has to negotiate not with just one doctor but with an establishment of highly skilled professionals. Without adequate protection, the right to self-determination could readily be compromised by these conditions. A model which has the rights of the particular patient as its cardinal point is more likely to secure this protection than a model that relies on standards set for or by the medical establishment and the objective man on the Clapham omnibus.

Utilitarian Justification

Another justification for consent is utilitarian: consent helps protect patients from treatment that they consider harmful or undesirable. Alternatively, it enables them to choose the treatment option that they consider beneficial or preferable. In this role, as guardian of their own health rather than passive

8 Manson NC and O'Neill O, *Rethinking Informed Consent in Bioethics*. Cambridge: Cambridge University Press 2007, pp. 10–11.

9 Rothman DJ, *Strangers at the Bedside: A History of How Law and Ethics Transformed Medical Decision-Making*. New York: Basic Books 1991.

10 O'Neill O, *Autonomy and Trust in Bioethics*. Cambridge: Cambridge University Press 2002, p. 20.

11 Ibid.

submissive recipient of medical care, they are more likely to have better health outcomes – clinicians recognise that giving patients information and involving them in their own care is associated with better health outcomes.[12] Indeed, the concept of an 'expert patient'[13] has evolved in recent times.

The utilitarian standpoint is by definition dependent on context – so long as utility (happiness, satisfaction and other perceived benefits) is maximised and disutility (distress, dissatisfaction and so on) is minimised, the criterion for utilitarian justification is met. Utilitarian ethics will not, therefore, always explain the basis of consent. When the underlying reason for providing information and seeking to gain a patient's agreement to treatment is simply the desire for a better health outcome (rather than to enable the patient to make an informed decision), then that goal is a different one from protection of the right to self-determination, and may even be diametrically opposite. Indeed, this approach has beneficence rather than self-determination as its ethical principle. It is arguable that when a physician obtains a patient's agreement to treatment solely for the purpose of enhancing therapeutic benefits, what the physician obtains from the patient is assent, not consent.

Respect for Persons; Self-determination

The most acclaimed ethical basis for consent can be found in the principle of respect for persons: treating persons as ends in themselves and not solely as means or instruments for other ends. Underlying this principle is the concept of a person's capacity for, and right to, self-determination. It is this principle that

12 Fallowfield LJ, Hall A, Maguire P, Baum M and A'Hern RP, Psychological effects of being offered choice of surgery for breast cancer (1994) 309 BMJ 448; Greenfield S, Kaplan SH, Ware Jr JE, Yano EM and Frank HJ, Patients' participation in medical care: effects on blood sugar control and quality of life in diabetes (1988) 3 J Gen Intern Med 448–457; Heisler M, Bouknight RR, Hayward RA, Smith DM and Kerr EA, The relative importance of physician communication, participatory decision making, and patient understanding in diabetes self-management (2002) 17 J Gen Intern Med 243–252; Jahng KH, Martin LR, Golin CE and DiMatteo MR, Preferences for medical collaboration: patient-physician congruence and patient outcomes (2005) 57 Patient Educ Couns 308–314; Little P, Everitt H, Williamson I, Warner G, Moore M, Gould C, Ferrier K and Payne S, Observational study of effect of patient centredness and positive approach on outcomes in general practice consultations (2001) 323 BMJ 908–911; Mandelblatt J, Kreling B, Figeuriedo M and Feng S, What is the impact of shared decision making on treatment and outcomes for older women with breast cancer? (2006) 24 J Clin Oncol 4908–4913; Mead N, Bower P and Hann M, The impact of general practitioners' patient-centredness on patients' post-consultation satisfaction and enablement (2002) 55 Soc Sci Med 283–299; Schulman BA, Active patient orientation and outcomes in hypertensive treatment (1979) 17 Medical Care 267–280.

13 Department of Health, *The Expert Patient: A New Approach to Chronic Disease Management for the 21st Century*. London: DH, September 2001.

gets the most emphasis in contemporary discussions of consent.[14] As Manson and O'Neill put it, '[t]he reason most commonly given for the expansion, entrenchment and elaboration of informed consent requirements is that they are needed to secure respect for individual autonomy'.[15]

The British Medical Association extols this principle:

> Seeking consent is a moral requirement, and the BMA believes that respect for others and their rights lies at the heart of this issue. Society emphasises the value and dignity of the individual. Competent adults have both an ethical and a legal right to self-determination and to respect for their autonomy. This entails their having choice about what happens to their bodies.[16]

As discussed in Chapter 2, rights thinking is on the ascendancy and underlies the push for protection of patient self-determination. However, it is feared that too much emphasis on self-determination in the consent process may result in replacement of paternalism 'with a distant and impersonal relationship of strangers negotiating rights and duties'.[17] The American College of Obstetricians and Gynaecologists (ACOG) asserts that if persons are to be respected and their well-being promoted, consent must be seen as expressing a fuller notion of relationship.[18] This interpretation of consent would be welcomed by those who advocate a duty-led approach, emphasising duty rather than rights as the cardinal ethic. Rights and duties may be described as opposite sides of a coin. If rights are heads and duties tails, then for champions of the duty approach the coin should always be tails up.

The idea that consent is not an end in itself but a means to responsible participation by patients in their own care and a means to a mutually rewarding relationship between clinician and patient is one that needs to be more widely promoted among health-care providers[19] and acknowledged by champions of the individual self-determination movement (whose adversarial approach has been criticised by O'Neill for being counter-productive[20]). All too often

---

14 See, for example, Maclean A, *Autonomy, Informed Consent and Medical Law: A Relational Challenge*. Cambridge: Cambridge University Press 2009; McLean SAM, *Autonomy, Consent and the Law*. Abingdon: Routledge 2010; Taylor JS, Autonomy and informed consent: a much misunderstood relationship (2004) 38 Journal of Value Inquiry 383; Wear, *Informed Consent*.

15 Manson and O'Neill, *Rethinking Informed Consent in Bioethics*, p. 185.

16 British Medical Association, *Medical Ethics Today: The BMA's Handbook of Ethics and Law*, 2nd edn. London; BMA and BMJ Books 2004, p. 71.

17 American College of Obstetricians and Gynecologists, *Informed Consent*. Washington DC: ACOG 2004.

18 Ibid.

19 This idea is also consonant with the ecological metaphor described in Chapter 1.

20 O'Neill, *Autonomy and Trust in Bioethics*.

clinicians consider consent primarily as protection against litigation or equate consent with the signing of a form.[21]

Clements suggests that we should be talking more about *choice* than consent. By this he means that the focus should be on the patient's expressed and informed choice, not on the doctor's preoccupation with avoidance of litigation.[22] He advocates dialogue between doctor and patient but sees preoccupation with consent formalities as an obstruction to this goal.[23] We will return, in Chapter 5, to Clements' proposition. Meanwhile, it is reiterated that the self-determination-protection goal is not mere choice but authentic choice – and scholars have questioned whether the law concerns itself with authentic choice (if in fact it has the wherewithal to do so in any case).[24]

Consent and Self-determination

In Chapter 2, the concept of self-determination was discussed and in the following chapter the evolution of the law of consent as a means of protecting the patient's right to self-determination was reviewed. For many years it was taken that the law of consent was so intricately bound to autonomy (however defined) that contemplating consent without autonomy was equivalent to speaking of *Hamlet* without the Prince of Denmark. In recent times, however, academic commentators have questioned this assumption.[25]

The first salvo appears to have been fired by Taylor, who declared that 'the conventional view that the ethical foundation of informed consent is concern for autonomy is mistaken'.[26] He advanced the proposition that 'the ethical foundation of informed consent is really concern for human well-being'.[27] His position is based on the premise that to undermine a patient's autonomy, the doctor must have the intention to exert control over the patient; if this intention is not present, the patient's autonomy has not been undermined.

> A person, then, can fail to give his informed consent to a medical procedure and yet not suffer from any diminution in his autonomy with respect to his

21 This is a paradigm of consent that will be contrasted with a broader paradigm in Chapter 5.

22 Clements RV, Informed choice: should we bin the consent form? (2005) 11 Clinical Risk 69–71.

23 Ibid., p. 70.

24 McLean, *Autonomy, Consent and the Law*, ch. 2.

25 Taylor, Autonomy and informed consent; McLean, *Autonomy, Consent and the Law*; Manson and O'Neill, *Rethinking Informed Consent in Bioethics.*

26 Taylor, Autonomy and informed consent, p. 383.

27 Ibid., p. 384.

> decision to undergo it. If concern for patient autonomy is the ethical foundation for requiring that a person give his informed consent to his medical treatment, then healthcare providers who negligently fail to secure informed consent from their patients would not be morally culpable for this, because this failure would not result in their patients' autonomy being compromised. But to hold that a healthcare provider who negligently fails to secure a patient's informed consent is not morally culpable for such failure is highly counterintuitive. Since this is so, it appears that concern for autonomy is not the ethical foundation for the doctrine of informed consent. It seems that if a healthcare provider such as Grant fails to inform his patients of the risks associated with their medical treatment, he will wrong them because this puts their well-being at risk. Thus, it appears that the true ethical basis for the doctrine of informed consent is not patient autonomy, but patient well-being.[28]

The point has been made in Chapter 2 that we are concerned here not with notions of how autonomy may or not be compromised but with the patient's right to self-determination. The starting point for the property approach advocated in this book is the patient's rights, not the doctor's intentions. Whatever the intention of the doctor may or may not be, the patient has a right to make an informed decision about his/her treatment, and the law should protect that right. As legal protection of self-determination is the focus of my proposition, further exploration of Taylor's view of the ethical basis of consent is not pursued. Attention is turned to the conception of autonomy applied by the courts.

Examining case law, McLean concluded that there is inconsistency regarding which conception of autonomy actually grounds the legal regulation of consent.[29] Consent law, she finds, does not adhere to a particular account of autonomy. This is because '[t]he law has imperatives of its own and often encapsulates policy and other considerations in deciding on the quality and standing of individual decisions'.[30] As a result of these imperatives, we find that while the courts stoutly proclaim the right to self-determination, they employ tests which look at what the hypothetical prudent doctor or prudent patient would want, rather than what the index patient wants. Critiquing a number of American and English cases relating to end of life and to pregnancy, cases where individual autonomy is confronted by relational considerations, McLean concludes disapprovingly that individual autonomy has been trumped and says:

28 Ibid., p. 387.

29 McLean, *Autonomy, Consent and the Law.*

30 Ibid., p. 4.

> … the law's ingenuity in simultaneously proclaiming adherence to individual autonomy yet using a more relational account to reject its application in hard cases knows no bounds.[31]

To be fair to the courts, they do to some extent recognise the problem of applying an objective yardstick while proclaiming individual autonomy, but are constrained by practicalities. This is reflected in Lord Scarman's speech in *Sidaway* v. *Board of Bethlem Royal Hospital*:

> Ideally, the court should ask itself whether in the particular circumstances the risk was such that this particular patient would think it significant if he was told it existed. I would think that, as a matter of ethics, this is the test of the doctor's duty. The law, however, operates not in Utopia but in the world as it is: and such an inquiry would prove in practice to be frustrated by the subjectivity of its aim and purpose. The law can, however, do the next best thing, and require the court to answer the question, what would a reasonably prudent patient think significant if in the situation of this patient. The 'prudent patient' cannot, however, always provide the answer for the obvious reason that he is a norm (like the man on the Clapham omnibus), not a real person: and certainly not the patient himself.[32]

Although this view was part of a minority judgment, it was subsequently adopted by the court in *Pearce* v. *United Bristol HC NHS Trust*.[33] So, while the courts may generally apply the objective test, recognising that the prudent patient is not the patient himself or herself leaves the door open for them to apply a more subjective test when feasible and conscionable. In *Montgomery*, the Supreme Court stated (regarding the materiality of a risk) that '[t]he test of materiality is whether, in the circumstances of the particular case, a reasonable person in the patient's position would be likely to attach significance to the risk, or the doctor is or should reasonably be aware that *the particular patient* would be likely to attach significance to it'.[34] (emphasis mine)

There is, indeed, discordance between the individual self-determination proclaimed by the courts and the relational account they implement. In some cases, however, particularly those involving life or death situations, the courts face difficult challenges, and contextual issues may account for this discordance. To elucidate the point, we have to go back to the discussion in Chapter 2 and,

31 Ibid., p. 152.

32 *Sidaway* v. *Board of Governors of the Bethlem Royal Hospital* [1985] AC 871.

33 *Pearce* v. *United Bristol HC NHS Trust* [1999] 48 BMLR 118.

34 [This is a repetition of the position stated in the Australian case *Rogers v Whitaker*]. *Montgomery (Appellant) v Lanarkshire Health Board (Respondent) (Scotland)* [2015] UKSC 11, at para 87.

particularly, to the point that individual autonomy does not exist in a vacuum but is itself socially contextualised. Ardent advocates of individual autonomy will, presumably, concede that the individual has to be alive in order to exercise autonomy. If individual autonomy is so highly valued, particularly as part of respect for persons as ends rather than means to an end, society should not be casual in allowing life to be extinguished. This is not to say that on no account should individuals be allowed to make informed choices in matters of life and death; rather, a fine balance has to be found on a case-by-case basis between respect for self-determination and respect for the sanctity of life. Commitment to finding this balance is implicit in adoption of the ecology paradigm described in Chapter 1. The law has shown a willingness to shift the balance in favour of self-determination – as Lord Donaldson MR stated in *Re T (Adult: Refusal of Treatment)*:

> This situation gives rise to a conflict between two interests, that of the patient and that of the society in which he lives. The patient's interest consists of his right to self-determination – his right to live his own life how he wishes, even if it will damage his health or lead to his premature death. Society's interest is in upholding the concept that all human life is sacred and should be preserved if at all possible. It is well established that in the ultimate the right of the individual is paramount.[35]

When cases involving life or death decisions are separated from others, a pattern emerges in relation to whether the individual or relational accounts of self-determination are upheld by the courts: in cases relating to the sanctity of life they recognise fundamentally valued relational interests, but in other cases (exemplified by *Chester* v. *Afshar*, discussed in Chapters 2 and 9[36]) they have progressively shown a willingness to give individual self-determination its due primacy. Although *MacFarlane* v. *Tayside Health Board*, a case where the court applied relational interests, did not involve a life or death situation, the essence of the case was about the value of a child's life (the value of a child is incalculable).[37] The claimants were a couple who had completed their family and decided to have permanent contraception by means of vasectomy. Following the procedure they were informed that the sperm count was nil, but they subsequently had a pregnancy and delivery of a healthy child. They sued for the pain and suffering attributable to the pregnancy and for the cost of bringing up the child. The House of Lords held that the couple could recover

35 *Re T (Adult: Refusal of Treatment)* [1993] Family Law 93, at 113.

36 *Chester* v. *Afshar* [2004] 4 All ER 587.

37 *MacFarlane* v. *Tayside Health Board* [2000] 2 AC 59.

for the physical harm of the pregnancy but could not recover for the costs of rearing a healthy child.

In *Rees* v. *Darlington Memorial Hospital NHS Trust* the claimant was a woman who had undergone voluntary sterilisation because she could not cope with looking after a baby as she was blind in one eye and had poor vision in the other eye.[38] As a result of the operation being negligently performed, she became pregnant and had a healthy child. The House of Lords held that the claimant could not recover for the costs of bringing up the child but, in addition to her claim for pain and suffering arising from the unwanted pregnancy, awarded a sum of £15,000 for the breach of her right to self-determination.

These cases suggest that the courts tend to protect self-determination within a socialised context, without necessarily aiming to apply one or other favoured account of autonomy. I would describe this pragmatic approach as 'applying not A or B but AB', where A (minimalist) and B (rational) are purist, theoretical conceptions of autonomy and AB is the practical, socially contextualised, 'ecologically' responsive conception of the principle of self-determination. This is the approach advocated in Chapter 2 where I attempted to articulate a contextualised conception of the principle of self-determination.

While McLean examines the legal context, Manson and O'Neil approach the debate from an ethics perspective.[39] Whereas others note that consent is at 'the cutting edge of the patient autonomy movement',[40] Manson and O'Neil criticise the prevailing minimalist conception of autonomy as lacking moral content and therefore as being incapable of providing the ethical basis of consent. The prevailing conception lacks moral content because it regards autonomy simply as independence, or freedom to choose, regardless of whether the choice leads to good or bad outcomes. If this minimalist, individual conception of autonomy is 'seen as fundamental to ethics',[41] then consensual activities that many persons (including libertarians) deem unacceptable could be ethically justified. The fact that these are deemed unacceptable means that there are other ethical principles – such as beneficence and respect for human dignity – that limit individual autonomy. Prevailing paradigms of consent, they state, have no difficulty in operationalising this conception of autonomy but are vacuous.

They also give three reasons why other conceptions of autonomy – autonomy as reasoned, reflective, rational choice – are inadequate.[42] Firstly, they are more cognitively demanding, so they set a higher bar for attainment of adequate consent. Secondly, if rational autonomy is seen as fundamental to ethics, then

38 *Rees* v. *Darlington Memorial Hospital NHS Trust* [2003] UKHL 52, [2003]; 4 All ER 987, HL.

39 Manson and O'Neill, *Rethinking Informed Consent in Bioethics.*

40 Wear, *Informed Consent*, p. 2.

41 Manson and O'Neill, *Rethinking Informed Consent in Bioethics*, p. 20.

42 Ibid., p. 21.

other principles such as beneficence 'would have to be seen as subordinate, or dismissed'.[43] The third, and in their view decisive, reason is that if consent were to be based on these rational conceptions, then it would be difficult for the prevailing paradigm of consent, which protects even unreflective choice, to operationalise this conception of autonomy.

These reasons for rejecting rational accounts of autonomy as providing justification of consent have been criticised by Bullock.[44] Arguably, however, this criticism is based on a misunderstanding of the position taken by Manson and O'Neill. Bullock criticises them for using the term 'fundamental to ethics' without clarification, as it could mean either that the principle referred to is the *only* ethical concern or that it is *one* of the primary ethical concerns.[45] However, this criticism is flawed because the only way this term could be interpreted, for the rest of the authors' account to make sense, is to regard it as meaning the principle that trumps any other principle. Bullock further argues, in respect of the third reason for rejecting rational autonomy as the justification of consent:

> Manson and O'Neill argue that rational autonomy cannot be the primary justification for informed consent procedures because '[i]nformed consent requirements protect actual choices, which are often not rational choices' (2007, 21). *They thus assume that a subject's irrational choice ought to be protected under the doctrine*, which cannot be the case if the justification for informed consent practice is a principle of respect for rational autonomy. Again, this argumentation seems incomplete; their reason for rejecting minimal accounts of autonomy was that they were permissive and allowed irrational choice to be a foundation for ethical decision-making. On the other hand, they present rational accounts as being too stringent because they fail to allow for irrational choices. Although for Manson and O'Neill the appeal to autonomy cannot be substantiated on either minimal or rational interpretations, the shift in their argument means that their rejection of autonomy as a justification for informed consent fails to be conclusive.[46] (emphasis mine)

The weakness in this argument is that Manson and O'Neill do not 'assume that a subject's irrational choice ought to be protected' by the doctrine of consent. On the contrary, their entire case for rethinking consent is motivated by, and based on, both dissatisfaction with the protection of irrational choice and a

43 Ibid.

44 Bullock E, Informed consent as waiver: the doctrine rethought? (2010) 17 Ethical Perspectives 529–555.

45 Ibid.

46 Ibid., p. 534.

desire to ensure protection of only those choices that are rational as well as associated with good outcomes.[47]

The Manson/O'Neill view on autonomy and consent has also been criticised for ignoring the growing literature on relational autonomy.[48] While it can rightly be said that they do not go into any depth about relational autonomy, it is fair to say they acknowledge its existence. They do say, as indicated above, that the prevailing paradigm of consent (by which, I take it, they mean the paradigm actually practised by clinicians) cannot operationalise the various rational concepts of autonomy.

Manson and O'Neill conclude that autonomy cannot and should not be the justification for consent:

> … appeals to individual autonomy, however conceived, are unlikely to provide convincing justifications for informed consent procedures. The question of justification has not been settled by decades of insistence that informed consent is required in order to respect individual autonomy.[49]

They propose instead a novel justification: consent as waiver, which is discussed below.

Consent as Waiver

When consent is given, specific ethical or legal or other requirements that are 'generally inviolable'[50] are waived by the person consenting. In the absence of such requirements, there is no consent to be obtained. An example given by the authors is that one does not need consent to cross the road – there is no requirement that has to be waived for one to do so. On the other hand, consent is needed to have a picnic in a neighbour's garden – his right to exclude has to be waived. The scope of consent is not set by autonomy but by the norms and expectations that have to be waived for the proposed treatment to be legitimate.[51]

The justification for obtaining this waiver is that but for it the outcome of the intended act would be 'pain, injury, damage, distress and even death';[52] but for it the act or intervention would do wrong to others or fail to meet legitimate expectations.

47 Manson and O'Neill, *Rethinking Informed Consent in Bioethics*, pp. 19–20.

48 Maclean, *Autonomy, Informed Consent and Medical Law*, p. 44.

49 Manson and O'Neill, *Rethinking Informed Consent in Bioethics*, p. 22.

50 Ibid., p. 76.

51 Ibid., p. 79.

52 Ibid., p. 74.

The procedures for obtaining consent and the specificity of consent sought and obtained must both take account of the underlying norms that are to be waived in particular cases.[53] This means that standards for consent will vary from case to case; there will be no uniformity of standards, it will all depend on the norms that would be breached but for consent. Applying this to medical practice, the standards for consent will be more rigorous for complex interventions than for straightforward, routine procedures, because it is likely that the former will carry more significant norms or expectations that have to be waived. Failure to recognise this and applying a blanket approach instead will show 'a lack of understanding of the reasons why consent matters'.[54]

Manson and O'Neill also say that '[t]he most significant ethical and legal norms may be so important that they cannot be waived by the consent of those affected'.[55] Although the examples they give in support of this (consensual cannibalism, torture or killing) are extreme, in theory this statement leaves open the question of what counts as significant norm and who determines this. Presumably, it is whatever society at large abhors. This then would justify the position taken by the courts in the cases involving sanctity of life, as discussed above – respect for the sanctity of life is a significant ethical norm which should not be waived.

The implication of the Manson/O'Neill distinction between these two justifications of consent (consent as protector of individual autonomy and consent as waiver) is as follows. When we justify consent on the basis of respecting individual autonomy we promote a conception of consent that relies heavily on disclosure of information; the patient makes an informed decision based on this information and autonomy is thus respected. The problem with this conception is that there is more to communication than mere disclosure of information, and apparent consent obtained without regard for various norms of communication may not be genuine consent. On the other hand, when consent is justified on the basis of waiver of otherwise inviolable requirements, we are obliged to adopt a transactional approach to consent, which entails two-way communication of intelligible, relevant and accurate information between doctor and patient. This transactional approach to consent is discussed in Chapter 5. Patient self-determination is not upheld simply by the passive transmission of information to the patient; the transactional approach provides for exchange of information between doctor and patient, facilitating mutual understanding and empowering the patient to make an informed decision.

One of the problems with the Manson/O'Neill analysis is that it fails to distinguish clearly between consent to participate in research and consent to

53 Ibid., p. 78.
54 Ibid., p. 82.
55 Ibid., p. 84.

treatment, sometimes actually conflating these two different activities. The argument for a gradient of consent standards, for example, is more applicable to research than to clinical practice. It is not difficult to accept that the consent requirements for recruiting a patient into a retrospectively conducted study using previously collected data or biological samples need not be as rigorous as those for recruiting into a clinical trial of a new drug never before tested on humans. When it comes to clinical practice, however, there is one ethical and legal norm that is not only important but also common to both routine and complex interventions – the patient's right to determine what may be done to his or her body – and as a minimum requirement or standard, this right has to be protected.

An even bigger problem with the Manson/O'Neill analysis is that it fails to distinguish between two paradigms of consent (which I discuss in Chapter 5): the paradigm designed to protect self-determination (described elsewhere as the 'autonomy-enhancing' or 'autonomous authorisation' paradigm[56]) and the one that actually operates in clinical practice (variously described as the 'institutional requirement' or 'harm avoidance' paradigm[57]). It has been pointed out that:

> The ethically and legally preferable model is one seeking to enhance the patient's autonomy and understanding of the medical decision through a process of active collaboration between the physician and patient. While the autonomy-enhancing model is widely recognized as being superior to the harm-avoidance approach, recent studies illustrate that the reality of medical practice remains closer to the latter.[58]

The Manson/O'Neill description of the disclosure model of consent fits with the latter paradigm, and their analysis would hold if it was concerned solely with that paradigm – but one hastens to point out that the 'institutional requirement' paradigm was not designed or intended to respect the principle of self-determination. In fact, the paradigm is perceived by doctors and patients as a means of avoiding litigation.[59]

56 Swintankowsky, *New Paradigm for Informed Consent*; Fadin RR and Beauchamp TL, in collaboration with King NMP, *A History and Theory of Informed Consent*. Oxford: Oxford University Press 1986, pp. 274–287.

57 Ibid.

58 Ali V, Consent forms as part of the informed consent process: moving away from 'medical miranda' (2003) 54 Hastings LJ 1575–1591.

59 Heywood R, Macaskill A and Williams K, Informed consent in hospital practice: health professionals perspective and legal reflections (2010) 18 Med L Rev 152–184.

Conclusions

In summary, the theory of consent is complex.[60] The consent model can be justified by a range of ethical principles the most sustainable of which is the rights-based approach of respect for patient self-determination. This justification has recently come under strong criticism, but when cognisance is taken of the distinction between consent as theoretically conceptualised by libertarian ethicists and consent as operationalised by clinicians, we find that Manson and O'Neill's criticism applies to the latter but not necessarily to the former. The position taken in this book is that respect for self-determination remains a valid ethical justification for requiring consent. In effect, the law (as described in the previous chapter) and ethics (as discussed in this chapter) of consent remain basically in harmony.

The emphasis on the duty of health professionals to be trustworthy and honest is welcome, and this duty is at the core of the property model articulated in Chapter 9. Also it could be difficult to move doctors from one paradigm of consent to another. An alternative way of addressing the concerns expressed by Manson and O'Neill, therefore, may be to consider an alternative model (such as the property model presented here) rather than seek to 'rethink' consent. Their concern about consent being founded on mere independence, or freedom to choose, regardless of whether the choice leads to good or bad outcomes, is valid, but only to an extent. While mere choice could be vacuous, insisting that self-determination should apply only when choice leads to a good outcome is self-defeating: judgments on what constitutes good or bad outcome are commonly value-laden, and what is good in the eyes of one person may be bad to another. It is not for the law to arbitrate on value judgments; rather it should allow free choice, within the framework of societal norms and policy considerations.

They advocate a transactional model of consent, on the basis that communication entails more than mere disclosure of information. A transactional approach to clinical consultation is an essential element of the property approach to protection of self-determination.

60 Swintankowsky, *New Paradigm for Informed Consent*, p. x.

Chapter 5
Limitations of the Consent Model

> [S]tandard accounts of informed consent, standard arguments for requiring consent in clinical and research practice and standard ways of implementing consent requirements lead to intractable problems.[1]

Laudable as the notion of consent to treatment is, there are limitations to its scope and effectiveness in protecting patient self-determination. Some of these limitations are intrinsic to the concept of consent as elaborated in bioethics, and scholars have sought to address this by reconceptualising or 'rethinking' consent,[2] and advancing alternative conceptions.[3] Some limitations arise not necessarily from the concept per se but from how it is operationalised. These include difficulties (such as pressures of time)[4] in applying the theoretical principles of consent in everyday clinical practice. These difficulties and related factors have resulted in discordance between the paradigm of consent espoused by bioethicists and the paradigm of consent that is actually practised by clinicians.[5] Limitations also arise from the judicial constructions of consent.[6] In this chapter, the dichotomy between theoretical and operational paradigms of consent is discussed. Other factors that limit the effectiveness of the consent model are discussed, and the alternative approaches proffered by Manson and O'Neill ('genuine consent')[7] and Maclean ('relational consent')[8] are considered. This sets the stage for a subsequent discussion of the possible role of a property approach in redressing the limitations of the consent model.

A convenient point from which to start this chapter is a discussion of the paradigms of consent. It is convenient to start at this point because in Chapter 4, it was argued that while the Manson/O'Neill reconceptualisation of consent

---

1 Manson NC and O'Neill O, *Rethinking Informed Consent in Bioethics*. Cambridge: Cambridge University Press 2007, p. viii.

2 Ibid.

3 Maclean A, *Autonomy, Informed Consent and Medical Law: A Relational Challenge*. Cambridge: Cambridge University Press 2009.

4 Heywood R, Macaskill A and Williams K, Informed consent in hospital practice: health professionals' perspectives and legal reflections (2010) 18 Med L Rev 152–184.

5 Swintankowsky IS, *A New Paradigm for Informed Consent*. Lanham, Md.: University Press of America 1998.

6 McLean SAM, *Autonomy, Consent and the Law*. Abingdon: Routledge 2010.

7 Manson and O'Neill, *Rethinking Informed Consent*.

8 Maclean, *Autonomy, Informed Consent and Medical Law*.

is intellectually robust, it conflates the two paradigms that I have distinguished above. Their criticism of the current concept of consent applies mostly to the paradigm practised by clinicians, rather than to the ethically-espoused paradigm. If their criticism is upheld, then what needs changing is not the *concept* of consent but the way in which that concept is operationalised.

Paradigms of Consent

Similar to the way in which the concept of autonomy has many conceptions, the concept of consent has been interpreted in many ways and explained with various theoretical models.[9] The various paradigms of consent can be categorised into three groups. The first group (Category 1 – which I term 'bona fide consent' or 'authentic consent') comprises paradigms of consent that are framed by both the law and bioethicists for the purpose of protecting the patient's right to self-determination. The second group (Category 2 – which I term 'contrived consent') comprises paradigms of consent that are actually implemented most of the time in clinical practice. The third group (Category 3 – 'null consent' in my terminology) is one that can be readily dismissed from further analysis. This group comprises paradigms of consent that amount to no consent, what one may call null or invalid consent or, in some cases, mere assent. None of these three groups is homogenous; within each group there are variations in conception but, generally, the differences between the categories are stark except that sometimes the way consent is operationalised in clinical practice (contrived consent) actually amounts to no consent at all (null consent). Any criticism of consent and any proposals for revamping the mechanisms for protecting the right to self-determination should recognise these differences and make it clear which paradigm is being addressed.

Randall and Downie identify four conceptions of consent:[10] (1) Consent as being told what is going to be done. This is the paternalistic approach, and it is arguable that this is not consent at all. From the legal perspective, this would be a null 'consent'. (2) Consent as simply agreeing or acquiescing to a treatment proposal. In this conception, consent equates to mere assent. (3) Consent as joint investigation. The patient makes his/her own choice from a range of options, with help from the physician. It fits into Category 1 outlined above; it is also consonant with the ecological metaphor described in Chapter 1. (4) Consent as

9 Alderson P and Goodey C, Theories of consent (1998) 31 BMJ 1313–1315.

10 Randall F and Downie RS, *The Philosophy of Palliative Care: Critique and Reconstruction.* Oxford: Oxford University Press 2006, pp. 60–61.

patient's self-assertion[11] or freedom to choose. This conception is consonant with the narrow construction of self-determination. The nature of 'choice' in this model must be clarified – choice in this case does not mean selecting from a range of options offered by the doctor (as in Randall and Downie's conception 3 above); rather it refers to the situation where the patient *demands* a form of treatment even if the doctor does not recommend it. An example would be Caesarean section performed at maternal request in the absence of a medical indication. Another example is that of a woman requesting (demanding?) hysterectomy for heavy menstrual bleeding when her doctor has offered less invasive but effective options such as ablation of the endometrium.[12]

One problem with this categorisation is that the true situation is not always as clear-cut as suggested by the four conceptions. For example, when a patient makes a choice it is not always clear whether he/she has done so within conception 3 or 4. If doctor and patient have jointly gone through options (including the risks, benefits and alternatives) and the well-informed patient has chosen an option different from the doctor's preference, does this fall under 'consent as joint investigation' or 'consent as self-assertion'? If the patient is requesting or demanding a treatment *that is known to be ineffective or dangerous*, then this would fall into conception 4 (and the doctor has professional and ethical issues to contend with). On the other hand, if he/she is demanding a treatment that is known to be effective but is not the doctor's preferred option (because it is more invasive or costs more or is outwith his/her technical competence or does not fit with his/her life values) would this be conception 3 or 4? Such judgments often involve value as well as medical considerations, and it has been argued that while doctors can define the limits of medical factors, it is not for them to also define moral or non-medical limits.[13] In any case, it is now well established not only by General Medical Council (GMC) guidance[14] but also by judicial pronouncement[15] that a doctor is not obliged to provide treatment that is ineffective or not in the best interests of the patient.

---

11 The authors use the term 'self-determination'; I have used 'self-assertion' instead, to avoid confusion with self-determination as defined in this book, and because I believe 'self-assertion' more appropriately describes the position the authors refer to.

12 Destruction (by burning) of the lining of the womb, in order to stop heavy menstrual bleeding.

13 For example, Lesser H, The patient's right to information. In Brazier M and Lobjoit M, *Protecting the Vulnerable: Autonomy and Consent in Health Care.* London: Routledge 1991, pp. 150–160, at p. 154.

14 General Medical Council, Consent: Patients and *Doctors Making Decisions Together.* London: GMC 2008.

15 *R (on the application of Burke)* v. *General Medical Council* [2005] EWCA Civ 1003. The principles of patient autonomy and choice were recognised; a competent person's wishes – apart from a right to demand a particular treatment – must be respected.

In summary, the first two conceptions in Randall and Downie's list can be consigned to my Category 3 (null consent) and will not be discussed further. The third conception falls into Category 1 (bona fide consent). On the basis that respect for self-determination does not include an obligation to provide any treatment demanded by the patient, their fourth conception is also consigned to Category 3.

Bona fide (Authentic) Consent

Concentrating now on Category 1, there are subtle or not so subtle differences between conceptions falling under this category. It is not surprising that this is the case, because as shown in Chapter 2, there is no standard model of doctor–patient relationship or consultation. The key point is that all conceptions in this category accord primacy to the patient's right to self-determination. Where they differ is in the *process* for obtaining consent. In the Randall and Downie conception described above, the process is one of joint investigation. This process combines respect for the patient's dignity and self-determination with respect for the physician's dignity and professional autonomy, and the authors say that it offers 'the best ethical-medical package'[16] for patient and doctor.

There are other accounts that propose a similar process for obtaining consent, which view consent as 'shared decision-making'.[17] Shared decision-making has the following key characteristics: (1) at least two participants – physician and patient – are involved; (2) the parties share information; (3) both parties take steps to build a consensus about the preferred treatment; and (4) an agreement is reached on the treatment to implement.[18] This conception of consent is advanced by the psychiatrist J Katz[19] and the (US) President's Commission,[20] but is opposed by Faden and Beauchamp, who say the essence of consent is that the patient authorises autonomously and not that patient and doctor reach a decision together.[21] The American College of Obstetricians and Gynecologists (ACOG) hints at the provenance of this paradigm:

16 Randall and Downie, *Philosophy of Palliative Care*, pp. 60–61.

17 Katz J, *The Silent World of Doctor and Patient.* New York: Free Press 1984; Elwyn G, Edwards A, Kinnersley P and Grol R, Shared decision making and the concept of equipoise: the competences of involving patients in healthcare choices (2000) 50 Br J Gen Pract 892–899.

18 Charles C, Gafni A and Whelan T, Shared decision-making in the medical encounter: what does it mean? (or it takes at least two to tango) (1997) 44 Soc Sci Med 681–692.

19 Katz, *Silent World of Doctor and Patient.*

20 President's Commission for the Study of Ethical Problems in Medicine and Biomedical and Behavioral Research, *Making Health Care Decisions*, vol 1. Washington DC: U.S. Government Printing Office 1982.

21 Faden RR and Beauchamp TL, in collaboration with King NMP, *A History and Theory of Informed Consent.* Oxford: Oxford University Press 1986, p. 279.

> If in the 1970s informed consent was embraced as a corrective to paternalism, the 1980s and 1990s exhibited a growing sense of the need for shared decision making as a corrective to the exaggerated individualism that patient autonomy had sometimes produced.[22]

The ACOG asserts that if persons are to be respected and their well-being promoted, consent must be seen as expressing a fuller notion of relationship.[23] Clements advocates minimum standards of dialogue between patient and doctor in the consent process.[24] These views are fundamentally the same as those expressed, albeit within a more theoretical framework, by ethicists such as Manson and O'Neill[25] and Randall and Downie[26] who see consent as more than mere disclosure of information. But does their richer conception of consent actually find application on the shop floor of medical practice? It appears not.

Ruth Faden and Tom Beauchamp distinguish between two conceptions of consent which they describe as *consent as autonomous authorisation* and *consent as a policy-oriented ritual*.[27] In the autonomous authorisation paradigm, a patient with (i) substantial understanding and (ii) in the substantial absence of control by others (iii) intentionally (iv) authorises a professional to undertake a particular intervention. A person whose act fulfils conditions i–iii but who refuses the intervention gives an informed refusal. The authors stress that only the patient authorises (that is the patient, not the doctor, makes the final decision) and it is not a prerequisite that agreement on the performance (or withholding) of the intervention should be reached through any particular method. By this emphasis, their intention is to clearly distinguish this paradigm from the 'shared decision-making' or 'joint investigation' paradigms. The authors go on to describe this notion of authorisation:

> In authorizing, one both *assumes responsibility* for what one has authorized and transfers to another one's authority to implement it. There is no informed consent unless one understands these features of the act and intends to perform

22 American College of Obstetricians and Gynecologists, *Ethical Dimensions of Informed Consent*, ACOG Committee Opinion: Committee on Ethics, No 108. Washington DC: ACOG 1992.

23 Ibid.

24 Clements RV, Informed choice: should we bin the consent form? (2005) 11 Clinical Risk 69–71.

25 Manson and O'Neill, *Rethinking Informed Consent*.

26 Randall and Downie, *Philosophy of Palliative Care*.

27 Faden and Beauchamp, *History and Theory of Informed Consent*, pp. 274–287.

> that act. That is, one must understand that one is assuming responsibility and warranting another to proceed.[28] (emphasis mine)[29]

In the Faden/Beauchamp *policy-oriented conception* of consent, effective authorisation is obtained from a patient through a procedure stipulated by institutional rules and regulations. Here, consent is 'effective' in the sense that it meets the regulations set by the hospital (or health-care facility) and is accepted by that institution as valid. Requirements for this paradigm of consent 'typically do not focus on the autonomy of the act of giving consent … but rather on regulating the behavior of the consent-seeker'.[30]

Writing a decade after Faden and Beauchamp, Irene Switankowsky also identifies two paradigms of consent: the *harm avoidance model* and the *autonomy-enhancing model*.[31] She states that the harm avoidance paradigm is the common framework within which physicians operate. In this model consent is considered to be a mere legal formality and a minimalist approach is adopted to disclosure of risks. In the autonomy-enhancing model, all treatments must be disclosed and discussed in detail with the patient. The risks and benefits of each treatment are disclosed, not just the treatment that is preferred by the physician.

Swintankowsky's two paradigms may appear similar to the Faden/Beauchamp paradigms but they are not identical. An important difference is the emphasis that Swintankowsky places on full disclosure in the autonomy-enhancing model. Faden and Beauchamp on the contrary decry such an emphasis; in their view it is understanding that counts, not disclosure – a patient can autonomously authorise an intervention in the absence of any disclosure, so long as the patient sufficiently understands the implications of the intervention (e.g. a general surgeon who needs to undergo a hernia operation does not need full disclosure before he/she can autonomously authorise it). This equates in legal terms to saying that the test for adequacy of information disclosure should be subjective.

The issue of disclosure of information and, in particular, the courts' concentration on standards of disclosure was discussed in Chapter 3 and it was shown that the courts have gradually moved away from relying on doctors to set the standards. It was also shown that the tension between the ideal of a subjective test and the pragmatism of an objective one calls for a continual balancing act by the courts. This tension and its resolution are discussed again in Chapter 9.

28 Ibid., p. 280.

29 The notion of authorisation involving assumption of responsibility is one to which I return below, and also when comparing the consent and property models in Chapter 9.

30 Ibid.

31 Swintankowsky, *New Paradigm for Informed Consent.*

Berg and colleagues recognise that consent as 'autonomous authorisation', consent as 'institutional requirement' and 'consent as shared decision-making' are interrelated, but they also emphasise that the distinctions between them are important and should be acknowledged:

> Acknowledging them permits us to see that sometimes strict adherence to the rules governing informed consent may actually undermine the dialogue involved in the process of shared decision-making, or may fail to enable a particular patient autonomously to authorise a treatment plan. Alternatively, placing too much emphasis on sharing the decision may undermine the decisional authority of some patients; for example, if they over-value maintaining a good relationship and comfortable interaction with their physicians, at the expense of expressing their own views. These patients may eventually be disappointed when they find that they, not their physicians, bear responsibility for what they authorised their doctors to do. Like the hypothetical homeowner who would like to be able to blame her painters for her own paint colour choice, patients may want to blame their physicians for choices they later regret. Recognising that in authorising another to act on one's behalf, one still retains responsibility for what is authorised, may help avoid misplacing blame. In order to be responsible for what they authorise, however, patients must be well informed and act autonomously.[32]

The idea of patients taking responsibility when they consent to treatment is one that needs more emphasis in clinical and legal practice, and will be revisited in Chapter 9. Suffice to say at this point that the theoretical conceptions of consent espoused by most bioethicists are broadly grouped as the Category 1 paradigm described above, but it is widely acknowledged that this paradigm is not always operationalised in clinical practice. It is important to distinguish between Category 1 and Category 2 paradigms because consent that is valid in the first paradigm may not be valid in the other, and vice versa. Crucially, any analysis of consent in relation to self-determination must make clear which one of these two paradigms is the subject of analysis. Attention is now turned to the dichotomy between the theoretically envisioned paradigm and the operationalised one.

32 Berg JW, Appelbaum PS, Lidz CW and Parker LS, *Informed Consent – Legal Theory and Clinical Practice*, 2nd edn. Oxford: Oxford University Press 2001, pp. 17–18.

Contrived Consent

In this paradigm of consent the patient is presented with a menu of choices (sometimes 'a menu of one item'[33]) and a 'yes or no' response is elicited. The menu may be accompanied by a large quantity of information, most of it generic rather than specific to the patient, or little or no information. The emphasis is not on comprehension of information but on the signal which indicates that the doctor may proceed with treatment. In most consultations the signal is verbal but for surgical operations and other interventional treatment it is usually a signature. From a theories-of-consent perspective, this paradigm of consent has been classified as 'Functionalist consent'.[34]

In practice, this paradigm is heavily dependent on the consent form, and in the minds of many clinicians consent is a signature on the form.[35] This paradigm of consent is boosted by the UK Department of Health's policy on consent, which appears to place undue emphasis on consent forms.[36] It appears that the current practice of health professionals in the UK matches this paradigm rather than what I have classified above as the bona fide or authentic paradigm of consent.[37] Clements paints this scenario:

> The preoccupation with the form inhibits, not encourages, dialogue. It leads to the ludicrous caricature often encountered in the anaesthetic room just before the patient is wheeled into theatre. The consultant surgeon, arriving late, puts his head round the door and enquires of the anaesthetist 'has she been consented?' Leaving aside the abuse of the intransitive verb, the question speaks volumes for the surgeon's understanding of the counselling process that should precede surgery.[38]

In a similar scenario, a woman in the throes of labour pains who signs a consent form minutes before she is whisked to the operating theatre for a Caesarean section is deemed to have given an institutionally valid consent, but almost certainly has not autonomously authorised the operation – in other words, contrived 'consent' may have been obtained but not bona fide consent. In Figure 5.1 a case further illustrating the difference between these two categories of consent is described.

33 O'Neill O, *Autonomy and Trust in Bioethics*. Cambridge: Cambridge University Press 2002, p. 38.

34 Alderson and Goodey, Theories of consent, p. 1314.

35 Clements, Informed choice.

36 Department of Health, *Good Practice in Consent Implementation Guide: Consent to Examination or Treatment*. London: DH 2009.

37 Manson and O'Neill, *Rethinking Informed Consent*.

38 Clements, Informed choice, pp. 70–71.

> A patient listed for hysterectomy is taken to the operating theatre on the day of the operation. When she arrived in the anaesthetic room, the consent form (which she had signed on the ward) was missing. The unit managers and theatre staff were minded to cancel the operation, in the belief that there was no valid consent. The surgeon explained that he had discussed the operation comprehensively with the patient before and during her admission into hospital, and these discussions (including her agreement) were documented in the health records and in a letter to the patient's general practitioner. In his opinion, the patient had given a valid consent and there was documentary evidence of this, even though there was no signed consent form. The managers and the theatre team then agreed that the operation should proceed. The institutional requirement for a consent form (Contrived or 'functionalist' consent) was not fulfilled but the operation was performed with the valid consent of the patient (Bona fide consent). In clinical audit of consent, this case would be flagged as bad practice, because it did not meet the institutional requirement for a signed consent form, and cases where a form was signed would be classified as good, regardless of the presence or absence of transactional communication between doctor and patient.

Figure 5.1 Case report distinguishing between Bona fide and Contrived consent

The British Medical Association has expressed concern that despite 'a considerable amount of written guidance on consent, from regulatory, professional, and indemnifying bodies as well as government departments',[39] the way in which consent was sought in practice was less than satisfactory.

Clearly this paradigm does not meet the requirements of the principles underlying Bona fide consent. This raises two questions: why is this so, and what can/should be done about it? The first question is addressed in this chapter and the second will be addressed in subsequent chapters.

There are barriers that circumscribe the potential application of the consent model in day-to-day clinical practice.[40] One of these is the difficulty in achieving optimal communication. Often there is not enough time or space for an adequate

39 British Medical Association, *Medical Ethics Today: The BMA's Handbook of Ethics and Law*, 2nd edn. London: BMA and BMJ Books 2004, p. 73. Also in 3rd edition. John Wiley 2012. Chapter 2.

40 Braddock CH III, Edwards KA, Hasenberg NM, Laidley TL and Levinson W, Informed decision making in outpatient practice: time to get back to basics (1999) 282 JAMA 2313–2320.

discussion, particularly in public sector hospitals (it must be stressed, however, that it is quality, not quantity of information that counts). At other times there may be language, cultural and social barriers inhibiting communication between clinicians and patients. These limiting factors are, however, relatively trivial compared to the factors discussed below.

Doctors' *Knowledge* and *Perception* of the Principles of Consent

There are a number of reasons why the operationalised paradigm of consent differs from the theoretical one. One of these is that doctors' knowledge regarding consent law is shockingly poor[41] and their perception of consent way off the mark established in bioethics. There is evidence that health professionals do not know enough about basic aspects of the law of consent, such as at what age can a child give consent or what happens when an adult is unable to give consent.[42]

Reflecting and/or reinforcing this knowledge deficiency is a misdirected perception of consent, firstly as an event, secondly as primarily a shield against litigation. Consciously or subconsciously, obtaining consent is often perceived by clinicians as an event marked by the signalling of an agreement (this signal often but not always being the signing of a form). In its broad construction, obtaining consent is a process which begins with an open discussion of the purpose, benefits and risks of the proposed intervention and the alternatives (including the alternative of no treatment), and does not end until the treatment has been delivered or declined. These issues are explored between doctor and patient in the context of the patient's values, goals and constraints.

The construction of consent as a process rather than an event, while accepted unequivocally by professional groups[43] and some academics,[44] has been challenged by Maclean who sees consent as a state of mind, and if it is a state of mind it should not also be regarded as a process.[45] In a sense, however, there is no conflict between the two sides, as they both accept that there is a process of communication between doctor and patient and that there is a signal given by the patient at the end of the process. The only difference is that while one school of thought uses the word consent to refer to the entire pathway from

41 Jackson E and Warner J, How much do doctors know about consent and capacity? (2002) 95 J R Soc Med 601–603.

42 Ibid.

43 BMA, p 73.

44 Meisel A and Kuczewiski M, Legal and ethical myths about informed consent (1996) 156 Arch Intern Med 2521–2526.

45 Maclean, *Autonomy, Informed Consent and Medical Law*, p. 122.

consultation to signal, the other regards only the signal as consent, everything else is 'the process leading to consent'.[46]

Doctors appear to be concerned principally with the signal, that is the event, and not so much with the process that precedes, informs and determines that signal. The signal is, of course, an expression of the patient's state of mind.

The point about *obtaining consent* being a process rather than an event is more than a matter of semantics. The patient's receipt, digesting and understanding of information is itself a process. When doctors take obtaining consent to be an event rather than a process, what they obtain is more likely to be an assent to what has been proposed (Category 3 paradigm) than a real consent to treatment. Also when the courts look at whether or not a valid signal (consent) has been given, they look at the preceding transaction.

The operational paradigm of consent tends to focus on the decision itself, paying insufficient attention to the process by which the decision is reached by patient and doctor. Any alternative model that takes due account of the communicative transaction leading up to the decision, rather than just focusing on the final decision, will meet the imperatives of cultural sensitivity while also upholding the principle of self-determination.

The other flawed perception is seeing consent as primarily a means of securing protection against litigation. Advising that it is time this perception was abandoned, Clements said:

> It is high time for a change of emphasis; we should no longer be looking over our shoulder at the lawyers so as to escape a charge of battery; rather, we should be seeking to improve the dialogue with the patient to make sure that she has the information necessary to express her choice of treatment.[47]

This misperception has been a longstanding attribute of the health professions, but there is evidence that it is beginning to change. In the first seven editions (1952–1971) of the iconic *Myles Textbook for Midwives*[48] there was no mention of consent, choice or information.[49] Consent was mentioned for the first time in the eighth edition, but what the author described is not a true consent:

> It is customary and expedient for midwives to request women admitted in labour to sign a permission slip for the obstetrician-in-charge to carry out any treatment or operation which may be considered necessary, including an anaesthetic. This is

46 Ibid., p. 123.

47 Clements, Informed choice, p. 71.

48 Fraser D, Cooper MA and Crawford J, *Myles' Textbook for Midwives*, 15th edn. London: Churchill Livingstone 2009.

49 I am grateful to Roger Clements for this insight.

> a wise precaution … particularly at the present time when unscrupulous persons may initiate litigation against medical staff or Area Health Authorities on the slightest pretext When any treatment, operation, or anaesthetic is required, the doctor will explain the situation to the patient so that she understands what is involved. When she signs the permissions form, she gives her informed consent. This is a wise precaution.[50]

In signing a 'permissions form' what the patient gave was not a bona fide consent but a null, or at best contrived, consent. Clearly, the purpose of 'consent' in this context was protection of the health-care professional from litigation. There was really no intention to uphold the patient's right to self-determination.

Subsequent editions of the textbook showed a shift from 'permissions' to 'choice':

> The midwife must take care not only to talk to the mother but to ask for her consent to what she plans to do and to invite her comments and questions. Promotion of informed choice is an essential element of contemporary midwifery care … It should be remembered that for some women their choice is to relinquish control and it should not … be assumed that all women desire or are capable of taking decisions about their care. They are, however, all entitled to information given in such a way as to assist their comprehension.[51]

The Consent Form

No distinction is made in this book between implied and expressed consent or between written and unwritten consent. Most clinical consultations do not entail the signing of a consent form but the doctor is still in these consultations required to obtain the patient's consent to any treatment that is proposed. Nevertheless, in the minds of doctors, particularly in secondary and tertiary care, consent is commonly equated to a signature on a consent form.[52] This is despite the fact that there is no requirement in common law, and only exceptionally in statute,[53] for consent to be written. Also, doctors and patients have different

50 Myles MF, *Textbook for Midwives, with Modern Concepts of Obstetric and Neonatal Care*, 8th edn. London: Churchill Livingstone 1975, pp. 242–243.

51 Bennett VR and Brown LK (eds), *Myles' Textbook for Midwives*, 13th edn. London: Churchill Livingstone 1999, p. 17.

52 Clements, Informed choice.

53 In relation to some aspects of mental health care and fertility treatment using gametes and embryos.

perceptions of what the form is about, with many patients thinking that the primary function of the consent form is to protect the hospital.[54]

In one study, most patients (68 per cent) thought consent forms allowed doctors to assume control.[55] Less than half of patients believed that consent forms reflected their wishes. One in every five patients did not know whether they could change their mind after they had signed the form, and 16 per cent incorrectly thought that signing a consent form removed their right to compensation if things went wrong. One in 10 patients reported that they did not know what they had agreed to when they signed the consent form, and approximately one-third were unsure whether the operation could be performed if they refused to sign the consent form. Nearly a quarter did not know whether the operation could be performed if they were unable to sign the consent form, and some mistakenly assumed it could not. The majority of patients (71 per cent) did not know that their next of kin could not sign on their behalf if they were unable to sign for themselves.[56]

Apart from failing to meet the requirements of patient self-determination, consent forms often fail the test of validity.[57] Consent may be valid in the absence of a signed consent form; on the other hand, consent may be invalid even though a consent form has been signed:

> The most outstanding finding of this study was the fact that 40% of the consent obtained for treatment was not valid immediately after the consent form was signed.[58]

Thus, for all of the attention focused on consent forms, the patients remained ill-informed and not in a position to assert their right to self-determination. This has led one clinician to suggest that the consent form should be binned:

> … the consent form is the single most important obstacle to the proper dialogue between doctor and patient … Preoccupation with the form inhibits not encourages dialogue.[59]

As stressed by the Bristol Inquiry, consent is about communication, not forms:

---

54 Heywood, Macaskill and Williams, Informed consent in hospital practice.

55 Akkad A, Jackson C, Kenyon S, Dixon-Woods M, Taub N and Habiba M, Patients' perceptions of written consent: questionnaire study (2006) 333 BMJ 528.

56 Ibid.

57 Ibid.; Tahir MAM, Mason C and Hind V, Informed consent: optimism versus reality (2002) 193 Br Dent J 221–224.

58 Tahir *et al.*, Informed consent, p. 224.

59 Clements, Informed choice, p. 69.

> The process of consent should apply not only to surgical procedures but to all clinical procedures and examinations which involve any form of touching. This must not mean more forms: it means more communication.[60]

If the Bristol recommendation for more communication rather than more forms is implemented, there would be a shift from Category 2 and Category 3 to Category 1 paradigm of consent, and the transactional approach recommended by Manson and O'Neill[61] (described below) could stand a better chance of being realised. National guidance produced by the English Department of Health, however, appears inadvertently to favour more forms, although it also encourages better communication.[62] The guidance includes four forms covering adults and children, and awake and anaesthetised patients. It even includes a 'consent form' for treating incompetent adults, despite the clear legal position that consent cannot be obtained from the patient or his/her relatives.

Manson and O'Neill note that the attempts to make consent more rigorous (in particular by making it more explicit and specific) have led to 'the development of increasingly complex, lengthy and (at worst) incomprehensible consent forms'.[63]

None of the above should be taken as meaning that there should be no place for documentation of consent. Binning the form does not mean that consent transactions should not be documented. Documentation of consent transactions constitutes what Manson and O'Neill describe as a 'second-order informational obligation'.[64] The obligation of clinicians to disclose information is a first-order obligation, and the obligation to ensure that this obligation is met is a second-order obligation.[65] The authors say that 'although the distinction between first and second-order obligation has received little attention in discussions of informed consent (in contrast to the relevant first-order informational obligations), it is an important distinction',[66] but they do not quite say how the second-order obligation derives any importance other than from the importance of its corresponding first-order obligation. Arguably, however, an obligation to document the consent transaction will help ensure that communication is effective (see discussion below). Such documentation

60 Bristol Royal Infirmary Inquiry, *Learning from Bristol: The Report of the Public Inquiry into Children's Heart Surgery at the Bristol Royal Infirmary 1984–1995*, Cm 5207(I). London: HMSO 2001, Recommendation 25.

61 Manson and O'Neill, *Rethinking Informed Consent.*

62 Department of Health, *Reference Guide to Consent for Examination or Treatment*, 2nd edn. London: DH 2009.

63 Manson and O'Neill, *Rethinking Informed Consent*, p. 10.

64 Ibid., p. 31.

65 Ibid.

66 Ibid.

could include letters to patients after the consultation.[67] These would help the patient understand what has been communicated, enable them to consider it in their own time, and reach an informed uncoerced decision.

Patients' Perception of the Consent Process

If doctors' perception of consent is flawed, it is no surprise that the patients' perception is problematic. In a study of the adequacy of the consent process as it is currently practised, the authors arrived at this conclusion:

> … there is substantial disparity between the ideals of the consent process as depicted in the bioethical model and how it is perceived and experienced by patients. These findings are disconcerting for healthcare professionals and patients alike and raise questions about how far current consent processes genuinely fulfill their aim of safeguarding autonomy and protecting patients' rights.[68]

Even when the consent process satisfies administrative and legal requirements, patients' needs may not be met, and some patients may, for example, even consent to surgery they do not want. Contrived consent has a lot to answer for.

In summary, a major limitation of the consent model is the apparent difficulty in translating the true essence of the model into clinical practice. From this perspective, it is somewhat surprising that there are not many more cases reaching the courts. Perhaps this is a reflection of the costs and difficulties of accessing the legal system and the hurdles of causation that have to be scaled in negligence law. Or could it simply be that, as Clements reminds us, '[i]n the great majority of contacts between doctor and patient, the patient is explicitly inviting … contact for she wants to be treated',[69] and he/she is loathe to sue the doctor? Whatever the case, the ethical-legal concept of consent has not permeated medical practice. When doctors conduct consent transactions the background context is not knowledge of the ethical or legal principles but fear of litigation. As Jones has stated, 'it seems likely that the law does not have a positive effect on the quality of doctor-patient communication'.[70]

---

67 Department of Health, *Copying Letters to Patients: Good Practice Guidelines*. London: DH 2003.

68 Akkad *et al.*, Patients' perceptions of written consent, p. 530.

69 Clements, Informed choice.

70 Jones MA, Informed consent and other fairy stories (1999) 7 Med L Rev 103–134, at p. 106.

Even in the cases that do reach court, there are factors that limit the effectiveness of the consent model in securing protection of the patient's right to self-determination. These factors relate to judicial constructions of consent.

Limitations Imposed by Deconstruction in Case Law

Apart from the limitations of consent in clinical practice discussed above, there are also limitations associated with the way in which the doctrine of consent has been deconstructed in case law. Although patient self-determination lies at the heart of contemporary discourse on consent, it was not the main factor underlying the development of consent principles from the outset. Consent initially developed to protect bodily security and only subsequently was it seen as a means of protecting self-determination.[71] Various authors argue that despite the development of the legal doctrine of 'informed' consent, the patient's right to self-determination is still not protected.[72]

In Chapter 3 I discussed the view that the UK courts have proved incapable of standing firmly on the side of self-determination because they fail to apply a subjective test and have usually opted for either the professional standard or an objective prudent patient standard instead. Critics point to the continuing inclination of the courts to respect medical opinion as one reason why patient self-determination has not been fully protected.[73] They also point out that the adoption of the objective rather than the subjective tests for disclosure standards fails to fully protect autonomy:[74]

> The need for consent was acknowledged (indeed rhapsodized) by the courts but proved to be ineffective all too often in the most problematic of cases. The underlying reason for this failure of English law always to uphold patient autonomy was the judiciary's deference to the medical profession. Emphasis upon the ethical duties and professional standards of doctors inevitably undermined consideration of the rights of patients. The HRA [Human Rights Act] acts as a reminder that this is unacceptable within a democratic society adhering to the rule of law.[75]

71 Randall and Downie, *Philosophy of Palliative Care*, p. 59.

72 For example, Manson and O'Neill, *Rethinking Informed Consent in Bioethics*; Maclean, *Autonomy, Informed Consent and Medical Law*; McLean, *Autonomy, Consent and the Law*.

73 McLean, *Autonomy, Consent and the Law*.

74 Mclean, *Autonomy, Consent and the Law*; Wicks E, The implications of the Human Rights Act 1998 – prioritizing consent. In Tingle J, Foster C and Wheat K. *Regulating Healthcare Quality*. Edinburgh: Butterworth Heinemann 2004, pp. 97–108.

75 Wicks, Implications of the Human Rights Act 1998, pp. 107–108.

Even after the test, appropriate or not, has been applied to determine whether disclosure met the reference standards, there is still the hurdle of causation. To establish a claim in clinical negligence one must prove not only breach of duty but also injury, causation and remoteness of damages.[76] The patient has to show that but for the failure to disclose the risk, he/she would not have suffered the injury; by traditional causation principles that held sway until *Chester* v. *Afshar*[77] appeared to put a spanner in the works, he/she had to convince the court that if the risk had been disclosed he/she would not have proceeded with the treatment. This means that even when an injury has occurred, a claim may not necessarily succeed; where there is no injury, no claim lies, even if there has been failure to disclose risks. More importantly, the emphasis is on harm caused rather than enhancement of patient self-determination – and this raises questions about the suitability of action in negligence as a vehicle for protecting self-determination.[78]

Lord Hope of Craighead, in *Chester* v. *Afshar*, recognised this problem:

> Liability for the non-disclosure of risks is judged by reference to the tort of negligence which looks to the nature of the doctor's duty and applies the *Bolam* test to it, rather than the validity of the consent of the patient to what would otherwise be a trespass. There are then two problems that face a patient who brings a claim for non-disclosure of risk: that of proving breach of duty and that of proving causation. *The greater the difficulties that stand in the way of the patient on these issues, the more difficult it is to say that the law of informed consent works as a means of protecting patient autonomy.*[79] (emphasis mine)

Beyond liability and causation, there are also limitations introduced when public policy considerations come to the fore.[80] These considerations include ethical and equitable use of limited resources and the need to protect the public good. Choice and communication issues may be limited by resource considerations, and allowing a competent minor to refuse life-saving heart transplantation, for example, may be seen as contrary to the public good.[81] However, I would argue that any model adopted for the legal protection of patient self-determination

76 Deakin S, Johnston A, Markesinis B QC, *Markesinis and Deakin's Tort Law*, 6th edn. Oxford: Oxford University Press 2007, p. 113.

77 *Chester* v. *Afshar* [2004] 4 All ER 587.

78 Jackson E, 'Informed consent' to medical treatment and the impotence of tort. In McLean SAM (ed), *First Do No Harm: Law, Ethics and Healthcare*. Aldershot: Ashgate 2006, pp. 273–286.

79 *Chester v. Afshar* [2004] 4 All ER 587, at para 57.

80 Symmons CR, The duty of care in negligence: recently expressed policy elements - Part 1 (1971) 34 MLR 394–409.

81 *Re M (A child) (Medical Treatment: Consent)* [1999] 2 FLR 1097.

cannot exist in a social vacuum and so must be subject to public policy considerations. The aim should not be to insulate such a model from public policy, but to have a legal framework that brings a degree of certainty to the relationship between the chosen model and public policy considerations. The consent model appears to lack this degree of certainty as there is no statutory framework and, despite the constraint imposed by precedence in case law, much is left to the whims and caprices of the judges in each case.

Finally the concept of therapeutic privilege[82] may also be seen as one limitation of the doctrine of consent. The doctor's therapeutic privilege allows him/her to withhold any information that might be harmful to the patient. In *Sidaway* Lord Scarman accepted this as an exception to the 'prudent patient' test.[83] This exception was reiterated in *Montgomery*:

> The doctor is however entitled to withhold from the patient information as to a risk if he reasonably considers that its disclosure would be seriously detrimental to the patient's health.[84]

The Supreme Court stated further that:

> It is a limited exception to the general principle that the patient should make the decision whether to undergo a proposed course of treatment: it is not intended to subvert that principle by enabling the doctor to prevent the patient from making an informed choice where she is liable to make a choice which the doctor considers to be contrary to her best interests.[85]

The extent to which therapeutic privilege compromises the principle of consent depends on how broadly or narrowly it is defined – too broad a definition defeats self-determination and restores paternalism. The narrow definition limits this privilege to cases where disclosure of information could cause a serious medical complication or render the patient incapable of exercising his/her right to self-determination.[86]

---

82 Johnston C and Holt G, The legal and ethical implications of therapeutic privilege – is it ever justified to withhold treatment information from a competent patient? (2006) 3 J Clin Ethics 146–151.

83 *Sidaway* v. *Board of Governors of the Bethlem Royal Hospital* [1985] AC 871, at 882.

84 *Montgomery (Appellant) v Lanarkshire Health Board (Respondent) (Scotland)* [2015] UKSC 11, para 88.

85 *Montgomery*, at para 91.

86 Faden and Beauchamp, *History and Theory of Informed Consent.*

Fears that therapeutic privilege could open the back door for re-emergence of medical paternalism are quelled by guidance from the professional bodies. The General Medical Council directs doctors as follows:

> You should not withhold information necessary for making decisions … unless you believe that giving it would cause the patient serious harm. In this context 'serious harm' means more than that the patient might become upset or decide to refuse treatment.
>
> If you withhold information from the patient you must record your reason for doing so in the patient's medical records, and you must be prepared to explain and justify your decision. You should regularly review your decision, and consider whether you could give information to the patient later, without causing them serious harm.[87]

Also, the American College of Obstetricians and Gynecologists says that:

> It is reasonable to argue that therapeutic privilege is almost never a basis for permanently overriding the obligation of informed *consent*. Ordinarily such overriding represents a temporary situation, one that will later allow the kind of communication conducive to the restored freedom of the patient.[88]

It could be argued, therefore, that the medical profession has, independent of legal guidance, introduced safeguards against undue use of therapeutic privilege to thwart patient self-determination. As noted by McLean, '[i]t is paradoxical that once embraced by the professions, the importance of respect for autonomy seems to have been taken more seriously by them than by the law'.[89] Given the sources from which this guidance has come, it is likely to be adopted by the courts. As the law currently stands, however, therapeutic privilege remains an intrinsic element of the consent model.

What is the Way Forward?

So far, ways in which the consent model could be limited in its ability truly to protect the patient's right to self-determination have been discussed. Two perspectives have been explored briefly: firstly, the difficulty in ensuring that

87 General Medical Council, *Consent*, p. 12.

88 American College of Obstetricians and Gynecologists. *Informed Consent*, Committee Opinion No 439. Washington DC: ACOG 2009, p. 7.

89 McLean, *Autonomy, Consent and the Law*, p. 96.

the operational paradigm of consent matches the theoretical paradigm which is rooted in the principle of respect for self-determination; secondly, the deconstruction of the principles of consent by the courts. If consent, despite its increasing sophistication in the twentieth and twenty-first centuries, is still not fully protective of patient self-determination, what is the way forward?

There is no shortage of suggestions.[90] The emphasis has been on the need to move from the professional standard of disclosure to the prudent patient standard – but, as discussed in Chapter 3, this would only be substantial if the subjective rather than objective prudent patient standard is applied, and that comes with problems of its own. Some have suggested that therapeutic privilege should be abolished[91] – but as stated above, the impact of this factor is diminishing anyway, given the strict professional regulatory guidance. Twerski and Cohen suggest that self-determination could be protected by allowing patients to recover for a violation of their right to participate in decision-making.[92] It would appear that currently the law focuses more on bad outcomes attributable to undisclosed risks than on the patient's traduced rights. However, the legal mechanism for attaining this remedy is yet to be articulated.

Almost all the suggestions for a way forward summarised above have one thing in common: they entail tinkering with the formulation and practice of consent. Perhaps what is needed is to give consideration to alternative models for protecting self-determination. Schultz has argued the case for development of a new course of action to protect self-determination as a distinct legal interest, but she falls back on traditional contract and tort analysis for the new course of action and, approaching a quarter of a century since her paper was published, there has been no movement in this direction.[93] In the early 1980s, the President's Commission in the USA suggested that 'the traditional monolithic legal model of informed consent may require re-thinking'.[94] Although the inadequacies of the consent model have long been identified, concrete suggestions of alternatives have been in short supply. For example, the psychiatrist Katz has been a prominent critic of consent law in the US,[95] but other critics have pointed out that 'despite [his] position as the most prominent theorist and

---

90 For example, Jackson, 'Informed consent' to medical treatment; McLean, *Autonomy, Consent and the Law*; Maclean, *Autonomy, Informed Consent and Medical Law*; Manson and O'Neill, *Rethinking Informed Consent*; Shultz MM, From informed consent to patient choice: a new protected interest (1985) 95 Yale LJ 219–299; Twerski A and Cohen N, Informed decision making and the law of torts: the myth of justiciable causation (1988) Univ Ill L Rev 607–665.

91 Berg *et al.*, *Informed Consent*, p. 84.

92 Twerski and Cohen, Informed decision making and the law of torts.

93 Shultz, From informed consent to patient choice.

94 President's Commission for the Study of Ethical Problems in Medicine and Biomedical and Behavioral Research, *Making Health Care Decisions*, Appendix C, p. 325.

95 Katz J, Informed consent – a fairy tale? (1977) 39 Univ Pittsbg L Rev 137–174.

critic of informed consent law, he has never formulated a comprehensive legal alternative to the current system'.[96] It is, therefore, refreshing that Manson and O'Neill, and Maclean have advanced new conceptions of consent.[97] For new conceptions to make a difference, however, they have to offer more than modest increments to the huge scholarship on consent. More importantly, they should be not just intellectually stimulating ethical manna but tangible conceptions capable of enactment into the law to protect self-determination. Further, as noted earlier, it may be more productive to consider novel approaches instead of trying too hard to make the unworkable work.

Conceptual Limitations in the Consent Model

Although Manson and O'Neill say that their approach 'is not novel or unfamiliar'[98] their recent critique of consent is groundbreaking. Theirs is not merely an incremental advancement on previous ideas for ensuring that the consent model serves its intended purpose; rather, they take an original as well as a nuanced approach to the subject. They identify two 'distortions' in the way informed consent is currently conceptualised: the first is the grounding of consent in individual autonomy; the second is the framework for information and communication in consent.[99]

They criticise consent, as currently operationalised, for concentrating on the content of communication – what information is disclosed – rather than the process of communication, and propose instead 'a less exorbitant and more plausible account of consent'.[100] Successful communication, they emphasise, is the transfer of meaning and calls for intelligibility, accuracy, honesty and relevance. These attributes cannot be achieved with what Manson and O'Neill describe as the 'container-conduit' model of communication which underlies the current approach to consent.[101] This model focuses on disclosure of information: the patient makes an informed choice on the basis of this disclosure and his/her right to self-determination is thus exercised. Information is seen as content; it is reified. The emphasis on full disclosure is misplaced, because communication is context-based. What is important is not how much information is communicated but how truthful it is, how relevant and how

96 Berg *et al.*, *Informed Consent*, p. 149.

97 Manson and O'Neill, *Rethinking Informed Consent*; Maclean, *Autonomy, Informed Consent and Medical Law*.

98 Manson and O'Neill, *Rethinking Informed Consent*, p. xi.

99 Ibid.

100 Ibid., p. 25.

101 Ibid., p. 35.

responsive to the needs of the patient. Thus the container/conduit metaphor has its uses but hides the richness of communication transactions.

As an alternative to the container/conduit model, Manson and O'Neill advocate an 'agency model'.[102] This model draws on each party's background knowledge and inferential competencies. The agent-based model augments the container/conduit view by emphasising that communication is a norm-governed activity between agents. The difference between the two models is best captured in this passage:

> When information is discussed in terms of the conduit/container model, it is thought of in abstraction from agents and from the speech acts by which they communicate. When we rely on this model, we think of information as 'flowing' or being 'transferred' between agents, who are thought of quite abstractly as 'originating' or 'receiving' messages. The message or content is highlighted, but the act of communicating is hidden.[103]

By contrast, when we view informing or communicating in terms of the agency model, we focus not only on content, but also on the speech acts by which agents communicate proposals, understand others' proposals and respond to them. The agency model takes account both of what is said (the speech content) and of what is done (the speech act).[104]

From these two models, the authors derive two accounts of informed consent: a disclosure-based model which is based on full disclosure of information to the patient and 'ignores the importance of reciprocal communication', and a transactional model of consent which 'defines better the justification, scope and standards of consent'.[105]

The disclosure-based account requires that those seeking consent should disclose relevant information to those who have to decide whether or not to consent to the proposal but, according to Manson and O'Neill, hides much of what is essential to giving or refusing genuine consent.[106]

Consent is a transaction,[107] and both the person asking for consent and the person giving consent should respect the norms for successful communication. This means that doctors should communicate truth-claims that are intelligible, relevant and adequately accurate, and patients should respond in ways that are

102 Ibid., pp. 65–66.
103 Ibid., p. 46.
104 Ibid.
105 Ibid., p. 89.
106 Ibid., p. 69.
107 Ibid., p. 89.

intelligible, relevant and adequately accurate. Without these, purported consent is defective.[108]

Manson and O'Neill may be over-emphasising or exaggerating the issue of full disclosure required in the 'disclosure-for-decision-making model of consent'.[109] The law of consent in the UK does not require the provision of maximal information or oblige doctors to obtain *'fully specific or fully explicit'*[110] consent; it simply requires that sufficient information be provided to enable the patient make an informed decision,[111] and it is the court that ultimately decides what sufficient information is. All that is required for a valid consent is that the patient is able to understand in broad terms the nature and purpose of the proposed treatment.[112]

Manson and O'Neill were not the first to suggest a focus on communication rather than standards of disclosure. Referring to the problems with consent, Faden and Beauchamp suggested that:

> the solution lies not in reformulations of conventional or proposed legal disclosure standards, but rather in the adoption of a different approach to understanding informed consent – an approach that focuses more broadly on issues of communication, while dispensing with abstract and disembodied issues about proper standards of disclosure.[113]

Maclean also asserts the importance of communication, although as discussed above, he distinguishes between consent itself and the process of obtaining consent:

> ...consent must be placed in the context of the professional-patient relationship and ... the approach to consent helps define that relationship. A good relationship requires mutual trust and respect, which includes an obligation to respect the other's autonomy.[114] This mutual respect requires open and honest communication allowing both parties to play their role within the relationship. If healthcare professionals are to respect their patients' autonomy, they must believe that the patient is consenting before they act. This belief can only be reliably achieved by communication of the consent.[115]

108 Ibid., pp. 84–94.
109 Ibid., p. 90.
110 Ibid., p. xi.
111 *Sidaway* v. *Board of Governors of the Bethlem Royal Hospital* [1985] AC 871.
112 *Chatterton* v. *Gerson* [1981] QB 432, at 443.
113 Faden and Beauchamp, *History and Theory of Informed Consent*, pp. 300–307.
114 This point is emphasised in the discussion of medical professionalism below.
115 MacLean, *Autonomy, Informed Consent and Medical Law*, p. 120.

Professional bodies also acknowledge that there is more to consent than simply providing loads of information. The guidance and standards set by professional bodies for obtaining consent are consistent with Manson and O'Neill's transactional model.[116] The British Medical Association states that '[i]nformation is useful only if it is provided in a manner that is accessible and intelligible to the patient, and is given at a pace at which the recipient can understand'.[117] It also says that 'consent is not a one-off event, but involves a process of information giving and explanation that facilitates informed decision making'.[118] This followed a report of a working party which concluded that:

> Greater emphasis needs to be placed on the initial explanation given to the patient, with provision for continuing opportunity for discussion in order that the patient can raise any concerns and/or questions.[119]

It is important that the patient understands the information provided by the doctor, and the transactional approach facilitates understanding. An alliterative demonstration of what amounts to a transactional model as proposed by Manson and O'Neill can be found in Clements' exhortation:

> To communicate choice effectively, we must first listen so as to gather data, so as to understand the patient and to develop a rapport and be able to respond to the patient's emotional needs. Communication in this context consists of:
>
> Engaging;
> Empathising;
> Educating;
> Enlisting.
>
> *Engaging* with the patient includes greeting and introduction, seating and body language, history taking, and determining her expectations.
>
> *Empathising* means having imagination for the needs of others 'To know what kind of person has a disease is as essential as to know what kind of disease a patient has'.
>
> *Education* includes the imparting of technical information in a form and in language the patient can readily understand.

116 British Medical Association, *Medical Ethics Today*; General Medical Council, *Consent*.

117 British Medical Association, *Medical Ethics Today*, p. 76.

118 Ibid., p. 73.

119 British Medical Association, *Report of the Consent Working Party: Incorporating Consent Tool Kit*. London: BMA 2001, Recommendation 2.

> Finally *enlisting*: only at this point in the interview does the clinician ask the patient to exercise choice and to indicate which treatment is preferred. It will always be appropriate to record that decision.[120]

The main objections to the disclosure model are that the subjective needs of the patient are subjugated and that the patient is exposed to the risk of cognitive overload, both of which are inimical to self-determination. Some critics are concerned that full disclosure leads to some patients unnecessarily refusing treatment and suffering unnecessary anxiety and sometimes dying as a result of untreated disease[121] but, as discussed earlier, this claim gives a nod to paternalism.

The difficulty in establishing what constitutes the optimal amount of information, as discussed in Chapter 3, bedevils the legal doctrine of informed consent. In the United States, ever-increasing amounts of information are being off-loaded onto patients and there is evidence that this information overload detracts from the value of consent.[122] The response of the patient to varying quantity, quality and formatting of information has been likened to the logarithmic dose-response relationship[123] seen in pharmacology: disclosure of too much information results in drowning of the message.[124]

Schwartz and Bergus pose the question:

> Because human beings have cognitive limitations on the amount of information they can process, informed consent processes can present only a subset of the information available about the trial interventions without overwhelming patients – which subset should be selected?[125]

These observations all underscore the need to shift focus from *amount of information disclosed* to ensuring that the patient has *adequate understanding* of the information that has been provided.

---

120 Clements, Informed choice, p. 69.

121 Kittay EF, Beyond autonomy and paternalism: the transparent caring self. In Nys T, Denier Y and Vandevelde T, *Autonomy & Paternalism: Reflections on the Theory and Practice of Health Care*. Leuven: Peeters 2007.

122 Faden and Beauchamp, *History and Theory of Informed Consent*, p. 324.

123 When the dose of drug exceeds the therapeutic range, no additional therapeutic effect is achieved and there may be adverse effects or harm from the excess dose.

124 Lynoe N and Hoeyer K, Quantitative aspects of informed consent: considering the dose response curve when estimating quantity of information (2005) 31 J Med Ethics 736–738.

125 Schwartz A and Bergus G, *Medical Decision Making: A Physician's Guide*. Cambridge: Cambridge University Press 2008, p. 184.

The General Medical Council exhorts doctors: 'You should check that the patient understands the terms that you use, particularly when describing the seriousness, frequency and likelihood of an adverse outcome.'[126]

Simpson also would like to see more emphasis on patient understanding than on physician disclosure.[127] The physician would have the burden of *ensuring* that the patient understands the information disclosed. Clearly such a prescriptive obligation, if regulatory, could work against patients' interests, as a doctor will not proceed with treatment if he has no way of being absolutely certain that the patient understands the information that has been provided. In any case, legal enforcement of such an obligation could be impracticable. What is legally enforceable is a requirement that doctors should be seen to have made a reasonable attempt to check that the patient understands information that has been given – in other words, that they have complied with the guidance given by their regulator, the General Medical Council.

The problem remains that efforts to make consent absolutely protective of patient self-determination could potentially mean that actual patient medical care is compromised. Furthermore, some argue, despite the importance of self-determination, that it may be that some patients want or need a measure of paternalism and it is possible that the courts will recognise this.[128] This is the position taken by critics who stress that the enforcement of the legal doctrine of consent should not cause patient harm instead of improving well-being.[129] These critics believe that many patients are unable to handle medical information in a way that results in meaningful decisions. They also say that patients often make decisions with very little reference to the information they have been given.[130]

If emphasis shifts from simply providing information to ensuring that the patient understands what has been said, then more attention will be focused on communication skills, on the way information is provided and on checking that the patient understands the meaning and implication of the information provided – just as would normally be the case in a property transaction. Emphasis on understanding is a central element of the *social construction theory* of consent:

> … decisions may involve a process of voluntariness or unwillingness, with complex desires and resistances. Desires and feelings can confuse understanding

126 General Medical Council, *Consent*, p. 11.

127 Simpson, R. Informed consent: from disclosure to patient participation in medical decision making (1981) 76 Northwest Univ L Rev 172–207.

128 Komrad MS, A defence of medical paternalism: maximising patients' autonomy (1983) 9 J Med Ethics 38–44.

129 Berg *et al.*, *Informed Consent*, p. 152.

130 Ibid.

> but also enrich it. Initially, patients often want to reject dangerous, unpleasant treatments. Before they can willingly consent, they have to journey from fear of the treatment into greater fear of the untreated condition, with growing trust in their health carers …
>
> Positivism tends to see patients' abilities as fixed personal attributes. Social construction sees them partly as responses in relationships, influenced by the professionals' abilities to explain, respect, and support.[131]

One of the implications of placing emphasis on the quality of *communication* in consent, in other words accepting the transactional approach, is that more attention will be paid to the obligations of both parties to the transaction – doctor and patient. As mentioned above, the consent model tends to focus on the obligations of the doctor while saying very little about the obligations and responsibility of the patient. In Chapter 9 I will explore the potential of the property model for achieving the right balance of rights and obligations between patients and doctors.

Manson and O'Neill's observations on the disclosure model and argument for a transactional approach are important. Indeed these reach to the roots of the principle of self-determination. It appears, however, that they apply to Categories 2 and 3 paradigms of consent, not necessarily to Category 1 consent. One of the criticisms levelled against Category 1 conceptions of consent is that they demand too much subjectivity, so it would be paradoxical if these conceptions were to subscribe to, or support, disclosure of large amounts of irrelevant and incomprehensible information. A lot of what the two scholars offer is new but, as shown above, closer scrutiny shows that quite a bit of what they suggest is reaffirmation of suggestions previously expressed by others within and outside ethics.

There are other criticisms of the model proposed by Manson and O'Neill. Maclean says that while Manson and O'Neill prioritise consent as communication, they do so primarily by focusing on the obligations of the health-care professional, which in turn means that attention shifts back to disclosure and truthful disclosure rather than to interaction between both parties.[132] He also makes the point that Manson and O'Neill have not addressed how their model would work in practice, given the institutional constraints (such as those discussed above, I presume) 'that have caused the liberal model of consent to mutate into a consumerist caricature'.[133] Incidentally it is this caricature that

131 Alderson and Goodey, Theories of consent, pp. 1313–1314.

132 Maclean, *Autonomy, Informed Consent and Medical Law*, p. 228.

133 Ibid., p. 229.

Manson and O'Neill mistake for the true model in their rethinking of consent, as I have discussed above.

Some of the criticism of the Manson/O'Neill account is, arguably, either unfair or based on wrong conclusions. For example, Maclean jumps to a wrong conclusion when he says that 'their assertion that autonomy is not the ethical justification for consent … means that they are not concerned with whether the person makes a good decision'.[134] The fact is that in their book and its forerunner, O'Neill's *Autonomy and Trust in Bioethics*,[135] it is argued that there should be no ethical justification for individual decision-making without taking account of the outcome (i.e. whether it is good or bad) of the decision.

Maclean's relational consent, another effort to overcome perceived shortcomings of the consent model, shares some attributes with the genuine consent model proposed by Manson and O'Neill.[136] Notably, both parties emphasise the importance of communication and context in consent transactions. They differ in their conceptual foundations, however, because while the latter dismiss the justification of consent based on autonomy, the former asserts autonomy as the primary justification.[137] The core element of Maclean's model seems to be that the agency and obligations of both the doctor and the patient are brought into play. This is based on the assumption that the libertarian model and the Manson/O'Neill model fail to find the right balance between agency and obligations in respect of both doctor and patient. In this model, consent is a permissive state of mind that waives the right to bodily integrity and can be denoted as $\text{consent}_{\text{P}}$.[138] The process leading to $\text{consent}_{\text{P}}$ includes *negotiation* or shared decision-making between doctor and patient, during which each party respects the other's autonomy. Following negotiation, *agreement* is reached between both parties, and this can be denoted as $\text{consent}_{\text{A}}$. The patient then gives permission, $\text{consent}_{\text{P.}}$ The signalling of $\text{consent}_{\text{P}}$ is an event distinct from, but integrated with, the process leading to it.

Any proposed alternative to the current conception of consent should not only have the potential of providing enhanced protection of self-determination, but should also ideally not be any more complex than what already exists. As it is, there is enough confusion about the meaning and scope of consent, and adding complexity will not make it easier to implement respect for self-determination. So when Maclean says that 'consent as agreement, while not an essential part of the theory of consent, should be incorporated as an attribute [of consent]',[139] he introduces ambiguity and complexity that make

134 Ibid., p. 228.

135 O'Neill, *Autonomy and Trust in Bioethics.*

136 Maclean, *Autonomy, Informed Consent and Medical Law.*

137 Ibid., p. 232.

138 Ibid., p. 113.

139 Ibid., p. 142.

his model susceptible to misinterpretation in clinical practice. If doctors don't know enough about consent as currently described by the law,[140] what are the prospects that they will distinguish clearly between consent as agreement and consent as permission, within one transaction? In any case, if agreement needs to be 'incorporated' why is it not part of the theory of consent? And if agreement is not essential, should negotiation be part of the process – surely the expectation when negotiations begin is that agreement can, should or will be reached. Expectations may differ, so the stage is set for conflict even before negotiation starts. If agreement is not reached, this could have an effect on trust in the relationship, and the negotiation may turn out to be an ill-afforded waste of time. It is difficult to imagine that negotiation does much for protection of patient self-determination in a situation where the informational (and often social) gradient between the parties is steep.

The problems associated with negotiation are accentuated by the model's advocacy of persuasion. The situation where the doctor may think of persuading a patient is when the patient's decision is different from the doctor's preference. What professionalism and respect for self-determination require in this situation is not for the doctor to persuade the patient but for him/her to explore the ramifications and implications of the decision and then leave it to the patient to make an informed choice. Anything more than this would be open to abuse – there is no sharp demarcation of where persuasion ends and coercion begins.

For the reasons outlined above, it is concluded that Maclean's approach to consent is too complex to find ready implementation in clinical and legal practice.

Conclusions

There are difficulties in translating the theoretical principles of consent into clinical practice: 'standard accounts of informed consent, standard arguments for requiring consent in clinical and research practice and standard ways of implementing consent requirements lead to intractable problems'.[141] These difficulties have resulted in an operational model of consent that differs from the theoretical model and which suffers the deficiencies that Manson and O'Neill have identified. From the medico-legal point of view, the value of the Manson/O'Neill conception of consent (or any other) will, however, be measured by the extent to which it finds application in the law. Applying their model in law may not be easy and the authors themselves have given an

140 Heywood *et al.*, Informed consent in hospital practice.

141 Manson and O'Neill, *Rethinking Informed Consent in Bioethics*, p. viii.

eloquent bioethical treatise, but relatively little idea of implementation in law and in clinical practice.

A working party of the British Medical Association stated in 2001 that 'the whole process of obtaining patient consent must be thoroughly reassessed'.[142] Manson and O'Neill have tried to do that, as has Maclean. In doing so they sought a radical departure from prevailing approaches. I would argue, however, that while their efforts are rich in intellectual content, they are too complex for application in clinical practice and for implementation in law. Perhaps it is time to consider alternative models to the consent model. In the following chapters, a fresh approach – property analysis – is examined as an alternative framework for protecting patient self-determination.

142 British Medical Association, *Report of the Consent Working Party*, Recommendation 2.

Chapter 6
Property and Proprietary Rights

> The meaning of 'property' varies according to its function in a particular context, and so we might conclude that it simply has no general meaning.[1]

> Property is a socially constructed concept; and former perceptions of property as a monopolistic right of control and exploitation have long since been eroded by wider conceptions of the public good.[2]

What is Property?

The first step in propounding a property approach is to be clear what we mean by property, but this is a first step on slippery ground for, as Gray and Gray put it, '[f]ew concepts are quite so fragile, so elusive and so often misused as the notion of property'.[3] As with autonomy, property is not a monolithic concept. It is arguable that property has no general meaning.[4] Property may be defined in layperson's terms and in economic, social and legal terms. To the layperson, property is tangible – land, house, car, book and so on. In the economic sense property is a means of distributing wealth. In the social sense property is a means of protecting liberty and autonomy – for example, the child asserting its identity by proclaiming that a toy is theirs. In this book we are concerned primarily with property in the legal sense of the word. However, the legal and social dimensions of property sit by side:

> Countless assumptions and claims are informed by the idea of property without reference to official agencies of the law. Furthermore the open-ended nature of many proprietary principles entails that, even when embodied in law, their official interpretation and implementation often interact with current social understandings of them.[5]

---

1 Allen T, *The Right to Property in Commonwealth Constitutions*. Cambridge: Cambridge University Press 2000, p. 119.

2 Gray K and Gray SF, *Land Law*, 5th edn. Oxford: Oxford University Press 2007, p. 32.

3 Ibid., p. 27.

4 Allen, *Right to Property*.

5 Harris JW, *Property and Justice*. Oxford: Oxford University Press 1996, p. 4.

The social dimension to the legal meaning of property is expressed in Demsetz's affirmation that '[i]n the world of Robinson Crusoe property rights play no role'[6] and in similar imagery by Underkuffler:

> The idea of a man's coconuts being his property makes no sense if he is stranded, irrevocably, on an uninhabited island; property has meaning only when human relations, or conflicting claims among people, are at stake.[7]

This point is expanded by Gold:

> … it is no good for me to claim ownership of a pen against the demands of a martian because the martian does not live by and under the rules imposed by our society. The pen is an instantiation of a norm – the exclusive rights of use and possession – that we, as members of this society at this time, have agreed or acquiesced in following. When we grant property rights to each other – assuming that we grant property rights for certain nonarbitrary reasons – we do so on the basis of one or more ways of valuing the object or the individual to whom we grant the rights. That is, the determination of who should get which rights to which object depends on how we, in society, value the object – as beautiful, as a luxury, or as a commodity – and the recipient of the right – as deserving, as having highly developed tastes, or as a consumer.[8]

This social dimension to the legal concept of property, the idea that we consider property not in isolation but in the context of the owner's relationships with others, parallels the observation made in Chapter 2 that the individual's right to self-determination exists not in a vacuum but in the context of relationships with other persons. This is the contextual emphasis that is captured by the ecology paradigm adopted in Chapter 1.

An underlying reason for (or perhaps a consequence of) the looseness of definitions in this subject is that the legal theory of property is dynamic. As Gray puts it, 'the definition of "property" is constantly on the move'.[9] In the same vein, Grubb states that 'the categories of property are never closed or static and shift with societal norms'.[10] Matthews proclaimed that:

6 Demsetz H, Toward a theory of property rights (1967) 57 Am Econ Rev 347–359.

7 Underkuffler LS, *The Idea of Property: Its Meaning and Power.* Oxford: Oxford University Press 2003, pp. 11–12.

8 Gold ER, *Body Parts: Property Rights and the Ownership of Human Biological Materials.* Washington DC: Georgetown University Press 1998, p. 3.

9 Gray K, *Elements of Land Law*, 2nd edn. London: Butterworths 1993, p. 927.

10 Grubb A, 'I, me, mine': bodies, parts and property (1998) 3 Med Law Int'l 299–317, at p. 316.

> the ambit of 'property' had broken its bounds, and there was no stopping it. Debts … became 'property', governed by the same principles. So did rights of action. Intellectual property was invented, and subsumed into the property framework. Shares in companies, confidential information and goodwill, all were taken under the property wing. In the twentieth century we see energy as property, and other forms of information, and maybe personality and image as well.[11]

Property as a Thing

The popular perception of property is that it is a 'thing'.[12] This perception, the reified notion of property, dates back to two centuries ago when William Blackstone described property rights as comprising:

> that sole or despotic dominion which one man claims and exercises over the external things of the world, in total exclusion of the right of any other individual in the universe.[13]

In contemporary society hardly anyone would argue that property confers absolute dominion. Property rights are subject to restrictions, for example, on what may be built where, and how the rights may or may not be enjoyed. This is more fully discussed later in this chapter.

A century ago, Strahan affirmed that property must be a physical object and categorically stated that debts, patent and copyright were not property.[14] At about the same time, however, Madison[15] produced this insightful conception of property:

> In the former sense, a man's land, or merchandize [*sic*] or money is called his property.
>
> In the latter sense, a man has property in his opinions and the free communication of them.
>
> He has a property of peculiar value in his opinions and the free communication of them.

11 Matthews P, The man of property (1995) 3 Med L Rev 251–274, at pp. 253–254.

12 Gray, *Elements of Land Law*; Grubb, 'I, me, mine'.

13 Blackstone W, *Commentaries on the Laws of England*. Chicago: University of Chicago Press, facsimile edn, 1979, II, p. 2.

14 Strahan JA, *Law of Property*, 3rd edn. London: Stevens & Sons 1901, p. 3.

15 Fourth President of the United States of America.

> He has property of peculiar value in his religious opinions and in the profession and practice dictated by them …
>
> He has property very dear to him in the safety and liberty of his person.
>
> He has an equal property in the free use of his faculties and free choice of the objects on which to employ them.
>
> In a word, as a man is said to have a right to his property, he may be equally said to have property in his rights.[16]

Despite the long existence of this broader concept of property, there are scholars who still uphold the narrower definition of property as a thing.[17] While Gray asserts that property is not a thing but a concentration of power over things (see below),[18] Penner maintains that 'property is what the average citizen … thinks it is: the right to a thing'.[19] He argues that the concept of property as a bundle of rights (i.e. not as a thing but as defining the relationship between two persons) lies at the root of property's identity crisis; it falls short of defining a particular legal relation and is not helpful to judges. For example, he asks, which of the rights in the bundle are essential, and are a critical number of rights essential?

He cautions against defining property in isolation:

> … property is a creature of its environment, the legal system. We make a mistake if we think we can just wrestle it to the ground, take its measurements and fingerprints, and set it on its way again, satisfied that we have done all we need to understand it. We must be ecologists, and see how it behaves in its environment, interacting with its fellow creatures. But we cannot go too far in the opposite extreme, either. Property is not just its interaction with others. If we are inattentive to the categories themselves, these interactions may make us lose a sense of where property ends and other legal concepts begin.[20]

In this quotation, Penner basically reiterates his point referred to earlier in this chapter, that the social and legal dimensions of property are intertwined. By warning of the consequences of going 'too far in the opposite extreme', he draws attention to the need for a conceptual framework which defines property in the legal sense.

---

16 Quoted in Underkuffler LS. On property: an essay (1990) 100 Yale LJ 127–148, at p. 135. Original citation: J Madison, Property. In *The Writings of James Madison*, ed. Hunt G, New York: GP Putnam's Sons 1906, vol 6, p. 101.

17 Penner JE, *The Idea of Property in Law*. Oxford: Oxford University Press 1997.

18 Gray, *Elements of Land Law*.

19 Penner, *Idea of Property in Law*, p. 2.

20 Ibid., p. 3.

Penner's advice that to understand property we must be ecologists echoes the ecology paradigm chosen for this book in Chapter 1. He associates property with a right to things, this right being defined by the 'exclusion thesis: the right to property is a right to exclude others from things which is grounded by the interest we have in the use of things'.[21] In his view, it is the concept of exclusion, not use, which is central to the definition of property:

> The right to property is thus a right to a liberty, the liberty to dispose of the things one owns as one wishes within a general sphere of protection. It is not the right to any particular use, benefit, or result from the use of property. The duty in rem of property correlates with the right to a liberty to dispose of property, not to a specific right in the value of property, or a right to any goal one may set on one's use of it, and so on.[22]

Penner supports this view by referring to the court's position in common law when faced with claims to property in news, events or information. In such cases the court does not ask whether the claimant has the *right* effectively to exclude the putative trespasser from the supposed property; rather, it asks whether the putative trespasser has a *duty* to exclude himself from it.

If property is a thing and property rights are rights to things, what 'things' can be property? Penner provides an answer in the separability thesis which he expresses as follows:

> Only those 'things' in the world which are contingently associated with any particular owner may be objects of poverty; as a function of the nature of this contingency, in theory nothing of normative consequence beyond the fact that the ownership has changed occurs when an object of property is alienated to another.[23]

In other words, '[t]o be conceived of as an object of property a thing must first be considered as separable and distinct from (i.e. "contingently associated" with) any person who might hold it, and is for that reason rightly regarded as alienable'.[24] Thus, our talents, personality, eyesight and friendships cannot be property. Similarly, rights such as the right to marry cannot be property rights – because they are not separable from the person. A taxi licence is property because it is freely alienable but a licence to practise medicine is not property

21 Ibid., p. 71.
22 Ibid., p. 73.
23 Ibid., p. 111.
24 Ibid., p. 113.

because it is not separable from the holder.[25] Applying this thesis to body parts, it could be argued that one's kidney is not property while it is *in vivo*, but becomes property when it has been removed from the body. On the same analogy, sperm would be an object of property once it had been ejaculated. In the same vein, the patient's right to self-determination cannot be property, since it is not separable from the patient.

Penner's analysis helps to clarify various attributes of property but is unlikely to withstand the tide of change that has been creating new objects of property, many of which are not tangible things.

In English law, property is classified as real or personal.[26] Real property is land. Personal property (or personalty) is all the property that is left once real property has been subtracted. Personal property may be chattels real (principally leasehold interests in land) or chattels personal (all other personal property). Chattels personal are divided into choses in possession and choses in action.

Choses in possession are tangible, movable things, and are called 'goods' when they are the subject of a sale. Proprietary interests in tangible personal property are defined in terms of possession and ownership, but these terms are not well defined. Proudhon ventures a comparison: 'a lover is a possessor, the husband a proprietor'.[27] A possessor may have property rights but no ownership. Proudhon states that the right in a thing (jus in re) rests with the possessor, but one does not have to be in possession to have the right to a thing (jus ad rem).[28] In contemporary law, the gap between personal and proprietary entitlement appears to be narrowing, and it has been suggested that human rights law bridges the gap between the two. The provisions of the European Convention on Human Rights relating to liberty and security (Article 5) and to private and family life and home (Article 8)[29] have legal implications for what can or cannot be done with realty, so, Gray and Gray argue, could be seen 'as creative of new forms of proprietary entitlement'.[30]

Unlike choses in possession, choses in action are intangible and cannot be physically possessed. Examples of choses in action are debts, shares in companies and intellectual property. According to Holdsworth, the term was originally used to cover rights associated with a personal action, such as trespass;

25 In a marital case (*Caratun* v. *Caratun*, [1992] OJ No. 1982), the Ontario Court of Appeal ruled that a dental licence was not property because, among other reasons, it was not transferable.

26 Bridge M, *Personal Property Law*, 3rd edn. Oxford: Oxford University Press 2002, pp. 1–13.

27 Proudhon P-J, *What is Property?*, ed and trans Kelly DR and Smith BG, Cambridge Texts in the History of Political Thought. Cambridge: Cambridge University Press 1993, p. 36.

28 Ibid.

29 Council of Europe, *European Convention on Human Rights as amended by Protocols Nos. 11 and 14*. Council of Europe Treaty Series, No 5. Strasbourg: Council of Europe 2010.

30 Gray and Gray, *Land Law*, p. 46.

only later was it applied to real action.[31] In the sixteenth century, choses in action 'were extended from a right to bring an action to the documents which were necessary evidence of such a right'[32] – so bonds and, later, stocks, insurance policies and similar intangibles became choses in action.

A chose in action is a property interest that can be enforced only through legal action (not by taking physical possession). Over a century ago, it was argued that a right of action in tort could be regarded as a chose in action.[33] In Chapters 8 and 9 it will be argued that the patient's right to self-determination can be protected as a chose in action.

Property as Commodity

Some commentators portray property not only as a thing but as something that can be bought and sold in a market. Steinbock describes this attribute as 'a very important element of property'.[34] However, while property may have this element, this is not necessarily or inevitably the case. Giving a dissenting judgment in the US case of *International News Service* v. *Associated Press*, Justice Brandeis said that the fact that a product had a value for which others were willing to pay was not sufficient to endow it with the legal attribute of property.[35]

Steinbock appears to be taking property as synonymous with commodity (something that can be turned to commercial or other advantage). In fact, property is sometimes *but not always* a commodity. This distinction is germane to any consideration of body or body parts as property. Some judges have dismissed property claims on the basis of inalienability of the object being claimed.[36] Radin, on the other hand, discounts the notion that market alienability is inherent in the concept of property.[37]

In *National Provincial Bank Ltd* v. *Ainsworth*, Lord Wilberforce described the hallmarks of a property right, stating that it must be 'definable, identifiable by third parties, capable in its nature of assumption by third parties, and have some degree of permanence or stability'.[38] This may have been helpful in distinguishing between property and personal rights, but it promotes the

31 Holdsworth WS, The history of the treatment of 'choses' in action by the common law (1920) 33 Harvard L Rev 997–1030.

32 Ibid., p. 1011.

33 Williams TC, Is a right of action in tort a chose in action? (1894) 10 LQR 143.

34 Steinbock B, Sperm as property. In Harris J and Holm S (eds), *The Future of Human Reproduction*. Oxford: Clarendon Press 1998, pp. 151–161, at p. 153.

35 *International News Service* v. *Associated Press* 248 US 215 (1918).

36 *Caratun* v. *Caratun* (1992) 96 DLR (4th) 404; In re Marriage of Graham 574 P.2d 75 (1978).

37 Radin M, Property and personhood (1982) 34 Stan L Rev 957.

38 *National Provincial Bank Ltd* v. *Ainsworth* (1965) AC 1175, at 1247–1248.

obsolete image of property as something merchantable. Property need not necessarily be alienable, nor does it have to be tangible.

Academic and judicial thinking that requires that an object be alienable in order to be regarded as property predates the biotechnology boom. In today's world, property does not have to be alienable – so the right to sufficient information and to make one's own informed decision cannot be excluded from the class of property simply on account of its inalienability. This right has assumed such high premium in contemporary western society that it arguably deserves the protection traditionally afforded to property.

It is arguable whether a core attribute of property is value; we would not usually attribute property rights to something that society does not value. To borrow a good illustration, a dead leaf fallen from a tree is not property but an accumulation of leaves in a compost pile is property.[39] On the other hand, Moses argues that '[q]uestions of value will affect whether anyone cares that something is classified as property, but value ought not be treated as essential to the very concept of property'.[40]

Generally, the more valuable the object becomes, the more precisely the property rights associated with it are defined and the more vigorously these rights are exercised. This is illustrated by the growing propertiness[41]of intellectual property.[42] This core attribute of property underlies Proudhon's famous assertion that 'property is theft':[43] property rights or interests protect value; that which has no value cannot be property or object of property rights. The multitudinous perception of property in everyday discourse, however, led Gray to say that:

> Proudhon got it all wrong. Property is not theft – it is fraud. Few other legal notions operate such gross or systematic deception. Before long I will have sold you a piece of thin air and you will have called it property. But the ultimate fact about property is that it does not really exist: it is mere illusion. It is a vacant concept – oddly enough rather like thin air.[44]

---

39 Dickens BM, Preface to Nwabueze RN, *Biotechnology and the Challenge of Property: Property Rights in Dead Bodies, Body Parts, and Genetic Information*. Aldershot: Ashgate 2007, p. vii.

40 Moses LB, The applicability of property law in new contexts: from cells to cyberspace (2008) 30 Sydney L Rev 639–662, at p. 650.

41 A word increasingly used in property law, referring to the spectrum of attributes that is used to characterise an object as property.

42 Menell PS, *The Property Rights Movement's Embrace of Intellectual Property: True Love or Doomed Relationship?* (February 2007). UC Berkeley Public Law Research Paper No 965083. Available at SSRN: http://ssrn.com/abstract=965083. Accessed 19 October 2012.

43 Proudhon, *What is Property?*, p. 13.

44 Gray K, Property in thin air (1991) 50 Cambridge LJ 252–307, at p. 252.

Property as Relationship with a Thing

Another approach to property is to see it not as a thing but as a relationship between a person and a thing. Some theorists, notably Margaret Radin, see property as forming part of our personality and social relationships.[45] According to Radin's 'property for personhood' theory, the control that one has over environmental resources is part of one's personality. Property for personhood defines a relationship that is essential to self-identification. She distinguishes between personal property (property that is bound up with a person) and fungible property (property that is held purely instrumentally). The former 'could be described as simply a category of property for personal autonomy or liberty',[46] and, she argues, should have greater legal protection. A wedding ring in a jeweller's shop is fungible property but a wedding ring on the finger of a loving wearer is personal property because it is constitutive of the wearer's personality. Extending that analogy, the body is personal property because it is also constitutive of the individual's personality. She goes on to say '[t]his line of thinking leads to a property theory for the tort of assault and battery: Interference with my body is interference with my personal property'.[47]

As will be seen in Chapter 7, this idea of property is used in arguments about commodification of the body. A weakness of the theory is that personality is defined in terms of a relationship with objects rather than a relationship with other persons.

Property as Rights against Others or Rights in, to or over a Thing

In everyday conversation, we usually speak of 'property' rather than 'property rights' but the contraction is misleading if it tends to make us think of property as things rather than as rights. A more modern view sees property not as a thing or a relationship between a person and a thing, but as rights against others, in or over things.[48] In other words, property can be seen as defining the obligations of persons with respect to a tangible or intangible object. When viewed in these terms – that is, property seen in terms of rights against others, rather than as a thing of commercial value – the concept of property rights in the human body would seem to have a more acceptable face. Intangibles to which property rights or interests have been attributed in contemporary discourse include

45 Radin MJ, *Reinterpreting Property*. Chicago: Chicago University Press 1993.

46 Ibid., p. 37

47 Ibid., p. 41.

48 Underkuffler, *The Idea of Property*.

welfare benefits,[49] franchises,[50] whiteness,[51] racial identity,[52] personhood,[53] university degrees[54] and air space.[55] Some have gone further to say that property establishes a legal relationship between persons, not necessarily with reference to things.[56]

A property interest indicates not necessarily that the holder owns something, but that someone owes him an obligation. Unlike contractual rights, which are enforceable against a particular person or persons (rights *in personam*), property rights are enforceable against the whole world (rights *in rem*). Rights against others can be seen as negative rights,[57] as expressed in Matthews' view of property:

> The common law sees property as essentially negative, the right to exclude others from something, or from some aspect of something. This negative right may be absolute, as for example 'This is my pen'. I can exclude everyone from everything in relation to it. Or it may be limited – even isolated as in for example 'I have a right to light over (your) land'. I can prevent you from building in a certain way on your land. Sometimes the negativity imposes a positive obligation on another person, as in 'You owe me £10'.[58]

The concept of property as rights against others owes its place in the annals of property law to the seminal work of Wesley Hohfeld.[59] He described four types of 'right': claim rights (A has a claim upon B and B has a reciprocal duty to A); liberty rights (A has the freedom to act in a certain manner or to enjoy a facility if he so desires, free of encumbrance from B, C or D); powers (A is statutorily empowered to act in a particular way); and immunities (A is 'immune' from the powers of B). It has been pointed out that these categories of rights are not mutually exclusive. Thus, A's rights to a particular property could include a claim right restraining B from using that property without A's permission, a

49 Reich CA, The new property (1964) 73 Yale LJ 733–787.

50 Ibid.

51 Harris CI, Whiteness as property (1993) 106 Harvard L Rev 1709–1791.

52 Chen J, Embryonic thoughts on racial identity as new property (1997) 68 Univ Colorado L Rev 1123.

53 Radin, Property and personhood.

54 *Woodworth* v. *Woodworth* (1983) 337 NW2d 332.

55 Gray K, Property in thin air; *Bernstein* v. *Skyviews & Gen* (1978) QB 479.

56 Vandevelde KJ, The new property of the nineteenth century: the development of the modern concept of property (1980) 29 Buffalo L Rev 325–367; Arnold C, The reconstitution of property: property as a web of interests (2002) 26 Harv Envtl L Rev 281–364.

57 In Chapter 7, I reiterate the point that property rights could generate positive claims.

58 Matthews, Man of property, p. 252.

59 Hohfeld WN, *Fundamental Legal Conceptions as Applied in Judicial Reasoning*, ed. Cook WW. New Haven: Yale University Press 1919. Reprint 1946.

liberty right allowing A to freely use the property, the power to sell the property, and immunity from the power of B to arbitrarily dispose of the property. Claim rights are categorised as 'positive' or 'negative'. Positive claim rights require an act of commission from the duty-bound party. For example, a right to be consulted before disposal of one's cryopreserved gametes is a positive right. On the other hand, negative claim rights simply require non-interference. Applying this to the doctor–patient relationship, it can be said that the patient has a negative claim right on the doctor not to be treated without his/her permission, or a positive claim right on the doctor to obtain his/her permission before proceeding with treatment. The patient who opts to die rather than undergo an amputation may be said to be exercising a liberty right which allows him/her to manage his/her body in the way deemed fit.

Honore utilised the Hohfeldian classification of rights as a framework to define ownership of property.[60] Ownership is established by the presence of a clutch of 'incidents', including the claim rights to possess, use, manage and receive income; the powers to transfer and exclude, the liberty to consume or destroy; immunity from expropriation; the duty not to use harmfully. The 'bundle of rights' definition of property is rather broad and does not distinguish between legal ownership and beneficial ownership as applies when items of property are held on trust. It also leaves open the categories of tangible and intangible things that could be objects of property, and some core attributes or rules could help restrain the subject. Grubb describes three such rules that define a proprietary relationship: *user entitlements* (which allow a person to exploit or enjoy the thing), *exclusionary control* (which prevents others from dealing with it) and *dispositional liberties* (which allow him to transfer it by gift, selling or other means).[61]

A different approach to defining 'the "propertiness" of property' is taken by Gray for whom the key criterion is 'excludability':

> … a resource can be propertised only if it is … excludable … [It] is excludable only if it is feasible for a legal person to exercise regulatory control over the access of strangers to the various benefits inherent in the resource.[62]

He goes on to say that a resource may be non-excludable for physical, legal or moral reasons, and a resource cannot be propertised if, on any of these grounds, it lacks the quality of excludability:

60 Honore AM, Ownership. In Guest AD (ed), *Oxford Essays in Jurisprudence* (First Series). Oxford: Clarendon Press 1961. Reprinted in Honore, Tony, *Making Law Bind: Essays Legal and Philosophical.* Oxford: Clarendon Press 1987, pp. 161–192.

61 Grubb, I, me, mine, p. 301.

62 Gray, Property in thin air, p. 268.

> … 'property' resides not in consumption of benefits but in control over benefits. 'Property' is not about *enjoyment of access* but about *control over access*. 'Property' is the power-relation constituted by the state's endorsement of private claims to regulate the access of strangers to the benefits of particular resources. If, in respect of a given claimant and a given resource, the exercise of such regulatory control is physically impracticable or legally abortive or morally or socially undesirable, we say that such a claimant can assert no 'property' in that resource and for that matter can lose no 'property' in it either. Herein lies an important key to the 'propertiness' of property.[63]

If property is about control over access, then the right to bodily integrity can be regarded as a property right. It is not morally, socially or legally undesirable for persons to have control over their body so, on Gray's analysis, a person can assert property rights over their body. In the context of doctor–patient communication, 'control over access' should entail being in a position to make an informed decision based on adequate information about the diagnosis or proposed treatment. Control over access should manifest as having the final say about whether information should be provided. The patient may not wish to know the diagnosis or the risks of treatment, and can exercise his/her right to self-determination by asking the doctor not to disclose this information. Thus the patient, in property terms, retains control over access, and his/her property right – or the right to self-determination – is upheld.

More recently, Gray has (with his co-author) described property as being 'not a *thing* but a *power relationship* – a power relationship of social and legal legitimacy existing between a person and a valued resource (whether tangible or intangible)'.[64] They further characterise property as not only a relationship but also one of socially approved control:

> Once property is recognised as a relationship of socially approved control, it becomes infinitely more accurate to say that one has property *in* a thing rather than to declare that something is one's *property*. To claim 'property' in a resource is, in effect, to assert a strategically important degree of control over that resource. 'Property' is simply the word used to describe particular concentrations of *power over* things and resources, and every claim of 'property' comprises the assertion of some *quantum* (or amount) of socially permissible power as exercisable in respect of some socially valued resource. The implications of this perspective are significant.[65]

63 Ibid., p. 294.

64 Gray and Gray, *Land Law*, p. 29.

65 Ibid., p. 30.

This description captures to an extent an underpinning concept of this book: while property is commonly viewed as a thing, as something tangible, it is more helpful to see it as the relationship between two or more parties with respect to a tangible or intangible object which has social value. While this distinction is important for our purpose, however, it is not enough. A more robust and comprehensive definition is needed. The law cherishes certainty, and the challenge is to synthesise a conceptual framework that will define property for today's as well as tomorrow's world.[66] Two attempts at formulating such a framework will now be discussed briefly.

Writers attempting to 'wrestle property to the ground'[67] tend to use a canvas that reflects their own specialisms,[68] and Harris is not different in this regard.[69] The title and context of his work reflects his specialisation in legal philosophy. The aims of his study are related to justifications for property institutions and questions of resource allocation, but it was essential as a starting point to define the features of property institutions. He posits that a property institution[70] has two essential elements: *trespassory rules* and *the ownership spectrum*. He defines 'trespassory rules' as

> any social rules, whether or not embodied in law, which purport to impose obligations on all members of a society, other than an individual or group who is taken to have some form of open-ended relationship to a thing, not to make use of that thing without the consent of that individual or group.[71]

Thus, for example, trespassory rules protect a patented idea from unauthorised use. The degree of trespassory protection afforded a property is dependent on the 'property-specific justice reasons' underlying that object, natural rights attracting extensive trespassory protection. Some things, such as sunlight and air, have no trespassory rules applied to them and are not property or the subject of proprietary rights.

The ownership spectrum is the range of open-ended relationships protected by trespassory rules, and any relationship along the spectrum is an 'ownership

---

66 Penner, *Idea of Property in Law*; Harris, *Property and Justice*; Underkuffler, *The Idea of Property*. Some writers feel that property defies definition; these three have tried to define it.

67 Penner, *Idea of Property in Law*, p. 3.

68 For example, Proudhon approaches the subject from the perspective of socio-political philosophy.

69 Harris, *Property and Justice*.

70 No distinction is made here between 'property' and Harris's 'property institution'. Although Harris describes property as 'points of reference within … the rules of a property institution', for practical purposes the terms are interchangeable when 'property' is used in the legal sense.

71 Harris, *Property and Justice*, p. 5.

interest'. At the lower end of the spectrum is 'mere property', and at the upper end is 'full-blooded ownership'. At the lower end, there are open-ended use-privileges and open-ended powers of control over uses made by others, but with restrictions on transmissibility. At the upper end, there is a *prima facie* assumption that the holder of the proprietary right is 'entirely free to do what he will with his own, whether by way of use, abuse or transfer'.[72] The ownership privileges are unlimited only in so far as they do not conflict with any property-independent prohibition or property-limitation rules.[73] Ownership interests are also subject to expropriation rules such as may be applied by the judicial system through the doctrine of proprietary estoppel[74] or by the legal system through a variety of legislation.[75] Similarly ownership interests are subject to appropriation rules, for example rules of succession to the property of deceased persons in certain circumstances. A summary of the Harris model of property is depicted in Figure 6.1.

Property =
trespassory rules + ownership interest
± property-limitation rules

Figure 6.1 The Harris model of property

Harris' trespassory rules are more or less conceptually similar to Penner's exclusion thesis. His ownership spectrum is not poles apart from Penner's separability thesis, but there are basic differences. In the separability thesis, property is intrinsically alienable. In the ownership spectrum, it is only interests in the upper half of the spectrum that are transmissible.

One problem with the Harris model is that the term 'ownership' is ambiguous. Harris himself acknowledges that '[a]ll attempts in the history of theorizing about property to provide a univocal explication of the concept of ownership, applicable within all societies and to all resources have failed'.[76] Also,

72 Ibid., p. 29.

73 For example, restrictions imposed by the tort of nuisance or by health and safety legislation.

74 Owners of property can be divested in favour of claimants who have suffered loss as a result of reliance on expectations created by the owner's conduct.

75 For example, fathers pursued by the Child Support Agency and owners divested by virtue of the Proceeds of Crime Act 1995.

76 Harris, *Property and Justice*, p. 5.

while ownership is central to the meaning of property in everyday language, there are some proprietary interests that do not entail ownership (e.g. rights of way and easements).

Any framework meant to define the meaning and scope of property should address the following key questions: What determines the extent to which one's property rights are protected? If the right to property is a right to exclude others from things, is this exclusion absolute for all time? To what extent is this protected in the face of competing public interests? Harris's definition of property addresses some but not all of these questions. A more comprehensive framework, which is also consistent with the 'ecologic' ethos of this book, is provided by Underkuffler.

Underkuffler: Property has Four Dimensions

Laura Underkuffler's framework for defining property is elegant as well as comprehensive.[77] She establishes that property has four dimensions. Reference has been made above to property as rights – such as rights to possess, use or sell, right to commercial gains, right of protection, right to exclude. These, including Penner's exclusion thesis, constitute the first dimension, which Underkuffler terms 'a theory of rights'.[78] Reference has also been made to property as a thing, the object to which the theory of rights applies – for example land, body parts, trade secrets. This is the second dimension, or the 'spatial dimension'[79] of property.[80] The third dimension is 'stringency (of protection)'[81] – not all property rights are given equal treatment, some are more protected than others. The right to exclude is almost absolute, but the right to sell is given little protection; the interest in anticipated gain and the right to use are also less protected. Similarly, some things are less protected than others: money less than real property. Also property involving the same rights and things may be afforded different protection under different circumstances. The fourth dimension of property is time – at what points in time are the above dimensions determined, and once determined is the right fixed or does it vary, potentially, thereafter?[82] To what extent are the property rights I acquire today protected against changes in legislation or perceived public interest tomorrow?

In demonstrating how this four-dimensional model of property can be applied, Underkuffler distinguishes between two conceptions of property

77 Underkuffler, *Idea of Property*.

78 Ibid., p. 16.

79 Ibid., p. 21.

80 Penner's separability thesis falls into this dimension.

81 Underkuffler, *Idea of Property*, p. 24.

82 Ibid., p. 28.

in law, the 'common conception' and the 'operative conception'.[83] The first two dimensions of property are common to both conceptions, but there are fundamental differences in relation to the other two dimensions. In the common conception, an assumption is made for equal protection of all property rights, and protection of individual interests against collective change is established for all time, bar a dire threat to public safety. In the operative conception, all property rights are not protected equally, and rights to exclude, use or transfer may be curtailed if deemed necessary for the public interest.

Which of these two conceptions we choose will affect what 'property rights' mean in law: the common conception strongly protects the individual's interest against competing public claims, the operative conception does not.[84]

Underkuffler's model, as summarised in Figure 6.2, is adopted in this book. This quaternary model has been chosen because it encapsulates the various conceptions and dimensions of property and provides a straightforward framework for what is a complex subject. It also provides the flexibility that allows new categories of property that may not necessarily be tangibles. When property analysis is deployed to explore the nature of the relationship between persons, in this case the relationship between doctor and patient, the more useful model is not that which simply reifies property but that which regards property as defining a relationship between two parties with respect to a tangible or intangible entity. Also, as the face of medicine is rapidly changing with advances in biotechnology, and as the range of objects regarded as objects of property is constantly changing, it is advantageous to have a model that takes into account both time and the stringency of protection accorded to objects of property, as this provides for adaptability without abandoning consistency.

Dimension	Common conception	Operative conception
Theory of rights	Explicit	Explicit
Spatial dimension	Explicit	Explicit
Stringency of protection	Equal protection	Unequal protection
Time	Frozen in time	Fluid in time

Figure 6.2 The Underkuffler model of property

83 Ibid., pp. 37–63.

84 Ibid., p. 62.

Is the Search for a Definition of Property Futile?

What emerges from all this is a realisation that the jurisprudence of property is cloudy. It may be argued that the search for a definition of property (and quasi-property) is futile, going by Paul Kohler's observation:

> We might well have views as to whether or not human body parts should be regarded as property but that is not because we have a definition of property to which they do or do not correspond but because we have certain views on the efficacy or otherwise of making them subject to such a regime. In other words it is not towards the definition of the subject matter, but the consequences of the categorization that we look, when we debate whether something should or should not be regarded as property. Thus society might in the near future recognize some form of property in *in situ* kidneys and whether or not it does has nothing to do with any definition of property to which it might subscribe but with the moral and practical consequences of adopting such a stance.[85]

Kohler's observation is exemplified by Steinbock's remarks:

> Cases like *Hecht* require judges to ask whether sperm is property because, if it is not, then it cannot be bequeathed by will. This suggests that we should first decide what property is, determine whether sperm is that sort of thing, and then conclude whether sperm can be bequeathed. However, this approach is backward. Whether sperm is property depends on what we think may permissibly be done with it. If there is a strong moral argument against allowing individuals to store sperm for the purpose of posthumous reproduction, then sperm should not be considered property for that purpose. If there is no such argument, sperm is rightly regarded as an asset that can be bequeathed by will.[86]

This position may be considered to be more in keeping with a social than a legal approach to property. On the other hand, it highlights the fact that sometimes legal rules and decisions have to follow public policy, a theme that recurs in this book. If what the law is prepared to accept as property simply reflects extant moral and ethical values, then the more sacrosanct the right to self-determination becomes, the more likely it is to be accorded the status of property – and as Chapter 9 seeks to establish, the right to self-determination has in recent times been regarded (more or less) as sacrosanct in English law.

---

85 Kohler P, The death of ownership and the demise of property (2000) 53 Current Legal Problems 237–282, at p. 243.

86 Steinbock, Sperm as property, p. 161.

Quasi-property

Difficulties in defining property have led to the notion of quasi-property. There are some interests or resources that are currently regarded as property, but which have not always been so regarded. In their transition from non-proprietary to proprietary status, many of these evolved through a category known as 'quasi-property'.[87] This category has been described as:

> a means of identifying things which whilst not property in the absolute meaning of the term, display (from certain perspectives at least) enough of a proprietary aspect to make the property parallel a useful tool of analysis.[88]

Most intellectual property passed through this category. In *International News Service* v. *Associated Press*, the majority judgment upheld the notion of a quasi-property in news.[89] Under the consent provisions of the Human Fertilisation and Embryology Act 1990, persons undergoing fertility treatment are granted some dispositional control over their sperm, eggs and embryos – and this may be regarded as quasi-property interest.

The concept of quasi-property has, however, been described as 'a legal fiction … a judicial contrivance that provides a legal basis for judicial remedy'[90] and as 'something evolved out of thin air to meet the occasion'.[91]

Rather than resort to legal fiction, this book adopts a Madisonian approach to property. The notion of property as a thing is discarded; Underkuffler's framework is adopted. Applying this framework to the context of this book, the rights to self-determination and bodily integrity belong to the first dimension described by Underkuffler, and the body itself is the second dimension. The right to self-determination is highly cherished by society and by the courts,[92] so will probably be given greater protection than some other property rights, but rights to exclude, use or transfer may need to be curtailed if and when deemed necessary for the public interest (third dimension). Finally, rapidly evolving bioethics and swift advances in biotechnology necessitate a protection of property that is fluid in time (fourth dimension).

87 Kohler, Death of ownership.

88 Ibid., p. 279.

89 *International News Service* v. *Associated Press* 248 US 215 (1918).

90 Nwabueze, *Biotechnology and the Challenge of Property*, p. 59.

91 Overton J in *State* v. *Powell* 497 So.2d 1188, at 1192 (1986). Also *Carney* v. *Knollwod Cemetry Assn* 514 NE2d 430 (1986).

92 As shown in *Chester* v. *Afshar*.

Property and Human Rights

In Chapter 2 the dominance of rights thinking in today's world was identified as one of the drivers of the retreat from paternalism. Just as rights discourse is on the ascendancy, so is the rhetoric of property. It has been observed that:

> the rhetoric of property has significant political purchase ... The successful characterisation of a thing as an object of property, a process which takes place in everyday language, in law, and in political discourse, can be of immense strategic value both in engineering and retarding social change.[93]

Underkuffler states that property has 'symbolic meaning and rhetorical power', and that 'it is the desire to capitalize on this symbolic meaning and rhetorical power that has motivated attempts to broaden the range of individual rights included within the concept of property'.[94]

In democratic societies, the right to own property is regarded as a basic right, but this has not always been the case. It was John Locke who famously put forward the theory that individuals had a natural right to property.[95] It must be stressed, however, that Locke took a broad view of property: it included not only one's possessions but also one's life and liberty. There is a close relationship between property, rights and self-determination. As Underkuffler observed, the historical (going back to Locke) view of property 'was tied to the notion of human beings as masters of themselves'.[96]

Some theorists argue that ownership of property is a fundamental human right that should be entrenched in a bill of rights, but others disagree.[97] In any case, property rights and personal rights interdigitate. Harris showed that there is a sense in which property may be said to be a human right, ranking below life but alongside liberty.[98] In *Lynch* v. *Household Finance Corp*, Justice Stewart declared the dichotomy between personal liberties and property rights a false

93 Davies M, From dominium to 'thin air': concepts of property. In Davies M and Naffine N (eds), *Are Persons Property? Legal Debates about Property and Personality*. Aldershot: Ashgate/Dartmouth 2001, p. 39.

94 Underkuffler LS. On property: an essay (1990) 100 Yale LJ 127–148, at p. 146.

95 Locke J, *Second Treatise of Government*, ed. Gough GW. Oxford: Basil Blackwell, 1976, ch. v.

96 Underkuffler, On property, p. 138.

97 Reich states that 'property is not a natural right but a deliberate construction by society' (New property, p. 771). Property is indeed a human construct, but arguably the right to it would, in a democratic dispensation, be regarded as natural. Harris exhaustively assessed natural property rights and arrived at 'largely negative' conclusions (*Property and Justice*, pp. 182–229).

98 Harris JW, Is property a human right? In McLean J (ed), *Property and the Constitution*. Oxford: Hart 1999, pp. 64–87.

one.[99] Indeed, property rights arguably derive their legitimacy from personal rights:

> Property is not thought to be a right because it is an enforceable claim; it is an enforceable claim only because and in so far as the prevailing ethical theory holds that it is a necessary human right.[100]

On some occasions rights have been in conflict: in *National Provincial Bank* v. *Ainsworth*, the property rights of the husband were allowed to override the personal rights of the deserted wife,[101] but in *Davis* v. *Johnson*, Lord Denning declared: 'Social justice requires that personal rights should, in a proper case, be given priority over rights of property.'[102] Increasingly the conflict is being resolved in favour of personal rights, on the basis of collective visions of the social good. Justice Murphy said in *Dornan* v. *Rogers* that property rights were limited by 'the interfaces between accepted and unaccepted social claims'.[103] Similarly, Gray asserted that:

> It has always been one of the fundamental features of a civilised society that exclusory claims of property stop where the infringement of more basic human freedom begins ... The law of property has always said more than is commonly supposed about the subject of human rights.[104]

He also remarks that the borderline between rights *in rem* and rights *in personam* is crucial:

> ... for it expresses an important social judgement. The designation of a right as 'proprietary' is a kind of social accolade which signifies that a certain importance is attached to the entitlement in question.[105]

The eminent rights scholar Joseph Raz objects to an individualist approach to rights:

> It regards rights as being by their very nature a way of protecting individual interests against the interests or claims of the public or collectivity, or against

99 *Lynch* v. *Household Finance Corp* (1972) 405 US 538, 552, 31 L Ed2d 424, 434–435.

100 Macpherson CB, The meaning of property. In Macpherson CB (ed), *Property: Mainstream and Critical Positions*. Oxford: Oxford University Press 1978, pp. 1–14, at p. 3.

101 *National Provincial Bank* v. *Ainsworth* [1965] AC 1175.

102 *Davis* v. *Johnson* [1979] AC 264, at 274f.

103 *Dornan* v. *Roger* (1982) 148 CLR 365, at 372.

104 Gray KJ, Equitable property (1994) 47 Current Legal Problems 157–214, at p. 211.

105 Gray, *Elements of Land Law*, p. 46.

> whatever reasons there are to promote the general good. The individualist view of rights is confrontational: Rights set the limits of the public sphere, in which each individual is sovereign over his or her own affairs, as against the public domain, where the public interest, as determined by political action prevails. Rights protect individuals against demands that they contribute to the public good, or to the welfare of other individuals.[106]

Favouring a broader approach, he goes on to argue that:

> the reason for caring about the violation of any one's right to property therefore transcends concern for the interest of *that* person in his property. Moreover, it transcends concern for the interest of all property owners in their property … My right in my property is based on my interest in having that property. But the weight given to my interest, the degree of protection it deserves, and the form that protection should take are morally determined by considerations which transcend concern for my interest in itself. They reflect the interest of other people in the common good of respect for property.[107]

Such public interest reasons are not difficult to identify, for as observed by the Supreme Court of New Jersey, 'property rights serve human values. They are recognised to that end and are limited by it.'[108] Thus if property rights were to be claimed over one's body, the boundaries of those rights would be influenced by society's vision of the common good as well as by the rising tide of rights thinking. It would also be influenced by the observation that:

> increasingly the courts fashion proprietary rights in order to give effect to what are thought to be the 'legitimate' moral expectations of litigants or the demands of conscionable conduct in their dealings.[109]

A narrow conception of property will be as atomistic as the narrow conception of self-determination that has bedevilled bioethical discourse. Advocating the more comprehensive concept of property, Underkuffler states that it:

> recognizes the individual's need to develop the capabilities of self in the context of relatedness to others; it stresses that individual autonomy and social context are in fact deeply intertwined. By viewing a collective context as necessary for

---

106 Raz J, Rights and Politics (1995) 71 Indiana LJ 27–44, at pp. 31–32; available at: http://www.repository.law.indiana.edu/ilj/vol71/iss1/2. Accessed 20 October 2012.

107 Ibid., p. 33.

108 *State* v. *Shark* (1971) 277 A2d 369, at 372.

109 Gray, *Elements of Land Law*, pp. 46–47.

> the definition and exercise of individual rights, the comprehensive approach to property forces us to rethink the relationship between the community and individual rights.[110]

Against the background of the above, and in keeping with the ecological metaphor adopted at the outset of this book, it is submitted that personal and proprietary rights must be defined and exercised in the context of public policy. It follows that the concept of property adopted in this book is available to the courts even where they have to take public policy into consideration when deciding cases concerning the patient's right to be involved in decision-making.[111]

The rise of rights thinking combined with the increasing strategic value of property rhetoric, as discussed above, means that there is fertile ground to grow the seeds of a property model in health-care decision-making. The question remains whether the courts will go with the tide, and this will be discussed in Chapter 9.

Conclusions

While the right to own property is fundamental in western democratic societies, the definition of property varies from one context to another, and is dynamic:

> Property is a socially constructed concept; and former perceptions of property as a monopolistic right of control and exploitation have long since been eroded by wider conceptions of the public good.[112]

Definitions of property advanced by various legal scholars have been described. At various times and in various places property has been taken to be a thing, a relationship with a thing or a relationship with other persons characterised by rights against others, to or over a thing. For the purpose of this book, the notion of property as a thing is rejected and a proprietary right is taken as defining a relationship with other persons characterised by rights against them to or over a fungible or infungible object. Underkuffler's framework[113] is adopted for two

110 Underkuffler, On property, p. 147.

111 For example, public policy was a factor in the House of Lords' decision in *Chester* v. *Afshar*. The court had to depart from traditional rules of causation in order to meet policy imperatives that made it unacceptable for the surgeon not to inform his patient of pertinent risks. In Chapter 9 it is suggested that the court would have found it easier and more logical to achieve this end by means of the property approach rather than consent.

112 Gray and Gray, *Land Law*.

113 Underkuffler, *Idea of Property*.

reasons: it is based on a broad conception of property and it has a robustness that facilitates legal certainty. In Chapter 9, this framework will be applied to the principle of self-determination and to leading consent cases.

Since the definition of property is constantly on the move, our chosen framework should ideally provide both certainty and flexibility. The dominance of rights thinking will lead to more proprietary rights being fashioned, and Underkuffler's framework accommodates this. The language of rights and the language of property have in common the command of strong socio-political force. Inevitably this force will come to bear on patient self-determination in health care.

Chapter 7
Property Rights in the Body

> In any legal system operating in a society which respects personal autonomy we would expect the law to allocate exclusive physical control over our own bodies and body parts to us.[1]

In the last chapter, an attempt was made to show that while property may have a spatial dimension, it is primarily about relationships. Also, the rights protected as property do not necessarily have absolute protection, nor are they necessarily protected for eternity. These four attributes are captured by the Underkuffler framework which was adopted as the model of property for the thesis put forward in this book.[2]

In applying property analysis to the subject of self-determination in health-care decision-making, there are two possible approaches. The more obvious one is to consider one's body as one's own property. There is considerable reluctance on the part of ethicists and the courts to regard the living human body, or parts of it, as property, primarily because of the fear of commodification.

An alternative approach is to regard the patient's right to make decisions about their treatment as a proprietary right. This is a much less travelled road, if not a novel approach, which will be explored in this book.

The association of property discourse with commodification of the human body will be a stumbling block in any attempt to promote a property model in doctor–patient consultations. To dispose of this obstacle, as well as cover the spatial dimension of the Underkuffler framework, this chapter elucidates the issue of property rights in the human body and in body parts and particles.

Lacks, Moore and Property Rights in the Human Body

Henrietta Lacks was a poor, young black woman who died of cervical cancer in 1951 in a segregated ward for black patients at the Johns Hopkins Hospital,

---

1 Clarke A and Kohler P, *Property Law: Commentary and Materials*. Cambridge: Cambridge University Press 2005, p. 6.

2 Underkuffler LS, *The Idea of Property: Its Meaning and Power*. Oxford: Oxford University Press 2003.

Baltimore, USA.[3] In the course of her treatment a sample of her cervical cells was, without her consent, sent to a research laboratory that was trying to grow human cells in culture. The cells became the first human cells to be discovered to multiply outside the body. Fifty years later, her cells continue to live on as the HeLa cell line. HeLa cells have contributed to numerous biomedical discoveries and can be ordered from tissue culture supply catalogues;[4] they have travelled the world and been shot into space (to determine whether human cells could survive zero gravity). They have been used to develop a vaccine for polio, in numerous other research studies (relating to cancer, AIDS, radiation and gene mapping) and to test human sensitivity to cosmetics and other products. The cells have given rise to a multibillion dollar industry, yet Lacks' family was never compensated, and they were unable to look after her unmarked grave.

Today, it would generally be accepted that to obtain the tissue without her consent was unethical.[5] The question arises as to whether she or her family are entitled to proprietary rights over the cell line. Her family did not test this in court, but someone else in a similar situation picked up the gauntlet.

John Moore had hairy cell leukaemia which necessitated removal of his spleen at the University of California Medical Centre, Los Angeles. Moore signed the customary consent form for splenectomy. He was not informed that his extirpated spleen was going to be used for research. His surgeon, Dr Golde, working with other colleagues, undertook research on Moore's T-lymphocytes, resulting in the development of a cell line and the Regents of the University of California were granted a patent for the method of producing this cell line as well as the use of this method to produce lymphokines.[6] During the period of the research, samples of blood, skin and bone marrow were taken from Moore. The Regents contracted with the Genetics Institute Inc. and Sandoz Pharmaceuticals Corporation to commercialise the research findings, the products of which were worth an estimated US$3 billion. In 1983, seven years after Moore's diagnosis was made, Moore was asked to sign a consent form permitting use of his body products and transferring rights in the products to the Regents. He declined and subsequently issued proceedings for *inter alia*, breach of fiduciary duty and conversion. He lost the claim of conversion but won on appeal, the Court of Appeal holding by a majority decision that Moore

3 Smith V, *Wonder Woman: The Life, Death, and Life After Death of Henrietta Lacks, Unwitting Heroine of Modern Medical Science*, Baltimore City Paper. 17 April 2002; available at http://www2.citypaper.com/news/story.asp?id=3426. Accessed 2 November 2014.

4 For example, http://www.biocompare.com/Transfection/12840-HeLa-Cell-Transfection-Reagents-Human-Cervical-Carcinoma-Henrietta-Lacks/?search=Hela. Accessed 2 November 2014.

5 *Moore* v. *Regents of the University of California* 249 Cal. Rptr. 494 (Cal. App 1988).

6 Substances released by blood cells as part of an immune response.

had property rights in his body part.[7] While acknowledging that there were relevant policy considerations in this regard, the court held that there was no reason to believe that this proprietary right would hinder medical research.[8] On appeal to the Supreme Court of California, a majority reversed this decision.[9] Moore was given leave to sue for failure to obtain consent and for breach of fiduciary duty, but not on the basis of the 'property' claim. One of the reasons given by the majority for taking this position was that granting Moore's property claim would hinder biotechnological development:

> In effect, what Moore is asking us to do is to impose a tort duty on scientists to investigate the consensual pedigree of each human cell sample used in research. To impose such a duty, which would affect medical research of importance to all of society, implicates policy concerns far removed from the traditional, two-party ownership disputes in which the law of conversion arose. Invoking a tort theory originally used to determine whether the loser or the finder of a horse had the better title, Moore claims ownership of the results of socially important medical research, including the genetic code for chemicals that regulate the functions of every human being's immune system.[10]

Another reason was that Moore's interest in his bodily integrity and privacy are protected by the requirement of informed consent, so there was no need to apply property analysis:

> … one may earnestly wish to protect privacy and dignity without accepting the extremely problematic conclusion that interference with those interests amounts to a conversion of personal property. Nor is it necessary to force the round pegs of 'privacy' and 'dignity' into the square hole of 'property' in order to protect the patient, since the fiduciary-duty and informed-consent theories protect these interests directly by requiring full disclosure.[11]

A third reason was that the scope of property rights in the body were better addressed by statute ('legislative resolution'[12]) than case law.

It is interesting to note that years before the Moore case, an American university regarded cell lines as its property. Leonard Hayflick, whose research was funded by the taxpayer, used the cells of an aborted foetus to create a

7 Ibid.

8 Ibid., 508.

9 *Moore* v. *Regents of the University of California* (1990) 51 Cal.3d 120.

10 Ibid., per Panelli J, at 135.

11 Ibid., 158.

12 *Moore* v. *Regents of the University of California* 793 P.2d 479 (Cal. 1990), at 493.

commercially profitable cell line (W!-38).[13] When he tried to sell the cell line, his university accused him of stealing public property and called in the police.

Whole communities have also suffered experiences similar to those of Lacks and Moore. An example is the case of the Tristan islanders who, on account of the extremely high prevalence of asthma in this remote South Atlantic island, were lured into providing blood samples to foreign researchers.[14] Subsequently genes associated with asthma were identified and patented and the patent rights were sold for US$70 million. The islanders had no property rights to their genes. In a similar case, a gene which might protect against HIV was extracted from blood samples taken from indigenous people in the Solomon Islands and New Guinea under the pretence of testing for diabetes, and only public pressure in the US forced the researchers to withdraw the patent of a gene.[15]

Mrs Lacks's forebears, as slaves, were regarded as the property of their masters. Slavery was abolished in 1772[16] but even in the twenty-first century the 'ownership' of human beings is widespread in practices such as baby-selling and sex slavery.[17] The opprobrium associated with ancient and modern slavery, and with cases such as those of Lacks and Moore, has influenced the wider debate about property rights to the body and body parts. As Alexandra George put it, images of slavery, exploitation and the degradation of humanity have a 'rhetorical force' that is 'at least partly responsible for driving the confused and inconsistent principles that govern this area of the law'.[18]

Self-ownership

While it is now established that no one can have property rights over another human, it remains contentious whether property rights can be claimed over one's own body or its parts, in life or after death.[19] Morgan asserts that '[t]he

13 Boffey PM, The fall and rise of Leonard Hayflick, biologist whose fight with U.S. seems over. New York Times, 19 January 1982.

14 Washington HA, Gene patenting produces profits, not cures. Huffington Post, July 2010, at http://www.huffingtonpost.com/harriet-a-washington/gene-patenting-produces-p_b_645862.html. Accessed 20 October 2012.

15 Hernández S, Panama: indigenous people fear genetic slavery. World News Inter Press Service, 17 December 1997.

16 Slavery Abolition Act 1833; Section LXIV.

17 Stange M, *Personal Property: Wives, White Slaves and the Market in Women.* Baltimore: Johns Hopkins University Press 1998.

18 George A, Is 'property' necessary? On owning the human body and its parts (2004) 10 Res Publica 15–24, at pp. 31–32.

19 Matthews P, The man of property [1995] 3 Med L Rev 251–274; Dworkin G and Kennedy I, Human tissue: rights in the body and its parts [1993] 1 Med L Rev 291–319.

"property in his own person" is less a metaphysical statement declaring self-ownership, more a political statement denying ownership by another'.[20]

In activities such as prostitution and surrogacy, the body is used as if it were one's property. It could be argued that men and women exercise property rights over their body and body parts when they part with their gametes in exchange for a sum of money, as happens in some surrogacy arrangements and gamete 'donation' programmes and in so-called 'rent-a-womb'[21] surrogacy arrangements. A socio-political activist even filed an application for a patent on herself.[22]

Kant deplored the notion of property in oneself:

> Man cannot dispose over himself because he is not a thing; he is not his own property; to say that he is would be self-contradictory; for in so far as he is a person he is a subject in whom the ownership of things can be vested, and if he were his own property, he would be a thing over which he could have ownership. But a person cannot be property and so cannot be a thing which can be owned, for it is impossible to be a person and a thing, the proprietor and the property.[23]

It will be noted here that Kant saw property as a thing – a notion of property rejected in this thesis. Locke, who affirmed that a person should be free from possession by others, thought of property in terms of the product of one's labour, and it is not surprising that his position differs from that of Kant:

> Though the earth, and all inferior creatures, be common to all men, yet every man has a property in his own person: this nobody has any right to but himself. The labour of his body, and the work of his hand, we may say, are properly his.[24]

The term self-ownership is applied to the sovereignty that individuals have over their body, skills, talents and labour. Jon Christman, who asserts that 'insofar as my body moves or acts, I should be the one who has the ultimate say over what

---

20 Morgan D, Where do I own my body? (And why?). In Morgan D, *Issues in Medical Law and Ethics*. London: Cavendish 2001, pp. 83–104, at p. 86.

21 Banerjee S and Basu S, *Rent a Womb: Surrogate Selection, Investment Incentives, and Contracting*. Pune, Maharashtra: Gokhale Institute of Politics and Economics 2007.

22 Meek J, Poet attempts the ultimate in self-invention – patenting her own genes. The Guardian, 29 February 2000; available at http://www.guardian.co.uk/science/2000/feb/29/genetics.uknews. Accessed 16 April 2015.

23 Kant I, Lectures on ethics, in Paton HJ (ed), *Groundwork of the Metaphysics of Morals*. London: Hutchinson 1953, p. 165.

24 Locke J, *Two Treatises of Government*. Minneapolis: Filiquarian 2007, p. 30.

it does and where it goes',[25] champions this sovereignty. He argues that there are two construals of this term:

> One can be called Lockean and the other Hegelian, referring to the bodies of thought that these positions most closely resemble. The Lockean defence of self-ownership expresses the idea that self-ownership is necessary as a kind of protection, in particular against invasions by the state into the private and personal aspects of one's life. The Hegelian view is that self-ownership is more than a mere negative barrier against intrusion, but rather a positive good that manifests a person's extension of her personality and will into the world. Self-ownership, on this view, is an expression of the person's embodiment in her own body and talents, and it is valuable because it is necessary for the self-expression that is constitutive of a truly human life.[26]

These two construals can be respectively described as 'self-ownership as non-interference' and 'self-ownership as self-control'. It is noteworthy that these two construals are respectively similar to the narrow and broad conceptions of property and also to the narrow and broad conceptions of individualism discussed earlier in the book. Christman argues that rights to trade one's talents are more difficult to justify on the basis of self-ownership when that principle is understood as the manifestation of a person's interest in self-control than when viewed as non-interference.[27] If self-determination in health care is simply about mere avoidance of unauthorised touch (battery) then the first construal will permit the application of property analysis to the protection of self-determination. Adopting, as has been done in this book, a definition of self-determination that is consistent with the ecology paradigm, the second construal ('self-ownership as self-control') enables application of property analysis, with Madison's broad conception of property being operative. This construal underlies the statement that '[t]he body is more than a utilitarian object: it is also a social, ritual, and metaphorical entity, and the only thing many people can really call their own'.[28]

The language of self-ownership could have the advantage of establishing that, at least in this respect, all persons are equal irrespective of gender, race or social standing, but this advantage is outweighed by disadvantages. While the notion of self-determination adopted in Chapter 2 unites one's values and

---

25 Christman J, Self-ownership, equality and the structure of property rights (1991) 19 Political Theory 28–46, at p. 39.

26 Christman J, *The Myth of Property: Toward an Egalitarian Theory of Ownership*. Oxford: Oxford University Press 1994, p. 149.

27 Ibid., p. 151.

28 Andrews L and Nelkin D, *Body Bazaar: The Market for Human Tissue in the Biotechnology Age*. New York: Crown 2001, p. 7.

aspirations with the physical self, forming one personality, the concept of self-ownership suggests a division between the physical body and the non-physical personality, with the latter claiming ownership of the former. This division also makes the body (the physical part of the person) an object of property; in other words, a thing. As discussed in Chapter 6, the notion of property as a thing is rejected in this thesis and the notion of property as defining relationships is preferred.

Dwelling on self-ownership would only help perpetuate and reinforce the perception of property as a thing, a perception which leads judges intuitively to link property in the body to commodification. Also, owning one's self could be seen as one step towards owning another. The case for a property model advanced in this book is therefore based not on self-ownership discourse, but on the property-as-defining-relationships-with-others concept of property.

The Increasing Application of Property Analysis to Body Parts and Particles

Increasingly, property analysis is being applied to the body and (especially) body parts and particles.[29] Attempts to exercise property rights have been extended to embryos, with divorcing couples seeking to exert claims on frozen embryos as if they were property.[30]

One driver for ascribing property to the body and body parts is the ascendancy of rights thinking (discussed in Chapter 2). If self-determination is a state in which individuals have control over material conditions which shape their character, then property, as seen in Chapter 6, offers a strong means of having and exercising control rights. Rights thinking, however, is arguably not the main driver for the increasing application of property analysis to body parts and particles. Although self-determination is an important enough principle to drive claims to property in the body or body parts, it is commercial interests in biotechnology that *currently* appear to be the principal driver.[31]

---

29 For detailed description and analysis of this trend, see Andrews and Nelkin, *Body Bazaar*; Dickenson D, *Property in the Body: Feminist Perspectives*. Cambridge: Cambridge University Press 2007; Hardcastle R, *Law and the Human Body*. Oxford: Hart 2007; Nwabueze RN, *Biotechnology and the Challenge of Property: Property Rights in Dead Bodies, Body Parts, and Genetic Information*. Aldershot: Ashgate 2007.

30 JFL, Embryos in a divorce case: joint property or offspring? (1989) 84 Pediatrics A54.

31 Dickenson, *Property in the Body*.

Biotechnology

With burgeoning biotechnology, the value of human tissue has increased astronomically and many more stories like that of Lacks may emerge. Some hospitals in the United States are forming partnerships with biotechnology companies to provide them with human tissue for research, treatment and drug development purposes.[32] Such arrangements raise concerns not only about compensation for the donors but also about commodification of the body and body parts. Perhaps it is such concerns that underlie the desire of some celebrities to acquire intellectual property rights in their own DNA.[33] Most importantly from a legal point of view, the increasing value of body parts raises questions about property rights to those parts. The patenting of genes and other biological materials derived from the human body essentially creates property rights in human material.[34]

Matthews sees this trend as part of a changing world:

> … all the societal pressures which a century ago pointed away from lawfully possessing and using human tissue now point towards it. The non-property solutions of yesterday are inadequate to the task of today.[35]

Richardson and Turner point out the 'paradoxical fictionalisation and reification'[36] of the human body: the body is fictionalised by its fragmentation to genetic codes, but at the same time reified by becoming a commodity in capitalist exchange relationships. They state that:

> Changes in contemporary biological sciences and their commercial application invite us to make a distinction between three levels of law and embodiment. In modern societies, law will in principle have to distinguish between:

32 US hospitals to ask patients for right to sell their tissue. BMJ, 16 September 2000, p. 653.

33 News report in *Metro*, North West edition, 23 August 2001.

34 Bovenberg JA, Inalienably yours? The new case for an inalienable property right in human biological material: empowerment of sample donors or a recipe for a tragic anti-commons? (2004) 1:4 SCRIPTed 545; available at http://www.law.ed.ac.uk/ahrc/script-ed/issue4/bovenberg.asp. Accessed 2 November 2014.

35 Matthews, Man of property, pp. 253–254.

36 Richardson EH and Turner BS, Bodies as property: from slavery to DNA maps. In Bainham A, Sclater SD and Richards M (eds), *Body Lore and Laws*. Oxford: Hart 2002, pp. 29–42, at p. 41.

1) rights to whole bodies (in practice therefore to persons)
2) rights to buy or to sell or to store parts of bodies (as in organ transplants)
3) rights over 'particles' of bodies (such as DNA codes, genetic material and material relevant to human reproduction, for example eggs and sperm), that is to phenomena below the whole organism.[37]

Munzer on the other hand does not see any advantage in distinguishing between body and body parts or particles, referring to this as the 'fallacy of division'.[38] If persons lack property rights in themselves it does not follow that they lack property rights in their parts and particles.

Posthumous Reproduction

The more acceptable posthumous reproduction becomes, the more likely it is that society will recognise property rights in gametes and embryos. For this reason, it is important to clarify the moral status of posthumous reproduction. In the UK, the direction in which the ship of public opinion is sailing was revealed by the widely publicised case of *R* v. *Human Fertilization & Embryology Authority, ex parte Blood*.[39] Stephen and Diane Blood had been in a relationship for 13 years, the last four as a married couple. Stephen was pronounced clinically dead on 2 March 1995, four days after contracting meningitis. At Diane's request, two samples of semen were retrieved from Stephen by electro-ejaculation while he was in a coma. These were cryopreserved at a second hospital, Diane Blood intending to use them to have her husband's child in due course. Her intention was frustrated by the Human Fertilisation and Embryology Authority (HFEA) on the grounds that the retrieval, storage and use of the sperm were unlawful. The court accepted Diane Blood's statement that she and her husband had decided to try for a baby, but had no difficulty in agreeing that the storage of the sperm contravened the consent provisions of the Human Fertilisation and Embryology Act 1990 – Stephen's written consent had not been obtained – and was unlawful.

Given that the use of her husband's sperm was unlawful in this jurisdiction, Diane Blood sought to have the sperm exported overseas where she could have treatment. For this to be possible, the HFEA would have had to make specific directions to the clinic holding the sperm. Section 24(4) of the 1990 Act grants HFEA the discretion to give general and specific 'directions' on the export of

---

37 Ibid., p. 39.

38 Munzer SR, An uneasy case against property rights in body parts. In Paul EF, Miller FD and Paul J (eds), *Property Rights*. Cambridge: Cambridge University Press 1994, pp. 259–286, at p. 275.

39 *R* v. *Human Fertilization & Embryology Authority, ex parte Blood* [1997] 2 All ER 687 (CA), (1997) 35 BMLR 1.

gametes. The HFEA declined to give the required specific directions, and Diane Blood sought judicial review of this decision.

The Court of Appeal accepted the argument that HFEA's decision not to give specific directions allowing the export of the sperm infringed Mrs Blood's rights under Articles 59 and 60 of the Treaty of Rome. These articles prohibit member states from imposing restrictions on rights to receive services, except where such a restriction is deemed necessary for sound reasons of public policy. The court held that HFEA's decision in the Blood case was not founded on the public interest, and referred the case back to the authority for review. Subsequently the HFEA withdrew its objection, and Mrs Blood has since had two children by her husband posthumously. It can be said that Diane Blood thwarted the consent provisions of the 1990 Act by gaining approval to export a property.

Storage and Use of Human Tissue

The Nuffield Council proffered the consent model as the appropriate approach to the acquisition and supply of human tissue.[40] Ignoring or rejecting notions of tissue as property, the Council called for changes in the manner of obtaining consent for the removal of human tissue during treatment.

While, however, consent is concerned primarily with the taking of tissue (as confirmed by the decision in *Moore*), property analysis addresses the taking as well as subsequent use and control of tissue. Grubb notes that English law provides significant protection to individuals' self-determination – by recognising a right to bodily integrity – such that the taking of any tissue from a competent adult person would be unlawful without the consent of the source but points out that the law is, however, solely concerned with the 'taking' rather than the 'use' of extra-corporeal organs or tissue and, by contrast, property law would have something to say about subsequent use and control.[41]

The Council of Europe tried to extend consent into the realms of further use and control when it declared that:

> When in the course of an intervention any part of the body is removed, it may be stored and used for a purpose other than that for which it was removed, only if this is done in conformity with appropriate information and consent procedures.[42]

40 Nuffield Council on Bioethics, *Human Tissue: Ethical and Legal Issues*. London: Nuffield Council on Bioethics 1995.

41 Grubb A, 'I, me, mine': bodies, parts and property (1998) 3 Med Law Int'l, 299–317.

42 Council of Europe, *Convention for the Protection of Human Rights and Dignity of the Human Being with regard to the Application of Biology and Medicine: Convention on Human Rights and Biomedicine*

In practice this is not easy. At the time the body part is removed, the donor may not be in the right frame of mind to look beyond the immediate purpose for which the part was removed – and this may vitiate any purported consent to future use. Further, some options for use of the tissue or organ may arise after it has been removed.

Beyleveld and Brownsword argue that the informed consent requirement of Article 22 quoted above presupposes that there is property in our own bodies; that 'the consent strategy presupposes the very property thesis that it tries to avoid': 'once we are contemplating rights of [use and control], we are in the natural territory of property rights'.[43] Their position is that if we do not accept that we have proprietary rights in our own bodies and body parts, then we do not accept that in every case we have the right to control the use of our own body parts once they have been removed.

The idea of continuing control through a property right was also expounded by Nwabueze,[44] who applied this to cases involving body parts and particles used for research[45] and organs donated for transplantation.

Although consent is important, the problems relating to the removal and use of human tissue cannot be resolved until proprietary rights are clarified.

This is further illustrated by the tangle the Nuffield Council got into when it tried to use the doctrine of abandonment to confer ownership of extirpated tissue on the hospital authority – the Council suggested that where tissue is removed during treatment, the tissue should be regarded as abandoned, a concept that applies to property.[46]

The Common Law Position

As acknowledged by Gage J, the common law position regarding property in the body or its parts is not firmly established.[47] Alexandra George describes the legal position regarding control of the body and body parts as 'a contradictory jumble of legal principles'.[48] There is substantial literature on property in the

(Convention on Human Rights and Biomedicine) 1997, Article 22; available at http://conventions.coe.int/Treaty/en/Treaties/Html/164.htm. Accessed 2 November 2014.

43 Beyleveld D and Brownsword R, 'My Body, My Body Parts, My Property' (2000) 8 Health Care Analysis 87–99, at p. 90.

44 Nwabueze RN, Donated organs, property rights and the remedial quagmire (2008) 16 Med Law Rev 201–224.

45 Such as *Washington University* v. *Catalona* 437 F.Supp.2d 985 (Dist. Ct. Missouri, 2006).

46 Nuffield Council, *Human Tissue*, at para 9.14.1, 13.26. An erudite critique of this is provided by Matthews, Man of property.

47 *AB* v. *Leeds Teaching Hospital NHS Trust* [2005] QB 506 at para 135.

48 George, Is 'property' necessary? p. 17.

corpse,[49] but a detailed review of the subject is unnecessary for the purposes of this book, which is about the living person's right to self-determination. Although it can be argued that the way the law treats the corpse gives an indication of how it will treat the living body, this is not necessarily so. Even in ordinary life the former is regarded differently from the latter. Take the case of a person who suffers a heart attack in a public facility, for example. If this person was taken to the hospital alive, the newspapers will report that 'Mr [or Mrs] Smith was taken to hospital'. If the person died, it will be reported that 'the body was taken to' (or 'deposited at') the hospital – what was previously a person becomes a thing to be deposited somewhere. The focus here will therefore be primarily on the living body, with only a few references to case law concerning the non-living body or body parts where appropriate.

According to *obiter dicta* in *Dobson* v. *North Tyneside Health Authority*, the body of a living person cannot be property.[50] Nevertheless, case law in English, American, Canadian and Australian jurisdictions has given human body parts and particles *some* of the attributes of 'property'.[51] In *Yearworth* v. *North Bristol NHS Trust* (see below), the Court of Appeal accepted the existence of property interests in parts or particles of the human body.[52] Body parts such as hair,[53] blood[54] and urine[55] have been regarded as property stolen from the person in possession, although it is not always certain whether it was the tissue itself or the container in which it was held that was treated as property. If it was the tissue rather than the container that was treated as property, then the courts are using separability as the criterion for defining property. As Radin said:

> The idea of property in one's body presents some interesting paradoxes. In some cases, bodily parts can become fungible commodities, just as other personal property can become fungible with a change in its relationship with the owner: Blood can be withdrawn and used in a transfusion; hair can be cut off and used by a wigmaker; organs can be transplanted. On the other hand, bodily parts

49 For an in-depth analysis, see Nwabueze, *Biotechnology and the Challenge of Property*.

50 *Dobson* v. *North Tyneside Health Authority* [1996] 4 All ER 474.

51 *Doodeward* v. *Spence* (1908) 6 CLR 406 (High Court of Australia); *Kate Jane Bazley* v. *Wesley Monash IVF Pty Ltd* [2010] QSC 118; *Jocelyn Edwards; Re the estate of the late Mark Edwards* [2011] NSWSC 478; *Hecht* v. *Superior Court* 20 Cal. Rptr. 2d 275 1993 (California Court of Appeals); *Yearworth* v. *North Bristol NHS Trust* [2009] EWCA Civ 37; [2010] QB 1.

52 *Yearworth* v. *North Bristol NHS Trust* [2009] EWCA Civ 37.

53 R v. *Herbert* (1960) Times, 22 December. The defendant was convicted of theft of a quantity of hair he had cut from the head of his female passenger.

54 R v. *Rothery* [1976] RTR 550. The defendant had provided a blood sample for alcohol test under the Road Traffic Act 1972. He was then released and he took with him the sample which he had retrieved while the officer's back was turned. He was convicted of theft.

55 R v. *Welsh* [1974] RTR 478. Similar circumstances to *Rothery*; the urine sample was poured down the sink when the officer left the room. He was convicted of theft.

> may be too 'personal' to be property at all. We have an intuition that property necessarily refers to something in the outside world, separate from oneself. Though the general idea of property for personhood means that the boundary between person and thing cannot be a bright line, still the idea of property seems to require some perceptible boundary, at least insofar as property requires the notion of thing, and the notion of thing requires separation from self. This intuition makes it seem appropriate to call parts of the body property only after they have been removed from the system.[56]

In the case of R v. *Kelly and Lindsay* it was held that parts of a dead body may be 'property'.[57] Kelly, an artist, had conspired with Lindsay, a technician, to remove anatomy specimens from the Royal College of Surgeons in London. They were both convicted of theft and appealed on the grounds, *inter alia*, that under common law the specimens did not constitute 'property'. In upholding their conviction, the Court of Appeal ruled that property lies in body parts that have acquired different attributes by virtue of the application of skill. Lord Rose speculated that, given the flexibility of the common law, property rights could be recognised in unaltered body parts in future cases.

The decision in *Kelly* mirrors that in the Australian High Court case of *Doodeward* v. *Spence* where it was held that a stillborn 'monster' that had been preserved with spirits for 40 years had become property.[58] In this case, Griffiths CJ said that:

> When a person has by the lawful exercise of work or skill so dealt with a human body or part of a human body in his lawful possession that it has acquired some attributes differentiating it from a *mere* corpse awaiting burial, he acquires a right to retain possession of it …
>
> … the common law does not stand still. It may be that if, on some future occasions, the question arises, the courts will hold that human body parts are capable of being property for the purposes of s4, even without the acquisition of different attributes, *if they have a use or significance beyond their mere existence.*[59] (emphasis mine)

His choice of words is instructive and it is open to speculation whether Griffiths CJ would have reached a different conclusion if the body or body part were that of a living person (with the dignity they are entitled to), not that of a '*mere*

56 Radin MJ, Property and personhood (1982) 34 Stan L Rev 957.

57 R v. *Kelly and Lindsay* [1998] 3 All ER 741.

58 *Doodeward* v. *Spence* (1908) 6 CLR 406.

59 Ibid., 414.

corpse' (emphasis added). Nonetheless his position was cited with approval in *AB* v. *Leeds Teaching Hospital NHS Trust*.[60] Both *Doodeward* and *Kelly* drew from the work of Locke who, per the quote earlier in this chapter, reasoned that property arises when a person invests effort in a thing that initially lacked value or existed in a natural state.

In the case of *Hecht* v. *Superior Court* the California appellate court ruled that frozen sperm was part of a deceased person's estate, able to be bequeathed like his other assets – in other words, that sperm was the object of a proprietary right.[61] Deborah Hecht and William Kane cohabited for five years. Mr Kane, who was contemplating suicide, 'assiduously' deposited vials of his semen with California Cryobank, Inc., with the knowledge and intention that Ms Hecht could have a child by him after his death. He made his intention clear in his will, his sperm banking directive, his final letter to his grown-up children (by a previous marriage) and his suicide note to Ms Hecht. His children contested the will. The judge at first instance decided in favour of the children, but was overruled by the Court of Appeal of California which concluded that he had decision-making authority over the use of his sperm and that this was sufficient to constitute property. This contrasts with the decision of the California Supreme Court in *Moore*. It would appear that the judge in *Hecht* was bound by public policy considerations not to thwart what was clearly Mr Kane's testament and intention. This is a clear example of the court adopting the property approach in order to meet a policy imperative. Notably, the Court of Appeal of California did not appear to regard the earlier decision of the California Supreme Court in *Moore* as binding.

Property rights in stored sperm have recently also been recognised by courts in the UK[62] and Australia,[63] with the Court of Appeal saying in *Yearworth* that:

> developments in medical science now require a reanalysis of the common law's treatment of and approach to the issue of ownership of parts or products of a living human body, whether for present purposes (*viz* an action in negligence) or otherwise.[64]

The claimants in that case (which is distinguished from *Dobson* in that it concerned material produced by a living human body) were six men who prior to undertaking courses of chemotherapy, and with the aim of preserving their ability to father children, had produced samples of semen for the purpose

60 *AB* v. *Leeds Teaching Hospital NHS Trust* [2005] QB 506.

61 *Hecht* v. *Superior Court* (1993) 20 Cal. Rptr. 2d 275 (Ct App).

62 *Yearworth* v. *North Bristol NHS Trust* [2009] EWCA Civ 37.

63 *Kate Jane Bazley* v. *Wesley Monash IVF Pty Ltd* [2010] QSC 118; *Jocelyn Edwards; Re the estate of the late Mark Edwards* [2011] NSWSC 478.

64 *Yearworth* v. *North Bristol NHS Trust* [2010] QB 1, at para 45a.

of cryopreservation and future use. The defendant Trust was responsible for freezing and storing the samples. Unfortunately, due to a fault with the storage facility, the samples thawed before they were used, and the sperm were irretrievably damaged. The men brought claims against the Trust in negligence, saying they had suffered personal injury and loss of property. The court held that the men had ownership of the sperm which they had produced. It stated, however, that its recognition of a property right was limited to the circumstances of this case, so it is uncertain whether property rights would be recognised in cases that involve donated body parts and particles. Rostill argues that 'the 'ownership' that the Court of Appeal purported to vest in each of the men was not a right *in rem*, a right 'binding the world' – each man had 'ownership' against the Trust and only against the Trust and, on a narrow view of property rights, this was not a property right.[65]

In limiting its finding of a property right to the circumstances of this case, the Court of Appeal intentionally or unintentionally placed property analysis on a leash, using it to achieve a desired objective but constraining its further application. This reflects the longstanding conservative approach of the courts to the question of proprietary rights in the human body or body parts.

The Statutory Position

Although discussion of body parts as property usually focuses on case law, ascription to human body parts and particles of *some* of the attributes of 'property' can also be found in statutes. The Human Fertilisation and Embryology Act 1990 s1(1) confers user entitlements and dispositional liberties on patients undergoing fertility treatment, in relation to the gametes they have provided and the embryos arising from same. It must be stressed that 'property' is used here in the broader sense, and there is no suggestion that the legislators intended to confer property rights on gametes and embryos or that they did consider these to be property. On the contrary, there is no indication that lawmakers disagreed with the position of the Warnock Committee which was opposed to treating embryos as property:

> Until now the law has never had to consider the existence of embryos outside the mother's uterus. The existence of such embryos raises potentially difficult problems as to ownership. The concept of ownership of human embryos seems

65 Rostill LD, The ownership that wasn't meant to be: *Yearworth* and property rights in human tissue [2014] 40 J Med Ethics 14–18.

> to us to be undesirable. We recommend that legislation be enacted to ensure that there is no right of ownership in a human embryo.[66]

An opportunity for legislative clarification of the issue of property rights to the body and its parts was spurned when the Human Tissue Act 2004 was enacted.[67] The act does not establish for certain whether or not body parts can be property but appears to acknowledge (in s 32(9)) the common law position that body parts could be property if they have been subjected to special skills.

Arguments against Treating Body Parts and Particles as Property

As can be seen from the common law cases discussed above, there is resistance to endowing property in the body and body parts. The courts have not always been articulate in explaining the case against treating the body and its parts and particles as property, but the main factor appears to be fear of commodification. Commodification aside, it could also be argued that treating the body as property is simply demeaning and affronts dignity, leads to fragmentation of the person and goes against public policy.[68] The basis for finding that the body is or could be property may be questioned. There is also the argument that our bodies, being interdependent with other bodies and the environment, do not just belong to us.[69] Each of these arguments will now be addressed.

Dignity

One school of thought holds that treating the body as property is an affront to human dignity.[70] This argument can be turned 180 degrees – there is a case for arguing that a denial of proprietary rights in our body or body parts affronts human dignity. On the basis that respecting dignity entails respect for the agent's capacity to make informed choices, Beyleveld and Brownsword argue

66 Warnock Committee, *Report of the Committee of Enquiry into Human Fertilisation and Embryology*. London: HMSO 1984, para 10.11.

67 Price D, The Human Tissue Act 2004 [2005] 68 MLR 798.

68 Murray TH, On the human body as property: the meaning of embodiment, markets, and the meaning of strangers (1986) 20 U Mich JL Reform 1055–1088.

69 Herring J and Chau PL, My body, your body, our bodies (2007) 15 Med L Rev 34–61.

70 Skene L, Arguments against people legally 'owning' their own bodies, body parts and tissue (2002) 2 Macquarie Law Journal 165–176; Munzer, Uneasy case against property rights in body parts.

that 'respect for human dignity is, if anything, an argument in favour of, rather than against, biocommerce'[71] in human body parts.

In the same vein, Mosk J giving his minority judgment in *Moore*, said that dignity is undermined when researchers profit from a person's body part to the exclusion of that person.[72]

Fragmentation

If persons have property rights to their bodies then, as discussed under self-ownership above, this implies a division between the physical body and the non-physical personality, with the latter claiming property rights to the former. This fragmentation of the body is a possible reason for opposing the idea of body as property. Radhika Rao articulates the position of this school of thought as follows:

> Property produces a fragmented relationship between the body and its owner, the person 'inside' the body, in contrast with privacy, which creates an indivisible corporeal identity. By uncoupling the body from the person and undermining the unity of the physical being, the property paradigm facilitates fragmentation of the body itself, both literally and figuratively.[73]

The fundamental problem with this argument has been discussed above: the argument is based on the notion of property as a thing, a notion that has been rejected in this thesis. A counter-argument is adduced here. If property is seen as defining the *relationship between persons*, then property analysis actually preserves and *mandates* unity of body and personality. Also, most (if not all) of the sticks in the bundle of incidents by which property is defined can be enjoyed only by the integral person, not by the mere physical body.

The other difficulty with this argument, as far as right to self-determination is concerned, is that the alternative model, consent, does not always address Rao's 'indivisible corporeal entity'. For example, battery (non-consensual touching) addresses the physical self, not necessarily the body-and-mind combination. As explained in the discussion of torts (Chapter 3), mere unauthorised touch is all that is required to establish liability in battery.

71 Beyleveld D and Brownsword R, *Human Dignity in Bioethics and Biolaw*. Oxford: Oxford University Press 2001, p. 218.

72 *Moore* v. *Regents of the University of California* 793 P.2d 479 (Cal. 1990), at 515.

73 Rao R, Property, privacy, and the human body (2000) 80 Boston Univ L Rev 359–460, at p. 364.

Definition of Property

It could be argued that the body does not meet the prerequisites to qualify as property, as defined by some scholars. These prerequisites, discussed in Chapter 5, include alienability and separability, but it has been argued in the previous chapter that property rights in the body are consistent with Underkuffler's framework of property. Also the idea of a thing having been processed or altered by the application of skill (an attribute of property developed in common law) does not apply to the living body.

Alexandra George argues that control over the human body and its parts should not be based on assumptions about the existence of property in the body; rather lawmakers should first decide the degree of control they wish to bestow, then use property if necessary, to enforce decisions about control.[74] This is an interesting point because the court in *Moore* appeared to be pre-occupied with whether there was property in the spleen, when it should have concentrated in the first instance on Mr Moore's right to self-determination, then applied property analysis afterwards.

Commodification

Possible commodification of the body is the central plank in the case against treating body parts and particles as property. If ascribing property to the body leads to commodification, this would be the opposite of what we wish to achieve, self-determination. Possible commodification of the body appears to be the main fear of those who are against treating body parts and particles as property. This is reflected in the views expressed by Arabian J in *Moore*:

> Plaintiff has asked us to recognize and enforce a right to sell one's own body tissue for profit. He entreats us to regard the human vessel – the single most venerated and protected subject in any civilized society – as equal with the basest commercial commodity. He urges us to comingle the sacred with the profane. He asks much.[75]

He went on to ask rhetorically: 'Does it uplift or degrade the "unique human persona" to treat human tissue as a fungible article of commerce?'[76]

Andrews and Nelkin, champions of the anti-commodification campaign, demonstrate the variable manifestation of commodification in the following observations:

74 George, Is 'property' necessary?

75 Moore v. Regents of the University of California (1990) 51 Cal.3d 120, at 140.

76 Ibid.

> The language of science is increasingly permeated with the commercial language of supply and demand, contracts, exchange, and compensation. Body parts are extracted like a mineral, *harvested* like a crop, or *mined* like a resource. Tissue is *procured* – a term more commonly used for land, goods, and prostitutes. Cells, embryos, and tissue are frozen, banked, placed in libraries or repositories, marketed, patented, bought or sold. Umbilical cords, whose stem cells are used for therapeutic purposes, are described as a 'hot clinical property'. The physician who patented John Moore's cell line apparently referred to his patient's body as a 'gold mine'.[77]

Some fear that in attaching property rights to human body or body parts, we may 'come to discover the price of everything but discover that we know the value of nothing'.[78] Concerns like this are pithy when we pause to consider what has happened to the brain of Albert Einstein (he wanted his body cremated so that people would not come to worship at his bones but the pathologist who conducted his autopsy removed the brain and has since been treating it as personal property)[79] and the bones of Alistair Cooke (which were stolen and sold to body parts dealers).[80]

The Council of Europe's Convention on Human Rights and Biomedicine stipulates that '(t)he human body and its parts shall not, as such, give rise to financial gain'.[81] This refrain is also to be found in Article 4 of UNESCO's Declaration on the Human Genome and Human Rights ('The human genome in its natural state shall not give rise to financial gains')[82] and a range of other sources.[83] These prohibitions are founded on the premise that commercialisation

---

77 Andrews and Nelkin, *Body Bazaar*, pp. 5–6.

78 Morgan, Where do I own my body?, p. 98.

79 Burrell B, The long, strange journey of Einstein's brain. In Burrell B, *Postcards from the Brain Museum: The Improbable Search for Meaning in the Matter of Famous Minds*. New York: Broadway Books 2004.

80 Jailed: gang which plundered Alistair Cooke's grave to sell body parts. Daily Mail, 23 October 2008.

81 Council of Europe, *Convention on Human Rights and Biomedicine*, Article 21; available at http://conventions.coe.int. Accessed 21 October 2012.

82 Universal Declaration on the Human Genome and Human Rights, adopted at the 29th session of the General Conference on 11 November 1997. Endorsed by the United Nations General Assembly (Resolution A/RES/53/152) on 9 December 1998.

83 For example, the Warnock Committee reported that 'it is inconsistent with human dignity that a woman should use her uterus for financial profit'; Warnock Committee, *Report of the Committee of Inquiry into Human Fertilisation and Embryology*, paragraph 8.10; Michael Trebilock reports that in America legal prohibitions support 'the commonly held notion that body parts are among those things which ought not to be bought and sold, because they are intrinsic to our personhood'; Trebilock MJ, *The Limits of Freedom of Contract*. Cambridge, Mass: Harvard University Press 1993, p. 38. Article 3 of the Charter of Fundamental Rights of the European Union prohibits 'making the human body and its parts a source of financial gain'. Canada's Royal

of the body or its parts[84] affronts human dignity. Objectors to the patenting of human genetic material employed similar arguments.[85] There are two problems with this argument. The first is that, as stated in Chapter 6, not all property rights are commercial property rights; property is sometimes *but not always*, a commodity.

Underlying the objection to commercialisation of the body or body parts is the idea that the body is different from other things, and its special status is defiled by placing a price on it. If all body parts were to be given equal treatment, this idea would be difficult to sustain, for if there is no objection to selling hair (a renewable body part), why should there be objection to selling blood (also a renewable body part). Commodification is not intrinsically evil; it only assumes that negativity when exploitation is present.

Apart from any intrinsic moral problem with commercialisation of human body parts, there is concern about the effect that financial inducement could have on vulnerable persons,[86] including pregnant ones.[87] This fear relates to the Kantian maxim, that the vulnerable may be seen not as ends in themselves but as means to an end. It is argued, for example, that if women were to have property interests in their foetal tissue, they might be induced to abort their foetuses for pecuniary advantage rather than carry them to term.[88] Such abortion-for-profit is a public policy concern that would outweigh the benefits of unfettered property rights. It is also argued that allowing women to sell their foetal tissue directly, or to exercise their right to share in profits resulting from commercial development of their foetal tissue, would be counter to the public interest.

Commission on New Reproductive Technologies said that 'Human beings, their reproductive capacities or tissues should not be treated as commodities to be traded for money or other goods'; *Proceed with Care, Final Report of the Royal Commission on New Reproductive Technologies*, vol ii, 30 November 1993, p. 718.

84 In the Convention on Human Rights and Biomedicine, the term 'body parts' applies to 'organs and tissue proper, including blood' but not to parts 'such as hair and nails, which are discarded tissues, and the sale of which is not an affront to human dignity'. Paragraphs 132 and 133 of the Explanatory Report to the Convention.

85 In the *Relaxin* case, it was argued that the 'isolation of the DNA relaxin gene from tissue taken from a pregnant woman is immoral, as it constitutes an offence against human dignity to make use of a particular female condition (pregnancy) for a technical process oriented towards profit' and that granting a patent would amount to 'a form of modern slavery since it involves the dismemberment of women and their piecemeal sale to commercial enterprises throughout the world' [1995] EPOR 541, 549 (paragraphs 6.1(a) and (b)).

86 Beyleveld and Brownsword, *Human Dignity in Bioethics and Biolaw*, pp. 207–215.

87 Field NE, Evolving conceptualisation of property: a proposal to de-commercialize the value of fetal tissue (1989) 99 Yale LJ 169–186.

88 Beyleveld and Brownsword, *Human Dignity in Bioethics and Biolaw*, pp. 207–215.

Similarly, trade in human organs generates the image of impoverished persons converted to organ farms to be harvested by the rich.[89]

Again, the problem with this line of argument is that where the self-determination of the individual is given prime consideration, a contract is not invalidated simply because some persons (or even the majority) consider the transaction harmful.[90] As the Court of Appeal said in respect of a pregnant woman declining treatment, whether or not her own life or that of the unborn child is at risk, 'her right is not reduced or diminished merely because her decision to exercise it may appear morally repugnant'.[91]

There is also an inconsistency in the argument: a person is allowed the self-determination to refuse blood transfusion or other treatment and die as a result, but not allowed the self-determination to sell a spare kidney. This inconsistency has arisen because the public interest considerations have been prioritised over individual self-determination. I would submit that public policy cannot be excluded from any analysis relating to the individual's right to self-determination in health care, and what I am proposing is a model that allows optimal exercise of self-determination while also accommodating public policy imperatives.

Ironically, while fear of commercialisation is the driving force of the anti-propertisation school, *Moore* shows that body parts can be commercialised *even while discountenancing property rights in them*: while disavowing a property approach, the court recognised that the claimant was entitled to a commercial interest in his body part. In other words, if it is the fear of commodification that we are concerned about, it is not rejection of property in the body that will allay our fears. Conversely, ascription of property rights to the body (or parts or particles) does not necessarily imply commodification.

In the final analysis, the answer to the commodification problem may lie somewhere in the middle, as acknowledged by some commentators:

> We do not see this issue as usefully approached as if it was all or nothing. Rather, we submit, it seems clear that some forms of commercialization will (and should) be allowed, some should absolutely be forbidden, and the real issue is which forms of commercialization, between these extremes, will be allowed or forbidden, and according to which principles or considerations.[92]

---

89 Leder D, Whose body, what body? The metaphysics of organ transplantation. In Cherry MJ (ed), *Persons and Their Bodies: Rights, Responsibilities, Relationships*. Dordrecht: Kluwer Academic 1999, pp. 233–264, at p. 242.

90 Beyleveld and Brownsword, *Human Dignity in Bioethics and Biolaw*, p. 209.

91 *St George's Healthcare NHS Trust* v. *S* [1998] 3 WLR 936, at 957.

92 Wear S, Freer J and Koczwara B, Commercialisation of human body parts: public policy considerations. In Cherry MJ (ed), *Persons and Their Bodies: Rights, Responsibilities, Relationships*. Dordrecht: Kluwer Academic 1999, pp. 363–384, at p. 375.

Sorting out which forms of commercialisation should be allowed is, however, beyond the scope of this book.

Interconnection of Bodies

Herring and Chau advocate a model that reflects, supports and respects the following nuances: 'our bodies are ours; are in relationship with others; are in constant flux; and yet central to our identity of ourselves'.[93] From intrauterine life through our entire life to death our bodies are interconnected with other bodies: examples include placenta, feto-maternal blood transfusion at birth, breastfeeding, shared genetic constitution and interdependence between carer and cared for. We are reminded that:

> Many of the things we most greatly value in life involve the sharing and interconnection of bodies: sex, sports, massage, shaking hands, to name but a few. It is in the meeting, intermingling and interaction of our bodies that many of life's most meaningful events occur.[94]

Also the interaction of the body with the wider environment – for example, through food, air and commensal bacteria – is essential to human life. The authors also refer to the mutability of our bodies: 'Our bodies are constantly changing [and] [b]y the time we die, there is little of us that is biologically the same as when we were born.'[95]

On the basis of the above – interconnection, interdependence and mutability – the authors argue the case for a moral obligation to allow one's bodily material to be used for the benefit of others. Each person owes this obligation to the world from which they benefit throughout their life. Also the body is not just that of the individual but the product of the interaction between this body, other bodies and the wider environment – so 'any argument that [the spleen] was just Mr Moore's should be resisted'.[96]

The affinity between this approach and the ecology paradigm espoused in Chapter 1 is immediately recognised at first glance, but getting to the root of the argument we meet with disappointment. The authors accept that 'our bodies are ours' (see above), then go on to say that there should be no property in the body. They do not offer any real reason why the body cannot be property; their analysis does not show that the body is not or cannot be property. Rather, what they have actually argued is that the body should belong not to the individual person

93 Herring and Chau, My body, your body, our bodies, p. 52.
94 Ibid., p. 48.
95 Ibid., p. 51.
96 Ibid., p. 55.

but to the world at large. This is idealistic communitarianism, divorced from the practicalities of life. Without individuals there can be no interdependence. Without individual nuances and characteristics, without a diversity of individual attributes and preferences, there cannot be the biological, genetic and social heterogeneity essential for sustenance of the environment – without diversity there is no ecology. Even the examples they give of interconnection between humans – sex, sports, massage, shaking hands – all require the consent (self-determination) of the partaking individuals.

A pragmatic rather than aspirational approach has been taken from the outset in this book. Just as the concept of absolute self-determination is rejected, so is the idea that the world is all about communities, with no individuals units at all. Accordingly the theory put forward by Herring and Chau is discountenanced.

Other Public Policy Considerations

Before looking at the other side of the coin, one must mention that public policy considerations other than commodification may be employed in arguing against property rights in body parts or particles. For example, objection to posthumous transfer or use of semen may be the basis for denying proprietary rights to stored sperm.[97] Conservative commentators and scholars could argue that it is not in the public interest to encourage post-mortem human reproduction.[98] As taking sperm to be the object of property facilitates postpartum reproduction, it is argued that sperm cannot be property. One problem with this argument is that, even if opposition to postpartum reproduction is a public policy matter (arguably, it is not), there are more direct ways of restricting it other than a denial of the concept of property in gametes.

Arguments for Treating Body Parts and Particles as Property

In the next few paragraphs it will be argued that people should benefit from exploitation of material derived from their body and that treating body parts and particles as property could foster self-determination and protect against commodification. It is argued that property generates positive obligations, and this is advantageous for protecting self-determination. It is also argued that the idea of quasi-property in the body is a fudge.

---

97 Steinbock B, Sperm as property. In Harris J and Holm S (eds), *The Future of Human Reproduction*. Oxford: Clarendon Press 1998.

98 Sperling D, *Management of Post-Mortem Pregnancy: Legal and Philosophical Aspects*. Aldershot: Ashgate 2006. See also McLean S, Post-mortem human reproduction: legal and other regulatory issues (2002) 9 J Law and Med 429–433.

Self-determination

The moral argument for treating the body and body parts, including genetic material, as property rests on the principle of self-determination – people should be allowed to use their body and body parts as they please, so long as others are not harmed. As Lord Tebbit has asserted:

> My body is mine. It may not be a very good one. Bits have been knocked off it and other bits have been broken. Parts have been removed to repair damage elsewhere, and it is held together with plastic reinforcement. It is past its best. If it were a car, it would not make a lot on a trade-in, but it might be cannibalized for spares. Nonetheless I own it. It does not belong to the state, the community or the BMA [British Medical Association]. So it is evident to me that I, and I alone, have the right to dispose of it, all or in part, before or after my death.[99]

A woman's right to abortion has also been defended on the principle that her body is her property.[100] On the other hand, a proprietary right in the body does not have to be established in order to uphold self-determination: without resorting to a property analysis, the common law in England has established that an adult of sound mind may refuse medical treatment even if such refusal could cost him his life.[101] Thus while property analysis is an appealing approach to the enhancement of self-determination, it is not the only (or until proven otherwise, preferable) one. The property model is compared with the consent model in Chapter 9.

People Should Benefit from Exploitation of Material Derived from Their Body

In relation to body parts, however, the common law has not found a way to grant continuing rights to the source of a body part or particle once it has been removed from the person. The law upholds the principle of bodily integrity through the requirement that consent be obtained before the tissue is taken from the patient. Once the tissue has been removed, however, the patient has no rights over subsequent use. The implication is that other parties are able to profit financially from property rights to the body part or particle, to the exclusion of the patient from whom the material was obtained. This does not

99 Lord Tebbit, Body politics. BMA News Review, June 2000, p. 34.

100 Goldberg JD, Involuntary servitudes: a property-based notion of abortion choice (1991) 38 UCLA LR 1597–1657.

101 *Re T (Adult: Refusal of Treatment)* [1993] Fam 95.

appear to be justice for all, but ethical justification for this position has been advanced.[102]

Property rights in one's body parts or particles would enable donors to share in the profits derived from commercialisation. However, while this may be of benefit to the individual, it may have deleterious effects on altruistic organ donation[103] and hinder scientific research and development. In *Moore* the Supreme Court of California said: 'The theory of liability that Moore urges us to endorse threatens to destroy the economic incentive to conduct important medical research.'[104]

It may be argued that all organ or tissue donation should be altruistic, that nobody should be allowed to make financial gains from their body parts. This was the preferred position of the Human Fertilisation and Embryology Authority (HFEA).[105] The Brazier Committee on surrogacy also adopted this position when it compared paid surrogacy to the sale of blood.[106] A requirement for all organ or tissue donation to be altruistic would, however, be based on moral rather than legal principles, and may not be a pragmatic approach where there is a dearth of donors – despite its moral stance, the HFEA opted to continue paying sperm and egg donors, given the effect that a total ban on payments would have on the availability of donated gametes and embryos.[107] We may abhor the idea of making money from such donations, but that is not to say that anyone wishing to profit in this way should be criminalised, as is the case in Australian jurisdictions where donors are prohibited from trading in their own tissue in the absence of ministerial permission.[108]

It is only fair that donors of genetic material should have some property right in their genetic material, and have a chance to benefit in some measure from financial benefits accruing from that material – after all, in relation to other objects that qualify as objects of proprietary rights the principle of equitable tracing will be applied.

Society stands to benefit from research in biotechnology, however, and it would be counter-productive if property rights in genetic material were to constrain research. If property rights were attached to body parts or tissue, then

102 Herring and Chau, My body, your body, our bodies.

103 Wear *et al.*, Commercialisation of human body parts, pp. 377–379.

104 *Moore* v. *Regents of the University of California* 271 Cal. Rptr. 146 (1990), at 162.

105 In 2007 the Human Fertilisation and Embryology Authority (HFEA) announced its decision to allow altruistic donation of eggs for research. London: HFEA Press release, 21 February 2007. See also HFEA 9th Annual Report and Accounts, 2000 (London: HFEA 2000, p. 28) for policy on payment of expenses to donors.

106 Brazier M, Campbell AV and Golombok S, *Surrogacy: Review for Health Ministers of Current Arrangements for Payments and Regulation: Report of the Review Team*. London: HMSO 1998.

107 Human Fertilisation and Embryology Authority (HFEA), HFEA agrees new policies to improve sperm and egg donation services. London: HFEA Press release, 19 October 2011.

108 Human Tissue Act 1983 (N.S.W.) ss 23–24.

there is the possibility that donors could restrict the use of these resources and so hamper research or inhibit equitable and altruistic medical intervention. This appeared to have been the policy consideration behind the decision in *Moore*. This argument underestimates the public's thirst for, and appreciation of, scientific advancement. For what is a pittance compared to the sums of money involved in biotechnology patents, the public readily volunteer to participate in clinical trials that entail bodily invasion, sometimes with near tragic complications.[109]

Protection against Commodification

Another argument for recognising property in body parts is that doing so minimises (paradoxically, it may seem) the potential for commodification of the body. This was the argument of Mosk J in his minority judgment in *Moore*: failure to recognise a man's property rights in his body or body parts leaves these objects vulnerable to ownership or exploitation by others.[110] In other words, while many scholars argue that recognising property rights in the body and its parts or particles opens the door to commodification, Mosk argues that it is a failure to recognise such property rights that actually opens this door.

Relaxation of moral or ethical restraints relating to commodification will certainly be a factor in the increased recourse to, and acceptability of, the property model, but a more enabling factor would be the more embracing definition of property. The less we think of property in terms of 'commodity', the more easily we are able to accommodate a view of gametes and embryos as property. In Chapter 6, a more embracing view of property was presented, emphasising that property is not necessarily a commodity, something merchantable. The arguments advanced above in support of property rights in the body and its parts assume that propertisation does not necessarily imply commodification but even the latter has its advocates, as noted by the late historian Roy Porter:

> The case for regarding (the body and its parts) as a commodity has been advanced by some American utilitarian philosophers: rational choice and market forces, they argue, would create an optimum trade in body commodities such as sperm, embryos, wombs and babies. A 'futures market' in organs has been proposed.[111]

---

109 Dyer O, Payment offered to injured trial participants has strings attached (2006) 332 BMJ 990.

110 *Moore* v. *Regents of the University of California* 793 P.2d 479 (Cal. 1990), at 515–516.

111 Porter R, *The Greatest Benefit to Mankind: A Medical History of Humanity from Antiquity to the Present*. London: Fountain Press 1999, p. 625.

Quasi-property and 'Limited Property' Analysis – Fudge

Sandwiched between the 'property' and 'no-property' approaches is the 'limited property' analysis put forward by Munzer, who remarks that:

> Too many incidents are lacking to say that persons own their bodies. Restrictions on transfer and the absence of a liberty to consume or destroy, for example, indicate that persons do not own their bodies in the way that they own automobiles and desks.[112]

He recognises that, as people can donate or sell their body parts, it is not quite right to say they have no property rights in them, but suggests that the rights to use, manage, dispose of, exclude others from or transfer a body part should be seen as limited property rights, rather than ownership.[113] There are problems with this viewpoint. Firstly, it is not quite right that 'too many incidents are lacking', but even if this were correct, there is no minimum number of incidents required for property to be established. Secondly, the fact that a person can refuse blood transfusion[114] or a life-saving Caesarean section[115] belies 'the absence of a liberty to consume or destroy'. Finally it seems counterintuitive to accept that 'rights to use, manage, dispose of, exclude others from, or transfer' could all add up to no more than 'limited' property rights. One cannot help feeling that this designation is simply a means of avoiding the dreaded word 'ownership'.

Thinking along the same lines as Munzer, Remigius Nwabueze proposes a 'limited but market-inalienable'[116] type of property right. 'Limited property rights' appears to be just another term for the so-called 'quasi-property' rights. Mason and Laurie's discussion of quasi-property shows that this is no more than a comfort zone for the middle-of-the-road traveller:

> To recognise a 'quasi-property' claim to material is to support a normatively strong connection to that material and, accordingly, to establish strong, justiciable legal interest; by the same token … 'full' property rights will only be recognised where there is little or no prospect of exploitation or other harm, which can include the 'harm' of disrespect for the dignity of the human organism.[117]

---

112 Munzer SR, *A Theory of Property*. Cambridge: Cambridge University Press 1990, p. 43.

113 Ibid., p. 45.

114 *Re T (Adult: Refusal of Treatment)* [1992] 4 All ER 649.

115 *St George's Healthcare NHS Trust* v. *S*; R v. *Collins and others, ex parte S* [1998] 3 All ER 673, [1998] Fam Law 52.

116 Nwabueze *Biotechnology*, p. 49.

117 Mason JK and Laurie GT, *Mason & McCall Smith's Law and Medical Ethics*, 7th edn. Oxford: Oxford University Press 2005, pp. 514–515.

The advocates of a limited or quasi-property category have not elaborated an adequate theoretical basis to justify this category. The category appears to be no more than a sanctuary for those who recognise the value of property analysis but cannot face the reality of applying property discourse to the human body.

In a nutshell, quasi-property is a fudge.

Conclusions

If we expect the law to allocate to us exclusive physical control over our own bodies and body parts,[118] then we must address the issue of whether our bodies and body parts or particles are property. On the basis of the foregoing arguments, it is concluded that body parts and particles and the body as a whole can be treated as property. The safeguard of legislative checks could be introduced as may from to time be agreed by society to restrain commercial trafficking. Given all the concrete and potential advantages of recognising property in the body, there is at least a *prima facie* case for doing so. Indeed it is the existence of a *prima facie* case that has kept the debate alive despite strong feelings and fears about commodification.

The analysis presented above shows that all of the reasons for rejecting the idea of property in the body have as their common denominator the reification of property – that is, the notion of property as a thing. This notion of property, however, is obsolete. Clinging on to Blackstone's concept of property in the twenty-first century will continue to fuel an emotional rather than rational approach to the matter of property in the body. Such emotional constraints are understandable given the history of slavery, exploitation and unethical, dehumanising medical experimentation. The mission to accelerate the abandonment of 'thingification' and entrench the modern notion of property calls for leadership. Unfortunately the law is slow to drive social change and some would say that it is not the role of the law to do so; that the purpose of the law is to reflect and protect social mores rather than to shape them. As far as driving the modern notion of property is concerned, both common law and the legislature have either explicitly rejected or implicitly spurned the opportunity to do so. The legislators had an opportunity to adopt a different approach when enacting the Human Tissue Act but fought shy of doing so. When legislators are tardy, the common law could show the way. As a 2008 editorial in *USA Today* stated:

> Sometimes, of course, courts do need to intervene to force morally and constitutionally necessary changes – such as mandating school integration

118 Clarke and Kohler, *Property Law*.

> and overturning bans on interracial marriage – when voters or their elected representatives won't do so.[119]

Regarding recognition of proprietary rights in the body, it does not appear that judges are keen to intervene and the task of driving the law on this subject falls on the shoulders of academic lawyers and commentators.

The interest we wish to protect is self-determination and it has been shown in this chapter that a valid notion of property *can* be applied to the body and its parts. The question arises, *why* is it necessary to consider applying a property analysis for protecting the right to self-determination in health care? The answer to this question is that the current approach, the consent model, has significant limitations that make it necessary for alternative or complementary models to be considered. These limitations were discussed in Chapter 5 and the proposed model is discussed in Chapter 9. Meanwhile attention is focused on a novel application of property analysis to health-care decision-making; one that has not previously been elaborated – property rights in the patient's expectation from a clinical consultation.

---

119 California ruling invites backlash against gay rights. *USA Today*, Friday, 23 May 2008, p. 7a. The editorial was in response to the ruling of the California Supreme Court in May 2008 allowing gay marriage.

Chapter 8
Property Rights in the Patient's Legitimate Expectations

> If we examine the modern legal meaning of property, we can see its enduring appeal as a means of asserting the autonomy of the individual.[1]

> As a man is said to have a right to his property, he may be equally said to have property in his rights.[2]

In the first few chapters of this book, it was seen that the doctor–patient relationship and the assertion of patients' right to self-determination have been influenced by, and evolved in tandem with, the ascendance of rights thinking and consumer advocacy. The relationship between consumers and the providers of goods and services is regulated by laws of contract, tort and property. The place of tort in the protection of patient self-determination has been discussed in Chapter 3. The place of contract has not been discussed, but its place in the UK medico-legal arena is limited to the relatively small size of the private sector, where doctors providing services privately are deemed to have a contractual relationship with their patients and can be sued in contract.[3] In the NHS, doctors do not legally have such a contractual relationship with their patients[4] although, as seen in Chapter 2, one model of the doctor–patient relationship could be described as contractual in nature.[5]

The subject of this book is the application of the third regulatory modality – property – to the doctor–patient relationship. One way of applying this is by

---

1 Davies M and Naffine N, *Are Persons Property? Legal Debates about Property and Personality*. Aldershot: Ashgate/Dartmouth 2001, p. 6.

2 Quoted in Underkuffler LS, On property: an essay (1990) 100 Yale LJ 127–148, at p. 135. Original citation: Madison J, Property. In *The Writings of James Madison*, ed Hunt G. 1906, vol. 6, p. 101.

3 De Cruz P, *Comparative Healthcare Law*. Abingdon: Psychology Press 2001, p. 234; *Pfizer Corp* v. *Ministry of Health* [1965] AC 512 (HL).

4 Department of Health, *NHS Indemnity Arrangements for Handling Clinical Negligence Claims against NHS Staff*, HSG (96)48. London: DH 1996.

5 Also, the General Medical Council refers to the duties outlined in its *Good Medical Practice* guidance as 'the contract between doctor and patient'. See General Medical Council (GMC) and the Conference of Post Graduate Medical Deaneries (COPMeD), *Memorandum of Understanding*. April 2007, Annexe A.

treating a person's body as his/her property, and on this basis treating the right to bodily integrity as a right to property. The arguments against this approach have been discussed in the previous chapter, and it has been concluded that the concept of property adopted in this book does not permit the commodification or other arguments to hold sway.

Once these arguments are disposed of, it would be logical for Lord Tebbit's assertion ('my body is my property')[6] to be backed by the law. On its own, however, the body-as-property approach would be inadequate for establishing a property model for protecting patient self-determination. One reason for saying so is that concentration on 'body as property' supports a narrow conception of property, whereas the case has been made in Chapter 6 for a broad, 'Madisonian'[7] conception. Secondly, a model founded solely on body-as-property will continue to elicit vocal opposition from those who maintain the commodification argument, thus stalling any moves to implement the property model as an alternative to the consent model. Thirdly, this approach based on a narrow conception of property will not fit easily with the Underkuffler framework that has been adopted in this book, and will therefore not have the advantages offered by this framework, such as the ability to define stringency of protection.

A key point is that property (as understood in this book) defines a *relationship*, not a thing. Moving away from the reification of property, a novel theory of property rights in the doctor–patient consultation is developed in this chapter. This theory ascribes property rights to the patient's expectations from the doctor–patient consultation, and the correlative duties of the doctor are regarded as fiduciary and at the core of medical professionalism. If the patient's legitimate expectations are accorded proprietary rights, they have the protection that property law offers, and this may have advantages over the consent model in securing self-determination. By thinking of legitimate expectations as giving rise to proprietary rights we move away from the notion of property as a thing and follow the alternative notion of property as defining relationships. This stance is also consonant with a social relational approach, which in turn is consonant with the ecology paradigm (discussed in Chapter 1).

Protecting the Vulnerable

It is not unusual for the law to protect the expectations of consumers. Consumer expectations are protected in product liability law. For example, the European

6 Lord Tebbit, Body politics. BMA News Review, June 2000, p. 34.

7 I use this eponym to refer to the broader conception of property advocated by the former US President James Madison.

Council Directive on General Product Safety 2001/95/EC states that the conformance of a product to a general safety requirement shall be assessed taking into account 'reasonable customer expectations regarding safety'[8] (among other considerations). Consumer protection law commonly upholds consumer rights by requiring providers to disclose detailed information about their goods and services, particularly where safety or public health is an issue.

In general, the law tends to protect the interests of the more vulnerable party by imposing obligations on the more powerful party. Academic commentators have made the case for the use of property rights to protect the interests of those affected by the closure of industrial plants in the USA,[9] the interests of individuals who are victims of takings[10] and the interests of employees in a publicly traded firm.[11] The case for these pleadings is based on the need to legally protect these interests and a recognition of the security associated with property rights.

Fundamentally, there is little difference between these interests and a patient's interest in being able to make informed decisions about his/her treatment; they all relate to basic human and consumer rights and it would not be out of place for the law to protect the patient's interests in the same way that it protects the vulnerable party in the examples given above. In transactions between two parties, what each party gets out of the transaction is usually a function of its power relative to the other. In the doctor–patient consultation, the patient is the more vulnerable party and, as argued in previous chapters, the consent model has proved incapable of offering the vulnerable party adequate protection in the face of a steep power gradient between doctor and patient. This gradient is partly responsible for the gap between the theoretical and the operationalised paradigms of consent and for the prevalence of Category III consent.[12]

If the consent model is not fit for purpose in this regard then, as argued earlier, the solution is not to tinker with this model but to explore alternative models. The starting point for one such approach is to recognise the patient's interest in making decisions on his/her own treatment; the right tool for protecting this interest can then be sought and applied. The patient has a legitimate expectation that the doctor will, in the course of the consultation, recognise and respect his/her right to self-determination. Respect for this right

8 European Parliament, Council, Directive 2001/95/EC of the European Parliament and of the Council of 3 December 2001 on general product safety, Article 3(f).

9 Singer JW, The reliance interest in property (1988) 40 Stan L Rev 611–750.

10 Yellin DS, Masters of their own eminent domain: the case for a reliance interest associated with economic development takings (2011) 99 Geo LJ 651–676.

11 Njoya W, *Property in Work: The Employment Relationship in the Anglo-American Firm*. Aldershot: Ashgate 2007.

12 See Chapter 5 for a discussion of the categories of consent.

entails engagement with the patient, provision of tailored information, taking reasonable steps to ensure comprehension and accepting the patient's decision.

This right to self-determination should be protected as a legal right in itself.[13] The legitimate expectation which flows from that right should be protected as a distinct legal interest. Property analysis has the potential to come to the rescue here: the legitimate expectation can be protected as a proprietary right. Property, as discussed in Chapter 6, defines the relationship between parties, and proprietary rights offer a means of protection to an otherwise vulnerable party in a transaction or relationship.[14] The patient's legitimate expectations from a consultation with the doctor constitute a chose in action. As discussed in Chapter 6, a chose in action is a property interest that can be enforced only through legal action; the term was originally used to cover rights associated with a personal action, and it was argued a century ago that a right of action in tort could be regarded as a chose in action. It is, therefore, not anomalous to suggest that the patient's legitimate expectation could be regarded as a chose in action.

Treating the patient's expectation as property would be similar to what happens with intellectual property and other intangible valuables:

> ... the owner of patent rights in a machine owns neither a particular machine nor the model or drawings of the machine submitted to the patent office, but rather the rights to control the use of his or her design for the machine. Immaterial, or even 'non-existent' entities can be subjugated to property regimes, if they are believed to have value, if they can be clearly conceptualized, and if they can be 'constructed' in such a way as to make property rights in them administrable. For example, the laws of slander and libel have been made to protect something as immaterial as a businessman's 'property in reputation'.[15]

In other words, there is nothing extraordinary in treating patient expectation as property and, as it meets the criteria outlined in this quote, there is no legal reason why it cannot be treated as such. In the following paragraphs the principle of property rights in expectation and how this principle could be applied to the doctor–patient transaction are explored. The central role of trust in this transaction is emphasised and, as one of the criticisms of the consent model is that it negates trust, the possibility that recognising the doctor's duties as fiduciary can help build trust is also explored. In the property model proposed in this book, the patient's legitimate expectations are accorded property rights

---

13 The argument for this is made in the next chapter.

14 Schultz D and Jann D, The use of eminent domain and contractually implied property rights to affect business and plant closings (1990) 16 Wm Mitchell L Rev 383–427.

15 Brewer J and Staves S (eds), *Early Modern Conceptions of Property*. London: Routledge 1995.

and, correlative to this, the doctor has fiduciary duties which include the duty to respect the right to self-determination. If this model works, therefore, it will enshrine trust while also upholding self-determination.

Expectation as Property

Expectation interest (the interest of a party to a breached contract in receiving the benefit of the bargain by being put in a position as good as that which would have resulted had the contract been performed) and reliance interest (the interest of a party to a breached contract in being compensated for detriments suffered in reliance on the agreement) are firmly embedded in contract law.[16]

Reliance interest is also established in divorce law.[17] The idea that expectation should in certain circumstances be protected by the law is therefore not new.

The idea that expectation could be treated as property is also not entirely new – what is new is its application to self-determination in health care and particularly, to the doctor–patient consultation. Jeremy Bentham declared that '[p]roperty is nothing but a basis of expectation'.[18] Powell noted that the law 'has recognised and protected even the expectation of rights as actual property'.[19] Demsetz theorised that property rights are an instrument of society, and posits:

> In the world of Robinson Crusoe property rights play no role. Property rights are an instrument of society and derive their significance from the fact that they help a man form those expectations which he can reasonably hold in his dealings with others. These expectations find expression in the laws, customs, and mores of a society.[20]

Patent law is now firmly established, but at its heart lies a recognition of property in the expectation of the patent holder.[21] Harris argued that expectations

---

16 Fuller LL and Perdue WR Jr, The reliance interest in contract damages: Parts 1 and 2 (1936–37) 46 Yale LJ 52 and 373; Hudec RE, Restating the reliance interest (1981–82) 67 Cornell L Rev 704.

17 Brinig MF and Carbone J, Reliance interest in marriage and divorce (1987–88) 62 Tul L Rev 855–905.

18 Bentham J, Security and equality of property. In CB Macpherson, *Property: Mainstream and Critical Positions*. Oxford: Blackwell 1978, pp. 39–58, at p. 51.

19 Powell JA, New property disaggregated: a model to address employment discrimination (1990) 24 USF L Rev 363–383, at p. 366.

20 Demsetz H, Toward a theory of property rights (1967) 57 Am Econ Rev 347–359, at p. 347.

21 Patents Legal Section, *The Patents Act 1977 (as amended)*. London: Intellectual Property Office, October 2011.

grounded on the privileges of being a white person amounted to property.[22] Further, Nwabueze has speculated that 'the need to protect certain societal expectations may lead to the emergence of new forms of property'.[23]

Expectation has also featured in the personhood theory of property (briefly discussed in Chapter 6). Radin, an exponent of this theory, said:

> This view of personhood [as a continuing character structure encompassing future projects or plans, as well as past events and feelings] also gives us insight into why protecting people's 'expectations' of continuing control over objects seems so important. If an object you now control is bound up in your future plans or in your anticipation of your future self, and it is partly these plans for your own continuity that make you a person, then your personhood depends on the realization of these expectations. This turn to expectations might seem to send property theory back toward Bentham, who declared that 'the idea of property consists in an established expectation.' But this justification for honoring expectations is far from Benthamite, because it applies only to personal property.[24]

An opportunity for a judicial test of the proposition that expectation could be property arose in the American case of *Local 1330, United Steel Workers of America* v. *U.S. Steel Corp.*[25] The claimant was a labour organisation representing the workers of a steel mill. The defendant, United States Steel Corporation, had been running a steel mill in Youngstown, Ohio, for many years but decided, in view of the age of its machinery and developments in technology and marketing, to shut down the steel mill. This was certain to lead to the economic demise of the community. The company declined the workers' offer to buy the plant. The labour union went to court on the matter. At the pre-trial hearing the judge said:

> Everything that has happened in the Mahoning Valley has been happening for many years because of steel. Schools have been built, roads have been built. Expansion that has taken place is because of steel. And to accommodate that industry, lives and destinies of the inhabitants of that community were based and planned on the basis of that institution: Steel.

---

22 Harris CI, Whiteness as property (1993) 106 Harvard L Rev 1707–1791.

23 Nwabueze RN, *Biotechnology and the Challenge of Property: Property Rights in Dead Bodies, Body Parts, and Genetic Information.* Aldershot: Ashgate 2007, p. 21.

24 Radin MJ, *Reinterpreting Property.* Chicago: University of Chicago Press 1996, p. 42.

25 *Local 1330, United Steel Workers of America* v. *U.S. Steel Corp* 631 F.2d 1264, 1980 U.S. App. 105 L.R.R.M. 2312; 89 Lab. Cas. (CCH) P12,220.

> We are talking about an institution, a large corporate institution that is virtually the reason for the existence of that segment of this nation ... It would seem to me that when we take a look at the whole body of American law and the principles we attempt to come out with – and although a legislature has not pronounced any laws with respect to such a property right, that is not to suggest that there will not be a need for such a law in the future dealing with similar situations – it seems to me that a property right has arisen from this lengthy, long-established relationship between United States Steel, the steel industry as an institution, the community in Youngstown, the people in Mahoning County and the Mahoning Valley in having given and devoted their lives to this industry. Perhaps not a property right to the extent that can be remedied by compelling U.S. Steel to remain in Youngstown. But I think the law can recognize the property right to the extent that U.S. Steel cannot leave that Mahoning Valley and the Youngstown area in a state of waste, that it cannot completely abandon its obligation to that community, because certain vested rights have arisen out of this long relationship and institution.[26]

Subsequently, the steelworkers sought an injunction, claiming that their long dependence on the plant entitled them to property rights in the plant. Their claim was unsuccessful, despite the views expressed by the judge at the pre-trial hearing. The district court denied relief, holding that the refusal to sell the plant to the workers did not constitute an antitrust violation; that the workers could not assert a property interest in their jobs.[27] The workers filed an appeal with the Sixth Circuit Court of Appeals,[28] and this appeal was supported by *amicus curiae* from the Center for Constitutional Rights which argued that companies such as the steel giant that received substantial public funding should be constrained by judicial control to act in the best interests of the community.

The appeal court expressed sympathy for the community interest that was the subject of appeal but ruled that there was no legal authority to support a property claim as advanced by the workers.[29] A couple of years after this ruling the steel plants were destroyed. This case is similar to the *Moore*[30] case in that the courts recognised the disadvantaged position of the claimant but felt uncomfortable with the idea of ameliorating this through application of property analysis. It appears that in both cases, the court's decision was strongly influenced by policy considerations (in the former, the impact of restraining

26 Ibid., paras 190–193, quoting the District Judge at the pre-trial hearing.

27 *United Steel Workers of America, Local 1330* v. *United States Steel Corporation*, 492 F. Supp. 1, 10 (N.D. Ohio 1980).

28 *Local 1330, United Steel Workers of America* v. *United States Steel Corporation*, 631 F.2d 1264, 1280 (6th Cir. 1980).

29 *Local 1330*, 631 F.2d at 1280–1282.

30 *Moore* v. *Regents of the University of California* (1990) 51 Cal.3d 120.

an industrial company from moving its operations as dictated by economic factors; and in the latter, the impact of the court's decision on scientific and technological innovation).

The decision in this case has been robustly criticised by Singer.[31] In a comprehensive analysis of a property in reliance interest, Singer argued that, contrary to the statement of the court in *US Steel Workers*, there was legal support for the property claim made by the workers. He cited public trust doctrine, adverse possession, easements by estoppel, easements by necessity and public rights of access as legal doctrines which provide relevant precedent for the property right described by Judge Lambros at the pre-trial hearing. He argues that:

> The doctrines of adverse possession, prescriptive easements, easement by estoppel and easement by necessity all stand for the same proposition: Where a non-owner of property comes to rely upon access to property, the law sometimes recognizes the non-owner's vulnerability and shifts some or all of the property rights from the title owner to the non-owner. The rules in force therefore protect the non-owner's reliance on her relationship with the owner that made access to the land possible.[32]

Interestingly, the doctrines which he refers to as providing the legal precedent to establishment of property in legitimate expectation are legal doctrines that apply in situations where the parties concerned are strangers to each other, in the sense that they did not have a pre-existing agreement. A parallel could be drawn between this situation and the situation in clinical practice described as 'Strangers at the Bedside'.[33]

Although the court did not recognise a property interest in this particular case, Singer's comprehensive analysis is convincing enough to support a belief that there are reasonable prospects of the courts upholding this right in future cases, bar countervailing policy considerations. In any case, the doctrines of easements are evidence that, regardless of the court's decision in a particular case, expectation and reliance interests may be regarded as property rights in law. The challenge is to show how and why this can be extended to the doctor–patient relationships

Expectation and reliance interests associated with the doctrines of easement have developed *in the course of* a continuing relationship between both parties. In the case of doctor and patient, the expectations that may be subject of property

31 Singer, Reliance interest in property.

32 Ibid.

33 Rothman DJ, *Strangers at the Bedside: A History of How Law and Bioethics Transformed Medical Decision Making*, 2nd edn. Piscataway, NJ: Transaction 2003.

rights arise *a priori* from the covenant between both parties. Underlying this covenant is medical professionalism. Medical professionalism specifies the duties of the doctor, and the patient, relying on professionalism, expects the doctor to act in accordance with professional norms. This reliance is an act of trust.

Medical Professionalism

Medical professionalism is the framework of values, attitudes and behaviour that defines the relationship between doctors and patients, in the context of society.[34] Medical professionalism is what distinguishes medicine as a profession from medicine as a commodity.[35] It is the bedrock of the trust implicit in a traditional patient–doctor relationship where it is normative that the doctor will always act in the best interest of the patient. The patient is, by virtue of illness and of inferior technical knowledge, in a vulnerable position, and reposes trust in the doctor to act in his or her best interests. The Tuskegee,[36] Willowbrook[37] and Shipman[38] disasters referred to in Chapter 2 are failures of medical professionalism.

When it comes to promoting patient self-determination in clinical practice, however, it is important to adopt the right strategy. Jones drew attention to the importance of looking at the shop floor when exploring the law of consent and its application.[39] It has been shown in empirical studies that clinicians' perception of what the law of consent requires is often different from what the law actually says.[40] The protection of patient self-determination may start with the law but it is operationalised in the consultation rooms, so it goes to the heart of medical professionalism.

The doctor must *a priori* see the patient as an individual, with his/her own values, attitudes, beliefs and knowledge. Wright and colleagues showed that patients wanted 'to be afforded the dignity and rights associated with being "a

34 Thistlethwaite J and Spencer J, *Professionalism in Medicine.* Oxford: Radcliffe 2008.

35 Swick HM, Toward a normative definition of medical professionalism (2000) 75 Acad Med 612–616, at p. 616.

36 Jones J, *Bad Blood: The Tuskegee Syphilis Experiment.* New York: Free Press 1981.

37 Goldby S, Krugman S, Pappworth MH and Edsall G, The Willowbrook letters: criticisms and defense (1971) The Lancet, 10 April, 8 May, 5 June and 10 July.

38 Shipman Inquiry, *Fifth Report. Safeguarding Patients: Lessons from the Past – Proposals for the Future*, Cm 6394. London: The Stationery Office 2004.

39 Jones M, Informed consent and other fairy stories (1999) 7 Med L Rev 103–134, at p. 123.

40 Heywood R, Macaskill A and Williams K, Informed consent in hospital practice: health professionals' perspectives and legal reflections (2010) 18 Med L Rev 152–184.

human being, somebody who has an opinion'".[41] Having elicited in a qualitative study the views and needs of patients, they said that:

> When individuals feel vulnerable in the face of major threats, they seek attachment figures to help them feel safe. Only a doctor who was believed to be expert, to value the patient as an equal, and to be committed to the patient in a unique relationship could fulfil this role. The starting point for study and training of clinical communication should therefore be patients' vulnerability and dependence on doctors.[42]

Medical professionalism should be taught at undergraduate, postgraduate and continuing education levels and the property model, enshrined in medical professionalism, should be part of the curriculum.

While there has been no difficulty in recognising the value of medical professionalism, there has been less certainty about what it actually entails. Traditional notions of professionalism have construed it in terms of trusteeship and altruism: Rosen and Dewer describe the traditional image of medical professionalism as that of 'a selfless clinician, motivated by a strong ethos of service, equipped with unique skills and knowledge, in control of their work and practising all hours to restore full health to "his" or "her" patients'[43] but some more recent notions have focused on delivery of technical expertise.[44] Also some older notions have been built on clinical autonomy, while newer definitions have been patient-centred.[45] It was once said that 'perhaps professionalism is like pornography: easy to recognize but difficult to define'.[46] This difficulty (in

41 Wright EB, Holcombe C and Salmon P, Doctors' communication of trust, care, and respect in breast cancer: qualitative study (2004) 328 BMJ 864–869, at p. 867.

42 Ibid., p. 868.

43 Rosen R and Dewer S, *On Being a Doctor: Redefining Medical Professionalism for Better Patient Care*. London: King's Fund 2004, p. 1.

44 Ibid., p. 13.

45 Project of the ABIM Foundation, ACP-ASIM Foundation and European Federation of Internal Medicine, Medical professionalism in the new millennium: a physician charter (2002) 100 Obstetrics Gynecology 170–172; Cohen JJ, Cruess S and Davidson C, Alliance between society and medicine: the public's stake in medical professionalism (2007) 298 JAMA 670–673; Kuczewski MG, The professionalism movement: can we pause? (2004) 4 Am J Bioethics 1–10; Swick HM, Professionalism: a key to weathering the storm (2001) 98 Obstetrics Gynecology 156–161; Smith R, Medical professionalism: out with the old and in with the new (2006) 99 J R Soc Med 48–50; Tallis RC, Doctors in society: medical professionalism in a changing world (2006) 6 Clinical Medicine 7–12; Wynia MK, Latham SR, Kao AC, Berg JW and Emanuel LL, Medical professionalism in society (1999) 341 N Engl J Med 1612–1616.

46 Swick, Toward a normative definition of medical professionalism, p. 612.

defining professionalism) has been removed by recent work which made explicit the domains and required standards for medical professionalism.[47]

The following are now established as core principles of medical professionalism:

> Principle of primacy of patient welfare. This principle is based on a dedication to serving the interest of the patient. Altruism contributes to the trust that is central to the physician–patient relationship. Market forces, societal pressures and administrative exigencies must not compromise this principle.
>
> Principle of patient autonomy. Physicians must have respect for patient autonomy. Physicians must be honest with their patients and empower them to make informed decisions about their treatment. Patients' decisions about their care must be paramount, as long as those decisions are in keeping with ethical practice and do not lead to demands for inappropriate care.
>
> Principle of social justice. The medical profession must promote justice in the health-care system, including the fair distribution of health-care resources. Physicians should work actively to eliminate discrimination in health care, whether based on race, gender, socio-economic status, ethnicity, religion or any other social category.[48]

The General Medical Council's guidance, *Good Medical Practice*,[49] sets out the principles and values on which good practice is founded; these principles together describe medical professionalism in action. The guidance is addressed to doctors, but it is also intended to let the public know what they can expect from doctors. 'Relationships with patients' is one of the seven headings of *Good Medical Practice* (the others being 'Good clinical care', 'Maintaining good medical practice', 'Teaching and training', 'Working with colleagues', 'Probity' and 'Health').

The guidance specifies the duties of a doctor registered with the General Medical Council as follows:

- Make the care of your patient your first concern
- Protect and promote the health of patients and the public
- Provide a good standard of practice and care

47 Project of the ABIM Foundation *et al.*, Medical professionalism in the new millennium; Royal College of Physicians Working Party, *Doctors in Society: Medical Professionalism in a Changing World.* London: RCP 2005.

48 Ibid.

49 http://www.gmc-uk.org/guidance/good_medical_practice.asp. Accessed 17 April 2015.

- Keep your professional knowledge and skills up to date
- Recognise and work within the limits of your competence
- Work with colleagues in the ways that best serve patients' interests
- Treat patients as individuals and respect their dignity
- Treat patients politely and considerately
- Respect patients' right to confidentiality
- Work in partnership with patients
- Listen to patients and respond to their concerns and preferences
- Give patients the information they want or need in a way they can understand
- Respect patients' right to reach decisions with you about their treatment and care
- Support patients in caring for themselves to improve and maintain their health
- Be honest and open and act with integrity
- Act without delay if you have good reason to believe that you or a colleague may be putting patients at risk
- Never discriminate unfairly against patients or colleagues
- Never abuse your patients' trust in you or the public's trust in the profession.[50]

Respect for the patient's right to self-determination is thus central to medical professionalism. Respecting the patient's right to self-determination is not an isolated process; it is part of a wider hallmark of professionalism that embraces recognition of the patient's values, expectations, fears, plans and social identity. Furthermore, certain expectations flow from the core principles of medical professionalism. The authors of a project report produced by the King's Fund stated: 'We have acknowledged the legitimacy of patients' expectations: their interests should lie at the heart of modern professionalism.'[51] I would submit that these expectations can be regarded as, and indeed are, property rights. Put in other words, the doctor's duty correlative to the patient's property rights (derived from legitimate expectations) is at the heart of medical professionalism. The property model thus harmonises the law and medical professionalism whereas, as argued in this book, there is a gap between the consent model and modern dictates of medical professionalism.

Legitimate Expectations from the Doctor–Patient Consultation

The patient's expectation and the importance of mutual trust between doctor and patient are reflected in the following vistas provided by Oxman and colleagues:

---

50 General Medical Council, *Good Medical Practice*. London: GMC 2006, inside front cover.
51 Rosen and Dewer, *On Being a Doctor*, p. 51.

The patient:

> If you expect me, as your patient, to accept the treatment you are prescribing for me, it is only fair that I inform you about my requirements. Firstly, I expect you to have consulted systematic reviews of reliable evidence about the relative merits and demerits of the various treatment alternatives available to me … I expect you to use the clinical skills, judgment, and intangible personal resources that characterise a thoughtful, reflective, evidence based practitioner.

The doctor:

> Patients vary in the amount of information that they want to give to and from their doctors. Most patients seem to get less information from their doctors than they want, but others would rather not be told some of the things that some doctors assume that they must want to know. Because you and I don't know each other yet, I'm going to need your help in learning how much information you want about your problem, and about the possible treatment options … You also need to know that I will never lie in response to a straight question from you, and if I don't know the answer I will do my best to find it for you.[52]

Doctors cannot be said to offer patient-centred care unless they actively seek to understand and meet patients' expectations. Most patients go into a medical consultation with explicit expectations.[53] The expectations relate to themes such as involvement in their care, the doctor's interpersonal manner, information about diagnosis and prognosis, and communication and clinical competence.[54] It is known that when these expectations are met, higher levels of satisfaction with health care are recorded.[55] Patients want not just more information but greater involvement in decision-making.[56] They want information that is adequate and accurate enough to enable them make informed choices from treatment options.[57] They should be told why a particular intervention is offered,

---

52 Oxman AD, Chalmers I and Sackett DL, A practical guide to informed consent to treatment (2001) 323 BMJ 1464–1466, at p. 1466.

53 Joos SK, Hickam DH and Borders LM, Patients' desires and satisfaction in general medicine clinics (1993) 108 Public Health Rep 751–759.

54 Dawn AG, McGwin G Jr and Lee PP, Patient expectations regarding eye care: development and results of the Eye Care Expectations Survey (ECES) (2005) 123 *Arch Ophthalmol* 534–541.

55 Kravitz RL, Cope DW, Bhrany V and Leake B, Internal medicine patients' expectations for care during office visits (1994) 9 J Gen Intern Med 75–81.

56 Richards T, Partnership with patients: patients want more than simply information; they need involvement too (1998) 316 BMJ 85–86.

57 Kravitz RL, Patients' expectations for medical care: an expanded formulation based on review of the literature (1996) 53 Medical Care Research and Review 3–27.

since 'the wide variations in practice, especially in operative procedures, are not related to need but to the advocacy and skill mix of local doctors'.[58]

Studies of patients' expectations of general practitioners show that 'explanation of the problem' is at the top of patients' values.[59] Unfortunately explanations are not always forthcoming and there is often a wide gap between patients' expectations and their experience.[60] Studies conducted in America show unmet expectations relating to doctor–patient communication were cited by one in six patients who attended outpatient consultations.[61]

When assessed using a 40-item questionnaire that covered the bio-physiological, functional, experiential, ethical, social and financial dimensions of patient knowledge, surgical patients reported that they received less knowledge than they needed.[62] Almost 50 per cent of women contributing to a survey for the UK National Sentinel Caesarean Section Audit indicated that they would like more information on risks and benefits of Caesarean sections.[63] Involvement in decision-making has a high impact on satisfaction with childbirth experience.[64] Surveys have pointed to the need for further research into ways by which doctors can elicit, measure and prioritise patients' expectations.[65]

Thus, while medical professionalism, as defined by the medical establishment, leads the patient to expect that his/her right to self-determination will be respected and that he/she will be provided with appropriate information and be involved in decision-making, the reality on the ground is that these expectations

---

58 Dr Jack Wennberg, of the Foundation for Informed Decision Making in the USA, quoted by Richards, Partnership with patients.

59 Williams S, Weinman J, Dale J and Newman S, Patient expectations: what do primary care patients want from the GP and how far does meeting expectations affect patient satisfaction? (1999) 16 Fam Pract 33–38.

60 Sanchez-Menegay C and Stalder H, Do physicians take into account patients' expectations? (1994) 9 J Gen Intern Med 404–406.

61 Kravitz RL, Callahan EJ, Paterniti D, Antonius D, Dunham M and Lewis CE, Prevalence and sources of patients' unmet expectations for care (1996) 125 Ann Intern Med 730–737.

62 Rankinen S, Salanterä S, Heikkinen K, Johansson K, Kaljonen A, Virtanen H and Leino-Kilpi H, Expectations and received knowledge by surgical patients (2007) 9 Int J Qual Health Care 113–119.

63 Royal College of Obstetricians and Gynaecologists, *National Sentinel Caesarean Section Audit*. London: RCOG Press 2001.

64 Waldenstrom U, Hildingsson I, Rubertsson C and Radestad I, A negative birth experience: prevalence and risk factors in a national sample (2004) 31 Birth 17–27 (lack of participation in decision-making identified as a risk factor for a negative birth experience); Hodnett ED, Caregiver support for women during childbirth (2002) Cochrane Database Systematic Reviews 1:CD000199.

65 Dawn AG and Lee PP, Patient expectations for medical and surgical care: a review of the literature and applications to ophthalmology (2004) 49 Surv Ophthalmol 513–524; Rao JK, Weinberger M and Kroenke K, Visit-specific expectations and patient-centered outcomes: a literature review (2000) 9 Arch Fam Med 1148–1155.

are often unfulfilled. As discussed in Chapter 5, the operationalised paradigm of consent lets the patient down in this respect. A more compelling approach is needed.

Treating Expectation as Property Endows a Positive Right

Whereas the right to do as one wishes with one's body is a right *in rem*, the expectation of truth-telling and involvement in decision-making in health care can be regarded as a right *in personam*, that is, it is a right held against a specific nameable person or persons. In respect of actions based on battery, consent does not confer any positive right on the patient. Rather, it confers immunity on the doctor (from litigation, and correlative disability on the patient). If any positive right is conferred by consent (as applied to actions in battery), it is a right of the doctor to breach the patient's bodily integrity. It could be said that consent in battery confers a negative right on the patient (a right to another person's forbearance).

Liability in battery may be established in consent cases only where there has been touching – a claim under battery would not apply unless the doctor has actually touched the patient. On the face of it, an action based on the principle of body-as-property (where the body is treated as property) is akin to an action in battery - trespass to the property would only occur where there has been bodily invasion. On scrutiny, however, a subtle but important difference emerges. A person may physically interfere with a neighbour's property (in other words, violate the integrity of the property) without 'touching' the property - by obstructing legitimate access to light. This would be regarded legally as a breach of a property right. Applying this to patient self-determination, in an action based on the principle of body-as-property the claimant could argue that the integrity of his or her body has been violated, even though he or she was not touched by the defendant. Thus, if a patient's legitimate expectations in respect of a medical consultation are not met (i.e. his or her self-determination has been breached), an action may be brought under the principle of body-as-property despite the absence of direct physical contact between doctor and patient. The patient may have a stronger case, however, if the action is based on the principle of legitimate-expectation-as-property, rather than (or as well as) body-as-property.

Whereas a right not to be touched without consent is a negative right, a property right in the expectation that one will be involved in decisions about one's own health care is a positive right, demanding positive action from the health-care provider. The demand for positive action can be formalised if the expectation of the patient from a medical consultation, his/her expectation that relevant and sufficient information will be provided and s/he will be engaged in all decisions about their care, is regarded as property. Treating the patient's legitimate expectations from a medical consultation as property allows the patient legal redress if these expectations are not met, regardless of whether or not the doctor has touched him/her. As this will be a positive right, however, it may be more difficult to justify and its limits will have to be very clearly defined.

If a doctor fails to inform a 37-year-old pregnant woman of the option of having a diagnostic test (such as amniocentesis) and the baby is found at birth to have Down syndrome, the woman has been denied an opportunity to be involved in making decisions about her care. In particular, the woman has been denied the chance to decide whether to undergo amniocentesis and, in the event of an abnormal karyotype result, to decide whether to have the pregnancy terminated. This was the story in an American case, *Karlson* v. *Guerinot.*[66] The claimant brought an action based on denial of consent but the court rebuffed this line of action on the basis that consent analysis was 'limited to those situations where the harm suffered arose from some affirmative violation of the patient's physical integrity such as surgical procedures, injections or invasive diagnostic tests'.[67] This was yet another manifestation of the consent model's inadequacies in protecting patient self-determination. Had property analysis been the basis of the action, and accepted by court, the claimant would have had a better chance of obtaining redress for the breach of her right to self-determination. At the age of 37 years, she had the legitimate expectation that her doctor would provide evidence-based information about the risk of having a baby with a chromosomal abnormality. This expectation, it is argued here, should be protected as a proprietary right. In addition, based on the analogy given above, the point about the absence of 'affirmative violation of the patient's physical integrity' can be countered.

Thus where there has been no touching, the patient cannot be protected by consent analysis (via battery) but could be protected by property analysis. Where there has been a failure to offer treatment (as in the amniocentesis case described above), the patient would not be able to rely on an action in battery; he/she could bring an action in negligence but will face the challenge of the causation hurdle and property analysis may provide more assured protection. Consent could offer protection where treatment has been given but the availability of an alternative and potentially preferable alternative was not disclosed to the patient (this equates to a lack of valid consent).[68]

Support for the idea of treating the patient's legitimate expectations as a property right can also be derived from analysis of the case of *Janet Birch*

66 *Karlson* v. *Guerinot* 57 App Div 2d 73, (at p 87); 394 NYS 2d 933 (N. 1977).

67 Ibid., 939.

68 *Janet Birch* v. *University College London Hospital NHS Foundation Trust* [2008] EWHC 2237 (QB).

v. *University College London Hospital NHS Foundation Trust.*[69] The claimant was a 55-year-old diabetic woman admitted to Watford General Hospital with suspected third nerve palsy. An urgent MRI scan was recommended to exclude the two differential diagnoses, posterior communicating artery aneurysm and cavernous sinus pathology. As there were no scanning slots available, she was transferred to the defendant's hospital, the National Hospital for Neurology, London. There, neurosurgeons decided to perform a catheter angiogram (the diagnostic test for an aneurysm) instead of an MRI scan. The risks of a catheter angiogram were explained to Mrs Birch, including the 1 per cent risk of a stroke, and written consent was obtained. Unfortunately this risk materialised. The claimant alleged that the decision to perform a catheter angiogram instead of an MRI scan was negligent but Cranston J, citing *Bolam* and *Bolitho*, found in favour of the defendant.

The claimant also alleged that she had not been provided with full information regarding the risk of a catheter angiogram compared with that of an MRI scan, and on this point Cranston J found for the claimant. He stated that although there was no requirement that a doctor should discuss alternative treatments in every case, special circumstances in this particular case warranted this discussion. On causation, the defence argued that had the claimant undergone an MRI scan she would still have had to undergo a catheter angiogram afterwards but, as in *Chester* v. *Afshar*,[70] the court prioritised the patient's right to self-determination over medical opinion.

On the face of it, this looks like a triumph of the consent model. Examined critically, however, there is little or no reason to believe that a similar outcome would be reached if a similar case should reach the English courts, as there are key facts which distinguish this case. The most notable of these was that the claimant had been offered an MRI scan at the referring hospital.

Also, had rules of causation been strictly applied, the decision may have favoured the defendant, for the claimant acknowledged that the doctor knew best, and there was merit in the defence that even if an MRI scan had been performed, the claimant would still have needed an angiogram.

A patient could not be said to have made a self-determining choice if the doctor has withheld information on alternative treatments – and it is not uncommon for doctors to exclude some options before presenting a patient with residual alternatives to choose from (or a 'menu of one item'). *Montgomery* establishes that the doctor is now under a duty to inform the patient of any reasonable alternative or variant treatments.

---

69 Ibid.

70 *Chester* v. *Afshar* [2004] UKHL 41; [2005] 1 AC 134; [2004] 3 WLR 927; [2004] 4 All ER 587.

Applying the property model to *Birch* would have yielded the same outcome for the claimant, but the legal precedent would have been a stronger, more certain one – there would have been greater legal certainty and no debates about this decision resting on the special circumstances of the case. Mrs Birch had a legitimate expectation that the doctors would explain to her the relative risks of an angiogram and an MRI scan, and explain why an angiogram was being proposed instead of an MRI scan. The court clearly placed high premium on this expectation and, had the case been argued on the basis of property analysis, it would have been reasonable for the court to recognise this as a proprietary right.

Also, had there been a transactional approach of the type implicit in the property model rather than application of the usual institutionally-valid paradigm of consent, Mrs Birch would have been informed of the comparative benefits and risks of both treatment options. The consent model focused on the duty of the doctors, and if an MRI scan had not previously been on the cards, it may well have been the case that the doctors did not have a duty to discuss this with Mrs Birch. The property model focuses on the claimant's right to make an informed choice regarding treatment options, and this right would apply whether or not an MRI scan had been discussed earlier. This positive right is complemented by a correlative fiduciary obligation on the doctor to provide the information required for making an informed choice.

Proprietary Rights and the Doctor's Fiduciary Role

In the above paragraphs, an attempt has been made to show that medical professionalism spells out certain duties expected of the doctor, and these include respect for self-determination. Further, the patient is entitled to a legitimate expectation that the doctor will fulfil these duties or obligations – that, after all, is the essence of professionalism. When the patient consults a doctor in the context of these legitimate expectations, there is a *bona fide* relationship of trust. Against this background, it is argued below that the doctor owes the patient fiduciary obligations that relate to patient self-determination, and that these obligations can be protected by the property approach.

A fiduciary relationship is *a relationship of trust* between two parties, A and B, where A (the principal) is in a comparatively vulnerable position and entrusts B (the fiduciary) with the management of property. B is obliged to act at all times in good faith and in the interests of A. The latter specifically reposes confidence, faith and trust in the former, and the former accepts this. The fiduciary duty owed to A by B is considered the highest standard of care in law, more demanding than the duty of care prescribed in the law of tort. Although fiduciary relationships most commonly arise in relation to the management of property (in particular, trusts of property), there are non-property situations where a fiduciary duty has been ascribed to one party: teacher–student; lawyer–client; priest–parishioner.[71]

Beauchamp and Childress state that:

> The patient-physician relationship is a fiduciary relationship – that is, founded on trust or confidence; and the physician is therefore necessarily a trustee for the patient's medical welfare.[72]

Various other academic commentators agree with this opinion[73] but, in general, the courts have not embraced it.[74] Canada is the only common law jurisdiction in the world that recognises the doctor–patient relationship as a fiduciary one.[75] In Australia and other parts of North America, however, the courts have variously found that a fiduciary relationship arises from some but not all of the doctor's duties to the patient.[76] These fiduciary duties relate to financial transactions, procurement of gifts, sexual relationships and disclosure of confidential information.[77] In one case, however, the duty to provide adequate information was regarded as a fiduciary duty:

> The duty of the doctor to inform the patient is a fiduciary duty. The patient is entitled to rely upon the physician to tell him what he needs to know about the condition of his own body. The patient has the right to chart his own destiny, and the doctor must supply the patient with material fact the patient will need in order to intelligently chart that destiny with dignity.[78]

71 Chodos R, The nature of fiduciary law and its relationship to other legal doctrines and categories (2011) 91 Boston Univ L Rev 837–849.

72 Beauchamp TL and Childress JF, *Principles of Biomedical Eethics*. New York: Oxford University Press 1994, p. 430.

73 Bartlett P, Doctors as fiduciaries: equitable regulation of the doctor-patient relationship (1997) 5 Med L Rev 193–224; Grubb A, The doctor as fiduciary (1994) 47 Current Legal Problems 311–340.

74 Bartlett, Doctors as fiduciaries.

75 *McInerney* v. *MacDonald* [1990] 2 SCR 138, 93 DLR (4th) 415.

76 *Breen* v. *Williams* (1996) 186 CLR 71; *Gannett* v. *Medical and Surgical Clinic* (1974) 315 NE2d 278; *McInemey* v. *MacDonald* (1992) 93 DLR (4th) 415 at 424 per La Forest J; *Norberg* v. *Wynrib* (1979) 92 DLR (4th) 449; *Emmett* v. *Eastern Dispensary and Casualty Hospital* (1967) 396 F.2d 931.

77 Ibid.

78 *Miller* v. *Kennedy* 522 P.2d 852 (Washington state Court of Appeal), at 860.

Also, in *Moore* Panelli J. stated that the doctor had a fiduciary duty to enable a competent patient to make self-determining decisions about his/her care.[79]

The English common law position on the matter was stated in *Sidaway* v. *Board of Governors of the Bethlem Royal Hospital and the Maudsley Hospital*[80] where Lord Scarman dismissed without giving any explanation the appellant's argument that the relationship between doctor and patient is of a fiduciary character:

> There is no comparison to be made between the relationship of doctor and patient with [*sic*] that of solicitor and client, trustee and *cestui qui* trust or the other relationships treated in equity as of a fiduciary character.[81]

It must be noted that *Sidaway* was not primarily about fiduciary duties, and to that extent cannot be the complete authority on fiduciary duties in the doctor–patient relationship in the UK. Despite Lord Scarman's statement, it is arguable that the doctor owes fiduciary duties to the patient in respect of the principle of self-determination. This argument is based on two observations. Firstly, when the duties of a doctor, as spelt out by the professional bodies cited above, are compared with the recognised duties of a fiduciary, it is difficult not to conclude that the former are within the ambit of the latter. Secondly, it is arguable that the term fiduciary should not be applied to particular *relationships* (e.g. doctor–patient, solicitor–client) but to particular *duties* expected of parties to the relationship.[82]

Rahaim states that a fiduciary must discharge duty with care, skill, prudence, diligence and up-to-date knowledge.[83] Berumen formulated the general duties of a fiduciary as follows:

- To take into account the reasonable expectations and interests of the 'fiduciaree'.
- To ensure they are sufficiently competent and knowledgeable to carry out their duties to professional standards
- To disclose to relevant parties any conflicts of interest, limitations or impediments that may interfere with their fiduciary responsibilities

79 *Moore* v. *Regents of the University of California* (1990) 793 P.2d 479 Supreme Court of California.

80 *Sidaway* v. *Board of Governors of the Bethlem Royal Hospital and the Maudsley Hospital* [1985] AC 871.

81 Ibid., 884.

82 Bartlett, Doctors as fiduciaries.

83 Rahaim CD, *The Fiduciary: An In-Depth Guide to Fiduciary Duties – From Studebaker to Enron.* Lincoln, Nebr.: iUniverse 2005, pp. 52–59.

- Not to misuse information or take undue advantage of their relationship or betray the confidences of the fiduciaree.[84]

These general duties are similar to those prescribed by the English Law Commission.[85] Significantly, these duties cover the same grounds as some of the duties outlined by the General Medical Council and the medical establishment, as shown above. The duty to act at all times in the best interests of the patient is clearly a fiduciary one. The duties of a doctor to respect the dignity of the patient, to work in partnership with patients and to respect their right to be involved in decision-making about their own care are duties that can be subsumed under the fiduciary duties listed above. In Canada, the courts have said that the doctor has a fiduciary duty to disclose medical error,[86] and it is argued by some commentators elsewhere that the doctor indeed has a fiduciary duty to disclose any mistakes he/she has made that have resulted in an adverse incident.[87]

If a fiduciary duty is recognised, the doctor will not be free to withhold information from the patient simply because he/she feels that this would influence the patient's decision. If the law and professional standards emphasise that the doctor has a fiduciary duty to disclose information to the patient, then doctors are likely to be more open with patients and the impact of the information gradient between doctor and patient will be reduced. Recognising the duty to respect patient self-determination as a fiduciary duty will also have a major implication for cases where the doctor has allegedly failed to fulfil this duty. The burden of proof will shift from the patient to the doctor, who will have to establish that he/she has competently performed the fiduciary duties.

Conclusions

Vulnerability in the face of a steep informational (and sometimes social) gradient between doctor and patient is a major threat to patient self-determination. Protection of the right to self-determination will remain inadequate for as long as vulnerability is not adequately addressed. The law has stepped in to protect the vulnerable party in various arenas, such as product liability and

84 Berumen ME, *Do No Evil: Ethics with Applications to Economic Theory and Business*. Lincoln, Nebr.: iUniverse 2003, pp. 333–334.

85 Law Commission, *Fiduciary Duties and Regulatory Rules (Consultation Paper)*. London: Stationery Office Books 1992.

86 *Vasdani* v. *Sehmi* [1993] OJ No. 44, 37 ACWS (3d) 856; *Gerula* v. *Flores* (1995) 126 DLR (4th) 506 [1995] OJ No. 2300.

87 Faunce TA and Bolsin SN, Fiduciary disclosure of medical mistakes: the duty to promptly notify patients of adverse health care events (2005) 12 JLM 478–482

consumer protection, and a similar approach could be made regarding patient self-determination. Property rhetoric intrinsically carries greater security, and patient self-determination gets stronger protection through a property model that recognises a proprietary right in the patient's expectation of engagement in decision-making. In this context, engagement means a transaction in which the doctor is aware of the patient's goals and provides tailored information that enables the patient to make a self-determining decision.

Where one party is particularly vulnerable, trust assumes greater significance. When the patient consults a doctor in the context of legitimate expectations generated by the medical establishment's own definition of medical professionalism, there is a *bona fide* relationship of trust. The doctor therefore can be argued to have a fiduciary duty to provide the patient with adequate information and to take into account the reasonable expectations and interests of the patient. This fiduciary duty is an essential element of the proposed property model; it is the correlative duty to the patient's right to make decisions about his/her treatment.

The concept of legitimate expectations constituting a chose in action fits with the concept of property as defining a relationship between persons. Recognition of a proprietary right in the patient's legitimate expectation from a consultation is not a huge leap forward, once the concept of property as defining relationships between persons (rather than between a person and a thing) is accepted. As argued in this book, the definition of property has to move with the times, and the legal concept of property as a thing or as defining the relationship between a person and a thing is obsolete. A modern account of property makes it appealing as a vehicle for promoting self-determination.[88] Further, to the extent that legitimate expectations are rights, a Madisonian concept of property can be applied: 'As a man is said to have a right to his property, he may be equally said to have property in his rights.'[89]

It is worth recalling at this juncture Underkuffler's 'four dimensions involved in any legally cognizable conception of property'.[90] The first of these dimensions is a theory of rights; the second is the spatial dimension. In Chapter 7 the concept of the body as object of property was discussed; this is the spatial dimension. This chapter has introduced the concept of property rights in the patient's expectations from consultation with the doctor, expectations that are legitimised by the dictates of medical professionalism and the duties prescribed by medical regulatory bodies. This constitutes Underkuffler's first dimension, a theory of rights.

88 Davies and Naffine, *Are Persons Property?*

89 Underkuffler, On property.

90 Underkuffler LS, *The Idea of Property: Its Meaning and Power.* Oxford: Oxford University Press 2003.

The third and fourth dimensions – stringency of protection and time – are less problematic in the context of this book and will be addressed in subsequent chapters which attempt to show how the property model compares with the consent model.

Chapter 9
Justification of the Property Model for Protecting Patient Self-determination

> Part of the imbalance between doctor and patient is due to the patient's lack of information, and, on one view, it is the function of the law to redress the imbalance by providing patients with the 'right' to be given that information, or perhaps more accurately imposing a duty on doctors to provide it.[1]

In Chapter 3, it was shown that the mechanism by which the law purports to 'redress the imbalance'[2] and uphold the patient's right to self-determination in medical decision-making is the law of consent. It was also shown that the consent model suffers from a number of weaknesses which limit its suitability for achieving what it is meant to achieve. One of the weaknesses is that, as applied in English courts, consent law protected the interests of a 'homogenised' patient rather than those of the index patient.[3] By definition, self-determination is referenced to the particular patient in question, not to a hypothetical person. Accordingly, the consent model cannot truly and effectively protect the patient's right to self-determination.

Traditionally, the English courts were not particularly keen on asserting the rights of the patient in medical decision-making; rather, they deferred to medical opinion – which made it difficult for the claimant to establish breach of duty in negligence cases brought against doctors. Gradually, they became more committed to upholding patient self-determination, but their efforts in this regard were hampered by the bluntness of the tool at their disposal – the traditional consent model, which was problematic, not least because the claimant had to establish not only breach of duty but also causation. The inadequacy of this tool in the wake of contemporary judicial thinking became most glaring in *Chester* v. *Afshar* where the court resorted to jurisprudential contortions in

---

1 Jones M, Informed consent and other fairy stories (1999) 7 Med L Rev 103–134, at p. 129.

2 Ibid.

3 I have borrowed the term 'homogenised' patient from McLean SAM, *Autonomy, Consent and the Law*. Abingdon: Routledge 2010; see pp. 83, 93 and 215.

order to protect the patient's right to self-determination.[4] Had an alternative model been available, the court could have reached the same decision through a more logical, less revisionist and less controversial analysis; one that is capable of being applied consistently in future cases and that does not entail departure from established legal principles of causation. Property analysis is presented as this alternative. The property model holds sacrosanct the patient's right to self-determination and imposes a duty on doctors to engage proactively with patients in decision-making.

This chapter seeks to identify the benefits that could flow from property analysis. With reference to landmark consent cases decided in UK courts – *Sidaway*,[5] *Chester* and *Montgomery* – and other case law, the chapter discusses the extent to which the principles (in particular, property analysis) enunciated in this book are consistent with principles espoused by Court of Appeal and House of Lords (Supreme Court) judgments.

It will be argued that the property model makes the doctor's duty to disclose information to the patient an affirmative one, precludes limitations imposed by the objective test applied in consent cases, hybridises the strengths of 'real consent'[6] and 'informed' consent, limits reliance on therapeutic privilege and fits with the courts' apparent shift towards a rights-based approach. Together, these attributes make the property model potentially better suited than the consent model to genuine protection of the patient's right to self-determination. It must be stressed here that the property model and the consent model are not mutually exclusive models; they have a lot in common but the property model has attributes, outlined above and tabulated below, which make it potentially better suited for what the law aims to achieve.

The Property Approach to Protecting Self-determination

In Chapter 2, the concept of self-determination underpinning my proposition was discussed. It is this concept of self-determination that the law of consent is meant to protect. For the avoidance of doubt it is stressed again that this is different from the notion of the patient having a right to choose or demand treatment regardless of cost, medical indication or other public-interest considerations. It is simply the patient's right to be the ultimate, informed decision-maker in respect of what should be done to his or her body. In essence, therefore, self-determination is a rights issue. It is about the rights of the patient, and the correlative duties of the doctor.

4 *Chester* v. *Afshar* [2004] 4 All ER 587 HL.

5 *Sidaway* v. *Bethlem Royal Hospital Governors* [1985] 1 All ER 643.

6 As expressed by Bristow J in *Chatterton* v. *Gerson* (1981) QB 432.

In the property model, the patient's right to self-determination is regarded as a proprietary right. Traditionally, the law and society at large have regarded proprietary rights as trumping most rights. So from the outset, adopting the property model signals the paramountcy of the patient's right to self-determination. The stringency with which this right is protected may vary from case to case, as the right is not absolute, but there is a default presumption that this right trumps most others. The theoretical underpinnings of this proprietary right and its structure have been discussed in the last three chapters. Essentially, the patient's bodily integrity is protected from unauthorised invasion and his/her legitimate expectation to be provided with the relevant information and opportunity to enable him/her to make an informed choice or decision regarding treatment is taken to be a proprietary right. The term 'proprietary right' is preferred to 'property right' in this book as, despite the arguments outlined in Chapter 6, 'property' carries the connotation of tangibility, ownership and commodification.

Two essential elements of the property model are now described: the transactional approach to doctor–patient communication and the bilateral distribution of responsibility between doctor and patient.

Effective Communication

Rights are meaningless without correlative duties, and the property model compels a fiduciary duty for the doctor to communicate effectively with the patient. This communication entails not only the provision of relevant information but also the taking of reasonable steps to ensure that the patient understands the information provided and that an informed decision is made by the patient. For this to happen, the doctor–patient consultation becomes a transactional activity rather than a unidirectional flow of data across a steep informational, and sometimes social, gradient. This transactional activity and the fiduciary duty that underlies it are embedded in medical professionalism as enunciated in Chapter 8 and by medical regulatory bodies.

Both judges[7] and academicians[8] have commented on the doctor's duty to check that the patient understands. Morland J said:

> When recommending a particular type of surgery or treatment, the doctor, when warning of the risks, *must take reasonable care* to ensure that his explanation of the risks is intelligible to his particular patient. The doctor should use language, simple but not misleading, which the doctor perceives from what knowledge and acquaintanceship that he may have of the patient (which might be slight), will

7 Morland J, in *Smith* v. *Tunbridge Wells HA* [1994] 5 Med LR 334.

8 O'Neill O, Paternalism and partial autonomy (1984) 10 J Med Ethics 173–178.

> be understood by the patient so that the patient can make an informed decision as to whether or not to consent to the recommended surgery or treatment.[9] (emphasis mine)

In the same vein, the UK Supreme Court judges recently said:

> ....the doctor's advisory role involves dialogue, the aim of which is to ensure that the patient understands the seriousness of her condition, and the anticipated benefits and risks of the proposed treatment and any reasonable alternatives, so that she is then in a position to make an informed decision. This role will only be performed effectively if the information provided is comprehensible. The doctor's duty is not therefore fulfilled by bombarding the patient with technical information which she cannot reasonably be expected to grasp, let alone by routinely demanding her signature on a consent form.[10]

These observations on the duty of the doctor in respect of the patient's understanding are not new. A quarter of a century ago, O'Neill asserted that:

> The onus on practitioners is to see that patients, as they actually are, understand what they can about the basics of their diagnosis and the proposed treatment, and are secure enough to refuse the treatment or to insist on changes.[11]

This duty tends to be overlooked in the consent model, as the model focuses on the amount of information disclosed rather than on what the patient actually understands (i.e. focus on content rather than the process of communication). If the focus shifts to ensuring that the patient understands what has been said, then clinicians will be legally obliged to pay more attention to communication skills, to the way information is provided and to checking that the patient understands the meaning and implication of the information provided – just as would normally be the case in a property transaction.

Other professionals dealing with clients are expected to adopt a similar approach; for example, financial advisers are asked to 'sense check' their recommendations against the customer's original objectives.[12] By adopting the transactional, rather than the conduit, approach to consultation, the clinician

9 Morland J, in *Smith* v. *Tunbridge Wells HA* [1994] 5 Med LR 334, at 339.

10 *Montgomery (Appellant) v Lanarkshire Health Board (Respondent) (Scotland)* [2015] UKSC 11, at para 90.

11 O'Neill, Paternalism and partial autonomy, pp. 175–176.

12 FSA calls on IFAs to 'sense-check' risk profiling approach. Money Marketing, 27 May 2011; available at http://www.moneymarketing.co.uk/adviser-news/fsa-calls-on-ifas-to-sense-check-risk-profiling-approach/1031694.article. Accessed 2 November 2014.

is more likely to meet Judge Morland's requirement to 'take reasonable care' to facilitate understanding.

The Doctor's Duty to Disclose Information to the Patient: An Affirmative Duty

Along with the duty to take reasonable steps to check the patient's understanding, the property model imposes an affirmative duty on the doctor to disclose tailored information to the patient. Regarding the doctor's duty to disclose information, Lord Templeman stated:

> The duty of the doctor … is to provide the patient with information which will enable the patient to make a balanced judgment if the patient chooses to make a balanced judgment … The court will award damages against the doctor if the court is satisfied that the doctor blundered and that the patient was deprived of information which was necessary for the purposes I have outlined.[13]

In describing the requirement that the doctor be under a duty to inform his patient of the material risks inherent in the treatment, Lord Scarman (in *Sidaway*) sought to impose an affirmative duty on the doctor. He made this unequivocal by saying:

> I think that English law must recognize a duty of the doctor to warn his patient of risk inherent in the treatment he is proposing: and especially so, if the treatment be surgery.[14]

It appears, however, that there was no juristic basis for this affirmative duty.. Recently, however, the UK Supreme Court has affirmed that:

> The doctor is … under a duty to take reasonable care to ensure that the patient is aware of any material risks involved in any recommended treatment, and of any reasonable alternative or variant treatments.[15]

It also asserted:

---

13 *Sidaway* v. *Board of Governors of the Bethlem Royal Hospital and the Maudsley Hospital* [1985] AC 871 HL, at 904.

14 Ibid., 889.

15 *Montgomery*, at para 87.

> It is … necessary to impose legal obligations, so that even those doctors who have less skill or inclination for communication, or who are more hurried, are obliged to pause and engage in the discussion which the law requires. This may not be welcomed by some healthcare providers; but the reasoning of the House of Lords in *Donoghue v Stevenson* [1932] AC 562 was no doubt received in a similar way by the manufacturers of bottled drinks.[16]

To the extent that I have indicated, English law should recognise a duty of the doctor to warn his or her patient of risk inherent in the treatment which he or she is proposing, such that the patient is able to obtain redress in the event that this duty is breached, regardless of whether or not a harm has resulted from the breach. A basis for such an affirmative duty to warn the patient of risks inherent in treatment can be provided by property analysis. Property analysis, as shown in Chapters 6–8, provides a legal as well as an ethical basis for assigning rights to the patient and correlative duties to the doctor.

Bilateral Distribution of Responsibility

While the doctor's duty to disclose information should be an affirmative one, the patient also has to take some responsibility for decision-making.[17] An example of how this applies is the issue of the patient's understanding of information provided by the doctor. It has been held that the legal duty of a doctor extends to provision of adequate information but not to ensuring that the patient has understood this information.[18] It must be acknowledged that imposing a duty on the doctor to ensure understanding could be both onerous and difficult to enforce. On the other hand, patient self-determination cannot be protected if there is no consideration of what the patient understands. It is submitted that one way of facilitating this is through a bilateral distribution of responsibility.

The right to self-determination should carry with it obligations not only on the part of doctor but also on the part of the patient: the patient should take some responsibility for the treatment received, by communicating with the doctor, providing contextual information relevant to his/her decision-making and communicating his/her understanding to the doctor. Unfortunately (for various reasons, a discussion of which is beyond the scope of this book), this does not always happen. Section 2b of the NHS Constitution lists the

---

16 *Montgomery*, at para 93.

17 Coulter A. Paternalism or partnership? (1999) 319 BMJ 719–20; Downie R and Randall F, Choice and responsibility in the NHS (2008) 8 Clin Med 182–185; Newman J and Vidler E, Discriminating customers, responsible patients, empowered users: consumerism and the modernisation of health care (2006) 35 J Soc Policy 193–209.

18 *Al Hamwi* v. *(1) Johnston (2) North West London Hospitals NHS Trust* [2005] EWHC 206.

responsibilities of patients.[19] These include the patient's responsibility to provide accurate information about his/her health, condition and status. The UK Supreme Court also recognised the importance of patients' responsibilities in the context of modern thinking:

> [Contemporary legal and social developments] point towards…..an approach to the law which, instead of treating patients as placing themselves in the hands of their doctors (and then being prone to sue their doctors in the event of a disappointing outcome), treats them so far as possible as adults who are capable of understanding that medical treatment is uncertain of success and may involve risks, *accepting responsibility for the taking of risks affecting their own lives, and living with the consequences of their choices.*[20] (emphasis mine)

The Court also speculated that this distribution of responsibility could reduce the incidence of litigation:

> ….in so far as the law contributes to the incidence of litigation, an approach which results in patients being aware that the outcome of treatment is uncertain and potentially dangerous, and *in their taking responsibility for the ultimate choice to undergo that treatment*, may be less likely to encourage recriminations and litigation, in the event of an adverse outcome, than an approach which requires patients to rely on their doctors to determine whether a risk inherent in a particular form of treatment should be incurred.[21] (emphasis mine)

It is recognised that in consent discussions '[t]he patient can make things impossible by acting on fixed or superstitious opinions or by failing to participate responsibly in her management or its planning'.[22] In *Sidaway*, Lord Scarman said that:

> a patient may well have in mind circumstances, objectives and values which he reasonably may not make known to the doctor but which may lead him to a different decision from that suggested by purely medical opinion.[23]

While it is the patient's prerogative to withhold information about his/her objectives and values from the doctor, it is also reasonable that the patient should take responsibility for the consequences of doing so.

19 Department of Health, *The NHS Constitution*. London: DH 2012, p. 10.
20 *Montgomery*, at para 81.
21 *Montgomery*, at para 93.
22 Gillett GR, Informed consent and moral integrity (1989) 15 J Med Ethics 117–123.
23 *Sidaway* v. *Bethlem Royal Hospital* [1985] AC 871, [1985] 2 WLR 480, [1985] 1 All ER 643 (HL, Lord Scarman at 652c–e).

The implementation of a model of doctor–patient relationship that is rooted in mutual trust – such as the property model incorporating the collaborative style of consultation adopted in Chapter 2 – will (because of enhanced trust) make it less likely for a patient to withhold from the doctor information that is relevant to his/her decision-making. Also, unless the patient discharges his/her own responsibility, the doctor will have to make an essentially arbitrary assessment of the patient's informational needs, which is the opposite of what the principle of self-determination seeks to protect.

The consent model does not create the right environment for patients to take responsibility in the decision-making process. One study found that at the point of signing a consent form, many patients are unaware that this is meant to be an exercise of their own right; they see it as an exercise to protect the doctor.[24] The authors of the study state that:

> while medical professionals may recognise the desirability of a two-way transaction, it may not operate this way in practice if patients fail to understand that the purpose of the consent process is to respect their autonomy.[25]

When obligations on both sides are addressed, tension between the patient's legitimate expectations and the doctor's duty is eased. This is the essence of a transactional approach to medical consultation. As stated in Chapter 5, a model which takes due account of the communicative transaction leading up to the decision, rather than just focusing on the final decision, will meet the imperatives of cultural sensitivity and uphold the principle of self-determination.

The emphasis on both the doctor's duty and the patient's responsibility manifests the property model's primary concern: the relationship between doctor and patient. The consent model does not take full account of the bi-directional dynamics of this relationship, and has appeared to be an impediment to the relationship. The newer, nuanced conceptions of consent have not changed this. Maclean says, for example, that while Manson and O'Neill prioritise consent as communication, they do so primarily by focusing on the obligations of the health-care professional, which in turn means that attention shifts back to disclosure and truthful disclosure rather than to interaction between both parties.[26]

---

24 Heywood R, Macaskill A and Williams K, Informed consent in hospital practice: health professionals' perspectives and legal reflections (2010) 18 Med L Rev 152–184.

25 Ibid., p. 157.

26 Maclean A, *Autonomy, Informed Consent and Medical Law: A Relational Challenge*. Cambridge: Cambridge University Press 2009.

Recognition of Patient Self-determination as a Distinct Legal Right

A fundamental weakness of the consent model is that its starting point is not the patient's rights but the doctor's duty. This is reflected in the following observation by Miller:

> The 1980 case of *Chatterton v. Gerson* seems to be the first reported opinion to hold that a doctor 'ought to warn of what may happen by misfortune, however well the operation is done, if there is a real risk of misfortune inherent in the procedure.' This duty to warn was derived from the physician's general duty of care, however, rather than from the patient's right to receive information. The court found that the physician's duty stemmed from his professional obligation to exercise the care of a responsible doctor in similar circumstances, as set forth in the landmark case of *Bolam v. Friern Hospital Management Committee*.[27] (references omitted)

To afford optimal protection to patient self-determination, the starting point has to be the patient's rights. One of the features of the proposed property model is that it seeks protection of the right to self-determination as a distinct legal right. Affording patient self-determination this degree of protection would be in keeping with Lord Munby's recent statement that rights issues 'have to be more than what Brennan J in the High Court of Australia once memorably described as "the incantations of legal rhetoric"'.[28] While recognising the importance of patient self-determination, the law has not moved to protect this as a right *per se*, independent of the outcome of a trespass to this right.[29] Schultz argued for the legal recognition of patient self-determination as a distinct legal right.[30] She drew a parallel between this argument and other legally protected rights such as the right to reputation. She further argued that legally protecting patient self-determination in this way would reduce rather than expand litigation, for it would promote better communication between doctors and patients.

Twerski and Cohen suggest that self-determination could be protected by allowing patients to recover for a violation of their right to make their own informed decision.[31] They state the case as follows:

---

27 Miller FH, Informed consent for the man on the Clapham omnibus: an English cure for an American disease? (1987) 9 W New Eng L Rev 169–190, at p. 173.

28 *Re G* [2012] EWCA Civ 1233, at para 34.

29 Shultz M, From informed consent to patient choice: a new protected interest (1985) 95 Yale LJ 219–299.

30 Ibid.

31 Twerski A and Cohen N, Informed decision-making and the law of torts: the myth of justiciable causation (1988) Univ Ill L Rev 607–665.

> The classic tort model for informed consent litigation, while simple in theory, is seriously flawed in practice. The model depends on constructing a causal bridge between the absence of the information and the decision of the plaintiff to proceed with the therapy or use the product. Except in the most blatant situations, the causal relationship between inadequate information and plaintiff decision making is … not practically justiciable. The law does and can only consider the information the health professional or product vendor should deliver. It does not and cannot consider the multitude of factors that influence the way people actually make decisions. To decide causation without looking at the latter is wholly illusory. On the other hand, to insist on such inquiry would involve the courts in the kind of investigation of human behaviour that would seriously compromise the judicial process … Rather than focusing on personal injury damages flowing from the hypothetical 'but for,' which seeks to determine what the plaintiff would have decided had the defendant provided the information, we suggest that the courts should identify and value the decision rights of the plaintiff which the defendant destroyed by withholding adequate information …
>
> The legal system should protect these rights and provide significant recompense for their invasion, rather than continue its single-minded and ill-considered attention to personal injuries allegedly *caused* by the lack of information.[32]

Other authors have also called for recognition of infringement of the right to self-determination as an independent cause of action,[33] and similar thoughts were expressed (albeit less forcefully) by Lord Hoffman in *Chester*:

> The remaining question is whether a special rule should be created by which doctors who fail to warn patients of risks should be made insurers against those risks.
>
> The argument for such a rule is that it vindicates the patient's right to choose for herself. Even though the failure to warn did not cause the patient any damage, it was an affront to her personality and leaves her feeling aggrieved.[34]

There are two fundamental reasons why patient self-determination should be protected as a distinct right. The first one is that, as Kennedy said, it is of profound importance:

---

32 Ibid., pp. 608–609.

33 Karako-Eyal N, Has non-US case law recognized a legally protected autonomy right? (2009)10 Minn J L Sci & Tech 671–726.

34 *Chester* v. *Afshar* [2004] 4 All ER 587, paras 32, 33.

> … when we consider the duty of the doctor to inform his patients we are concerned with a *profoundly important human right*: the right to control one's own destiny by knowing what it is that will be done by way of treatment, so that one may say no, if so minded.[35] (emphasis mine)

In the same vein, Lord Steyn (in *Chester*) said:

> A patient's right to an appropriate warning from a surgeon when faced with surgery ought normatively to be regarded as an important right which must be given effective protection whenever possible.[36]

The second reason is that this right originates independently of any harm that the claimant may suffer. As Jackson said:

> we should remember why it is important to give patients information. Patients need information in order to make informed choices about their care, not in order to protect themselves against medical accidents.[37]

Where there has been a failure to disclose risks and alternatives, the property model entitles the claimant to a remedy once breach of the duty of care is proven, without any requirement to prove causation. In other words, the property model treats interference with the patient's right to self-determination as a cause of action in itself, as distinct from harm to the physical well-being of the patient.

Arguably, a disadvantage of recognising the patient's right to make his/her own informed decision as an independent cause of action, not requiring any assessment of harm and its causation, is that damages awarded would be nominal.[38] This should not necessarily be the case: it is logical that the compensation for infraction of this right should reflect the reason why it was deemed worthy of special protection, which is that it is '*a profoundly important human right*'.[39] This point is emphasised by the use of property analysis to secure the required protection; property rhetoric is powerful. In any case, the quantum

---

35 Kennedy I, *Treat Me Right: Essays in Medical Law and Ethics*. Oxford: Clarendon Press 1988, p. 389.

36 *Chester* v. *Afshar* [2004] 4 All ER 587, at para 17.

37 Jackson E, 'Informed consent' to medical treatment and the impotence of tort. In McLean SAM, *First Do No Harm: Law, Ethics and Healthcare*. Aldershot: Ashgate 2006, pp. 273–288, at p. 274.

38 Shultz, From informed consent to patient choice; Twerski and Cohen, Informed decision-making and the law of torts.

39 Kennedy I, *Treat Me Right*, p. 389.

of damages is not the key issue – what matters most is the vindication of the right rather than financial recompense.

In the Absence of Physical Harm, the Patient may be Left with Nothing

The impact of a requirement to prove causation is illustrated by Lord Bingham's judgement in *Chester*. Lord Bingham allowed the appeal, on the ground that the 'but for' test was not satisfied: 'a claimant is not entitled to be compensated, and a defendant is not bound to compensate the claimant, for damage not caused by the negligence complained of'.[40] He explains his decision not to allow the appeal by saying that the law should not hold a defendant liable where the defendant's violation of the claimant's right to be warned has not been 'shown to have worsened the physical condition of the claimant'.[41] In other words, he stuck to the conventional principle of causation. Unlike the majority, he did not appear prepared to bend this principle. The reason for this could not be that he did not appreciate the importance of the patient's rights. He recognised this right but appeared to be more concerned about the quantum of damages:

> The patient's right to be appropriately warned is an important right, which few doctors in the current legal and social climate would consciously or deliberately violate. I do not for my part think that the law should seek to reinforce that right by providing for the payment of potentially very large damages by a defendant whose violation of that right is not shown to have worsened the physical condition of the claimant.[42]

In deciding not to go with the majority Lord Bingham, like Lord Bridge, failed to make a clear distinction between the patient's right to relevant information for informed decision-making (a right which in itself deserves protection) and the occurrence of harm of which the patient had not been warned.

Lord Hoffman, who also decided for the defendant on the basis that the 'but for' test was not satisfied, appeared to distinguish between physical harm and infringement of personality:

> The remaining question is whether a special rule should be created by which doctors who fail to warn patients of risks should be made insurers against those risks. The argument for such a rule is that it vindicates the patient's right to

---

40 *Chester (Respondent)* v. *Afshar (Appellant)* [2004] UKHL 41, at para 9.

41 Ibid.

42 Ibid.

> choose for herself. Even though the failure to warn did not cause the patient any damage, it was an affront to her personality and leaves her feeling aggrieved.
>
> I can see that there might be a case for a modest solatium in such cases.[43]

A focus on physical harm detracts from protection of patient self-determination as a fundamental right. If the law truly seeks to protect patient self-determination, then a remedy should be available to the patient whose right has been breached, regardless of whether he/she has suffered demonstrable harm and, in the event that there is such harm, without the burden of proving that this harm would not have occurred but for the breach.

Support for the recognition of patient self-determination as a distinct legal right could be drawn from Lord Hope's assertion that the doctor's duty was 'unaffected in its scope by the response which Miss Chester would have given had she been told of these risks';[44] this being the case, the doctor should be liable for any breach of the duty, regardless of what flows or results from the breach. The consent model fails in this regard, except in relation to battery where there is no requirement to prove harm – but battery is, as discussed in Chapter 3, considered an inappropriate form of action in cases relating to non-disclosure of information. Lord Hoffman's acknowledgement that 'there might be a case for a modest solatium'[45] in cases of affront to personality, however, opens a door by means of which an alternative model could be introduced with the aim of achieving what consent fails to deliver.

Personality as a Legally Recognised Interest

Recognition of the patient's right to self-determination as a distinct right would not be unparalleled in jurisprudence; it would be akin to the protection afforded in some jurisdictions to one's right to honour and dignity.[46] In South Africa, for example, personality is a legally recognised interest protected through a modern form of the *actio iniuriarum*.[47] The *actio iniuriarum* is an action for negligent behaviour that affronts the dignity, reputation or bodily integrity of the claimant.[48] Rooted in Roman law, it had by the nineteenth century fallen

43 Ibid., paras 32–34.

44 *Chester* v. *Afshar* [2004] All ER (D) 164, [2004] UKHL 41, at para 55.

45 *Chester (Respondent)* v. *Afshar (Appellant)* [2004] UKHL 41, at para 34.

46 Burchell J, The legal protection of privacy in South Africa: a transplantable hybrid (2009) 13.1 Electronic Journal of Comparative Law; available at http://www.ejcl.org/131/art131-2.pdf. Accessed 17 April 2015.

47 Ibid.

48 Zimmermann R, *The Law of Obligations: Roman Foundations of the Civilian Tradition*. Oxford: Oxford University Press 1996, pp. 1083–1084.

out of favour in jurisdictions (such as Germany) where it had hitherto featured prominently, but has recently made a comeback.[49] As Zimmermann put it, '[t]hrown out by the front door, the actio iniurarium has managed to sneak in through the back window – in the guise and under the cover of the general right of personality'.[50] It was applied in the Scottish case of *Stevens* v. *Yorkhill NHS Trust* in which a mother brought an action against the doctors who, without her consent, had removed (at a post-mortem examination) and retained the brain of her baby.[51] Whitty was not cited in *Stevens*, but had earlier argued that 'the actio iniuriarum, in its modern form as a doctrine of rights of personality, provides a principled legal framework within which the Scottish post-mortem cases naturally, and indeed historically, belong'.[52]

Adoption of Property Analysis: Receptivity of the Courts to New Developments

For property analysis to establish firm roots, the courts will have to be prepared to give it a chance. Given the courts' reluctance to recognise property rights to the human body as discussed in Chapter 7, some degree of scepticism is tenable. On the other hand, Lord Scarman's statement in *Sidaway* gives a ray of hope:

> The common law is adaptable: it would not otherwise have survived over the centuries of its existence. The concept of negligence itself is a development of the law by the judges over the last hundred years or so …
>
> Unless statute has intervened to restrict the range of judge-made law, the common law enables the judges when faced with a situation where a right recognized by law is not adequately protected, either to extend existing principles to cover the situation or to apply an existing remedy to redress the injustice.[53]

This leads one to believe that the apex court left the door open for new developments – such as property analysis – but it must be borne in mind that Lord Scarman was one of the more liberal members of the court.

49 The reasons for the dormancy of *actio iniuriarum* have been discussed elsewhere and are beyond the scope of this book. See Whitty NR, Rights of personality, property rights and the human body in Scots law (2005) Edin L Rev 9 194–237, at p. 201.

50 Zimmermann, *The Law of Obligations*, p. 1092.

51 *Stevens* v. *Yorkhill NHS Trust* [2006] CSOH 143.

52 Whitty, Rights of personality, p. 197.

53 *Sidaway* v. *Bethlem Royal Hospital and the Maudsley Hospital Health Authority and Others* [1985] UKHL 1, at 8–9.

From *Sidaway* to *Chester*: The Appellate Courts in Transition

The position of the courts in relation to the patient's right to self-determination has progressively shifted in the last couple of decades. It is important to trace this shift because it shows that the time may be right for consideration of the advantages that a property model potentially offers.

For three decades, the seminal UK case regarding the patient's right to be adequately informed about his or her treatment has been *Sidaway*, the facts of which were discussed in Chapter 3. Although the court found in favour of the defendant, all of the judges recognised that the claimant had a fundamental right to decide whether to accept or reject any treatment proposed by the doctor. What differed between them was the distance they were prepared to travel in order to protect that right. The more adventurous Lord Scarman travelled the farthest, but even he found in favour of the defendant.

Lord Scarman's Rights-based Position

Lord Scarman appeared to be well ahead of his time, and was recently described as 'one of the greatest and most socially sensitive judges of his generation'.[54] He narrowed the issues at stake to these questions:

> Has the patient a legal right to know, and is the doctor under a legal duty to disclose, the risks inherent in the treatment which the doctor recommends? If the law recognizes the right and the obligation, is it a right to full disclosure or has the doctor a discretion as to the nature and extent of his disclosure?[55]

These questions and the way Lord Scarman addressed them are underpinned by rights-based thinking. He opined that the patient's right to make his own decision 'may be seen as a basic human right protected by the common law'[56] and went on to say:

> If, therefore, the failure to warn a patient of the risks inherent in the operation which is recommended does constitute a failure to respect the patient's right to make his own decision, I can see no reason in principle why, if the risk materialises and injury or damage is caused, the law should not recognize and enforce a right in the patient to compensation by way of damages.[57]

54 Lord Justice Munby in *Re G* [2012] EWCA Civ 1233, at para 48.

55 *Sidaway* v. *Board of Governors of the Bethlem Royal Hospital and the Maudsley Hospital* [1985] UKHL 1, at 2.

56 Ibid., 7.

57 Ibid., 9–10.

Lord Scarman acknowledged that in cases relating to informing the patient of the benefits, risks and alternatives of treatment, 'the court is concerned primarily with a patient's right'[58] and that '[t]he doctor's duty arises from his patient's right'.[59] Still placing the patient's rights in pole position, he goes on to say:

> If one considers the scope of the doctor's duty by beginning with the right of the patient to make his own decision whether he will or will not undergo the treatment proposed, the right to be informed of significant risk and the doctor's corresponding duty are easy to understand: for the proper implementation of the right requires that the doctor be under a duty to inform his patient of the material risks inherent in the treatment.[60]

If the law accords primacy to protection of the patient's rights, and in particular the patient's right to adequate information and involvement in decision-making, then property analysis is advantageous in so far as it protects the patient's rights more stringently than the consent model does. Lord Scarman's view of the patient's right to make his or her own decision as a basic human right is consistent with the case made above for this right to be protected as a distinct legal interest under the property model. It is also encompassed in the concept, enunciated in Chapter 8, of property rights in the patient's expectation of sufficient disclosure of information during a medical consultation.

The other judges did not adopt the rights-based approach of Lord Scarman. There are a number of reasons for this, as reflected in the judgments. One reason was the then prevalent deference to the medical profession. The other was the prevailing social norm which did not prize individual self-determination in the way that contemporary society does.

Deference to the Medical Profession

Lord Diplock held that the *Bolam* test should be applied.[61] In this regard, and in the tone of his judgment, he was diametrically opposite to Lord Scarman. In his view, the doctor's duty of care had always been and should continue to be

58 Ibid., 13.

59 Ibid. (Alternatively, *Sidaway* v. *Board of Governors of the Bethlem Royal Hospital and the Maudsley Hospital* [1985] 1 BMLR 132, at 145.)

60 Ibid.

61 'The test [in determining the standard of care required of a doctor in advising and treating his patient] is the standard of the ordinary skilled man exercising and professing to have that special skill ... it is sufficient if he exercises the ordinary skill of an ordinary competent man exercising that particular art.' Per McNair J, *Bolam* v. *Friern Hospital Management Committee* [1957] 2 All ER 118.

'treated as single comprehensive duty covering all the ways in which a doctor is called upon to exercise his skill and judgment',[62] and the entirety of this duty of care is subject to the *Bolam* test. He did not see any reason to distinguish the duty to inform the patient of risks from the more technical aspects of care, and pointed out that even the *Bolam* case itself included a claim of failure to warn:

> This general duty is not subject to dissection into a number of component parts to which different criteria of what satisfy the duty of care apply, such as diagnosis, treatment, advice (including warning of any risks of something going wrong however skilfully the treatment advised is carried out). The *Bolam* case itself embraced failure to advise the patient of the risk involved in the electric shock treatment as one of the allegations of negligence against the surgeon.[63]

As the duty to warn is not, in Lord Diplock's view, separable from diagnosis and treatment, expert evidence in this regard should be treated the same way – that is, the professional standard applied:

> To decide what risks the existence of which a patient should be voluntarily warned and the terms in which such warning, if any, should be given, having regard to the effect that the warning may have, is as much an exercise of professional skill and judgment as any other part of the doctor's comprehensive duty of care to the individual patient, and expert medical evidence should be treated in just the same way. The Bolam test should be applied.[64]

This view that the patient should be told not what he/she expects to be told but what the medical profession feel he/she should be told was subsequently followed by the Court of Appeal in two cases.[65] In *Gold* v. *Haringey Health Authority* the claimant became pregnant and had her fourth child, despite having been sterilised in 1979 at the defendants' hospital.[66] She brought an action in negligence, and alleged that she was not warned of the risk of failure of the sterilisation. The court was told that a substantial body of medical opinion in 1979 would not have informed the patient of the possibility that a sterilisation operation could fail. In spite of this professional opinion, the court found for the claimant. On appeal, the Court of Appeal found in favour of the defendants.

---

62 *Sidaway* v. *Board of Governors of the Bethlem Royal Hospital and the Maudsley Hospital* [1985] UKHL 1, at 18.

63 Ibid.

64 Ibid., 20.

65 *Blyth* v. *Bloomsbury* [1993] 4 Med LR 151, CA; *Gold* v. *Haringey Health Authority* [1987] 2 All ER 888, CA.

66 *Gold* v. *Haringey Health Authority* [1987] 2 All ER 888, CA.

This position was, however, strongly criticised by academic commentators who have argued, with good reason, that the duty to inform patients of benefits, risks and alternatives should be separated from the more technical aspects of care such as details of diagnosis and treatment.[67] On the other hand, there is some logic in Lord Diplock's view that the provision of information is part of the duty of care, just as is making a diagnosis or providing safe care. While it is accepted that there is a difference between the strictly technical aspects of care and the discussion of risks, benefits and alternatives, the divergence between the two when it comes to the law (whereby one test is applied to a part of the duty of care but a different test is applied to another component of that duty) only serves to underscore the inadequacy of the consent model – discussion of risks, benefits and alternatives had to be extricated from the duty of care in order for consent to work as a legal means of protecting patient self-determination (otherwise the *Bolam* test applied). Potentially, this can be avoided by exploring the option of a property model. With the property model, the question of whether *Bolam* applies to information-giving does not arise; once the proprietary right is breached, the patient is entitled to redress.

The First Steps of Departure from Bolam

It could be argued that the shift away from the *Bolam* test in determining disclosure standards actually started with *Sidaway* itself. Although Lord Scarman was alone in taking the view that the patient's right to information trumped professional opinion, three of the other four judges – Lord Bridge, Lord Keith and Lord Templeman – did take small but significant steps in this direction, by advocating a modified *Bolam* test.

Lord Bridge, with whose judgment Lord Keith agreed, invoked the 'realities of the doctor/patient relationship' as one reason why a doctrine enforcing the patient's right to self-determination would be 'quite impracticable in application'.[68] His view of the relationship is a vertical and paternalistic one. He said that the doctor 'cannot set out to educate the patient to his own standard of medical knowledge of all the relevant factors involved'[69] (a statement that emphasises a vertical relationship) and expressed concern that disclosure of risk 'may lead to that risk assuming an undue significance in the patient's calculations'[70] (a concern that is paternalistic). Vertical doctor–patient relationships and paternalism are both anachronistic. Had Lord Bridge adopted

67 These include Margaret Brazier, 'Patient autonomy and consent to treatment: the role of the law?' (1987) 7 Legal Studies 169–193 and McLean, *Autonomy, Consent and the Law*.

68 *Sidaway* v. *Board of Governors of the Bethlem Royal Hospital and the Maudsley Hospital* [1985] UKHL 1, at 24.

69 Ibid.

70 Ibid.

the collaborative model of doctor–patient relationship described and advocated in Chapter 2, there would have been no great barrier to the enforcement of patient self-determination.

The *tour de force* of Lord Bridge's speech was the following:

> [A] decision what degree of disclosure of risks is best calculated to assist a particular patient to make a rational choice as to whether or not to undergo a particular treatment must primarily be a matter of clinical judgment. It would follow from this that the issue whether non-disclosure in a particular case should be condemned as a breach of the doctor's duty of care is an issue to be determined primarily on the basis of expert medical evidence, applying the Bolam test.[71]

However, what he says subsequently carries immense significance because it indicates a modified *Bolam* position:

> But I do not see that this approach involves the necessity 'to hand over to the medical profession the entire question of the scope of the duty of disclosure, including the question whether there has been a breach of that duty'.[72]

It appears that the judge was keen to uphold patient self-determination but preferred an incremental rather than a radical approach to achieving it: *Bolam* applies, but where the court deems fit, the appropriate standard of care regarding disclosure of information will be set not by medical opinion but by the court. What we see here is the beginning of a shift from the *Bolam* position.

Lord Templeman said that, regarding results and options for treatment, 'the doctor must decide in the light of his training and experience and in the light of his knowledge of the patient what should be said and how it should be said',[73] but he goes on to say that:

> At the same time the doctor is not entitled to make the final decision with regard to treatment which may have disadvantages or dangers. Where the patient's health and future are at stake, the patient must make the final decision. The patient is free to decide whether or not to submit to treatment recommended by the doctor and therefore the doctor impliedly contracts to provide information which is adequate to enable the patient to reach a balanced judgment, subject always to the [therapeutic privilege].[74]

71 Ibid., 25.
72 Ibid.
73 Ibid., 29.
74 Ibid.

Thus, Lord Templeman also takes a similar modified *Bolam* position, holding up the *Bolam* test as the appropriate test in this situation but also affirming the patient's rights as final arbiter of what treatment may or may not be given. It is arguable that the modified *Bolam* test is nebulous, and simply reflected the reluctance of the judges to take a definitive step forward in the manner that Lord Scarman attempted to do. Further demonstrating the inadequacy of the consent model, Lord Templeman also said that 'the relationship between doctor and patient is contractual in origin'[75] – a statement that suggests he was mindful of the obligation (regarding disclosure of information) owed to the patient by the doctor, but he was unable to enforce that obligation in this case.

Medical Opinion Must Withstand Logical Scrutiny: Bolitho v. City and Hackney Health Authority

In *Bolitho*, the court showed that it was prepared to depart from the traditional position of excessive deference to the medical profession.[76] Lord Brown-Wilkinson asserted that for expert medical opinion to be acceptable to the court it must be capable of withstanding logical scrutiny:

> These cases demonstrate that in cases of diagnosis and treatment there are cases where, despite a body of professional opinion sanctioning the defendant's conduct, the defendant can properly be held liable for negligence (I am not here considering questions of disclosure or risk). In my judgment that is because, in some cases, it cannot be demonstrated to the judge's satisfaction that the body of opinion relied on is reasonable or responsible. In the vast majority of cases, the fact that distinguished experts in the field are of a particular opinion will demonstrate the reasonableness of that opinion. In particular, where there are questions of assessment of the relative risks and benefits of adopting a medical practice, a reasonable view necessarily presupposes that the relative risks and benefits have been weighed by the experts in forming their opinions. But if, in a rare case, it can be demonstrated that the professional opinion is not capable of withstanding logical analysis, the judge is entitled to hold that the body of opinion is not reasonable or responsible. I emphasise that, in my view, it will very seldom be right for a judge to reach the conclusion that views genuinely held by a competent medical expert are unreasonable. The assessment of medical risks and benefits is a matter of clinical judgment which a judge would not normally be able to make without expert evidence.[77]

---

75 Ibid.

76 *Bolitho* v. *City and Hackney Health Authority* (1997) 39 BLMR 1 at 10, and [1997] 3 WLR 1151.

77 *Bolitho* v. *City and Hackney Health Authority* [1997] 3 WLR 1151, at 1160.

For a jurisdiction that appeared beholden to the medical profession this was a major development, and it was followed in a case relating to disclosure of information.[78] While *Bolitho* has the appearance of a landmark case, however, the court's position regarding the reasonableness of medical opinion was not novel. Sir John Donaldson, Master of the Rolls, had earlier said that:

> the definition of the duty of care is not to be handed over to the medical or any other profession. The definition of the duty of care is a matter for the law and the courts. They cannot stand idly by if the profession, by an excess of paternalism, denies its patients real choice. In a word, the law will not allow the medical profession to play God … I think that, in an appropriate case, a judge would be entitled to reject a unanimous medical view if he were satisfied that it was manifestly wrong and that the doctors must have been misdirecting themselves as to their duty in law.[79]

Also, in *Smith* v. *Tunbridge Wells Health Authority* the court affirmed the patient's right to make an informed decision but stated that the materiality of risk was for the court (and not the medical profession) to determine.[80] The judge said:

> In my judgement by 1988, although some surgeons may still not have been warning patients similar in situation to the plaintiff of the risk of impotence, that omission was neither reasonable nor responsible.[81]

The patient has a Right to be Informed of Significant Risks: Pearce v. United Bristol Healthcare NHS Trust[82]

Mrs Pearce brought an action in negligence against the defendants after she suffered a stillbirth. The pregnancy with her sixth child had been uncomplicated until it went two weeks beyond the estimated due date. At this point she asked her specialist for labour to be induced or the baby to be delivered by Caesarean section. The specialist declined her request, on the grounds that induction of labour would be risky and a Caesarean section would entail a longer stay in hospital. She accepted his recommendation that nature should take its course, but a few days later the baby died in the womb. Mrs Pearce claimed that the doctor should have informed her of the increased risk of stillbirth associated

78 *Pearce* v. *United Bristol Healthcare NHS Trust* (1998) 48 BMLR 118.

79 *Sidaway* v. *Bethlem Royal Hospital Governors* [1984] 1 All ER 1018, at 1028.

80 *Smith* v. *Tunbridge Wells Health Authority* [1994] 5 Med LR 334.

81 Ibid., 338.

82 *Pearce* v. *United Bristol Healthcare NHS Trust* [1999] PIQR 53. (Also [1998] EWCA Civ 865.)

with expectant management beyond 42 weeks of pregnancy, and that if she had been given this information she would not have opted for this line of management. At first instance her claim was dismissed, and she appealed, but the Court of Appeal also dismissed her claim.

In dismissing the appeal, Lord Woolf followed the footsteps of the majority in *Sidaway* by agreeing that the patient was entitled to be informed by the doctor of any information that would be relevant to her decision-making, and took cognisance of the decision in *Bolitho*. According to Lord Woolf:

> In a case where it is being alleged that a plaintiff has been deprived of the opportunity to make a proper decision as to what course he or she should take in relation to treatment, it seems to me to be the law, as indicated in the cases to which I have just referred, that if there is a *significant* risk which would affect the judgment of a reasonable patient, then in the normal course it is the responsibility of a doctor to inform the patient of that *significant* risk, if the information is needed so that the patient can determine for him or herself as to what course he or she should adopt.[83] (emphases mine)

Having acknowledged the patient's entitlement to information, Lord Woolf nonetheless proceeded to dismiss the appeal on the basis of medical opinion that the risk of stillbirth in this case was not significant. This was not a favourable outcome for the claimant whose right to self-determination had been breached by the doctor's failure to disclose relevant information, but progress had been made because of the pronouncement that the standard of disclosure was to be determined not by the *Bolam* test but by the reasonable patient test.

If the position of the individual judges in *Sidaway* is examined in isolation, it seems clear that the apex court in the UK was not quite ready for a property analysis approach to the disclosure of information. When their Lordships' modification of the *Bolam* test is taken into account and, more importantly, when the decisions of the Court of Appeal (*Pearce*) and the House of Lords (*Bolitho*) in subsequent years are considered, there is a clear shift in the courts' position, in the direction of the position taken by Lord Scarman in *Sidaway*. This shift to a more patient-oriented stance opens the door to a re-evaluation of the consent model, and perhaps even a conclusion that it should be replaced.

The Courts' Shift towards a Rights-based Approach: *Chester* v. *Afshar*

Lord Woolf, Lord Chief Justice of England and Wales, admitted in a lecture given at University College London in January 2001 that the courts had been

83 Ibid., 59.

'over-differential' to the medical profession but asserted that this had not only changed but had 'changed for the better'.[84] He cited as one of the reasons for this change the increasing awareness of patients' expectations and said that 'the move to a rights-based society has fundamentally changed the behaviour of the courts'.[85] The most striking manifestation of this changed behaviour was in *Chester* v. *Afshar*.[86]

Miss Carole Chester, a journalist, underwent a spinal operation in the hands of Mr Fari Afshar, a neurosurgeon. The risk of cauda equina syndrome complicating this operation was about 1–2 per cent but this risk materialised, and it was established at first instance that Mr Afshar did not warn Miss Chester of the risk. At first instance, Judge Robert Taylor held that Mr Afshar was not negligent in his conduct of the operation. However, if Miss Chester had been informed of the risk of nerve damage, she would have taken time to consider her options and would not have had the operation on 21 November 1994. Since she would not have had the operation at the time it was performed, there was a causal link between the failure to warn and the injury suffered by the claimant. Mr Afshar appealed but by a majority of 3:2 the House of Lords decided in favour of Miss Chester.

In doing so, the court broke (or at the very least, bent) the traditional rule of causation which required the claimant to show that had she been warned of the risk that materialised, she would not have undergone the operation. The court was concerned that she had not been warned of the risk of cauda equina syndrome, but Miss Chester's truthfulness (that, if she had been warned of the risk of cauda equine syndrome, she still would have had the operation albeit on another day) left it in a quandary: it was keen to protect her right to be informed of risks that may determine her decision whether to proceed, but causation was a stumbling block. While two of the judges stuck to the traditional causation rule, the majority felt that the right to self-determination was so fundamental that it had to be upheld at the expense of a legal tradition. The majority judges were unequivocal in asserting the primacy of self-determination.

Concern for Self-determination and Dignity

Lord Walker recalled that Lord Scarman, in *Sidaway*, had described the patient's right to make his own decision as a basic human right, and he pointed out that, although Lord Scarman was delivering a dissenting speech, the whole House recognised this right. Lord Hope said that 'during the 20 years which have

---

84 Lord Woolf, Are the courts excessively deferential to the medical profession? (2001) 9 Med L Rev 1–16, at p. 1.

85 Ibid., p. 3.

86 *Chester* v. *Afshar* [2004] UKHL 41, [2004] 3 WLR 927.

elapsed since Sidaway the importance of personal autonomy has been more and more widely recognised'.[87]

Lord Steyn felt that a patient's right to be informed of the risks of surgery 'ought normatively to be regarded as an important right which must be given effective protection whenever possible'.[88] He prefaced this opinion by acknowledging that 'not all rights are equally important',[89] which is the basis on which some rights are deemed worthy of special protection as property. Emphasising the fundamental nature of the right to self-determination, he said that patients 'have the right to make decisions which doctors regard as ill advised'.[90]

Clearly, Lord Steyn manifested a Scarmanesque concern for the importance of patient self-determination. That he was willing to depart (and it could be argued that this departure was more than 'narrow and modest'[91]) from time-honoured legal principles of causation for the sake of granting Miss Chester relief showed his strong commitment to protecting the patient's right to self-determination. On the other hand, in maintaining that '[t]he court is the final arbiter of what constitutes informed consent',[92] Lord Steyn shows that so long as the consent model is the preferred model, protection of patient self-determination will be dependent on malleable judicial opinion rather than the legal certainty offered by the property model.

Concern for the Protection of Rights and Remedies

Lord Walker was of the opinion that where a surgeon has failed in his professional duty and the claimant has suffered injury directly within the scope of that duty, such a claimant should have a remedy, 'even if it involves some extension of existing principle'.[93]

While Lord Steyn said that consent 'ensures that due respect is given to the autonomy and dignity of each patient',[94] his conclusion that Miss Chester's 'right of autonomy and dignity can and ought to be vindicated by a narrow and modest departure from traditional causation principles'[95] shows that the consent model is actually inadequate for protecting this right without recourse to juridical gymnastics. His abandonment of firm adherence to traditionalist

87 Ibid., para 92.
88 Ibid., para 17.
89 Ibid.
90 Ibid., para 14.
91 Ibid., para 24.
92 Ibid.
93 Ibid., para 101.
94 Ibid., para 18.
95 Ibid., para 24.

causation analysis in favour of a greater emphasis on policy and corrective justice showed that protection of self-determination has become a policy objective and reaffirmed a view long held in the academic legal community that the consent model as implemented in English courts often deprived the patient of corrective justice.

Lord Hope spoke of Miss Chester's right to be informed of the risks inherent in the proposed surgery, and said 'the function of the law is to protect the patient's right to choose'.[96] He put forward 'the proposition that the law which imposed the duty to warn on the doctor has at its heart the right of the patient to make an informed choice as to whether, and if so when and by whom, to be operated on',[97] and said that:

> The function of the law is to enable rights to be vindicated and to provide remedies when duties have been breached. Unless this is done the duty is a hollow one, stripped of all practical force and devoid of all content. It will have lost its ability to protect the patient and thus to fulfil the only purpose which brought it into existence.[98]

> The choice between these alternatives was for her to take, and for her alone. The function of the law is to protect the patient's right to choose. If it is to fulfil that function it must ensure that the duty to inform is respected by the doctor. It will fail to do this if an appropriate remedy cannot be given if the duty is breached and the very risk that the patient should have been told about occurs and she suffers injury.[99]

He accepted that Miss Chester's claim could not be upheld on the basis of conventional causation principles and turned to policy grounds for dismissing the appeal. As with his fellow judges Lord Steyn and Lord Walker, his willingness to modify the normal approach to causation in the interest of justice manifests a deep commitment to rights protection. He highlights the difficulty faced by the law in providing an appropriate remedy when the consent model is applied. This difficulty could be avoided by adoption of property analysis, as causation does not have to be established. Establishing a breach of the property right will be sufficient to draw a remedy.

96 Ibid., para 56.
97 Ibid., para 86.
98 Ibid., para 87.
99 Ibid., para 56.

Chester is Welcome, but Does Not Go Far Enough

With the decision in *Chester*, it could be said that the prudent patient has now, contrary to the assertion of Sir John Donaldson (then Master of the Rolls), been removed to the courts from his/her natural habitat, to the benefit of patients.[100] The figurative appearance in court of the prudent patient is not, however, an end in itself. The court's decision in *Chester* was welcomed by academic commentators[101] but, while the court was unequivocally clear about its commitment to patient self-determination, it did not go far enough towards freeing the potential claimant from the shackles of the consent model. For a start, the claimant was awarded damages not for the infraction of her right to self-determination *per se*, but for the injury she suffered. As argued above, the right to self-determination should be protected as a distinct legal right.

Also noteworthy in *Chester* is that the House of Lords did not abandon causation. It could be said that the court found for the claimant by interpreting causation in the context of policy. The court held (by a majority) that, on policy grounds, causation had been fulfilled despite the absence of a statement by the claimant that but for the failure to warn her she would not have undergone the operation. An alternative viewpoint is that the court actually sidestepped causation, and the explanation of the decision lies in their Lordships' exploration of the scope of the duty of care which led them to 'a normative conclusion … (the doctor *ought* to be liable for this injury) rather than a causative one (the doctor *caused* this injury)'.[102] Regardless of which explanation is preferred, *Chester* does not obviate causation. This means that the hurdle of proving causation in cases of failure to disclose information remains.

The conclusion is that while *Chester* demonstrates a changed attitude and a strong commitment to protecting patient self-determination, it also shows that the courts need a suitable framework for translating this avowed commitment into real benefit for the patient – it is worth exploring the prospects of a model other than the consent model.

---

100 Sir Donaldson said: 'I suspect that [the prudent patient] is a fairly rare bird and I have no doubt that his removal to the courts from his natural habitat, which would, I assume, be a seat or hand rail on the Clapham omnibus, would do nothing for patients or medicine, although it might do a great deal for lawyers and litigation.' *Sidaway* v. *Bethlem Royal Hospital* [1985] 2 WLR, at 791.

101 Mason K and Brodie D, Bolam, Bolam – wherefore art thou Bolam? (2005) 9 Edin L Rev 298–306.

102 Hogg M, Duties of care, causation, and the implications of *Chester* v *Afshar* (2005) 9 Edin L Rev 156–167, at pp. 156–157.

The Demise of the Professional Standard: *Montgomery (Appellant) v Lanarkshire Health Board (Respondent) (Scotland)*[103]

The facts of this case were summarised in Chapter 5. Expert evidence had indicated that a body of responsible practitioners would, like the obstetrician in this case, not have given the patient information about the risks of shoulder dystocia and its possible consequences. The court, however, rejected the professional standard. The judges dissected the judgement in *Sidaway* and subsequent case law, and concluded:

> It would therefore be wrong to regard *Sidaway* as an unqualified endorsement of the application of the *Bolam* test to the giving of advice about treatment. Only Lord Diplock adopted that position.[104]

The apex court also observed that:

> Since *Sidaway*, ... it has become increasingly clear that the paradigm of the doctor-patient relationship implicit in the speeches in that case has ceased to reflect the reality and complexity of the way in which healthcare services are provided, or the way in which the providers and recipients of such services view their relationship. One development which is particularly significant in the present context is that patients are now widely regarded as persons holding rights, rather than as the passive recipients of the care of the medical profession.[105]

It stated categorically that:

> [r]esponsibility for determining the nature and extent of a person's rights rests with the courts, not with the medical professions.[106]

and concluded that:

> the analysis of the law by the majority in *Sidaway* is unsatisfactory, in so far as it treated the doctor's duty to advise her patient of the risks of proposed treatment as falling within the scope of the *Bolam* test.[107]

---

103 *Montgomery (Appellant) v Lanarkshire Health Board (Respondent) (Scotland)* [2015] UKSC 11.
104 *Montgomery*, at para 57.
105 Ibid., para 75.
106 Ibid., para 83.
107 Ibid., para 87.

It clarified the current legal position to be as follows:

> The correct position, in relation to the risks of injury involved in treatment, can now be seen to be substantially that adopted in *Sidaway* by Lord Scarman, and by Lord Woolf MR in *Pearce*, subject to the refinement made by the High Court of Australia in *Rogers v Whitaker*. An adult person of sound mind is entitled to decide which, if any, of the available forms of treatment to undergo, and her consent must be obtained before treatment interfering with her bodily integrity is undertaken. The doctor is therefore under a duty to take reasonable care to ensure that the patient is aware of any material risks involved in any recommended treatment, and of any reasonable alternative or variant treatments. The test of materiality is whether, in the circumstances of the particular case, a reasonable person in the patient's position would be likely to attach significance to the risk, or the doctor is or should reasonably be aware that the particular patient would be likely to attach significance to it.[108]

This is a landmark case, because for the first time the professional standard has been abandoned in the English and Scottish jurisdictions, in favour of the prudent patient standard. This is not an unexpected development, given the transition discussed above. Nonetheless, it is ground-breaking.

The Index (or Particular) Patient versus the Hypothetical Patient

The shift from the reasonable doctor test to the prudent patient test for disclosure of information may on the surface appear to be a major victory for champions of patient self-determination. Experience in other jurisdictions, however, shows that even with this shift the battle is not yet half-won. Gerald Robertson, for example, has shown that in Canada the adoption of a prudent patient test has not resulted in more successes for claimants.[109] The reasons for this are firstly, that the element of causation is a major stumbling block and, secondly, that patient self-determination is best protected by application of a subjective test for assessing disclosure of information. The problem posed by the substitution of the interests of a homogenised patient for those of the particular patient has been discussed in Chapter 3 where this was identified as a weakness of the consent model.

The most striking difference between Lord Scarman's speech and those of the other judges in *Sidaway* is that, while others had the medical profession as

108 Ibid., para 87.

109 Robertson GB, Informed consent: 20 years later (2003) Health Law Journal Special edition 153–159.

their focal point, Lord Scarman had the patient (and his/her rights) as his focal point. This focus was maintained by the majority in *Chester* and by all judges in *Montgomery*. Perhaps the greatest strength of the property model is that it shifts the starting point from the doctor's duty to the rights of the particular patient, and does so without the inconsistencies demonstrated by the consent model. An example of such inconsistency in the consent model is the use of a *subjective* test for *causation* (would this patient have made a different decision if she had been well informed?) in contrast to an *objective* test for the *standard of disclosure* (what would a reasonable patient have expected to be told?).

In focusing on the patient, however, it will usually not be helpful to the index patient if an objective test is applied. In *Sidaway*, Lord Scarman referred to this weakness when commenting on the prudent patient test:

> The 'prudent patient', however, cannot always provide the answer for the obvious reason that he is a norm (like the man on the Clapham omnibus), not a real person: and certainly not the patient himself.[110]

Lord Scarman was concerned that the law should address the position of the particular claimant, but felt that this line of inquiry 'would prove in practice to be frustrated by the subjectivity of its aim and purpose',[111] accordingly, he applied the objective test.

Three decades after *Sidaway*, UK society has become so heterogeneous that the gap between the 'prudent patient' and the index patient has widened considerably. The growing heterogeneity of values and diminishing social consensus in the UK is described by one commentator as follows:

> Like many Western societies UK society has become more diverse and individualistic in the past half-century, with a diminished underpinning of social consensus. Values are still collectively held, but there are now many collectivities, and they are internally diverse. The individualisation of society ... is amplified by the effect of consumerism, which encourages people to express personal uniqueness through their valuation of particular experiences. So it is very risky to try to predict the values of an individual on any given issue, even if we believe we can locate that individual socially and culturally. In the end we can only rely on the individual to know their own values.[112]

110 *Sidaway* v. *Bethlem Royal Hospital Governors* [1985] AC 871, at 889.

111 Ibid.

112 Wilmot S, A fair range of choice: justifying maximum patient choice in the British National Health Service (2007) 15 Health Care Anal 59–72, at p. 65.

Lord Hope also alluded to this in *Chester*:

> ... the law which imposed the duty to warn on the doctor has at its heart the right of the patient to make an informed choice as to whether, and if so when and by whom, to be operated on. Patients may have, and are entitled to have, different views about these matters. All sorts of factors may be at work here – the patient's hopes and fears and personal circumstances, the nature of the condition that has to be treated and, above all, the patient's own views about whether the risk is worth running for the benefits that may come if the operation is carried out.[113]

If the patient's right to self-determination is to be better protected by a consent model then the subjective test (what does this patient want to know?) should be consistently applied, and this version of the consent model shares some, but not all, attributes of the property model. The subjective standard has its strengths as discussed above, but is not without possible disadvantage. Concern has been expressed that application of the subjective standard may foster defensive medicine and hinder the doctor–patient relationship. Lord Scarman acknowledged that 'the danger of defensive medicine developing in this country clearly exists',[114] and there is some evidence that it actually happens.[115] As the property model is built on a foundation of trust and effective communication between doctor and patient, there should be no fear that defensive medicine will be fostered.

The property approach hybridises the 'real consent' of English law and the 'informed consent' of some US jurisdictions, taking the elements of both that are appropriate to contemporary legal, ethical and social thinking, but adds a subjective element to decision-making. In real consent, there is only a requirement for broad information to be provided, the standard is set by the medical profession and either the objective or, less commonly, the subjective test is applied. In informed consent, all material risks are disclosed, the standard is set by the law and an objective test is applied (what would the reasonable patient want to know?). In the property model, all material risks are disclosed, the standard of disclosure is set by the law, but a subjective test is applied.

Property analysis addresses the position of the particular claimant, not that of a hypothetical person. The doctor is obliged to communicate with, rather than merely inform, the patient. As stated in the quotation above, in a heterogeneous

113 *Chester* v. *Afshar* [2004] UKHL 41, [2004] 3 WLR 927, at para 86.

114 *Sidaway* v. *Bethlem Royal Hospital Governors* [1985] 1 All ER 643, at 653.

115 Summerton N, Positive and negative factors in defensive medicine: a questionnaire study of general practitioners (1995) 310 BMJ 27–29; Kessler DP, Summerton N and Graham JR, Effects of the medical liability system in Australia, the UK, and the USA (2006) 368 The Lancet 240–246.

multicultural society it is risky to try to predict the values of an individual on any given issue. Apart from the problem of determining what is reasonable for a particular patient, the courts, litigants and health professionals would be better served by certainty than by the whims of judges. In the property model, the patient has a protected right to make informed decisions about treatment based on his or her own values and circumstances. The doctor has a fiduciary duty to discuss the treatment options against the background of the patient's particular circumstances and take reasonable steps to ensure that the patient makes an informed decision.

In *Sidaway*, Lord Diplock drew a sharp line between information given voluntarily and information given in response to questioning, and placed the onus on the patient to ask questions – a far cry from Lord Scarman's position which sees the patient's right as the starting point. He also manifested elitist thinking when he suggested that what was good for the goose might not necessarily be good for the gander:

> … when it comes to warning about risks, the kind of training and experience that a judge will have undergone at the Bar makes it natural for him to say (correctly) it is my right to decide whether any particular thing is done to my body, and I want to be fully informed of any risks there may be involved of which I am not already aware from my general knowledge as a highly educated man of experience, so that I may form my own judgment as to whether to refuse the advised treatment or not.[116]

To acknowledge that a man of training and experience can correctly assert the right to be fully informed and to decide what is done to his body, then go on to say that for everyone else such information does not have to be provided unless they specifically ask for it, is the height of elitism. In Montgomery, the court said that:

> [t]he significance attached in *Sidaway* to a patient's failure to question the doctor is … profoundly unsatisfactory' because, among other reasons, 'it is those patients who lack … knowledge, and who are in consequence unable to pose [the appropriate] questions and instead express their anxiety in more general terms, who are in the greatest need of information.[117]

Positions such as that expressed by Lord Diplock would be regarded as politically incorrect in today's world. It also suggests that the subjective test is appropriate

116 *Sidaway* v. *Bethlem Royal Hospital Governors* [1985] 1 All ER 643, at 659.

117 *Montgomery*, at para 58.

for the elite but an objective test has to be applied for others. The property model would pre-empt such elitism and ensure a level playing field for all.

Discussion of Alternatives

Another criticism of the consent model is that, reflecting the fact of its starting position being the doctor's duty rather than the patient's rights, it concentrates too much on disclosure of information about the particular treatment being offered, and not enough on alternative treatments:

> English case law (and academic discussion) places relatively little emphasis on the disclosure of information about alternatives. If a patient is well-informed about, say, a surgical intervention which may alleviate back pain, the patient would usually be regarded as able to give 'informed consent' to it. However, there may be non-surgical alternatives about which the patient is unaware. For the patient, information about alternatives will sometimes be at least as important as information about the proposed procedure.[118]

A step towards redressing this in case law was taken in *Janet Birch* v. *University College London Hospital NHS Foundation Trust*, which was briefly referred to above.[119] Citing and extending the principle established in *Sidaway*, *Pearce* and *Chester* that the doctor had a duty to disclose significant risks that would affect the decision of a patient, Cranston J held that this duty was not discharged if the patient was not made aware of the comparative risks of alternative available treatments. While this case goes some way to addressing the criticism quoted above, it cannot be assumed that a similar finding will apply in similar cases. The judge said there were 'special circumstances' in the case which influenced his decision, and it is possible that, in the absence of special circumstances, a different decision may have been reached. Reassuringly, Lady Hale stated in *Montgomery* [para 109] that 'it is not possible to consider a particular medical procedure in isolation from its alternatives'.

In the property model, the focus is not on getting the patient to agree to a particular treatment (as in the consent model), but on giving the patient the best opportunity to make an informed decision on which treatment option (including the option of no intervention) best serves his or her values and interests. The transaction between doctor and patient would necessarily include discussion of alternatives as well as the treatment being offered.

---

118 Skegg PDG, English medical law and 'informed consent': an antipodean assessment and alternative (1999) 7 Med L Rev 135–165, at p. 150.

119 *Janet Birch* v. *University College London Hospital NHS Foundation Trust* [2008] EWHC 2237.

Therapeutic Privilege

Even if the risk be material, the doctor will not be liable if upon a reasonable assessment of his patient's condition, he takes the view that a warning would be detrimental to his patient's health.[120] Although Lord Scarman cited therapeutic privilege as capable of trumping consent,[121] this is unlikely to be a major issue in contemporary practice, given the professional safeguards against it that were described in Chapter 5. The Supreme Court warned in *Montgomery* that the therapeutic privilege was not intended to subvert the principle of patient self-determination. Experience elsewhere also shows that 'the defence [therapeutic privilege] has been so narrowly interpreted … that it has come to occupy an almost untenable position in Australia's medical jurisprudence'.[122] In any case, by taking the patient's right as the default position, the property model places a heavier burden than the consent model on the doctor to justify any withholding of information under any circumstances.

Application of the Property Model to the Facts of *Sidaway*, *Chester* and *Montgomery*

Against the background of the above narrative and analysis, the property model is applied to the facts of *Sidaway*, *Chester* and *Montgomery* as follows.

The facts of the *Sidaway* case were outlined in Chapter 3, but are repeated here for ease of reference. Mrs Sidaway had suffered persistent neck and shoulder pain. She was relieved of this pain for some years after the defendant surgeon, Mr. Falconer, operated on her in 1960. She informed Mr. Falconer in 1973, that the pain had returned, and investigation showed a disc causing pressure on a nerve root. Mr Falconer proceeded to operate. Mrs. Sidaway's spinal cord was damaged during this operation, and she became partially paralysed as a result. She acknowledged that the operation was not negligently performed, but sued the hospital on the grounds that she had not been informed of the risk of nerve damage. Mr Falconer had died before the trial, so was unable to give his own account of what was disclosed, but the judge found that Mrs Sidaway had not been warned of the 1–2 per cent risk of spinal cord injury. As discussed above, the professional standard prevailed, and the court found in favour of the defendant.

120 *Obiter dicta*, Lord Scarman in *Sidaway* v. *Bethlem Royal Hospital Governors* [1984] 1 All ER 1018.

121 Ibid.

122 Mulheron R, The defence of therapeutic privilege in Australia (2003) 11 J Law Med 201–213, at p. 201.

Applying property analysis, the starting point is Mrs Sidaway's right to be given information that puts her in a position to make an informed decision about her care. This is what Lord Scarman attempted to do when he considered the scope of the doctor's duty 'by beginning with the right of the patient to make his own decision'.[123] This right would be protected as a distinct right, and Mrs Sidaway would not have needed to prove causation. In the property model, this right imposed a correlative fiduciary duty on Mr Falconer to effectively communicate with Mrs Sidaway and take reasonable steps to ensure that she understood information that he had provided. There would not have been a requirement to provide information on all possible risks, the emphasis being on quality rather than quantity of information.

In keeping with the transactional approach to consultation required by the property model, Mr Falconer would have advised Mrs Sidaway of any alternatives to the operation he had decided to perform, including the option of not operating. It was stated as a fact in court that what Mr Falconer proposed to do was 'an operation of choice rather than necessity'.[124] Mr Falconer apparently offered Mrs Sidaway what O'Neill describes as 'a menu of one item'.[125] This means that Mr Falconer failed in the fiduciary duty imposed by the property model. As Mrs Sidaway's legitimate expectation that her surgeon would inform her of relevant risks as well as alternative treatments constituted a proprietary right, she had a claim in breach of property right against Mr Falconer.

The professional standard does not apply in the property model, and the adequacy of disclosure of information would be assessed by forensic examination of the process of consultation between Mrs Sidaway and Mr Falconer. Medical opinion on what is usually disclosed or not disclosed in relation to the particular diagnosis would be relevant but not determinative.

Further, although Mrs Sidaway could not successfully bring an action in battery (because she had given a valid consent to be touched by Mr Falconer) under the consent model, she may validly claim trespass to bodily integrity under the property model (as well as the proprietary right in her legitimate expectation from the consultation), as her body is one dimension (the spatial dimension) of the property framework adopted in this book, (and a party may breach another's property right without having physical contact with the property).

Although she did not have to prove causation in this model, the damages awarded would not be merely nominal, for the property model includes a dimension which defines stringency of protection. This dimension accords highly stringent protection to the patient's right described above, as it is a

123 *Sidaway* v. *Bethlem Royal Hospital*, [1985] 2 WLR, at 494.

124 Ibid., 486.

125 O'Neill O, *Autonomy and Trust in Bioethics*. Cambridge: Cambridge University Press 2002, p. 38.

profoundly important right. Accordingly, compensation for infraction of this right will reflect this degree of protection and the concomitant need for deterrent remedy.

In summary, a different outcome would be expected if the property model is applied to the facts of *Sidaway*: patient self-determination would have triumphed and Mrs Sidaway would have been awarded damages.

In the case of *Chester*, Mr Afshar's failure to warn his patient of the risk of cauda equina syndrome constituted a breach of Miss Chester's proprietary rights, on the basis of the principles described above. The 'starting point' for Lord Steyn was Miss Chester's right to self-determination.[126] Had the property model been applied, this would also have been the starting point for all five judges in this case, and the position of the dissenting judges would have been different (especially as the causation hurdle would have been absent).

The court had a close look at the communication between Mr Afshar and Miss Chester, which itself speaks strongly for the importance attached to the transactional approach in the property model. Lord Hope summarised what transpired as follows:

> Miss Chester's account, which was the version which the trial judge accepted, was that she told Mr Afshar that she had heard a lot of horror stories about surgery and that she wanted to know about the risks, but that none of this was explained to her. She did not mention paralysis specifically as one of the risks that she wanted to be told about, and this was not mentioned as a risk of surgery by Mr Afshar. The reply which she got from him, as a throw away line, was that he had not crippled anybody yet. She agreed to the surgery because he made it all sound so simple.[127]

It is clear from this account that if property analysis is applied, it would be concluded that Mr Afshar did not take a transactional approach to communication with Miss Chester and did not discharge his fiduciary obligation as required by the property model. He thus breached Miss Chester's proprietary rights, and she was entitled to damages on this analysis, without any requirement for the court to consider causation.

As there is no imperative to prove harm and causation in the property model, there would have been no place for Lord Bingham's reservations about 'the payment of potentially very large damages by a defendant whose violation of that right is not shown to have worsened the physical condition of the claimant'.[128] As stated above regarding Mrs Sidaway, the quantum of

126 Per Lord Steyn in *Chester* v. *Afshar* [2004] UKHL 41, [2004] 3 WLR 927, at para 9.

127 Ibid., para 44.

128 Ibid., para 9.

damages would reflect the value placed by the public and the law on patient self-determination.[129]

Clearly, the speeches of the majority judges in *Chester* showed that they concurred with one of the tenets of the property model: the primacy of the patient's right to self-determination. As shown in the narrative above, the judges were also keen to protect this right regardless of the obstacle posed by causation – which supports another tenet of the property model, the protection of the right as a distinct legal right. Thirdly, the judges focused on the doctor–patient relationship and on Miss Chester's legitimate expectation from her consultation with Mr Afshar; both of these are the essence of property analysis and her legitimate expectation was a chose in action.

In summary, applying the property model to the facts of *Chester* yields the same outcome (the majority judgement), but without any jurisprudential contortions, no departures from established legal rules. As it stands, *Chester* is not necessarily a precedent for future cases – given the departure from traditional rules of causation, it may be treated as a special case, with future cases distinguished from it. Had property analysis been applied, it would have become firmly established as setting the law for protection of patient self-determination.

Application of the property model to the facts of *Montgomery* would have yielded the same outcome as reached at the apex court (but different to the judgement of the lower courts). The pursuer's right to information about the risk of shoulder dystocia and about the possible consequences of shoulder dystocia would be protected as a distinct right, and she would not have needed to prove causation. The obstetrician would have had a fiduciary duty to discuss her patient's anxieties (rather than use this as a reason to withhold information), disclose the risks of the treatment options, and support the pursuer in making an informed choice. The pursuer would have taken responsibility for her choice.

There are echoes of the transactional approach intrinsic to the property model in the observations of Lords Kerr and Reed:

> …the doctor's advisory role involves dialogue, the aim of which is to ensure that the patient understands the seriousness of her condition, and the anticipated benefits and risks of the proposed treatment and any reasonable alternatives, so that she is then in a position to make an informed decision. This role will only be performed effectively if the information provided is comprehensible. The doctor's duty is not therefore fulfilled by bombarding the patient with technical

129 In *Chester*, Lord Steyn stated: 'the decision announced by the House today reflects the reasonable expectations of the public in contemporary society'. *Chester* v. *Afshar* [2004] UKHL 41, [2004] 3 WLR 927, at para 25.

> information which she cannot reasonably be expected to grasp, let alone by routinely demanding her signature on a consent form.[130]

Further, the property model would reduce or eliminate the unpredictability which the Supreme Court recognised as a possible disadvantage of the retreat from Bolam:

> [We] would accept that a departure from the *Bolam* test will reduce the predictability of the outcome of litigation, given the difficulty of overcoming that test in contested proceedings. It appears to us however that a degree of unpredictability can be tolerated as the consequence of protecting patients from exposure to risks of injury which they would otherwise have chosen to avoid. The more fundamental response to such points, however, is that respect for the dignity of patients requires no less.[131]

I submit that the framework for a property approach described in this book (and its subsequent development) potentially removes the 'degree of unpredictability' that the legal system has to tolerate as a consequence of protecting self-determination under the consent model.

Alternative Approaches to Protection of Patient Self-determination: Human Rights and Contract

In attempting to secure protection of the patient's right to self-determination and clarify the doctor's corresponding duties, it may be helpful to consider briefly human rights discourse and the law of contract (which applies to a bilateral relationship, with one party having a personal right to demand and expect performance from the other, and the other party having a duty to perform accordingly), as these potentially offer alternatives to property analysis.

Human Rights Law as an Alternative Means of Protecting Patient Self-determination

In Chapter 2, the patient's right to self-determination was described as a foundational right, the ascendancy of rights thinking was given as one of the factors underlying the fall of paternalism and the impact on case law was outlined. The consent model is supposed to protect patient self-determination. As I have attempted to show, however, consent has not quite lived up to its

130 *Montgomery*, para 90.

131 Ibid., para 93.

billing. The question arises as to whether human rights law could be called to the rescue. Judges attempting to view information disclosure primarily from the scope of the doctor's duty may, at least in theory, be constrained by human rights legislation which has the patient's rights, not the doctor's duty, as its starting point. The European Convention on Human Rights, particularly Article 8 (right to private and family life), could be invoked in respect of a failure to disclose material information, and it is unlawful for the NHS to act in breach of the Convention.[132] It has also been suggested that a doctor who delivers treatment of an experimental nature without obtaining the patient's valid consent could be in breach of Article 3 (which prohibits inhuman or degrading treatment or punishment).[133]

Following in the footsteps of the European Convention is the European Charter of Patients' Rights[134] which was produced by the Active Citizenship Network, a network of European civic organisations. It has not been incorporated in statute, but it contains two articles (out of 14) that are particularly germane to patient self-determination:

> Article 4. Right to Consent
>
> Every individual has the right of access to all information that might enable him or her to actively participate in the decisions regarding his or her health; this information is a prerequisite for any procedure and treatment, including the participation in scientific research.
>
> Article 5. Right to Free Choice
>
> Each individual has the right to freely choose from among different treatment procedures and providers on the basis of adequate information.

When the European Convention on Human Rights was incorporated into UK domestic law by the Human Rights Act 1998, analysts anticipated that it would make a difference to the protection (or lack of it) afforded to patient self-determination:[135]

---

132 Section 6 of the Human Rights Act 1998.

133 Havers P and Neenan C, Impact of the European Convention on Human Rights on medical law (2002) 78 Postgrad Med J 573–574.

134 http://www.activecitizenship.net/images/patientsrights/ec_english.pdf. Accessed 15 November 2012.

135 Samanta A and Samanta J, The Human Rights Act 1998 – why should it matter for medical practice? (2005) 98 J R Soc Med 404–410; Hewson B, Why the Human Rights Act matters to doctors (2000) 321 BMJ 780–781.

> The current definition of 'informed consent' – meaning, loosely, what the doctor decides you should know – may be altered in favour of a version of informed consent more common in the United States in which patients are told 'everything.' The Bolam test is another tenet of medical law which may be reviewed. This test defines the standard of care which doctors must meet, if they are not to be negligent. At present doctors set the standard of care themselves: the test is, would a responsible body of medical opinion support the act in question? But patients' lawyers are keen to argue that it should not be a sufficient defence to a medical accident (especially when life is lost) to say that other responsible professionals would have done the same thing.[136]

In *Pretty* v. *UK* the European Court of Human Rights stated that:

> Although no previous case has established as such any right to self-determination as being contained in Article 8 of the Convention, the Court considers that the notion of personal autonomy is an important principle underlying the interpretation of its guarantees.[137]

The court further stated that treating a competent adult without his/her consent could be interpreted as an infringement of Article 8 of the Convention.[138] It was also feared that the Human Rights Act would open the floodgates of litigation but this has not materialised.[139] It remains to be seen whether the European Charter of Patients' Rights will have a significant legal impact.

The apparent lack of impact of the Human Rights Act on litigation may be attributed to the aspirational nature of the Convention: it sets out broad rights that are generally accepted by society but does not specifically spell out correlative duties or obligations. Also, the Human Rights Act applies only to the actions or inactions of public bodies, and not to transactions at the doctor/patient level which are matters of private law.

It is submitted that human rights law does not provide a resolution of the problems identified with consent. Human rights analysis does, however, provide justification for a property approach: if patient self-determination is a foundational or human right, then it should be afforded the protection that property analysis offers.

136 Hewson, Why the Human Rights Act matters to doctors, p. 781.

137 European Court of Human Rights. Fourth section. Case of *Pretty* v. *The United Kingdom (Application no. 2346/02)*. Published in Reports of Judgments and Decisions 2002-III, para 61.

138 Ibid., para 63.

139 Hagger LE, The Human Rights Act 1998 and medical treatment: time for re-examination (2004) 89 Arch Dis Child 460–463.

Contract Law as an Alternative Means of Protecting Patient Self-determination

In *Lee* v. *South West Thames Regional Health Authority* (a case concerning disclosure of communication files relating to a brain-damaged infant), the judge suggested that the plaintiff could bring an action in contract for breach of the duty to inform.[140] The potential use of contract law to secure stronger protection of patient self-determination is worth considering.

It goes without saying that recognising the patient's right to self-determination as a distinct legal right imposes correlative duties on the doctor. In this regard, it is important that clarity and balance are achieved. This in turn requires that attention be paid to the power relations between doctor and patient. A lop-sided distribution of power could easily result in paternalism (if the doctor is so dominant) or wanton consumerism (if the patient is all-powerful). The transactional approach to consultation advocated in Chapter 5 aims to ensure that a power gradient conducive to bilateral flow of information is maintained. It is stressed that the duty referred to here is the duty to provide information and to take action to promote understanding:

> It is important, therefore, that this crucial distinction between the types of duties that doctors owe to their patients is borne in mind. On the one hand, there is the set of technical duties ... and on the other there is the moral or ethical (but also legal) duty which demands information disclosure. The latter duty is defined not by the amount of information that the doctor thinks the patient should know, could handle or might want to know, but by the amount of information that the patient needs so that they are able to make an autonomous choice.[141]

The relationship between patient and doctor has sometimes been described as contractual, and the law of contract is essentially about the relationship between two parties in relation to a defined tangible or intangible object:

> [The] remedy, in the case of obligations, was always an action in personam: the plaintiff was not asserting a relationship between a person and a thing (in the sense that he could bring his remedy against whoever was, by some act, denying the plaintiff's alleged right to the object in question – that was the crucial point in an action in rem), but rather a relationship between two persons; the plaintiff set out to sue the particular defendant because he, personally, was under a duty towards him, and not because (for instance) he happened to be in possession

140 *Lee* v. *South West Thames Regional Health Authority* [1985] 2 All ER 385.

141 McLean SAM, *A Patient's Right to Know: Information Disclosure, the Doctor and the Law*. Aldershot: Ashgate 1999, pp. 80–81.

> of some of the plaintiff's property. If one translates this into the language of substantive law, one can say that the law of obligations is concerned with rights in personam, whilst rights in rem are the subject matter of property.[142]

Contract could, therefore, potentially be employed to protect patient self-determination. It is, however, subject to a major limitation: the doctrine of consideration.[143] Accordingly, only fee-paying patients have a legally-enforceable contract with the doctor. This means that in the UK, a patient who has not been provided with adequate information regarding his/her treatment can bring an action in contract if he/she was a private patient but not if he/she was an NHS patient. Also, while there may be legal merit in describing the doctor–patient relationship as contractual, in practice a contract approach may nurture consumerism, with patients feeling entitled to any treatment of their choice regardless of resource and other public interest considerations. It is submitted that while contract analysis aligns patient's rights and doctor's duties, it does not meet the degree of protection that property analysis provides to patient self-determination.

Consent, Property and Battery

In *Chatterton* v. *Gerson*, Bristow J declared that 'once the patient is informed in broad terms of the nature of the procedure which is intended, and gives her consent, that consent is real'[144] and the cause of action for alleged failure to disclose risks is negligence, not trespass. As Lord Scarman put it, 'damage is the gist of the action in the tort of negligence'.[145] Placing emphasis on harm caused rather than on enhancement of patient self-determination raises questions about the suitability of the action in negligence as a vehicle for protecting self-determination. As mentioned in Chapter 3, Kennedy has called for expansion of the tort of battery in order to provide better protection of the patient's right to self-determination, particularly in cases of failure to disclose adequate

142 Zimmermann, *Law of Obligations*, pp. 6–7. It should be noted that the concept of property underlying this quote is different from the one adopted in this book.

143 The doctrine stipulates that each party to a contract must exchange an item of value (such as money or service), if the contract is to be legally valid. This limitation has often led the courts to expand the law of torts – see Jaffey AJE, Contract in tort's clothing (1985) 5 Legal Studies 77–103.

144 *Chatterton* v. *Gerson* [1981] QB 432; *Chatterton* v. *Gerson* [1981] 1 All ER 257, at 432.

145 *Sidaway* v. *Board of Governors of the Bethlem Royal Hospital and the Maudsley Hospital* [1985] AC 871, 883H. Repeated verbatim by Lord Steyn in *Chester* v. *Afshar* [2004] UKHL 41.

information on risks and benefits.[146] A similar proposition has been argued for by other commentators.[147] Hockton speculated that the rise of human rights law could lead to greater use of this tort in consent cases, but this does not appear to have happened.[148]

Calls for wider application of battery in this context are themselves implicit acknowledgements of the inadequacies of negligence and the consent model in protecting patient self-determination. Also, although the court in *Chester* did not base its decision on battery, it has been argued that the weakening (or sidestepping) of the causation requirement in that case made the action of negligence akin to a battery action.[149]

Brazier advances two reasons why trespass to the person is unlikely to be developed into a suitable form of protection for patient self-determination in cases of inadequate disclosure of information.[150] Firstly, (as discussed in Chapter 3) the courts have expressed strong opposition to the application of battery in such cases. Secondly, since trespass requires touching, cases where there has been no touching (such as prescription of drugs without adequate information of risks and benefits) will not be covered by an action in battery.

For these reasons, there is a gap between what is needed (a form of action that prohibits infringement of the patient's rights regardless of the occurrence of harm) and what is feasible in the common law. This gap can be filled by the property model. Action for breach of the proprietary right to one's body can be an alternative to battery in cases of unauthorised invasion of bodily integrity. As the courts have shown great reluctance to accommodate cases against doctors brought in battery, this would be an alternative which provides the protection sought by advocates of an expansion of battery without eliciting judicial discontent.

There is a further reason why the way forward does not lie in battery. As discussed in Chapter 3, a broad explanation of the treatment will usually be adequate defence to an allegation of battery, but more detailed discussion will usually be required in order to meet the duty of care in negligence. What is needed is a form of action that combines the advantages of an action in battery with the detailed (tailored) discussion required by the duty of care in negligence. The property model meets this need. In this model, the patient can

---

146 Kennedy I, The fiduciary relationship and its application to doctors and patients. In Birks P (ed), *Wrongs and Remedies in the Twenty-First Century*. Oxford: Clarendon Press 1996, pp. 111–140.

147 Feng TK, Failure of medical advice: trespass or negligence? (1987) 7 Legal Studies 149–168.

148 Hockton A, *The Law of Consent to Medical Treatment*. London: Sweet & Maxwell 2002, pp. 17 and 29.

149 Mohindra R, *Medical Law Handbook*. Oxford: Radcliffe 2008.

150 Brazier, Patient autonomy and consent to treatment.

say, 'you have trespassed my property' (referring to the spatial dimension of property; this would be an alternative to battery) and/or say 'you have breached my proprietary right by not providing adequate information to enable me make an informed choice'. As argued in Chapter 8, an action may be brought under the principle of body-as-property despite the absence of direct physical contact between doctor and patient. The model thus combines the strengths of two torts while also overcoming their inadequacies.

Conclusions

To summarise, there is little doubt that the consent model is not ideal for the purpose of protecting the patient's right to self-determination. Rather than remain fixated on this model in the hope of achieving the desired end, it would be preferable to consider what insights can be gained from an alternative model. The case of *Chester* v. *Afshar* illustrates this. The challenge, however, has been to identify the alternative model. Human rights law and contract law are putative alternatives but they have limited practical application in this context. It is submitted that the property model meets the requirements of both patient and doctor, and serves as both a shield (in the sense that a doctor fulfilling the fiduciary duty under this model gets legal certainty and protection) and a sword (placing the patient on stronger footing to exercise his/her rights in decision-making). It resolves the deficits of the consent model, and is consistent with recent guidelines from professional bodies.

The attributes of both models are summarised in Table 9.1, which shows that there are some shared attributes but also key attributes that confer advantage to the property model.

Table 9.1 The consent and property models compared

	Consent model	**Property model**
Self-determination is protected as a distinct legal right	No	Yes
Primary focus	Duty of the doctor	Rights of the patient

Table 9.1 (cont.)

	Consent model	Property model
Effective as a means of protection against unwanted treatment	Yes (to a degree)	Yes
Effective in ensuring that all treatment options are discussed	Marginally effective	Optimally effective
Doctor–patient communication	Largely unidirectional and passive (the conduit paradigm)	Transactional
Doctor has an explicit fiduciary duty regarding communication with patient	No	Yes
Promotes bilateral distribution of responsibility between patient and doctor	No	Yes
Provides defence against battery	Yes	Yes
Harm has to have occurred before patient can bring an action	Yes	No
Causation has to be established	Yes	No

In conclusion, while it is widely recognised that the consent model is not fit for purpose, no suitable model has been devised to complement or supplant it. The property model appears to be more fit-for-purpose and offers the prospect of being the sought-after answer to the deficiencies of the consent model.

Chapter 10
Conclusion

> If the legitimate interests of patients are to be safeguarded by law, there is a need for developments which involve more than fine tuning of the law of torts.[1]

> [P]atients 'need to be able to choose which dance they want, know the steps needed and be able to hear the music'.[2]

Self-determination has traditionally been highly valued in western societies. With the ascendancy of rights thinking, the right to self-determination has become even more highly valued, and this change has induced shifts in the medical and legal arena. In the sphere of medical investigation, diagnosis and treatment, it has led to the decline of paternalism. In the courts, deference to the medical profession has given way to a desire to uphold patient self-determination.

Unfortunately, the current legal framework (the consent model) for dealing with breach of the patient's right to self-determination has been relatively static and has not responded sufficiently to changing times and priorities. Although it is well recognised that the consent model is sub-optimal for protecting patient self-determination, suitable alternatives have not been proposed and one commentator has hinted at a need for lateral thinking:

> Criticism of the *Sidaway* decision, and the hope that the House of Lords will come to adopt a different approach, has dominated English academic writing relating to 'informed consent' for much more than a decade. It has distracted attention from the important question of whether the law of torts can ever have much of a role in protecting the legitimate interests of patients to be informed about risks and alternatives. It has also distracted attention from the question whether there are other ways in which the law could play a more significant role, and the related question of whether any other form of legal regulation is likely to do more harm than good.[3]

---

1 Skegg PDG, English medical law and 'informed consent': an antipodean assessment and alternative (1999) 7 Med L Rev 135–165, at p. 165.

2 The Health Foundation. Quoted in Laitner S, Shared decision making leads to a better patient experience. The Guardian, 3 October 2012; available at http://www.guardian.co.uk/healthcare-network/2012/oct/03/nhs-patients-shared-decision-making. Accessed 17 April 2015.

3 Skegg, English medical law and 'informed consent', pp. 146–147.

What is needed is more than a fine tuning of the law as it currently stands. In Chapter 1, I made the point that as a general principle when a tool, system or strategy is not delivering the required end-product, consequent to fundamental flaws, it is often more productive to think laterally and consider alternative approaches, rather than persist with efforts to rescue the failing one. Sticking to the failing model when the situation calls for an alternative model could become a fixation, and it is well recognised in psychology and business that fixation increases the probability of poor judgment, poor decision-making, error and adverse outcomes.[4] Fixation with consent in the face of contemporary developments in medical law could have similar consequences. The case of *Chester* v. *Afshar* was a missed opportunity for lateral thinking and departure from fixation on consent.[5] The answer lies not in a refashioning of consent but in consideration of a different model.

This book has attempted to explore an alternative way – the property model – in which the law could seek to protect the patient's right to self-determination. In preceding chapters, an effort has been made to show not only that the property model offers greater stringency of protection of patient self-determination than the consent model does, but also that it could be more robust than contract and human rights law in providing this protection. It has also been shown that the property model is consistent with the evolution of UK case law relating to patient involvement in medical decision-making, and with current professional guidance and professionalism. The model provides the judiciary with an appropriate tool for implementing the commitment to patient self-determination that was demonstrated in *Chester*, and in *Montgomery*.[6] In essence, the decision in *Chester* was based on policy considerations, and I submit that the property model is consistent with public policy.

The Two Models Compared

The consent and property models are not mutually exclusive – they have some properties in common (see Table 9.1). For example, the underlying principles of the property model are almost identical to those of the social construction theory of consent.[7] There could be an argument for ameliorating consent rather than, as it were, throwing away the baby with the bathwater. The point has been

4 Murphy JD, *Flawless Execution: Use the Techniques and Systems of America's Fighter Pilots to Perform at Your Peak and Win the Battles of the Business World.* New York: Regan Books 2005, pp. 118–122. See also Job M, 'Hey – what's happening here?' In *Air Disaster* vol 1. Fyshwick ACT: Aerospace Publications 1994, pp. 98–111.

5 *Chester* v. *Afshar* [2004] 4 All ER 587, HL.

6 *Montgomery (Appellant)* v *Lanarkshire Health Board (Respondent) (Scotland)* [2015] UKSC 11.

7 Alderson P and Goodey C, Theories of consent (1998) 31 BMJ 1313–1315.

made in Chapter 1 and reiterated above, however, that it is often preferable to think laterally and consider a new model instead of remaining fixated with a current model that is not fit for purpose. As discussed in Chapter 5, scholarly efforts to make consent more protective of self-determination are unlikely to have practical application in courts or in clinical practice.

For the patient, the property model removes some of the barriers he/she has to contend with under the consent model, making it more likely that his/her right to self-determination will be respected by the doctor and easier to obtain a remedy when the doctor's duty to communicate effectively has been breached.

For the doctor, the property model makes clear (at least compared to the consent model) what his/her duties are with respect to the patient's need for information and the patient's role as ultimate decision-maker. For doctor and patient, the property model promotes communication (a two-way process) and promotes a collaborative model of their relationship. For the courts, the property model provides simplicity, clarity and certainty, and a means to protect patient self-determination without the type of controversial judicial contortion shown in *Chester*.

In the consent model the right to accept treatment is relative, whereas the right to refuse treatment is inalienable. In the property model, the right to self-determination is inalienable regardless of whether this is expressed as agreement to, or refusal of, treatment.

Fundamentally, the property model is not intended to, and does not, confer or create any new rights. It is simply presented as a model affording more robust protection of a right (the right to self-determination) that is legally and ethically acknowledged.

No constitutional, professional or other conflict is generated by applying the property model to patient self-determination. For example, there is no conflict with human rights legislation or with professional regulation.

Communication between Doctor and Patient

Without effective communication, patients will be unable to choose which dance they want or to hear the music.[8] Until the vulnerability of the patient arising from the informational gradient is addressed, there cannot be adequate protection for patient self-determination. Communication between doctor and patient is essential for meaningful expression of the patient's right to self-determination, but this does not appear to feature in the consent model and

8 The Health Foundation. Quoted in Laitner, Shared decision making leads to a better patient experience.

Jones has stated that 'it seems likely that the law does not have a positive effect on the quality of doctor-patient communication'.[9]

Case law on consent has been concerned mostly with information disclosure, particularly the question of how much information should be disclosed and who determines this. Further, most of the cases relating to disclosure of information that have reached the courts have focused on disclosure of risk. In clinical practice this has led to undue emphasis on risk, with particular focus on what percentage of occurrence warrants disclosure. A study of hospital clinicians reported that '[i]n order to meet the legal obligations relating to consent, the nature of the information provided to patients centres mainly on risk disclosure'.[10]

While Manson and O'Neill have emphasised the importance of communication in consent,[11] Maclean points out that they have focused on the obligations of the health-care professional, which shifts the discourse back to disclosure rather than to interaction between both parties.[12] The property model is rooted in the kind of transactional process between doctor and patient that Manson and O'Neill recommend, rather than a unidirectional flow of information. This emphasis on communication has ethical as well as legal foundations:

> A narrative approach to ethics emphasizes the subjective experience and assumes that individuals experience health and illness differently. Its starting point therefore is that the individualized, subjective, partial and personal are important in the consultation in general, and in sharing information specifically. Immediately, information provision for the purposes of consent ceases to be a process whereby an expert professional gives a passive patient a version of esoteric and inaccessible knowledge that has taken the clinician years to acquire … both the clinician and the patient are engaged in a shared endeavour where there is more than one way of knowing, experiencing and conceptualizing health and illness … No longer is the clinician an expert vessel for the transfer of specialist knowledge to the non-participative patient. Rather, both patient and clinician are actively engaged in explaining, listening, negotiating and responding

9 Jones MA, Informed consent and other fairy stories (1999) 7 Med L Rev 103–134, at p. 106.

10 Heywood, R, Macaskill A and Williams K, Informed consent in hospital practice: health professionals' perspectives and legal reflections (2010) 18 Med L Rev 152–184, at p. 161.

11 Manson NC and O'Neill O, *Rethinking Informed Consent in Bioethics*. Cambridge: Cambridge University Press 2007.

12 Maclean A, *Autonomy, Informed Consent and Medical Law: A Relational Challenge*. Cambridge: Cambridge University Press 2009.

> to each other in a shared and transformative process that affords each party respect and dignity.[13]

Recognition of the importance of the transactional approach renders redundant much of the debate on how much information should be given to patients, at least from an ethical standpoint:

> … the ethical challenge is not to identify how statistically significant a risk has to be before it is disclosed but to focus on that essential humanity. It is by sharing information and adapting it according to the needs, interests and priorities of individual patients that clinicians foster autonomy and give meaning to familiar terms such as choice, trust and care.[14]

At least two commentators have advocated a shift from consent to choice.[15] Skegg states:

> Consent does, of course, involve choice. However the choice is usually a matter of deciding whether or not to consent to a particular proposal. The role of consent is often seen to be that of protecting a practitioner from a risk of legal proceedings: information is disclosed to ensure that the consent is 'legally effective'.
>
> A shift of emphasis to 'informed choice' could give greater prominence to the provision of information about alternatives, and to the provision of information by people who will not themselves be involved in carrying out the particular procedure to which consent may eventually be given.[16]

The property model, unlike the consent model, mandates the doctor to discuss alternative treatments with the patient. The doctor is also obliged to take reasonable steps to ensure that the patient understands, and to present the patient with the information required to make an informed choice. With this emphasis on effective communication, the property model obviates the ethical problems associated with mere choice and empowers the patient to make a choice consistent with his/her own values, regardless of whether that choice may in the eyes of others appear risky or irrational.

---

13 Bowman D, Spicer J and Iqbal R, *Informed Consent: A Primer for Clinical Practice*. Cambridge: Cambridge University Press 2012, p. 33.

14 Ibid., p. 35.

15 Skegg, English medical law and 'informed consent'; Clements RV, Informed choice: should we bin the consent form? (2005) 11 Clinical Risk 69–71.

16 Skegg, English medical law and 'informed consent', p. 149.

Self-determination and the Question of Trust

The protection of patient self-determination should not be seen as merely recognising the patient's right to make a decision and acceding to this right. Rather, it should also entail creating the right environment for this right to be fully exercised and acknowledging that the patient's personal and social context underlies his/her exercise of this right. As stated in Chapter 2, the doctor must *a priori* see the patient as an individual, with his/her own values, attitudes, beliefs and knowledge. The property model aims to achieve this through its emphasis on the nature of the doctor–patient relationship. This emphasis on relationships is in keeping with the ecology paradigm described in Chapter 1. Ideally, the partnership between patient and doctor should rest on mutual trust and respect – the patient should repose trust in the doctor, and the doctor must respect the self-determination of the patient.[17] Doctors have a responsibility not to betray the trust of their patients, and this is reflected in the view of the Royal College of Physicians that '[m]edical professionalism signifies a set of values, behaviours and relationships that underpin the trust the public has in doctors'.[18]

The consent model appears to have been weakened by the erosion of trust in the doctor. Conversely, doctors sometimes do not trust patients to make decisions about their own health care. Distrust of doctors has implications for patient self-determination:

> All possible measures aimed at reducing informational asymmetries can be effective and successful insofar as those who carry them out are trusted by the public. A source of information can be highly competent and honest, but if it is not trusted, those concerned will not be confident of its advice.[19]

As a judge said in the US case of *Arato* v. *Avedon*, the trust which the patient has in the doctor during the decision-making process imposes an obligation on the doctor which transcends arm's-length transactions.[20]

17 Coulter A, Paternalism or partnership? (1999) 319 BMJ 712–719; Teff H, Consent to medical procedures: paternalism, self- determination or therapeutic alliance (1995) 101 LQR 450.

18 Royal College of Physicians Working Party, *Doctors in Society: Medical Professionalism in a Changing World.* London: RCP 2005, p. 14.

19 Moro G, Choice. In Marinker M, *Constructive Conversations about Health.* Oxford: Radcliffe 2006, pp. 51–62, at p. 57.

20 *Arato* v. *Avedon* 858 P.2d *598* (1993) Supreme Court of California. This is an American case that illustrates deception and intentional non-disclosure in health care. Miklos Arato had a non-functioning kidney removed. During the operation, a tumour was found in the tail of his pancreas and this was removed. After the operation, his surgeon told Mr Arato and his wife that the entire tumour had been removed and he referred Mr Arato for adjuvant chemotherapy and radiation. Mr Arato was not given a prognosis and he died approximately one year after the

The property model, by demanding a transactional approach to communication and emphasising the fiduciary responsibility of the doctor, has the potential to reinforce trust between both parties. It offers a platform for Pellegrino and Thomasma's 'beneficence-in-trust' model of the doctor–patient relationship, a model in which the doctor acts in the best interest of the patient while keeping trust in his or her moral values.[21]

The Issue of Causation

In the consent model damages are awarded for injuries suffered by the claimant, where a causal link is established; in the property model the claimant receives a remedy for the breach of the right to self-determination and is not required to have suffered an injury or to prove causation. In the consent model, the patient will have no remedy if the risk to which she was exposed without her knowledge did not result in an injury.

The protection of a right deemed paramount should not be dependent on the presence or absence of injury resultant on undisclosed but materialised risk. In the property model, the patient gets a remedy once the breach of her right to self-determination is established. The quantum of the remedy may, however, be partly determined by the damage resulting from the breach.

Potential Arguments against Property Analysis

There are two main arguments that could be made against the property model. The first one is the commodification argument which has been discussed in

initial diagnosis. His wife and children sued the surgeon and oncologist for not informing Mr Arato prior to chemotherapy that approximately 95 per cent of patients with pancreatic cancer die within five years, arguing that if Mr Arato had known that at best chemotherapy would only have prolonged his life by a few months, he would not have undergone this treatment and would have tidied up his financial affairs before his death. The failure to do so resulted in substantial financial losses to his estate. The defence argued that non-disclosure was justifiable on the grounds that disclosure would have caused Mr Arato avoidable anxiety – the classic justification for paternalism. The jury returned a verdict in favour of the physicians, but this was reversed at the California Court of Appeals, and the matter went to the California Supreme Court, which decided in favour of the physicians. The Supreme Court held that the standard for determining whether a particular risk should be disclosed is its materiality to the patient's decision, and said the jury was in the best position to determine this and had found that the defendants had reasonably disclosed to Mr Arato information material to his decision whether to undergo the proposed chemotherapy/radiation treatment.

21 Pellegrino ED and Thomasma DC, *For the Patient's Good: The Restoration of Beneficence in Health Care*. Oxford: Oxford University Press.

Chapter 7. As Moses said, 'even where a classification of property is otherwise appropriate, there is an understandable reluctance to treat something as an object of property where to do so poses moral or practical problems'.[22] As shown in Chapter 7, the commodification argument can be, and has been, defeated.

Also, as the property model endorsed in this book is not that of property-as-a-thing but property-as-a-relationship, the moral problems referred to by Moses do not arise on this occasion. Furthermore, this model is consistent with the contemporary legal conception of property. It is even arguable that the notion of property as defining relationships between persons rather than relationships with things is founded on ancient precepts: one hundred years ago, it was said that:

> The term 'legal relation' should always be used with reference to two persons, neither more nor less … There can be no such thing as a legal relation between a person and a thing. The relation of A to his house is a physical relation; but A has many legal relations to other persons with respect to his house.[23]

The social dimension to the legal concept of property, the idea that we consider property not in isolation but in the context of the owner's relationships with others, parallels the observation made in Chapter 2 that the individual's right to self-determination exists not in a vacuum but in the context of relationships with other persons. This contextual emphasis reflects the ecology paradigm adopted in Chapter 1.

The second potential concern about the property model relates to the risk of absolute individualism – the fear that the property approach could promote atomism, engender consumerism and hamper the relationship between patient and doctor. This concern has also been addressed in this book. In keeping with the ecology paradigm adopted at the outset, the proprietary right advocated in this book is, as Kennedy would put it, a *prima facie* right, not an absolute right, meaning that it is 'to be observed in the absence of any powerful justifying argument which allows [it] to be overridden [and], of course, any such justification must itself be derived from a morally sound principle'.[24] It does not confer on the patient a right to demand a particular treatment, and it is antithetical to the supermarket concept of health-care delivery which offers 'mere, sheer choice'.[25] Far from introducing barriers to the doctor–patient

22 Moses LB, The applicability of property law in new contexts: from cells to cyberspace (2008) 30 Sydney L Rev 639–662, at p. 660.

23 Corbin AL, Legal analysis and terminology (1919–1920) 29 Yale LJ 163–173, at p. 165.

24 Kennedy I, *Treat Me Right: Essays in Medical Law and Ethics*. Oxford: Clarendon Press 1988, p. 387.

25 Manson and O'Neill, *Rethinking Informed Consent in Bioethics*, p. 70.

relationship, it calls for a collaborative model of relationship and a transactional approach to provision of information – both of which reduce the social and informational gradient between doctor and patient. The fiduciary role of the doctor is emphasised.

Implementation of the New Model

The proposed property model can be implemented by legislation, in common law or by incorporation into professional codes and guidance. It can also be introduced via a commission established for this purpose, along the lines suggested by Brazier[26] in the wake of *Sidaway*.[27] Except in emergency situations, it takes years to introduce new statutes in the UK. Law-making by judicial pronouncement is also slow and is dependent on the right cases reaching the courts, particularly the Supreme Court. The quickest way to get the proposed model into practice is by adopting it in professional codes. As shown in Chapter 8, some recent professional codes already have key elements of the property model and it should not be difficult to formally incorporate the property model, once mental blocks are lifted. Two decades ago the term 'clinical governance' was non-existent, but following its introduction at the end of the last millennium, it has speedily been established in professional codes and clinical practice.[28] There is no reason why the same cannot apply to the property model, and clinical governance can itself be one of the vehicles for implementing this novel model.

In clinical practice, medical paternalism is ebbing; in the legal arena, it is 'bye-bye Bolam';[29] in both arenas it is time to welcome the property model which, to borrow an apt description, is 'well suited to cut the Gordian knot of indeterminacies surrounding … consent'.[30]

---

26 Brazier M, Patient autonomy and consent to treatment: the role of the law? (1987) 7 Legal Studies 169–193.

27 *Sidaway* v. *Bethlem Royal Hospital Governors* [1985] 1 All ER 643.

28 Scally G and Donaldson LJ, Clinical governance and the drive for quality improvement in the new NHS in England (1998) 317 BMJ 61–65.

29 Brazier M and Miola J, Bye-bye Bolam: a medical litigation revolution? (2000) 8 Med L Rev 85–114.

30 Gillett GR, Informed consent and moral integrity (1989) 15 J Med Ethics 117–123, at p. 121.

Bibliography

ABIM Foundation (American Board of Internal Medicine), ACP-ASIM Foundation (American College of Physicians-American Society of Internal Medicine) and European Federation of Internal Medicine. Medical professionalism in the new millennium: a physician charter (2002) 136 Ann Intern Med 243–246.

Akkad A, Jackson C, Kenyon S, Dixon-Woods M, Taub N and Habiba M, Patients' perceptions of written consent: questionnaire study (2006) 333 BMJ 528.

Alderson P and Goodey C, Theories of consent (1998) 317 BMJ 1313–1315.

Ali V, Consent forms as part of the informed consent process: moving away from 'medical miranda' (2003) 54 Hastings LJ 1575–1591.

Allen T, *The Right to Property in Commonwealth Constitutions*. Cambridge: Cambridge University Press 2000.

American College of Obstetricians and Gynecologists, *Ethical Dimensions of Informed Consent*, ACOG Committee Opinion: Committee on Ethics, No 108. Washington DC: ACOG 1992.

American College of Obstetricians and Gynecologists, *Informed Consent*. Washington DC: ACOG 2004.

American College of Obstetricians and Gynecologists. *Informed Consent*, Committee Opinion No 439. Washington DC: ACOG 2009. Also at (2009) 114 Obstet Gynecol 401–408.

American Hospital Association. The Patient Care Partnership. Understanding Expectations, Rights and Responsibilities. AHA; 2003. Available at http://www.aha.org/advocacyissues/communicatingpts/pt-care-partnership.shtml. Accessed 17 April 2015.

Andrews L and Nelkin D, *Body Bazaar: The Market for Human Tissue in the Biotechnology Age*. New York: Crown 2001.

Annas GJ, Why the British courts rejected the American doctrine of informed consent (and what British physicians should do about it) (1984) 74 Am J Public Health 1286–1288.

Annas GJ, *Some Choice – Law, Medicine and the Market*. New York: Oxford University Press 1998.

Arnold C, The reconstitution of property: property as a web of interests (2002) 26 Harv Envtl L Rev 281–364.

Atkins K, Autonomy and the subjective character of experience (2000) 17 J Appl Philos 71–79.

Banerjee S and Basu S, *Rent a Womb: Surrogate Selection, Investment Incentives, and Contracting*. Pune, Maharashtra: Gokhale Institute of Politics and Economics 2007.

Barry C, Bradley CP, Britten N, Stevenson FA and Barber N, Patients' unvoiced agendas in general practice consultations: qualitative study (2000) 320 BMJ 1246–1250.

Bartlett P, Doctors as fiduciaries: equitable regulation of the doctor-patient relationship (1997) 5 Med L Rev 193–224.

Beauchamp TL and Childress JF, *Principles of Biomedical Ethics*. New York: Oxford University Press 1994.

Beauchamp TL and Childress JF, *Principles of Biomedical Ethics*, 5th edn. Oxford: Oxford University Press 2001.

Bennett VR and Brown LK (eds), *Myles' Textbook for Midwives*, 13th edn. London: Churchill Livingstone 1999.

Bentham J, Security and equality of property. In Macpherson CB (ed), *Property: Mainstream and Critical Positions*. Oxford: Blackwell 1978, pp. 39–58.

Berg JW, Appelbaum PS, Lidz CW and Parker LS, *Informed Consent – Legal Theory and Clinical Practice*, 2nd edn. Oxford: Oxford University Press 2001.

Bergsma J and Thomasma DC, *Autonomy and Clinical Medicine: Renewing the Health Professional Relation with the Patient*. Dordrecht: Kluwer Academic 2000.

Berumen ME, *Do No Evil: Ethics With Applications to Economic Theory and Business*. Lincoln, Nebr.: iUniverse 2003.

Beyleveld D and Brownsword R, *Human Dignity in Bioethics and Biolaw*. Oxford: Oxford University Press 2001.

Beyleveld D and Brownsword R, My body, my body parts, my property (2000) 8 Health Care Analysis 87–99.

Birks P (ed), *Wrongs and Remedies in the Twenty-first Century*. Oxford: Clarendon Press 1996.

Blackstone W, *Commentaries on the Laws of England*, vol II, facsimile edn. Chicago: University of Chicago Press 1979.

Boffey PM, The fall and rise of Leonard Hayflick, biologist whose fight with U.S. seems over. New York Times, 19 January 1982.

Bovenberg JA, Inalienably yours? The new case for an inalienable property right in human biological material: empowerment of sample donors or a recipe for a tragic anti-commons? (2004) 1:4 SCRIPTed 545; available at http://www.law.ed.ac.uk/ahrc/script-ed/issue4/bovenberg.asp. Accessed 20 October 2012.

Bowman D, Spicer J and Iqbal R, *Informed Consent: A Primer for Clinical Practice*. Cambridge: Cambridge University Press 2012.

Braddock CH III, Edwards KA, Hasenberg NM, Laidley TL and Levinson W, Informed decision making in outpatient practice: time to get back to basics (1999) 282 JAMA 2313–2320.

Brandt AM, Racism and research: the case of the Tuskegee Syphilis Study (1978) 8 Hastings Cent Rep 21–29.

Brazier M, Patient autonomy and consent to treatment: the role of the law? (1987) 7 Legal Studies 169–193.

Brazier M, Campbell AV and Golombok S, *Surrogacy: Review for Health Ministers of Current Arrangements for Payments and Regulation: Report of the Review Team.* London: HMSO 1998.

Brazier M and Miola J, Bye-bye Bolam: a medical litigation revolution? (2000) 8 Med L Rev 85–114.

Brewer J and Staves S (eds), *Early Modern Conceptions of Property*. London: Routledge 1995.

Bridge M, *Personal Property Law*, 3rd edn. Oxford: Oxford University Press 2002.

Brinig MF and Carbone J, Reliance interest in marriage and divorce (1987–1988) 62 Tul L Rev 855–905.

Bristol Royal Infirmary Inquiry, *Learning from Bristol: The Report of the Public Inquiry into Children's Heart Surgery at the Bristol Royal Infirmary 1984–1995*, Cm 5207(I). London: HMSO 2001; available at http://www.bristol-inquiry.org.uk/final_report/the_report.pdf. Accessed 13 October 2012.

British Medical Association, *Consent Tool Kit*, 5th edn. London: British Medical Association, undated.

British Medical Association, *Medical Ethics Today: The BMA's Handbook of Ethics and Law*, 2nd edn. London: BMA and BMJ Books 2004. 3rd edn. John Wiley, 2012

British Medical Association, *Report of the Consent Working Party: Incorporating Consent Tool Kit.* London: BMA 2001.

Britten N, Stevenson F, Barry C, Barber N and Bradley C, Misunderstandings in general practice prescribing decisions: qualitative study (2000) 320 BMJ 1246–1250

Brownsword R, The cult of consent: fixation and fallacy (2004) 15 King's College Law J 223–252.

Buchanan A, Medical paternalism (1978) 7 Philos Public Aff 370–90.

Bullock E, Informed consent as waiver: the doctrine rethought? (2010) 17 Ethical Perspectives 529–555.

Burchell J, The legal protection of privacy in South Africa: a transplantable hybrid (2009) 13.1 Electronic Journal of Comparative Law; available at http://www.ejcl.org/131/art131-2.pdf. Accessed 20 November 2012.

Burrell B, The long, strange journey of Einstein's brain. In Burrell B, *Postcards from the Brain Museum: The Improbable Search for Meaning in the Matter of Famous Minds*. New York: Broadway Books 2004.

Byrne PS, The passing of the 'eight' train (1968) 15 J R Coll Gen Pract 409–427.

California ruling invites backlash against gay rights. USA Today, Friday, 23 May 2008.

Care Quality Commission, *Briefing Note: Inpatient Survey Results 2010*. Care Quality Commission 2011; available at www.nhssurveys.org/survey/1016.

Carnerie F, Crisis and informed consent: analysis of a law-medicine malocclusion (1986) 12 Am J Law & Med 55–97.

Chadwick R, Genetics, choice and responsibility (1999) 1 Health Risk Soc 293–300.

Charles C, Gafni A and Whelan T, Shared decision-making in the medical encounter: what does it mean? (or it takes at least two to tango) (1997) 44 Soc Sci Med 681–692.

Charles C, Whelan T and Gafni A, What do we mean by partnership in making decisions about treatment? (1999) 319 BMJ 780–782.

Chen J, Embryonic thoughts on racial identity as new property (1997) 68 Univ Colorado L Rev 1123.

Chervenak FA and McCullough LB, The threat of the new managed practice of medicine to patients' autonomy (1995) 6 J Clin Ethics 320–323.

Chodos R, The nature of fiduciary law and its relationship to other legal doctrines and categories (2011) 91 Boston Univ L Rev 837–849.

Christman J, Autonomy in moral and political philosophy. In *Stanford Encyclopaedia of Philosophy* (2009); available at http://plato.stanford.edu/entries/autonomy-moral/. Accessed 3 March 2015

Christman J, Self-ownership, equality and the structure of property rights (1991) 19 Political Theory 28–46.

Christman J, *The Myth of Property: Toward an Egalitarian Theory of Ownership*. Oxford: Oxford University Press 1994.

Clapham A, *Human Rights: A Very Short Introduction*. Oxford: Oxford University Press 2007.

Clarke A and Kohler P, *Property Law: Commentary and Materials*. Cambridge: Cambridge University Press 2005.

Clarke G, Hall R and Rosencrance G, Physician-patient relations: no more models (2004) 4 Am J Bioethics W16–W19.

Clarke J, Newman J, Westmarland L, Smith N and Vidler E, *Creating Citizen-Consumers: Changing Publics and Changing Public Services*. London: Sage 2007.

Clements RV, Informed choice: should we bin the consent form? (2005) 11 Clinical Risk 69–71.

Cloutier-Steele L, *Misinformed Consent: Women's Stories about Unnecessary Hysterectomy*. Chester, NJ: Next Decade 2003.

Coggon J, Varied and principled understandings of autonomy in English law: justifiable inconsistency or blinkered moralism? (2007) 15 Health Care Anal 235–255.

Cohen JJ, Cruess S and Davidson C, Alliance between society and medicine: the public's stake in medical professionalism (2007) 298 JAMA 670–673.

Corbin AL, Legal analysis and terminology (1919–1920) 29 Yale LJ 163–173.

Coulter A, Paternalism or partnership? (1999) 319 BMJ 712–719.

Coulter A, *Trends in Patients' Experience of the NHS*. Oxford: Picker Institute Europe 2005.

Council of Europe, *Convention on Human Rights and Biomedicine*. 1997; available at http://www.conventions.coe.int/Treaty/Commun/QueVoulezVous.asp?NT=164&CL=ENG

Accessed 3 March 2015.

Council of Europe, *Convention for the Protection of Human Rights and Dignity of the Human Being with Regard to the Application of Biology and Medicine: Convention on Human Rights and Biomedicine*, 1996; available at http://www.conventions.coe.int/Treaty/en/Treaties/Html/164.htm. Accessed 3 March 2015.

Council of Europe, *European Convention on Human Rights as amended by Protocols Nos. 11 and 14*, Council of Europe Treaty Series, No 5. Strasbourg: Council of Europe 2010.

Da Silva CHM, Cunha RLG, Tonaco RB, Cunha TM, Diniz AC, Domingos GG, Silva JD, Santos MV, Antoun MG and de Paula RL, Not telling the truth in the patient-physician relationship (2003) 17 Bioethics 417–424.

Davies M and Naffine N, *Are Persons Property? Legal Debates about Property and Personality*. Aldershot: Ashgate/Dartmouth 2001.

Dawn AG and Lee PP, Patient expectations for medical and surgical care: a review of the literature and applications to ophthalmology (2004) 49 Surv Ophthalmol 513–524.

Dawn AG, McGwin G Jr, Lee PP, Patient expectations regarding eye care: development and results of the Eye Care Expectations Survey (ECES) (2005) 123 Arch Ophthalmol 534–541.

Deakin S, Johnston A and Markesinis B QC, *Markesinis and Deakin's Tort Law*, 6th edn. Oxford: Oxford University Press 2007.

De Cruz P, *Comparative Healthcare Law*. Abingdon: Psychology Press 2001.

Demsetz H, Toward a theory of property rights (1967) 57 Am Econ Rev 347–359.

Department of Health, *Copying Letters to Patients: Good Practice Guidelines*. London: DH 2003. Department of Health, *Equity and Excellence: Liberating the NHS*, Cm 7881. London: The Stationery Office 2010.

Department of Health, *The Expert Patient: A New Approach to Chronic Disease Management for the 21st Century*. London: DH 2001.

Department of Health, *Good Practice in Consent Implementation Guide: Consent to Examination or Treatment*. London: DH 2009.

Department of Health, *The NHS Constitution*. London: DH 2012.

Department of Health, *NHS Indemnity Arrangements for Handling Clinical Negligence Claims against NHS Staff*, HSG (96)48. London: DH 1996.

Department of Health, *The NHS Plan: A Plan for Investment, a Plan for Reform*, Cm 4818-I. London: The Stationery Office 2000.

Department of Health, *The Patient's Charter*. London: DH 1991.

Department of Health, *Reference Guide to Consent for Examination or Treatment*, 2nd edn. London: DH 2009.

Department of Health, *Report on the Effect of the NHS Constitution*. London: DH 2012.

Dickenson D, *Property in the Body: Feminist Perspectives*. Cambridge: Cambridge University Press 2007.

Downie RS, The doctor-patient relationship. In Gillon R (ed), *Principles of Health Care Ethics*. Chichester: John Wiley 1994, pp. 343–352.

Downie RS and Macnaughton RJ, *Bioethics and the Humanities: Attitudes and Perceptions*. Abingdon: Routledge-Cavendish 2007.

Downie R and Randall F, Choice and responsibility in the NHS (2008) 8 Clin Med 182–185.

Drake JF, The many faces of competency (1985) 15 Hastings Cent Rep 17–21.

Dryden J, Autonomy: overview; available at http://www.iep.utm.edu/autonomy/. Accessed 3 March 2015.

Dworkin G, *The Theory and Practice of Autonomy*. New York: Cambridge University Press 1988.

Dworkin G and Kennedy I, Human tissue: rights in the body and its parts (1993) 1 Med L Rev 291–319.

Dyer O, Payment offered to injured trial participants has strings attached (2006) 332 BMJ 990.

Dyer O, Shipman murdered more than 200 patients, inquiry finds (2002) 325 BMJ 181.

Edwards A and Elwyn G, Inside the black box of shared decision making – distinguishing between the process of involvement and who makes the decision (2006) 9 Health Expectations 307–320.

Elwyn G, Edwards A, Kinnersley P and Grol R, Shared decision making and the concept of equipoise: the competences of involving patients in healthcare choices (2000) 50 Br J Gen Pract 892–829.

Emanuel EJ and Emanuel LL, Four models of the physician-patient relationship (1992) 267 JAMA 2221–2226.

Engelhardt HT Jr, *The Foundations of Bioethics*. Oxford: Oxford University Press 1986.

Entwistle VA and Watt IS, Patient involvement in treatment decision-making: the case for a broader conceptual framework (2006) 63 Patient Educ Couns 268–278.

Faden RR and Beauchamp TL, in collaboration with King NMP, *A History and Theory of Informed Consent.* Oxford: Oxford University Press 1986.

Fallowfield LJ, Hall A, Maguire P, Baum M and A'Hern RP, Psychological effects of being offered choice of surgery for breast cancer (1994) 309 BMJ 448.

Fallowfield LJ, Hall A, Maguire P, Baum M and A'Hern RP, A question of choice: results of a prospective 3-year follow-up study of women with breast cancer (1994) 3 The Breast 202–208.

Faunce TA and Bolsin SN, Fiduciary disclosure of medical mistakes: the duty to promptly notify patients of adverse health care events (2005) 12 JLM 478.

Feinberg J, Legal paternalism (1971) 1 Can J Philos 105–24.

Feng TK, Failure of medical advice: trespass or negligence? (1987) 7 Legal Studies 149–168.

Field NE, Evolving conceptualisation of property: a proposal to de-commercialize the value of fetal tissue (1989) 99 Yale LJ 169–186.

Francis R, *Report of the Mid Staffordshire NHS Foundation Trust Public Inquiry.* London: The Stationery Office 2013.

Fraser D, Cooper MA and Crawford J, *Myles' Textbook for Midwives*, 15th edn. London: Churchill Livingstone 2009.

Freidson E, The changing nature of professional control (1984) 10 Ann Rev Sociology 1–20.

Freidson E, *Profession of Medicine: A Study of the Sociology of Applied Knowledge.* Chicago: University of Chicago Press 1988.

Fuller LL and Perdue WR Jr, The reliance interest in contract damages: Parts 1 and 2 (1936–1937) 46 Yale LJ 52 and 373.

Gann B, From NHS choices to the integrated customer service platform (2013) 30 Health Info Libr J 1–3.

Geisen D, *International Medical Malpractice Law: A Comparative Law Study of Civil Liability Arising from Medical Care.* London: Nijhoff 1988.

General Medical Council, *Consent: Patients and Doctors Making Decisions Together.* London: GMC 2008.

General Medical Council, *Good Medical Practice.* London: GMC 2006.

General Medical Council, *Good Medical Practice.* London: GMC 2009.

General Medical Council (GMC) and the Conference of Post Graduate Medical Deaneries (COPMeD), *Memorandum of Understanding*, Annexe A. April 2007.

George A, Is 'property' necessary? On owning the human body and its parts (2004) 10 Res Publica 15–24.

Gillett GR, Informed consent and moral integrity (1989) 15 J Med Ethics 117–123.

Gold ER, *Body Parts: Property Rights and the Ownership of Human Biological Materials.* Washington DC: Georgetown University Press 1998.

Goldberg JD, Involuntary servitudes: a property-based notion of abortion choice (1991) 38 UCLA L Rev 1597–1657.

Goldby S, Krugman S, Pappworth MH and Edsall G, The Willowbrook letters: criticisms and defense (1971) The Lancet 10 April, 8 May, 5 June and 10 July.
Gray K, *Elements of Land Law*, 2nd edn. London: Butterworths 1993.
Gray K, Property in thin air (1991) 50 Cambridge LJ 252–307.
Gray K and Gray SF, *Land Law*, 5th edn. Oxford: Oxford University Press 2007.
Gray KJ, Equitable property (1994) 47 Current Legal Problems 157–214.
Greener I, Towards a history of choice in UK health policy (2009) 31 Sociology of Health and Illness 309–324.
Greenfield S, Kaplan SH, Ware JE Jr, Yano EM and Frank HJ, Patients' participation in medical care: effects on blood sugar control and quality of life in diabetes (1988) 3 J Gen Intern Med 448–457.
Grubb A, The doctor as fiduciary (1994) 47 Current Legal Problems 311–340.
Grubb A, 'I, me, mine': bodies, parts and property (1998) 3 Med Law Int'l 299–317.
Hagger LE, The Human Rights Act 1998 and medical treatment: time for re-examination (2004) 89 Arch Dis Child 460–463.
Hardcastle R, *Law and the Human Body*. Oxford: Hart 2007.
Harris CI, Whiteness as property (1993) 106 Harvard L Rev 1709–1791.
Harris JW, Is property a human right? In McLean J (ed), *Property and the Constitution*. Oxford: Hart 1999, pp. 64–87.
Harris JW, *Property and Justice*. Oxford: Oxford University Press 2002.
Haug M and Lavin B, *Consumerism in Medicine: Challenging Physician Authority*. London: Sage 1983.
Haug MR, A re-examination of the hypothesis of physician deprofessionalization (1988) 66 Milbank Quarterly 48–56.
Havers P and Neenan C, Impact of the European Convention on Human Rights on medical law (2002) 78 Postgrad Med J 573–574.
Hayry H, *The Limits of Medical Paternalism*. London: Routledge 1991.
Healy J, *Medical Negligence: Common Law Perspectives*. London: Sweet & Maxwell 1999.
Heisler M, Bouknight RR, Hayward RA, Smith DM and Kerr EA, The relative importance of physician communication, participatory decision making, and patient understanding in diabetes self-management (2002) 17 J Gen Intern Med 243–252.
Hellsten S, *In Defense of Moral Individualism*. Helsinki: Philosophical Society of Finland 1997.
Hernández S, Panama: indigenous people fear genetic slavery. World News Inter Press Service 17 December 1997.
Herring J and Chau PL, My body, your body, our bodies (2007) 15 Med L Rev 34–61.
Hewson B, Why the Human Rights Act matters to doctors (2000) 321 BMJ 780–781.

Heywood R, Macaskill A and Williams K, Informed consent in hospital practice: health professionals' perspectives and legal reflections (2010) 18 Med L Rev 152–184.

Higgs R, Truth-telling. In Kuhse H and Singer P (eds), *A Companion to Bioethics*, 2nd edn. Chichester: Wiley-Blackwell 2009, pp. 520–529.

Hilton S, Education and the changing face of medical professionalism: from priest to mountain guide (2008) 58 Br J Gen Pract 353–361.

Hockton A, *The Law of Consent to Medical Treatment*. London: Sweet & Maxwell 2002.

Hodnett ED, Caregiver support for women during childbirth (2002) Cochrane Database Syst Rev 1:CD000199.

Hogg M, Duties of care, causation, and the implications of *Chester v Afshar* (2005) 9 Edin L Rev 156–167.

Hohfeld WN, *Fundamental Legal Conceptions as Applied in Judicial Reasoning*, ed. Cook WW. New Haven: Yale University Press 1919. Reprint 1946.

Holden J and O'Donnell S, Shipman proposals will alter general practice profoundly (2003) 326 BMJ 280.

Holdsworth WS, The history of the treatment of 'choses' in action by the common law (1920) 33 Harvard L Rev 997–1030.

Honore AM, Ownership. In Guest AD (ed), *Oxford Essays in Jurisprudence* (First Series). Oxford: Clarendon Press, 1961. Reprinted in Honore A, *Making Law Bind: Essays Legal and Philosophical*. Oxford: Clarendon Press 1987, pp. 161–92.

Hudec RE, Restating the reliance interest (1981–82) 67 Cornell L Rev 704.

Human Fertilisation and Embryology Authority (HFEA), HFEA agrees new policies to improve sperm and egg donation services. HFEA Press release, 19 October 2011.

Imison C, Naylor C and Maybin J, *Under One Roof: Will Polyclinics Deliver Integrated Care?* London: King's Fund 2008.

Jackson E, 'Informed consent' to medical treatment and the impotence of tort. In McLean SAM, *First Do No Harm: Law, Ethics and Healthcare*. Aldershot: Ashgate 2006, pp. 273–286.

Jackson E and Warner J, How much do doctors know about consent and capacity? (2002) 95 J R Soc Med 601–603.

Jackson J, Telling the truth (1991) 17 J Med Ethics 5–9.

Jaffey AJE, Contract in tort's clothing (1985) 5 Legal Studies 77–103.

Jahng KH, Martin LR, Golin CE and Di Matteo MR, Preferences for medical collaboration: patient-physician congruence and patient outcomes (2005) 57 Patient Educ Couns 308–314.

Jailed: gang which plundered Alistair Cooke's grave to sell body parts. Daily Mail 23 October 2008.

JFL, Embryos in a divorce case: joint property or offspring? (1989) 84 Pediatrics A54.

Job M, 'Hey – what's happening here?' In *Air Disaster* vol 1. Fyshwick ACT: Aerospace Publications 1994, pp. 98–111.

Johnston C and Holt G, The legal and ethical implications of therapeutic privilege – is it ever justified to withhold treatment information from a competent patient? (2006) 3 J Clin Ethics 146–151.

Jones J, *Bad Blood: The Tuskegee Syphilis Experiment.* New York: Free Press 1981.

Jones MA, Failed sterilization and omission to warn: the causation problem (1998) 4 Clinical Risk 12–16.

Jones MA, Informed consent and other fairy stories (1999) 7 Med L Rev 103–134.

Jones P, *Rights.* London: Macmillan 1994.

Joos SK, Hickam DH and Borders LM, Patients' desires and satisfaction in general medicine clinics (1993) 108 Public Health Rep 751–759.

Kant I, Lectures on ethics, in Paton HJ (ed), *Groundwork of the Metaphysics of Morals.* London: Hutchinson 1953.

Kaplan SH, Greenfield S and Ware JE Jr, Assessing the effects of physician-patient interactions on the outcomes of chronic disease (1989) 27 (suppl 3) Med Care S110–27.

Karako-Eyal N, Has non-U.S. case law recognized a legally protected autonomy right? (2009) 10 Minn J L Sci & Tech 671–726.

Katz J, Informed consent – a fairy tale? (1977) 39 Univ Pittsbg L Rev 137–174.

Katz J, *The Silent World of Doctor and Patient.* New York: Free Press 1984.

Kennedy I, The fiduciary relationship and its application to doctors and patients. In Birks P (ed), *Wrongs and Remedies in the Twenty-first Century.* Oxford: Clarendon Press 1996, pp. 111–140.

Kennedy I, *Treat Me Right: Essays in Medical Law and Ethics.* Oxford: Clarendon Press 1988.

Kennedy I and Grubb A, *Medical Law: Text with Materials*, 2nd edn. London: Butterworths 1994.

Kessler DP, Summerton N and Graham JR, Effects of the medical liability system in Australia, the UK, and the USA (2006) 368 The Lancet 240–246.

Kittay EF, Beyond autonomy and paternalism: the transparent caring self. In Nys T, Denier Y and Vandevelde T, *Autonomy & Paternalism: Reflections on the Theory and Practice of Health Care.* Leuven: Peeters 2007.

Kohler P, The death of ownership and the demise of property (2000) 53 Current Legal Problems 237–282.

Komrad MS, A defence of medical paternalism: maximising patients' autonomy (1983) 9 J Med Ethics 38–44.

Kravitz RL, Patients' expectations for medical care: an expanded formulation based on review of the literature (1996) 53 Medical Care Research and Review 3–27.

Kravitz RL, Callahan EJ, Paterniti D, Antonius D, Dunham M and Lewis CE, Prevalence and sources of patients' unmet expectations for care (1996) 125 Ann Intern Med 730–737.

Kravitz RL, Cope DW, Bhrany V and Leake B, Internal medicine patients' expectations for care during office visits (1994) 9 J Gen Intern Med 75–81.

Kravitz RL and Melnikow J, Engaging patients in medical decision making (2001) 323 BMJ 584.

Krugman S and Giles JP, Viral hepatitis: new light on an old disease (1970) 212 JAMA 1019–1029.

Kuczewski MG, The professionalism movement: can we pause? (2004) 4 Am J Bioethics 1–10.

Laitner S, Shared decision making leads to a better patient experience. The Guardian, 3 October 2012; available at http://www.guardian.co.uk/healthcare-network/2012/oct/03/nhs-patients-shared-decision-making. Accessed 4 October 2012.

Law Commission, *Consent in the Criminal Law: A Consultation Paper*, Law Commission Consultation Paper Series 139. London: HMSO 1995.

Law Commission, *Fiduciary Duties and Regulatory Rules (Consultation Paper)*. London: Stationery Office Books 1992.

Leder D, Whose body, what body? The metaphysics of organ transplantation. In Cherry MJ (ed), *Persons and Their Bodies: Rights, Responsibilities, Relationships*. Dordrecht: Kluwer Academic 1999, pp. 233–264.

Legal Correspondent, Consent to treatment: the medical standard reaffirmed (1984) 288 BMJ 802–803.

Legare F, Ratte S, Gravel K and Graham ID, Barriers and facilitators to implementing shared decision-making in clinical practice: update of a systematic review of health professionals' perceptions (2008) 73 Patient Educ Couns 526–535.

Lesser H, The patient's right to information. In Brazier M and Lobjoit M, *Protecting the Vulnerable: Autonomy and Consent in Health Care*. London: Routledge 1991, pp. 150–160.

Levinson W, Kao A, Kuby A and Thisted RA, Not all patients want to participate in decision making: a national study of public preferences (2005) 20 J Gen Intern Med 531–535.

Lin TE, Social norms and judicial decision making: examining the role of narratives in same-sex adoption cases (1999) 99 Columbia L Rev 739–794.

Lippman A, Choice as a risk to women's health (1999) 1 Health Risk Soc 281–291.

Little P, Everitt H, Williamson I, Warner G, Moore M, Gould C, Ferrier K and Payne S, Observational study of effect of patient centredness and positive approach on outcomes in general practice consultations (2001) 323 BMJ 908–911.

Locke J, *Two Treatises of Government*. Minneapolis: Filiquarian 2007.
Locke J, *Second Treatise of Government*, ed Gough GW. Oxford: Basil Blackwell 1976.
Lupton D, Consumerism, reflexivity and the medical encounter (1997) 45 Soc Sci Med 373–381.
Lynoe N and Hoeyer K, Quantitative aspects of informed consent: considering the dose response curve when estimating quantity of information (2005) 31 J Med Ethics 736–738.
McCullough LB, Was bioethics founded on historical and conceptual mistakes about medical paternalism? (2011) 25 Bioethics 66–74.
McFarlane G, Clinical negligence – risk management and reporting (2001) 2 J Personal Injury Law 164.
McKinstry B, Do patients wish to be involved in decision making in the consultation? A cross sectional survey with video vignettes (2000) 321 BMJ 867–871.
McKinstry B, Ashcroft RE, Car J, Freeman GK and Sheikh A, Interventions for improving patients' trust in doctors and groups of doctors (2006) 3 Cochrane Database Syst Rev CD004134.
Maclean A, *Autonomy, Informed Consent and Medical Law: A Relational Challenge*. Cambridge: Cambridge University Press 2009.
Maclean A, From *Sidaway* to *Pearce* and beyond: is the legal regulation of consent any better following a quarter of a century of judicial scrutiny? (2012) 20 Med L Rev 108–129.
McLean S, Post-mortem human reproduction: legal and other regulatory issues (2002) 9 J Law and Med 429–433.
McLean SAM, *Autonomy, Consent and the Law*. Abingdon: Routledge 2010.
McLean, SAM (ed) *First Do No Harm: Law, Ethics and Healthcare*. Aldershot: Ashgate 2006.
McLean SAM, *A Patient's Right to Know*. Aldershot: Dartmouth 1989.
McMullan M, Patients using the Internet to obtain health information: how this affects the patient-health professional relationship (2006) 63 Patient Educ Couns 24–28.
Macpherson CB, The meaning of property. In Macpherson CB (ed), *Property: Mainstream and Critical Positions*. Oxford: Oxford University Press 1978, pp. 1–14.
Madhok S, Autonomy and human rights. In Smith RKM and van den Anker C, *The Essentials of Human Rights*. London: Hodder Arnold 2005.
Mandelblatt J, Kreling B, Figeuriedo M and Feng S, What is the impact of shared decision making on treatment and outcomes for older women with breast cancer? (2006) 24 J Clin Oncol 4908–4913.
Manson NC and O'Neill O, *Rethinking Informed Consent in Bioethics*. Cambridge: Cambridge University Press 2007.

Marinker M, Health policy and the constructive conversationalist. In Marinker M, *Constructive Conversations about Health.* Oxford: Radcliffe 2006, pp. 1–16.

Mason JK and Laurie GT, *Mason & McCall Smith's Law and Medical Ethics*, 7th edn. Oxford: Oxford University Press 2005.

Mason JK and McCall-Smith RA, *Law and Medical Ethics*, 5th edn. London: Butterworths 1999.

Mason K and Brodie D, Bolam, Bolam – wherefore art thou Bolam? (2005) 9 Edin L Rev 298–306.

Matthews P, The man of property (1995) 3 Med L Rev 251–274.

Mead N, Bower P and Hann M, The impact of general practitioners' patient-centredness on patients' post-consultation satisfaction and enablement (2002) 55 Soc Sci Med 283–299.

Medical Professionalism Project, Medical professionalism in the new millennium: a physicians' charter (2002) 359 The Lancet 520–522.

Meek J, Poet attempts the ultimate in self-invention – patenting her own genes. The Guardian, 29 February 2000; available at http://www.guardian.co.uk/science/2000/feb/29/genetics.uknews. Accessed 20 October 2012.

Meisel A and Kuczewiski M, Legal and ethical myths about informed consent (1996) 156 Arch Intern Med 2521–2526.

Menell PS, *The Property Rights Movement's Embrace of Intellectual Property: True Love or Doomed Relationship?* UC Berkeley Public Law Research Paper No 965083. February 2007; available at SSRN: http://ssrn.com/abstract=965083. Accessed 3 March 2015.

Miller FH, Informed consent for the man on the Clapham omnibus: an English cure for an American disease? (1987) 9 W New Eng L Rev 169–190.Mohindra R, *Medical Law Handbook*. Oxford: Radcliffe 2008.

Moreno J, *Undue Risk: Secret State Experiments on Humans.* New York: Routledge 2001.

Morgan D, Where do I own my body? (And why?). In Morgan D, *Issues in Medical Law and Ethics*. London: Cavendish 2001.

Morgan M, The doctor-patient relationship. In Scrambler G (ed), *Sociology As Applied to Medicine*, 5th edn. Edinburgh: Saunders 2003, pp. 49–65.

Moro G, Choice. In Marinker M, *Constructive Conversations about Health.* Oxford: Radcliffe 2006, pp. 51–62.

Moses LB, The applicability of property law in new contexts: from cells to cyberspace (2008) 30 Sydney L Rev 639–662.

Moulton B and King JS, Aligning ethics with medical decision-making: the quest for informed patient choice (2010) 38 J Law, Med Ethics 85–97.

Mulheron R, The defence of therapeutic privilege in Australia (2003) 11 J Law Med 201–213.

Munzer SR, An uneasy case against property rights in body parts. In Paul E, Miller F and Paul J (eds), *Property Rights*. Cambridge: Cambridge University Press 1994, pp. 259–286.

Munzer SR, *A Theory of Property*. Cambridge: Cambridge University Press, 1990.

Murphy JD, *Flawless Execution: Use the Techniques and Systems of America's Fighter Pilots to Perform at Your Peak and Win the Battles of the Business World*. New York: Regan Books 2005.

Murray TH, On the human body as property: the meaning of embodiment, markets, and the meaning of strangers (1986) 20 U Mich J L Reform 1055–1088.

Myles MF, *Textbook for Midwives, with Modern Concepts of Obstetric and Neonatal Care*, 8th edn. London: Churchill Livingstone 1975.

Nairne K, Case: diagnosis of multiple sclerosis withheld for eight years from the patient, *Gary Dimmock* v *East Sussex NHS Trust* (2007) 13 Clinical Risk 224–225.

Nedelsky J, *Law's Relations: A Relational Theory of Self, Autonomy, and Law*. New York and Oxford: Oxford University Press 2012.

Nedelsky J, Re-conceiving autonomy: sources, thoughts and possibilities (1989) 1 Yale J Law and Feminism 7–36.

Newman J and Vidler E, Discriminating customers, responsible patients, empowered users: consumerism and the modernisation of health care (2006) 35 J Soc Policy 193–20.

NHS Greater Glasgow and Clyde, *Integrating Patient Focus and Public Involvement into Clinical Governance*, Learning Note. 2 October 2008; available at http://otbds.org/assets/uploaded_files/project/Learningnote2-IntegratingPatientFocusandPublicInvolvementintoClinicalGovernanc.pdf. Accessed 3 March 2015.

NHS Scotland, *Educational resources. Clinical governance*; available at http://www.clinicalgovernance.scot.nhs.uk. Accessed 12 October 2012.

Njoya W, *Property in Work: The Employment Relationship in the Anglo-American Firm*. Aldershot: Ashgate 2007.

Nuffield Council on Bioethics, *Human Tissue: Ethical and Legal Issues*. London: Nuffield Council on Bioethics 1995.

Nwabueze RN, *Biotechnology and the Challenge of Property: Property Rights in Dead Bodies, Body Parts, and Genetic Information*. Ashgate: Aldershot 2007.

Nwabueze RN, Donated organs, property rights and the remedial quagmire (2008) 16 Med Law Rev 201–224.

O'Donnell S, Shipman proposals will alter general practice profoundly (2003) 326 BMJ 280.

O'Neill O, *Autonomy and Trust in Bioethics*. Cambridge: Cambridge University Press 2002.

O'Neill O, Paternalism and partial autonomy (1984) 10 J Med Ethics 173–178.

Oxman AD, Chalmers I and Sackett DL, A practical guide to informed consent to treatment (2001) 323 BMJ 1464–1466.

Patents Legal Section, *The Patents Act 1977 (as amended)*. London: Intellectual Property Office 2011.

Patients Association, *Information, What Information? Information Challenges of Shared Decision Making*. Harrow: Patients Association 2011.

Patients Association, *The NHS Constitution: Fact or Fiction*? Harrow: Patients Association 2012.

Pellegrino ED and Thomasma DC, *For the Patient's Good: The Restoration of Beneficence in Healthcare*. Oxford: Oxford University Press 1988.

Penner JE. *The Idea of Property in Law*. Oxford: Oxford University Press 1997.

Petersen CJ, Reproduction and family planning: individual right or public policy? In Wacks R (ed), *Hong Kong, China and 1997: Essays in Legal Theory*. Hong Kong: Hong Kong University Press 1993, pp. 261–306.

Porter R, *The Greatest Benefit to Mankind: A Medical History of Humanity from Antiquity to the Present*. London: Fountain Press 1999.

Powell JA, New property disaggregated: a model to address employment discrimination (1990) 24 USF L Rev 363–383.

President's Commission for the Study of Ethical Problems in Medicine and Biomedical and Behavioral Research, *Making Health Care Decisions*, vol 1. Washington DC: U.S. Government Printing Office 1982.

Price D, The Human Tissue Act 2004 (2005) 68 MLR 798–821.

Project of the ABIM Foundation, ACP-ASIM Foundation and European Federation of Internal Medicine, Medical professionalism in the new millennium: a physician charter (2002) 100 Obstetrics Gynecology 170–172.

Proudhon P-J, *What is Property*?, ed and trans Kelly DR and Smith BG, Cambridge Texts in the History of Political Thought. Cambridge: Cambridge University Press 1993.

Radin MJ, Property and Personhood (1982) 34 Stan L Rev 957–1015.

Radin MJ, *Reinterpreting Property*. Chicago: Chicago University Press 1993.

Radin MJ, *Reinterpreting Property*. Chicago: University of Chicago Press 1996.

Rahaim CD, *The Fiduciary: An In-Depth Guide to Fiduciary Duties – From Studebaker to Enron*. Lincoln, Nebr.: iUniverse 2005.

Randall F and Downie RS, *The Philosophy of Palliative Care: Critique and Reconstruction*. Oxford: Oxford University Press 2006.

Rankinen S, Salanterä S, Heikkinen K, Johansson K, Kaljonen A, Virtanen H and Leino-Kilpi H, Expectations and received knowledge by surgical patients (2007) 9 Int J Qual Health Care 113–119.

Rao R, Property, privacy, and the human body (2000) 80 Boston Univ L Rev 359–460.

Rao JK, Weinberger M and Kroenke K, Visit-specific expectations and patient-centered outcomes: a literature review (2000) 9 Arch Fam Med 1148–1155.

Raz J, Rights and politics (1995) 71 Indiana LJ 27–44; available at http://www.repository.law.indiana.edu/ilj/vol71/iss1/2. Accessed 3 March 2015.

Reich CA, The new property (1964) 73 Yale LJ 733–787.

Richards MA, Ramirez AJ, Degner LF, Fallowfield LJ, Maher EJ and Neuberger J. Offering choice of treatment to patients with cancers: a review based on a symposium held at the 10th annual conference of the British Psychosocial Oncology Group, December 1993 (1995) 31 European Journal of Cancer 112–116.

Richards N and Coulter A, *Is the NHS Becoming More Patient-centred? Trends from the National Surveys of NHS Patients in England 2002–07*. Oxford: Picker Institute Europe 2007.

Richards T, Partnership with patients: patients want more than simply information: they need involvement too (1998) 316 BMJ 85–86.

Richardson EH and Turner BS, Bodies as property: from slavery to DNA maps. In Bainham A, Sclater SD and Richards M (eds), *Body Lore and Laws*. Oxford: Hart 2002, pp. 29–42.

Robertson G, Informed consent to medical treatment (1981) 97 LQR 102–126.

Robertson G, Informed consent 10 years later: the impact of *Reibl v. Hughes* (1991) 70 Can Bar Rev 423–447.

Robertson GB, Informed consent: 20 years later (2003) Health Law Journal Special edn 153–159.

Rosen R and Dewer S, *On Being a Doctor: Redefining Medical Professionalism for Better Patient Care*. London: King's Fund 2004.

Rostill LD, The ownership that wasn't meant to be: *Yearworth* and property rights in human tissue (2014) 40 J Med Ethics 14–18.

Rothman DJ, *Strangers at the Bedside: A History of How Law and Bioethics Transformed Medical Decision Making*, 2nd edn. Piscataway, NJ: Transaction 2003.

Rothman DJ, Were Tuskegee & Willowbrook 'studies in nature'? (1982) 12 Hastings Cent Rep 5–7.

Royal College of Obstetricians and Gynaecologists, *National Sentinel Caesarean Section Audit*. London: RCOG Press 2001.

Royal College of Obstetricians and Gynaecologists, *Obtaining Valid Consent*, 2nd edn, Clinical Governance Advice 6. London: RCOG Press 2008.

Royal College of Physicians Working Party, *Doctors in Society: Medical Professionalism in a Changing World*. London: RCP 2005.

Samanta A and Samanta J, The Human Rights Act 1998 – why should it matter for medical practice? (2005) 98 J R Soc Med 404–410.

Sanchez-Menegay C and Stalder H, Do physicians take into account patients' expectations? (1994) 9 J Gen Intern Med 404–406.

Say R, Murtagh M and Thomson R, Patients' preference for involvement in medical decision making: a narrative review (2006) 60 Patient Educ Couns 102–114.

Scally G and Donaldson LJ, Clinical governance and the drive for quality improvement in the new NHS in England (1998) 317 BMJ 61–65.

Schermer M, *The Different Faces of Autonomy: Patient Autonomy in Ethical Theory and Hospital Practice*. Dordrecht: Kluwer Academic 2002.

Schulman BA, Active patient orientation and outcomes in hypertensive treatment (1979) 17 Medical Care 267–280.

Schultz D and Jann D, The use of eminent domain and contractually implied property rights to affect business and plant closings (1990) 16 Wm Mitchell L Rev 383–427.

Schwartz A and Bergus G, *Medical Decision Making: A Physician's Guide*. Cambridge: Cambridge University Press 2008.

Shaw I and Aldridge A, Consumerism, health and social order (2003) 2 Soc Pol Soc 35–43.

Shell SM, *Kant and the Limits of Autonomy*. Boston: Harvard University Press 2009.

Shinebourne EA and Bush A, For paternalism in the doctor-patient relationship. In Gillon R (ed), *Principles of Healthcare Ethics*. Chichester: John Wiley 1994, pp. 399–408.

Shipman Inquiry, *First Report. Death Disguised*. London: The Stationery Office 2002; available at http://www.the-shipman-inquiry-org.uk/firstreport.asp.

Shipman Inquiry, *Fifth Report. Safeguarding Patients: Lessons from the Past – Proposals for the Future*, Cm 6394. London: The Stationery Office 2004.

Shultz MM, From informed consent to patient choice: a new protected interest (1985) 95 Yale LJ 219–299.

Simpson R, Informed consent: from disclosure to patient participation in medical decision making (1981) 76 Northwest Univ L Rev 72–207.

Sinding C and Wiernikowski J, Treatment decision-making and its discontents (2009) 48 Social Work in Health Care 614–634.

Singer JW, The reliance interest in property (1988) 40 Stan L Rev 611–750.

Skegg PDG, English medical law and 'informed consent': an antipodean assessment and alternative (1999) 7 Med L Rev 135–165.

Skene L, Arguments against people legally 'owning' their own bodies, body parts and tissue (2002) 2 Macquarie LJ 165–176.

Slowther A, The concept of autonomy and its interpretation in health care (2007) 2 Clin Ethics 173–175.

Slowther A, Truth-telling in health care (2009) 4 Clin Ethics 173–175.

Smith R, Medical professionalism: out with the old and in with the new (2006) 99 J R Soc Med 48–50.

Smith V, *Wonder Woman: The Life, Death, and Life After Death of Henrietta Lacks, Unwitting Heroine of Modern Medical Science*, Baltimore City Paper. 17 April 2002; available at http://www.citypaper.com/news/story.asp?id=3426. Accessed 20 October 2012.

Sperling D, *Management of Post-Mortem Pregnancy: Legal and Philosophical Aspects*. Aldershot: Ashgate 2006.

Spiro HM and Mandell HN, When doctors get sick (1998) 128 Ann Intern Med 152–154.

Stange M, *Personal Property: Wives, White Slaves and the Market in Women*. Baltimore: Johns Hopkins University Press 1998.

Stauch M, Court-authorised Caesareans and the principle of patient autonomy (1997) 6 Nott LJ 74.

Steinbock B, Sperm as property. In Harris J and Holm S (eds), *The Future of Human Reproduction*. Oxford: Clarendon Press 1998.

Stirrat GM, Truth-telling, autonomy and paternalism in healthcare: a commentary on the case of Gary Dimmock v. East Sussex NHS Trust (2007) 13 Clinical Risk 226–228.

Stirrat GM and Gill R, Autonomy in medical ethics after O'Neill (2005) 31 J Med Ethics 127–130.

Strahan JA, *Law of Property*, 3rd edn. London: Stevens & Sons 1901.

Summerton N, Positive and negative factors in defensive medicine: a questionnaire study of general practitioners (1995) 310 BMJ 27–29.

Swick HM, Toward a normative definition of medical professionalism (2000) 75 Acad Med 612–616.

Swick HM, Professionalism: a key to weathering the storm (2001) 98 Obstetrics Gynecology 156–161.

Swintankowsky IS, *A New Paradigm for Informed Consent*. Lanham, Md.: University Press of America 1998.

Symmons CR, The duty of care in negligence: recently expressed policy elements – Part 1 (1971) 34 MLR 394–409.

Symonds A, Reactions to perceived risk: defensiveness in clinical practice (2003) 9 Clinical Risk 182.

Szasz TS and Hollender MH, The basic models of the doctor-patient relationship (1956) 97 Arch Intern Med 585–592.

Tahir MAM, Mason C and Hind V, Informed consent: optimism versus reality (2002) 193 Br Dent J 221–224.

Tallis RC, Doctors in society: medical professionalism in a changing world (2006) 6 Clinical Medicine 7–12.

Taylor JS, Autonomy and informed consent: a much misunderstood relationship (2004) 38 Journal of Value Inquiry 383–391.

Taylor K, Paternalism, participation and partnership – the evolution of patient centeredness in the consultation (2009) 74 Patient Educ and Couns 150–155.

Tebbit, Lord, Body politics. BMA News Review, June 2000.

Teff H, Consent to medical procedures: paternalism, self-determination or therapeutic alliance (1995) 101 LQR 432–453.

Thistlethwaite J and Spencer J, *Professionalism in Medicine*. Oxford: Radcliffe 2008.

Thorpe, Lord Justice, Consent for Caesarean section: Part 2 – autonomy, capacity, best interests, reasonable force and procedural guidelines (1999) 5 Clinical Risk 209–212.

Tingle J, Foster C and Wheat K, *Regulating Healthcare Quality*. Edinburgh: Butterworth Heinemann.

Trebilock MJ, *The Limits of Freedom of Contract*. Cambridge, Mass: Harvard University Press 1993.

Trotter MI and Morgan DW, Patients' use of the Internet for health related matters: a study of Internet usage in 2000 and 2006 (2008) 14 Health Informatics J 175–81.

Tuckett AG, Truth-telling in clinical practice and the arguments for and against: a review of the literature (2004) 11 Nursing Ethics 500–513.

Twerski A and Cohen N, Informed decision-making and the law of torts: the myth of justiciable causation (1988) Univ Ill L Rev 607–665.

Tyreman S, The expert patient: outline of UK government paper (2005) 8 Med Health Care Philos 149–151.

Underkuffler LS, On property: an essay (1990) 100 Yale LJ 127–148.

Underkuffler LS, *The Idea of Property: Its Meaning and Power*. Oxford: Oxford University Press 2003.

United Nations. *The Universal Declaration of Human Rights*; available at http://www.un.org/Overview/rights.html. Accessed 3 March 2015.

US hospitals to ask patients for right to sell their tissue. BMJ 16 September 2000, p. 653.

van den Brink-Muinen A, van Dulmen SM, de Haes HC, Visser AP, Schellevis FG and Bensing JM, Has patients' involvement in the decision-making process changed over time? (2006) 9 Health Expectations 333–342.

Vandevelde KJ, The new property of the nineteenth century: the development of the modern concept of property (1980) 29 Buffalo L Rev 325–368.

van Kleffens T, van Baarsen B and van Leeuwen E, The medical practice of patient autonomy and cancer treatment refusals: a patients' and physicians' perspective (2004) 58 Soc Sci Med 2325–2336.

Veatch A, *Theory of Medical Ethics*. New York: Basic Books 1983.

Veatch RM, *The Patient-Physician Relation: The Patient as Partner, Part 2*. Bloomington: Indiana University Press 1991.

Veatch RM and Spicer CM, Against paternalism in the patient-physician relationship. In Gillon R (ed), *Principles of Healthcare Ethics*. Chichester: John Wiley 1994, pp. 409–19.

Vick S and Scott A, Agency in health care: examining patients' preferences for attributes of the doctor-patient relationship (1998) 17 J Health Econ 587–605.

Wald HS, Dube CE and Anthony DC, Untangling the Web: the impact of Internet use on health care and the physician-patient relationship (2007) 68 Patient Educ Couns 218–224.

Waldenstrom U, Hildingsson I, Rubertsson C and Radestad I, A negative birth experience: prevalence and risk factors in a national sample (2004) 31 Birth 17–27.

Warnock Report, *Report of the Committee of Enquiry into Human Fertilisation and Embryology*. London: HMSO 1984.

Washington HA, Gene patenting produces profits, not cures. Huffington Post, July 2010 at http://www.huffingtonpost.com/harriet-a-washington/gene-patenting-produces-p_b_645862.html. Accessed 20 October 2012.

Wear S, *Informed Consent – Patient Autonomy and Clinical Beneficence within Health Care*, 2nd edn. Washington DC: Georgetown University Press 1998.

Wear S, Freer J and Koczwara B, Commercialisation of human body parts: public policy considerations. In Cherry MJ (ed), *Persons and Their Bodies: Rights, Responsibilities, Relationships*. Dordrecht: Kluwer Academic 1999, pp. 363–384.

Wennberg JE, *Tracking Medicine: A Researcher's Quest to Understand Health Care.* Oxford: Oxford University Press 2010.

Wertheimer A, *Coercion*. Princeton, NJ: Princeton University Press 1990.

Whitty NR, Rights of personality, property rights and the human body in Scots law (2005) 9 Edin L Rev 194–237.

Wicks E, The implications of the Human Rights Act 1998 – prioritizing consent. In Tingle J, Foster C and Wheat K, *Regulating Healthcare Quality*. Edinburgh: Butterworth Heinemann 2004, pp. 97–108.

Wiggins NM, Stop using military metaphors for disease (2012) BMJ 345: e4706.

Williams S, Weinman J, Dale J and Newman S, Patient expectations: what do primary care patients want from the GP and how far does meeting expectations affect patient satisfaction? (1999) 16 Fam Pract 33–38.

Williams TC, Is a right of action in tort a chose in action? (1894) 10 LQR 143.

Wilmot S, A fair range of choice: justifying maximum patient choice in the British National Health Service (2007) 15 Health Care Anal 59–72.

Woodiwiss A, *Human Rights*. Abingdon: Routledge 2005.

Woolf, Lord, *Access to Justice: Final Report to the Lord Chancellor by Lord Woolf.* London: HMSO, July 1996.

Woolf, Lord Are the courts excessively deferential to the medical profession? (2001) 9 Med L Rev 1–16.

World Medical Association, *International Code of Medical Ethics*; available at http://www.wma.net/en/30publications/10policies/c8/. Accessed 3 March 2015.

World Medical Association, *The Declaration of Geneva*; available at http://www.wma.net/en/30publications/10policies/g1/ . Accessed 3 March 2015.

Wright EB, Holcombe C and Salmon P, Doctors' communication of trust, care, and respect in breast cancer: qualitative study (2004) 328 BMJ 864.

Wynia MK, Latham SR, Kao AC, Berg JW and Emanuel LL, Medical professionalism in society (1999) 341 N Engl J Med 1612–1616.

Yellin DS, Masters of their own eminent domain: the case for a reliance interest associated with economic development takings (2011) 99 Geo LJ 651–676.

Zimmermann R, *The Law of Obligations: Roman Foundations of the Civilian Tradition*. Oxford: Oxford University Press 1996.

Index

For Product Safety Concerns and Information please contact our EU representative GPSR@taylorandfrancis.com
Taylor & Francis Verlag GmbH, Kaufingerstraße 24, 80331 München, Germany

www.ingramcontent.com/pod-product-compliance
Ingram Content Group UK Ltd.
Pitfield, Milton Keynes, MK11 3LW, UK
UKHW022014180926
475701UK00003B/352

* 9 7 8 0 3 6 7 5 9 8 8 4 6 *